Contents

ALSO BY VÁCLAV HAVEL

Václav Havel or: Living in Truth
(essays by and about Havel)
(1987)

The Power of the Powerless
(co-author)
(1985)

The Memorandum
(1980)

Sorry: Two Plays (Audience and Private View)
(1978)

The Increased Difficulty of Concentration
(1972)

The Garden Party
(1969)

LETTERS TO
OLGA

LETTERS TO OLGA

June 1979–September 1982

With a New Author's Preface
for the Owl Book Edition

Translated from the Czech
with an Introduction by
Paul Wilson

An Owl Book

Henry Holt and Company · New York

Published by Henry Holt and Company, Inc., 115 West 18th Street,
New York, New York 10011. Published by arrangement with
Alfred A. Knopf, Inc.
Published in Canada by Fitzhenry & Whiteside Limited,
195 Allstate Parkway, Markham, Ontario L3R 4T8.

Library of Congress Cataloging-in-Publication Data
Havel, Václav.
  [Dopisy Olze. English]
  Letters to Olga : June 1979–September 1982 / Václav Havel :
translated from the Czech with an introduction by Paul Wilson.
    p.   cm.
  Translation of: Dopisy Olze.
  "An Owl Book."
  Includes index.
  ISBN 0-8050-0973-6 (pbk.)
  1. Havel, Václav—Correspondence.   2. Havel, Olga—
Correspondence.   3. Authors, Czech—20th century—
Correspondence.   4. Authors, Czech—20th century—Imprisonment—
Czechoslovakia.   5. Political prisoners—Czechoslovakia—
Correspondence.   I. Title.
PG5039.18.A9Z48413   1989
891.8'625—dc19   88-36835
                                                      CIP

Henry Holt books are available at special discounts for bulk purchases
for sales promotions, premiums, fund-raising, or educational use.
Special editions or book excerpts can also be created to specification.
For details contact: Special Sales Director, Henry Holt and Company,
Inc., 115 West 18th Street, New York, New York 10011.

Originally published in Germany as *Briefe an Olga* by Rowohlt
Taschenbuch Verlag GmbH, Reinbek bei Hamburg.
Published in Canada as *Dopisy Olze* (červen 1979—září 1982) by
Sixty-Eight Publishers Corp., Toronto, in 1985.
First published in hardcover in the United States by Alfred A. Knopf,
Inc., in 1988, by arrangement with Rowohlt Verlag GmbH, Reinbek bei
Hamburg.

First Owl Book Edition—1989

Printed in the United States of America
10   9   8   7   6   5   4   3

"Letters From Prison" by Václav Havel, translated by Paul Wilson was
originally published in the Spring 1987, Number 21 issue of *Granta*.

Grateful acknowledgment is made to Macmillan Publishing Company
for permission to reprint an excerpt from *Letters and Papers from Prison:
The Enlarged Edition*, by Dietrich Bonhoeffer, edited by Eberhard
Bethge. Copyright © 1953, 1967, 1971 by SCM Press Ltd. Reprinted
by permission.

Author's Preface

Just over ten years ago, my friends and I in VONS (Czech acronym for the Committee to Defend the Unjustly Prosecuted) were arrested, and my almost four years in prison began. Looking back on it now, I realize, perhaps more clearly than I did when I was first released early in 1983, how important my letters home were to me. Not only were they my only means of communication with the outside world, they were my only opportunity for some kind of creative expression; I was not allowed to write anything else.

The conditions in which I wrote these letters were harsh. All sorts of restrictions imposed by the prison authorities, some possible, some impossible, had to be abided by before the letters could even be sent. There was a desperate lack of space, time, and tranquillity for writing them. At first, my two fellow inmates and I were allowed only to write about family matters. Gradually, however, we began to smuggle more and more general comments into our letters, and the prison censors gradually got used to these. I soon realized that the more abstract and incomprehensible these meditative letters were, the greater their chance of being sent, since the censors did not permit any comments to be mailed that they could understand. Slowly, I learned to write in a complex, encoded fashion which was far more convoluted than I wanted and certainly more complicated than the way I normally write.

Writing these letters became my passion; they were constantly on my mind. I developed them in my head while I was at work, or attending to other prison duties. They made me feel I was doing something worthwhile and that my years in prison were not completely wasted. In short, they gave meaning to my life in prison, and helped me to endure.

Out of all that came this strange book. I am always moved when I learn that someone has read it, or been enriched by it, or felt that it was speaking to them. It is an odd and happy sensation to discover that something you had written originally only for yourself, for your wife, and at most for a handful of friends, and not for a wider readership, suddenly appears in the marketplace and through it finds its way to sensitive and observant readers.

I am most grateful to the publishers of these letters for their understanding and their courage to take the risks that publishing a book like this entails. And I am especially grateful to Paul Wilson, for his sensitive and conscientious translation and for his informative introduction.

—Václav Havel, Prague,
January 1, 1989

Preface

Not long after Václav Havel was released from prison, the first edition of his *Letters to Olga* appeared. It was a professionally bound, typewritten edition of about a dozen copies with the title stamped on the spine, and it proved again, if proof were needed, how flexible, responsive and alert a medium *samizdat*—or self-publishing, Soviet style—can be. Translation and publication in the West are a somewhat more leisurely and cumbersome affair, but in the five years that have passed since Havel's release from prison, the letters have lost nothing of their relevance.

Havel's original intention was to publish only the letters he considered of lasting interest, but fortunately his friends, old associates from *Tvář* magazine, intervened. Here we have a classic illustration of practical literary criticism in the pre-post-Gutenberg world of *samizdat:* Jan Lopatka (a critic who has saved many a writer from self-censorship) persuaded Havel to publish the letters more or less exactly as he wrote them. The argument, according to Jiří Němec, who also helped dissuade Havel from his first plan, was this: that since the letters indelibly bear the mark of their origin, to present them as anything other than prison letters would be to act against their essential nature.

Consequently, of the 144 letters that Havel wrote to Olga between June 4, 1979, and September 4, 1982, all but nineteen were kept. Of those nineteen, four (11, 24, 34 and 124) were never delivered (more, in fact, were not delivered but Havel found out about these in time to alter his own numbering) and fifteen (6, 8, 22, 26, 42, 43, 56, 57, 59, 84, 85, 88, 98, 101, 125) were dropped from the original edition either because they repeat practical information contained in other letters, or the meditations they contain are present in a more lively and complete form in other letters.

The English version of *Letters to Olga* is approximately one-sixth shorter than the Czech edition, and the principles we followed in making cuts were more or less the same as those followed by the Czech editor. That is, nothing has been excluded that in any essential way alters the quality of the original collection. Two more letters (36 and 50) have been dropped, and cuts were made wherever we felt there were unnecessary repetitions. All exclusions longer than a sentence or two are indicated in the text by three dots. Many names mentioned in the letters are identified in an alphabetical Glossary of Names at the back of the book. We have also included a Notes section that explains some of the more obscure references in the text.

Translation is always more work than one bargains for, and this book—with its special difficulties—was no exception. I would not have been able to accomplish the work without the help, encouragement, and support of many people. Thanks to Deborah Karl for setting this project off on the right foot; to Vratislav Brabenec, Jana Převratská, Aleš Březina, Jiří Grusa, Josef Škvorecký, Ivo Uhlíř, Jan Vladislav, and Jiří Němec for their invaluable help in solving some of the translation problems and illuminating obscure points in the text; to Joachim Brus, G. Brain, Jacques Rupnik, John Keane, Petr Chudožilov, Jiří Boreš and the Libánský family for collegial discussions and hospitality; to Marketa Goetz-Stankiewicz for her excellent study of Havel's plays, and Gordon Skilling for sharing his wide knowledge of independent Czechoslovak intellectual life; to Helena and Vilém Prečan for their kind hospitality at the Documentation Center for the Promotion of Independent Czechoslovak Literature, in West Germany; to Karel Hvížďăla for permission to quote from his lengthy interview with Havel; to Bobbie Bristol at Knopf for her patience in delay, her firm hand in editing and her unwavering belief in the book; to Václav Havel himself, for his help in unravelling some of the mysteries of the text, and for his confidence and encouragement; and finally, and perhaps above all, to my wife Helena, not only for her linguistic assistance, but for her steady support, which was always there when I needed it.
—Paul Wilson, Toronto

LETTERS TO
OLGA

On October 22 and 23, 1979, a trial was held in the Prague Municipal Court of six imprisoned signatories of Charter 77 who were also members of the Committee to Defend the Unjustly Prosecuted.

The senate, presided over by JUDr. Antonín Kašpar, found the defendants guilty of the crime of subversion of the republic (Section 98, Subsections 1 and 2, a and b, of the Criminal Code) which they were alleged to have committed by assembling, copying and distributing, both on the territory of the Czechoslovak Socialist Republic and abroad, written material which the senate considered indictable. It concerned mainly information contained in the communiqués of the Committee to Defend the Unjustly Prosecuted, that is, information about unjust judicial and extrajudicial procedures and practices in present-day Czechoslovakia.

The senate passed the following sentences:

Otta Bednářová	—3 years in prison
Václav Benda	—4 years in prison
Jiří Dienstbier	—3 years in prison
Václav Havel	—4 1/2 years in prison: all the above sentences to be served in a First Category Correctional Institution
Dana Němcová	—2 years in prison; conditionally suspended for 5 years
Petr Uhl	—5 years in prison; to be served in a Second Category Correctional Institution

Prague, October 23, 1979

Introduction

There remains an experience of incomparable value. We have for once learnt to see the great events of world history from below, from the perspective of the outcast, the suspects, the maltreated, the powerless, the oppressed, the reviled—in short, from the perspective of those who suffer. . . . We have to learn that personal suffering is a more effective key, a more rewarding principle for exploring the world in thought and action than personal good fortune. This perspective from below must not become the partisan possession of those who are eternally dissatisfied; rather, we must do justice to life in all its dimensions from a higher satisfaction, whose foundation is beyond any talk of "from below" or "from above."

—Dietrich Bonhoeffer,
LETTERS AND PAPERS FROM PRISON

At five o'clock in the morning of May 29, 1979, the Czechoslovak State Security police began arresting members of the Committee to Defend the Unjustly Prosecuted, otherwise known by its Czech acronym, VONS. Fifteen people were rounded up and ten of these, including Václav Havel, were detained in Ruzyně prison and later indicted under Article 98 of the Criminal Code for "subversion," a crime against the state that carries a maximum sentence of ten years.

VONS had been formed a year earlier as a direct outgrowth of Charter 77, the Czechoslovak human rights movement, and its purpose was, in the words of its first official document, "to monitor the cases of people who have been indicted or imprisoned for expressing their beliefs, or who are victims of abuses by the police and the courts." The members of VONS gathered information and circulated typewritten reports of their findings both to official institutions, and to the public. By the time of the arrests, 155 of these reports had been issued. They comprised the only hard evidence in the state's case against VONS.

Between the Warsaw Pact invasion in 1968 and the appearance of Charter 77 in 1977, Czechoslovakia had undergone a deepening crisis. All the social, political and economic ills in the system, ills the short-lived Prague Spring had attempted to correct, now became endemic. One of the earliest, and still one of the best, descriptions of that period was Havel's open letter to President Husák, written in 1975. It was a sign of the times that Havel fully expected to be arrested for writing it. (He claims that for a long time afterward, he carried an emergency kit wherever he went, containing things like toothpaste, cigarettes and razor blades, in case he was arrested in the street.)

It was also a sign of the times that he was not arrested. By the mid-seventies the authorities appeared to have come to a certain negative accommodation with its recalcitrant intellectuals and they more or less tolerated—or more precisely did not specifically prosecute—occasional delinquencies like the letter to Husák or the various *samizdat* publishing ventures like Petlice or Havel's own Edice Expedice. There even appeared to be a tacit understanding that writers like Havel who already had a reputation outside Czechoslovakia could continue to publish and have their plays produced abroad—provided, of course, they declared their income and paid their taxes.

No one liked this state of affairs, least of all the writers themselves, because they felt it gave them an artificial "protected" status, like an endangered species. Havel was again one of the first to articulate the idea that writers could only be effective in helping others if they were prepared to assume the same risks as everyone else. After a trial in 1976 in which some artists and musicians from the Czech musical underground were sentenced to terms in prison essentially for songs they had written and performed, Havel publicly repudiated what he called "the world of 'rear exits,' "[1] by which he meant the "privilege" he and his colleagues enjoyed of being left alone while others less well-known were persecuted.

When Charter 77 appeared, this uneasy truce came abruptly to an end and the regime began to employ a fuller range of repressive tactics. Shortly after the Charter manifesto was released in January 1977 Havel, as one of the three spokesmen, was arrested and held in Ruzyně until May 20, when he was released in circumstances that caused him a lot of personal pain. While still in prison, he had written what he thought was a clever but entirely routine request to be let out; the day of his release, the official media published parts of his letter out of context, making it appear that he had bartered a promise to curtail his activities in Charter 77 in exchange for personal freedom. As the authorities had intended, Havel was humiliated and though his fellow Chartists were understanding he could not help feeling that the whole incident had been his own fault, that he had let his guard down, and failed to keep trust as a Charter spokesman. Recalling this incident in his letters, (Letters 138 and 139), he came to see it as one of central importance in his life.

Havel continued to be active in Charter 77 (he even became spokesman again for a time), and the state continued to increase the pressure on him. In October 1977 he was sentenced to fourteen months in prison for "subversion," but this was conditionally suspended for three years. He was arrested again in January 1978 but released in March without charges having been laid. Then in late 1978, the police began a focused campaign of harassment designed to break Havel's nerve and compel him either to give up or emigrate. He was followed everywhere, a permanent detail of police was stationed outside his Prague apartment whenever he was in town, and just outside Hrádeček, a farmhouse he and Olga had renovated in North Bohemia, the police built a permanent observation post that looked like a small, portable classroom on stilts (Havel called it the "Lunochod," after the Soviet remote-controlled moon module) where they could observe his movements and monitor his guests. There were even absurdly transparent attempts to make it appear as though people were against him: his car was vandalized and local repair shops received orders not to repair it. Havel cataloged these and other abuses, which continued well into 1979, in two defiantly sardonic essays on what he called his "House Arrest and Attendant Phenomena." In his own civilized way, Havel was serving notice that he was not about to be broken.

By the time the trial of VONS was held in October 1979, four of the original ten detainees had been dropped from the indictment leaving, besides Havel, Otta Bednářová, a former television journalist; Václav Benda, a mathematician and prominent Catholic layman; Jiří Dienstbier, a former foreign correspondent; Dana Němcová, a child psychologist; and Petr Uhl, an engineer and revolutionary socialist who had spent four years of the last decade in prison. Even by Czech standards the trial was a travesty of judicial procedure. The state made no effort to prove that subversion, motivated by "hostility" toward society, had actually taken place and the defense attorneys offered only the most cursory arguments for their clients' innocence. (Benda's lawyer even congratulated the prosecutor on the indictment and apologized for having to enter a plea of not guilty.) In his final statement to the court, Havel concluded by mentioning an odd circumstance that in effect undercut the state's position: "Two months ago, while in prison," he said, "I was asked whether I would not consider accepting an invitation I'd received for a working visit to the United States. I don't know what might have happened had I accepted that offer, but I cannot exclude the possibility that I might have been sitting in New York at this very moment. If I am standing in this courtroom now, it is quite possibly by my own choice, a choice which certainly does not suggest that I am hostile toward this country."[2]

The appeal was quashed on December 20, 1979, and soon afterward the five VONS members who had received "straight" sentences (Dana Němcová's sentence of two years was suspended) were sent under escort from Ruzyně to their various prisons. Otta Bednářová went to serve her three years in the Opava woman's prison; Peter Uhl was sent to a maximum-security prison in Mírov, and the remaining three—Dienstbier, Benda and Havel—against all expectations and for reasons no one quite understands, were all assigned to the same prison, Heřmanice, in Ostrava, a large mining and steel-manufacturing city in Northern Moravia, close to the Polish border.

Because of the strict censorship Havel's letters contain almost nothing about his everyday life in prison. Even after his release he remained reluctant to talk about it, not because the experience had been too harrowing to relive, but because he felt that the real meaning of his imprisonment could not be conveyed by mere facts. Nevertheless, we can surmise something of what that life was like from what his fellow prisoners have said, from things Havel revealed later, and even from the letters themselves.

Havel's days were filled with hard labor. His first job in Heřmanice was making heavy steel mesh with a spot welder. The quotas were deliberately set high—double what they would be in civilian life, Havel estimated—and it was some time before he could meet them. Failure meant working extra hours, less food and pocket money and the loss of privileges. When his health began to show signs of deteriorating (and coincidentally, just as he was beginning to fulfill the quotas), he was shifted to a physically less demanding job with an oxyacetylene cutting torch. Later, in Plzeň-Bory, he worked in two places, first the prison laundry (where the work was easier but the presence of informers made it more unpleasant), then in a scrap metal depot, stripping the insulation off wires and cables. Despite long hours, physical discomfort and frequent aches and pains, Havel looked forward to work because he said that you were less likely to be harassed and bullied at the workplace.

The absolute ruler of the Heřmanice prison was a self-professed admirer of Hitler, a sadistic, frustrated man near the end of his career, the high point of which had occurred when he'd been in command of a Stalinist prison camp in the 1950s. Havel, Dienstbier and Benda arrived, branded as notorious dissidents and enemies of the state, and for the warden it was like a return to the good old days. He took great delight in tormenting them. Letters home were one of his favorite targets, and they became the theater of a titanic battle between this man's vindictiveness and the wit and ingenuity of his prisoners. "We were allowed to write one four-page letter home a week," Havel said later. "It had to be legible, with nothing corrected or crossed out, and there were strict rules about margins and graphic and stylistic devices (we were forbidden, for example, to use quotation marks, to underline words, use foreign expressions, etc.). . . . We could write only about 'family matters.' Humor was banned as well: punishment is a serious business, after all, and jokes would have undermined the gravity, which is one reason why my letters are so deadly serious."[3]

Havel seems to have been a favorite target for abuse. In an afterword to the Czech *samizdat* edition of *Letters to Olga,* Jiří Dienstbier recalls: "His very decent and polite manners may have first persuaded the warden and some of the guards that he was soft and easily broken. It was a wrong impression. Havel was visibly ill at ease in the presence of crude and threatening behavior, but instead of the expected submission, this was usually followed by a quiet and persistent refusal to back down. They would confiscate a letter in which there were too many 'thoughts.' 'What's all this crap about "the order of the spirit" and "the order of Being?"' the warden would roar. 'The only order you have to worry about is the rules of prison order!' So Havel would write a letter about something else. When the warden told him he could write only about himself, he began a series of letters about his fifteen moods. After the eighth, the warden forbade him to number them. So seven moods are unnumbered, but they are there, nonetheless."

By contrast, the other prisoners—unless they were informers or provocateurs—treated the three "dissidents" with kindness and respect, sharing their food with them and teaching them some of the survival techniques that make prison life more bearable. The prisoners obviously drew their own conclusions about what kind of "criminals" the three men were, and before long they were coming to them for assistance, from legal, psychological and marital advice to arbitration in disputes over the rules of poker. The trust they enjoyed among their fellow prisoners enraged the warden, who said he'd be damned if they were going to set up a branch of VONS in his prison. Once he sent Havel and Benda to solitary confinement after he discovered they'd been writing letters for an illiterate gypsy.

Despite the difficulties—or perhaps because of them—Havel, Dienstbier and Benda tried to turn their own letter writing into a game. The basic censorship code was clear enough, but the way the censor interpreted it was not; consequently, they would read each other's letters, attempting to guess which ones would make it through. "Eventually," Dienstbier says, "we realized that an intellectual desire to discover order and logic in such things is as pointless behind bars as it is on the outside. The only rule was the momentary whim of the warden and the other censors."

Havel was not allowed any other form of writing, and eventually, his weekly letter to Olga was the only thing that gave his stay in prison a meaning. "The letters gave me a chance to develop a new way of looking at myself and examining my attitudes to the fundamental things in life. I became more and more wrapped up in them, I depended on them to the point where almost nothing else mattered. All week long I would develop the essays in my head—at work, when exercising before going to bed—and then on Saturday, amid constant interruption, I would write them out in a kind of wild trance. Later I discovered ways of writing out a rough draft, but then the problem became where to hide it, since searches were part of the daily routine. In Bory I hid my rough drafts in a mountain of dirty sheets stained by millions of unborn children, and I would revise them during the noon break, while trying to avoid being seen by informers. Once I'd written out a fair copy, I couldn't change anything or cross anything out, much less copy it again. I'd hand it in, and then there'd be a short, suspenseful wait: would it get through or not? Since I wasn't allowed to keep a copy, I eventually lost track of what I had written, and which letters had been sent—which is why there are so many gaps, repetitions, and flaws in logic. In time I learned how to think ahead and arrange my thoughts in thematic cycles, and to weave the motifs in and out of them and thus—in a rather uneven fashion—to build, over time, my own little structure, putting it together something like my plays. . . . The letters, in fact, are endless spirals in which I've tried to enclose something. Very early on, I realized that comprehensible letters wouldn't get through, which is why the letters are full of long, compound sentences and the complicated ways of saying things. Instead of writing 'regime,' for instance, I would obviously have had to write 'the socially apparent focus of the non-I,' or some such nonsense."

Perhaps understandably for someone surrounded by walls, Havel became preoccupied with the image of a horizon, the outer rim of the discernible, intelligible or imaginable world. He often calls it his "concrete horizon," or his "home," which in Czech—*domov*—expresses a notion that is close to what we mean by "a sense of belonging." Since he was allowed to write to only one person, it is not surprising that Olga, his wife since 1964, became the focus or the center of this feeling.

Readers have remarked that some of the passages addressed specifically to Olga are unpleasantly finicky, fussy, lacking in warmth. In his earlier letters, Havel inundates her with demands, requests, tasks to be performed, lists of things to send him, "directives" he calls them, not without a touch of irony. He worries about their farmhouse, Hrádeček, not only because it needs constant upkeep, but because, as he discovers to his dismay, the housing authorities appear ready to condemn it. He urges her to think about exchanging their flat for another one, to buy new furniture, get a job, learn to drive. He complains that she doesn't write often enough, that she doesn't answer his questions, that her news, when it comes, is not specific enough, that he can't form a clear picture of her daily routines, and so on.

Behind the nagging, one senses the deep anxiety Havel felt at suddenly being cut off from the community of his friends and colleagues. Apart from occasional visits from his lawyer, Olga was his only point of contact with that life, and he depended on her to tell him what was going on. When he urges her to "be sociable," he is expressing his need, through her, to go on participating in the life of his community. He wanted to know things he couldn't get away with asking about directly: the underground concerts, the unofficial seminars, the new *samizdat* books and journals that had come out, the discussions, debates and controversies, and the gossip. His community was under siege, and every event, every change of mood within it, was immensely important to him.

"Olga and I are very different," Havel said later. "I'm a child of the middle class and ever the diffident intellectual, Olga's a working-class girl, very much her own person, sober, unsentimental, and she can even be somewhat mouthy and obnoxious; in other words, as we say, you can't get her drunk on a bun. I grew up in the loving and firm embrace of a dominant mother and I needed an energetic woman beside me to turn to for advice and yet still be someone I could be in awe of. . . . In Olga, I found exactly what I needed: someone who could respond to my own mental instability, to offer sober criticism of my wilder ideas, provide private support for my public adventures. All my life, I've consulted with her in everything I do (the wags claim I even require her agreement to the sins through which I hurt her, and that I seek her advice in the problems my occasional emotional centrifugality bring me). She's usually the first to read whatever I write, and if not, then she's certainly my main authority when it comes to judging it."

Thus, although none of Olga's letters to Havel are included in this volume, she has a vividly felt presence in the letters. In her silences and Havel's frustration at them, one senses a strong personality establishing its own identity in his absence. The editor of the Czech edition of the letters, Jan Lopatka, even suggests that the letters may be read as a romantic epistolary novel, a novel of "maturing love." The progress of Havel's relationship with Olga, from the petulant dependence of the early letters, to the greater serenity of the later letters when he has recognized her independence and accepted the qualities in her he perceived as limitations, is one of the most moving of the letters' implicit themes.

"Olga and I have not professed love for each other for at least two hundred years, but we both feel that we are probably inseparable," Havel said. "It's true that you won't find many heartfelt, personal passages specifically addressed to my wife in my prison letters. Even so, I think that Olga is their main hero, though admittedly hidden. That was why I put her name in the title of the book. Doesn't that endless search for a firm point, for certainty, for an absolute horizon that fills those letters say something, in itself, to confirm that?"

Havel's letters also have their place in a long, continuing conversation among Czechs and Slovaks about the fate of their society, of their country, of Central and Eastern Europe, and ultimately, of the modern world.

This conversation—which should be understood almost literally, for the Czechs and Slovaks are a convivial people who love a good argument and take the idea of discourse very seriously—has a long history stretching back to the beginning of the modern Czech nation in the nineteenth century, when the language and culture were revived and re-created by several generations of patriotic artists, writers, composers, journalists, politicians and intellectuals who based their work on foundations laid by generations of ordinary people who had preserved and enriched the language orally. The conversation bore fruit: at the end of World War One, Czechoslovakia emerged triumphantly as a modern liberal democracy headed by the "philosopher-president" Tomáš G. Masaryk, who embodied the country's cultural paternity.

The 1920s and 1930s were a crucial period in Czech history. The rise of Nazi Germany on one side and Soviet Russia on the other provided the ominous framework for a debate—with strong utopian undertones—on the social responsibility of intellectuals. The towering figure in Czech literature at this time was the playwright and essayist Karel Čapek who introduced the world (in his play *R.U.R.*) to an enduring symbol of the appropriation of human faculties by machines—the robot. Čapek was an eloquent observer and critic of cultural and political trends. By the 1930s, a majority of Czech intellectuals were leftist, and the prevailing belief among them was that some form of socialism was the only answer to the rise of fascism, and that they should therefore put their shoulders to that particular wheel. Čapek saw the real threat to democracy in an intellectual tendency common to both nazism and communism, in which public discourse was increasingly dominated by demands for unanimity, culture by a denigration of the past and a functional view of the present, and politics by a belief in the benefits of single party rule.

After the Second World War, the main question facing Czechoslovakia became what new social order should arise from the wreckage of Nazi occupation. At this stage, a significant number of intellectuals got firmly behind the communist cause. After the Communist party took power in 1948, those who hesitated or resisted were sent to prison, compelled to emigrate or left to withdraw into privacy. For the next eight years, orchestrated public jubilation over the "victories of socialism" combined with political terror to reduce the ancient conversation to muted whispers, and when the Stalinist cloud at last began to lift around 1956, the main item on the agenda, hidden at first, but increasingly aboveboard, was reform (or simply change, if you were a noncommunist). By 1968, when the reform communists came to power under Alexander Dubček and abolished censorship, the discussion went public for a brief, bright period (when Prague suddenly became a vibrant city with a visible public life) and its terms became specific: how to loosen the deadening grip of Soviet-style socialism and create a socialism—or perhaps just a society—that was more democratic, more pluralistic, more liveable. Such openness—i.e., genuine public debate unregulated by the party—was judged by the Soviet leaders to be tantamount to chaos, and they called in the Warsaw Pact troops to put an end to it.

In the 1970s and 1980s, for the first time in Czechoslovakia's modern history, the artists, writers and scholars who were the natural heirs of that idealistic, patriotic, "nation-building" intellectual tradition were completely severed from public life. Their disputes, their discussions, and their visions were no longer a part of public life. The trauma of this separation—engineered by censorship and epitomized by prison and exile—did not stop the discussion, but it radically transformed the way it was carried out. With the press denied to them, dissenters now found themselves in a pre-Gutenberg world where manuscripts, not printed works, had to become the precious lifeblood of their community. Paradoxically, the attempt to destroy literature succeeded in prolonging the life of one of the few surviving old-fashioned literary communities left in Europe, a fact that has provoked several Western authors (John Updike and Philip Roth among them) into sending fictional emissaries over to examine what was going on. The instincts of these authors— that something interesting is going on there—is true, but sometimes a combination of pity and envy can deflect their attention away from what makes this community truly unique—the ideas that preoccupy it.

Ever since the mid-seventies, Czech and Slovak intellectuals have seriously and systematically been examining, from inside, a process that is central to an understanding of our century: the process by which Utopia becomes Dystopia, by which bright ideas turn into tarnished, uninhabitable realities. Socialism (or at least the Marxist version of it) is no longer a subject for anatomy, but rather for autopsy, and the system under which they live is studied with the same passionate involvement, and for the same reasons, that pathologists and immunologists study epidemics. Not surprisingly, since totalitarianism is a modern human institution, they have discovered disquieting evidence that their own disease has features in common with some of the ills of humanity at large.

Many of the subjects Havel meditates upon in his letters—the nature of belief, the dehumanizing tendencies in the modern world, the struggle between the "order of life" and the "order of death," the origins of fanaticism, and (perhaps the most central one) the nature and meaning of responsibility and individual human identity—are all related to the megathemes that underlie not only his own writing, but the writing of many Central European intellectuals. In his open letter to Husák and in "The Power of the Powerless," an essay on dissent from 1978, he discusses these and other subjects in concrete terms, with great precision. Prison censorship makes his treatment of some of those same themes gingerly abstract, but it has also driven him deeper into their essence. The glory of his letters is that they need not be "decoded" to be understood; they can be read "as is."

Václav Havel's central place in modern Czech thought, and his power as a writer, derive not so much from his originality as from tradition: he represents a direct link, a continuity, with the noblest strand of Czech thought, its democratic traditions or rather, since its experience of democracy was so brief, its commitment to democratic and humane principles even when those principles seemed hopelessly lost. They also derive from his way of writing. "The *novum* that Havel brought into Czech literature," says psychologist Jiří Němec, a fellow VONS member and longtime friend of Havel's now living in Vienna, "was that he has always written as though censorship did not exist. If he didn't want to write about something, he didn't write about it; and if he did, then he wrote about it only in a way that he believed was true."

Another factor in Havel's special power as a writer is his capacity to see things from below, from outside the purview of power and advantage and particular interest. It is a crucial ability for a playwright, of course, but he carries it over into his other writing as well. Havel attributes this ability to the "apparent disadvantage" of having been born into a wealthy family and grown up under a communist regime, which deliberately penalized him for his background. Prevented from attending high school in the early 1950s, he got his diploma at night school while working in a chemical lab during the day. Consequently his early literary efforts were extracurricular. He was inspired in those efforts by encounters with banned poets like Jaroslav Seifert, Vladimír Holan and Jiří Kolář, beside whose work the official Stalinist culture of the time seemed thin, artificial and unrepresentative. In the fall of 1956, when Havel was barely twenty, he challenged a conference of young writers and cultural *apparatniks* to recognize officially the existence of writers like Kolář and Seifert. For the rest of the three-day conference, Havel's appeal was the main topic of conversation and debate. How dare Havel talk about some "forgotten poets," someone demanded, when socialism was fighting for its life on the streets of Budapest? What's the point of holding an expensive conference on Czech poetry, Havel shot back, if we can't talk about important Czech poets?

It was in many small ways such as this that the invisible struggle between the inert, conservative regime and the forces of change in society gradually began to surface. At first, the only legal, institutional representation these forces had were the so-called reform communists, or "antidogmatists" as Havel calls them, party members who still called themselves Marxist but favored a more liberal interpretation of Marxism in practice. By 1965, large segments of the literary establishment—the leadership of the Writers' Union, the publishing houses, the editorial boards of literary magazines and newspapers—were in the hands of the "antidogmatists." Many saw this as a sign of hope, but Havel believed that the antidogmatists were dangerously irresolute when it came to resisting pressure from the party hard-liners.

In 1965, Havel joined the Czechoslovak Writers' Union and at the same time became a member of the editorial board of a small literary magazine called *Tvář* that had recently been founded by some young, non-Communist writers and was under increasing pressure from the Union, its official publisher, to toe the line or shut down. Havel led a spirited campaign inside the Union to save the magazine's life and its identity, and though the campaign failed, it taught him an important lesson. The Union leaders had argued that their pursuit of bigger game—liberalization—made small concessions to the "center" in "less important" matters, such as the banning of *Tvář*, necessary. The Tvářists replied that conditions could only be improved by refusing to compromise in precisely such "unimportant" matters as the publication of a particular book or little magazine. "We introduced a new model of behavior: don't get involved in diffuse, general ideological polemics with the center, to whom numerous concrete 'causes' are always being sacrificed; fight 'only' for those concrete causes, and be prepared to fight unswervingly to the end."

The 1960s were also the only time in Czech postwar history when a vital theater not only existed, but was an important part of this complex cultural and social renewal that was taking place largely out of sight. Since 1960, Havel had been working at a small avant-garde theater called the Theatre on the Balustrade, first as a stagehand and then as resident playwright and dramaturge. Between 1963 and 1965, he wrote and produced two full-length plays of his own—*The Garden Party* (1963) and *The Memorandum* (1965). These plays soon established his reputation among a wider Czech audience that may not have been in a position to follow the intricacies of literary politics, but could and did respond to his dramatic vision with a deeply instinctive understanding. The public's enthusiasm taught Havel another important lesson: "Every act of social self-awareness—that is, every time a new work was genuinely and deeply accepted, identified with and integrated into the spiritual reality of the time—immediately opened the way for even more radical acts. Each new work weakened the repressive system. It was like an acceleration in the metabolic process that goes on between art and the age, and it was immensely inspiring and productive in an institution as social as theater."[4]

As 1968 approached, Havel's public activity intensified. At the famous IVth Writers' Congress in June 1967, he delivered a stinging attack on the lack of democracy in the union. During the Prague Spring he helped establish, within the union, a Circle of Independent Writers, and was subsequently elected its chairman. In the same period, he published an influential article "On the Theme of an Opposition," calling for a second political party, to be based on Czechoslovak democratic and humanitarian traditions. His third full-length play, *The Increased Difficulty of Concentration*, opened at the Theatre on the Balustrade in April 1968. In May and June he spent six weeks in the United States where *The Memorandum* was performed in Joseph Papp's New York Shakespeare Festival. (Later that year, it won an Obie.) *Tvář* resurfaced, and with Havel as chairman of the editorial board, it put out eight issues before being shut down again in June 1969.

All this activity did not suddenly stop with the Soviet invasion in August 1968. All through that fall and winter, Havel struggled to defend the existence of the Circle of Independent Writers. In early 1969 he engaged in a public polemic with Milan Kundera over the fate of the nation. Kundera took a position—very similar to the one being propagated more subtly by the remnants of the liberal party press—that the ideals of the Prague Spring had placed Czechoslovakia at the center of world history and that the disciplined, passive resistance of the Czechs to the Soviet invasion offered hope that the ideals of the Prague Spring would prevail. Havel labeled this attitude "pseudocritical illusionism" and argued that "freedom and legality are the sine qua non of any normal, healthy social organism, and if a country attempts to renew them after years of absence, it is not doing anything historically earth-shaking, but is simply trying to shed its own abnormality, regardless of whether it calls itself socialist or not."[5]

In March 1969, Havel discovered a listening device in the ceiling of his Prague flat. Attacks on him and others who had been active and unrepentant after the invasion began appearing in the press and on the air. In the fall of 1969 he and others were charged with "subversion" for signing a petition against the politics of "normalization" instituted by Gustav Husák, who by now had replaced Alexander Dubček as head of the party; the trial was adjourned and the case never resumed. The old Writers' Union was dissolved and Havel's books, along with works by other "unnormalized" writers, were removed from all school and public libraries, and his plays were banned from the stage.

In the early seventies, Havel and Olga moved into their farmhouse in North Bohemia and from then on divided their time between Hrá-deček and Prague. Away from the day-to-day activity of the theater and literary politics, Havel had more time to write and think. His old sparring partners, the "antidogmatists," were banned as well, and for a while he turned his attention in a more general direction. He wrote three full-length plays in this period: *The Conspirators,* set in an unspecified military dictatorship; *The Beggar's Opera,* a reworking of John Gay's original play, not Brecht's version of it; and *The Mountain Hotel,* a highly formal drama that he analyzes at some length in his letters.

Havel's best-known dramatic works from the 1970s, however, are three one-act plays, sometimes referred to as the Vaněk trilogy after the main character, Ferdinand Vaněk, a soft-spoken dissident writer very like Havel himself. Here Havel deals directly with the problem of how the system impinges on people who are not "dissidents," ordinary people trapped in jobs that are degrading not because they are menial but because to keep them these people must demean themselves, hide their humiliation by indulging in mindless consumption, make their uneasy peace with the regime and then feel that the cause of justice is best served by their silence. These plays are the heartbeat of Havel's present activism and his compassion for the voiceless victims of totalitarianism, who are far worse off than the dissidents because they have no way of making themselves heard. As the morose brewmaster in *Audience* tells Vaněk: "You always got a chance, but what about me? Who's gonna stick their neck out for me? Who's afraid of me? Who's gonna write about me? Who's gonna help me? Who even gives a shit? I'm just the manure that makes your fancy principles grow." Vaněk has no answer to this outcry because there is none. There is only action, not "on behalf" of those who suffer, but as one of them.

Havel's prison letters are unlike anything else he has ever written. They were not, as most of his other nontheatrical writing has been, intended to stir up discussion around a specific cultural and political situation. Jan Lopatka suggests that the letters might also be read as a novel of "character and destiny." The hero starts out on a quest, determined to withstand any test fate puts in his way. But he soon discovers that the reality is worse, and different, than he had imagined and the nature of the quest undergoes a subtle change. He masters the mysteries of this strange way of writing and transcends the physical difficulties that go with it only to find himself locked in an even more primordial struggle: he must discover the meaning of his life and snatch it from the jaws of nothingness. His existence, his very Being depend upon it. Havel's letters climax in a dramatic spiral of pure thought mingled with an experience of almost religious intensity.

Havel meant his final sixteen letters to be read as a unit. In fact they were published separately in a *samizdat* edition, along with a commentary by "Sidonius" (a Prague philosopher), who draws a suggestive parallel between those letters and Boethius's *Consolation of Philosophy*. Boethius was a prominent Roman senator condemned to death in the sixth century A.D. for publicly defending a fellow senator against charges of treason, and he wrote the *Consolation* while awaiting execution. It was conceived as a conversation between himself and Philosophy, who visits his cell in the person of a woman and talks to him about questions—such as free will versus fate—that would preoccupy Western philosophers and theologians for centuries to come. In an analagous way, "Sidonius" says, Havel was "visited" by the spirit of philosophy and we can read his final letters not as "the philosophical opinions of the Czech dramatist and writer Václav Havel" but as the unfolding of a philosophically articulated vision that is addressed, through Havel and his experience, to our time.

Readers familiar with modern philosophy will recognize, in some of the language Havel uses, his debt to Martin Heidegger and the schools of phenomenology and existentialism that Heidegger's work inspired. Expressions like "Being" (capitalized) or "existence-in-the-world" or "thrownness" (translations of the Czech words "bytí," "pobyt" and "vrženost," which in turn are standard Czech renderings of the Heideggerian terms "Sein," "Dasein" and "Geworfenheit") abound. But as Havel warns us in the letters, he does not use them with anything like the rigor normally associated with philosophical writing, and rather than seeking clarification outside the text, we should perhaps allow their meaning to emerge from the letters themselves.

The influence of phenomenology, however, is not just something peculiar to Havel's thinking; phenomenology is now a symptomatic, or typical, feature of the independent intellectual landscape in Central Europe today. It is not hard to see why this is so. Phenomenology offers a way of describing the world that frees thought (and, by implication, action) from the assumptions of the mechanistic determinism that still lies behind much of our scientific and political thinking. It seeks the meaning of things, beings, relations and events in how they present themselves to us, not in how they are mediated to us by an ideology or a scientific theory. Phenomenology's stress on personal responsibility is an implicit critique of the predisposition of ideologies to see responsibility for the state of the world primarily as blame to be assigned to a "class enemy" or an "evil empire," for example, rather than as an obligation to be assumed by each individual. Human rights, in this view, are not a political device to be granted as reward and taken away as punishment, but rather a set of principles designed to allow individual responsibility to flourish in society, in the belief that only through such a flourishing can the world be continually revitalized.

The person chiefly responsible for introducing phenomenology to Czech and Slovak intellectuals was the philosopher Jan Patočka, whose life was a living parable of thought in action. He was a student of Husserl and Heidegger and, since the communist takeover in 1948, had virtually been excluded from university life, with the exception of a brief period from 1968-1972. Havel recalls that in the 1960s, Patočka would come to the Theatre on the Balustrade and hold informal discussions with the actors and writers on phenomenology, existentialism and other philosophical questions. "These unofficial seminars," Havel says, "took us into the world of philosophizing in the true, original sense of the word: not the boredom of the classroom, but rather an inspired, vital search for the meaning of things and the illumination of one's self, of one's situation in the world."[6]

In an eerie way Havel's final encounter with Patočka prefigures the world of *Letters to Olga.* As Charter spokesmen, Havel and Patočka had both been summoned to Ruzyně prison for interrogation, and during the noon break they sat in the prisoners' waiting room, discussing philosophy. "At any moment," Havel recalls, "they could have come for us, but that didn't bother Professor Patočka: in an impromptu seminar on the history of the idea of human immortality and human responsibility, he weighed his words as carefully as if we had all the time in the world ahead of us."[7] Two months later, Patočka died of a brain stroke after a long and intense interrogation by the secret police. Yet in a way, Patočka and Havel's conversation continues in these letters.

Havel's last published letter is dated September 4, 1982, but he was not released until the following January. Presumably Havel continued to write letters which were not included in the final volume; in any case, his health was deteriorating, and there were signs that the regime was looking for a way to let him go. Once, in the fall of 1982, he was visited by his Prague investigators who told him he had only to write a single sentence asking for pardon and he would be home within the week. Perhaps mindful of his painful experience in Ruzyně in 1977, and perhaps out of simple solidarity with those who were still in prison, he refused.

Then in late January 1983, Havel suddenly came down with a high fever. The attack was so severe he thought he might be dying, and so, evidently, did his jailers, for a few days later he was rushed to the Pankrác prison hospital in Prague—a journey of about fifty miles—in the back of a police van, in his pajamas, handcuffed and with a temperature of over 104. When his temperature subsided and his appetite began to return, Havel wrote a detailed letter to Olga describing his plight, gambling that the censorship from Pankrác would be less stringent. The letter got through, Olga quickly alerted Havel's friends outside the country, and interventions on his behalf began arriving from all over the world.

"One evening, which I shall never forget, just as I was getting ready to go to sleep, into my cell there suddenly stepped several guards, a doctor and a woman official of some kind, who informed me that the District Court of Prague 4 was terminating my sentence. I was flabbergasted and asked them if I could spend one more night in prison. They said it was out of the question because I was now a civilian. I asked them what I was supposed to do now, in my pajamas? An ambulance was waiting to take me to a civilian hospital, they said. It was a shock to hear the doctor suddenly calling me 'Mr. Havel' instead of just 'Havel.' I hadn't heard myself addressed that way in years."

Havel spent a month in the hospital, entertaining a stream of friends and admirers, catching up on the gossip, reading the new *samizdat* texts, basking in the fellowship, the attention, the sudden ease. He said it was the most beautiful month of his life; even the secret police were affable. "Released from the burden of prison but not yet encumbered by the burden of freedom, I lived like a king. . . . The world—beginning with loved ones and friends and ending with the doctors, nurses and fellow patients—showed me its kindest face. I had no responsibilities, only rights. I was no longer in prison, and at the same time, I did not yet know the postprison depression suffered by a returnee who is suddenly cast loose into the absurd terrain of freedom.

"But the beautiful dream had to end. The day came when I had to step back into the world as it really was . . . and I've been moving along its uncertain surface ever since."

—Paul Wilson

1. Václav Havel, "The Trial," October 11, 1976. There is a translation of this essay in *Charter 77 and Human Rights in Czechoslovakia*, by H. Gordon Skilling (London: George Allen & Unwin, 1981), pp. 201–4.
2. Václav Havel, "Defence Speech," October 22–23, 1979. Translated and printed in Skilling, *Charter 77*, pp. 299–306. A dramatized version of the trial exists: *Procès a Prague: Le V.O.N.S., comité de défense des personnes injustement poursuivies, devant ses juges, 22–23 octobre 1979*. Paris: François Maspero, 1980.
3. Unless otherwise indicated, all subsequent quotations, including this one, have been taken from Karel Hvížďála's interview with Václav Havel, published in Czech as *Dálkový výslech* (Purely, Surrey, England: Rozmluvy, 1986).
4. From the "Author's Afterword" to an edition of Havel's plays from the 1970s, *Václav Havel: Hry 1970–1976 (Václav Havel: Plays 1970–1976)* (Toronto: Sixty-Eight Publishers, 1977).
5. From "Cesky udel?" ("The Czech Destiny?") by Václav Havel, in *Václav Havel: O lidskou identitou (Václav Havel on Human Identity)*, ed. Vilém Prečan and Alexander Tomský (London: Rozmluvy, 1984), pp. 198–9.
6. From "The Last Conversation," by Václav Havel, 1977. Published in *Václav Havel: O lidskou identitou (Václav Havel on Human Identity)*, ed. Vilém Prečan and Alexander Tomský (London: Rozmluvy, 1984), pp. 152–5.
7. Ibid.

I. Letters 1–17

Pretrial Detention in Ruzyně Prison, Prague

June 1979–January 1980

1

Dear Father, dear Puzuk, dear Květa,

Greetings from another of my sojourns in Ruzyně. Don't worry about me; I'm not about to vanish. I'm sending this letter for Olga to you because I don't know where she is and what arrangements have been made for mail in Hrádeček.

V.

＊

Dear Olga,

It appears the astrologers were right when they predicted prison for me again this year and when they said the summer would be a hot one. As a matter of fact, it's stifling hot here, like being in a perpetual sauna. I feel sorry about the many complications my new stint in jail will probably cause you. I think you should stay in Hrádeček and look after the place—tend the meadow, make improvements to the house, take the dogs for walks to the pond, etc. There are always family or friends who might want to spend their holidays there with you. There's no reason to stay in Prague—you can't be of any help to me here and what would you do all day? And anyway, we've sublet the flat. Of course, you should learn to drive so you can do the shopping and so on without having to rely on someone else all the time. In short, you should lead a completely normal life, as though I were off on a trip somewhere. This is how you can help me the most, if I know you're well and taken care of. I don't know, of course, how long this trip will last; I'm not harbouring any illusions, and in fact I hardly think about it at all. I don't think much about our "case" either—since there's nothing to think about. The matter is clear and it is also clear to me (after all we've been through) what I have to do and how.

I think about quite different matters, and it's too bad I can't write about them. Prison as such is, of course, a terrible bore; it's no fun staring at the walls day after day, but with each stay I find it easier to bear because a lot that I once found disturbing no longer surprises or upsets me. What bothers me the most is the thought that some people outside might be harassed on my account; please write to me about it. I'm terribly pleased that Dr. Danisz will be defending me, though I don't suppose it will be for long. Many greetings to Andulka and please give her this letter to read. I'm sorry I won't be able to write her, but perhaps she could write to me. Every evening I listen to children romping about in a nearby playground, so I do have contact of sorts with the outside world after all. I am trying to do a little yoga, but quarters are cramped and every movement must be worked out to within a millimeter. And it's pretty hot for it, too. If you send me a parcel, make it the usual: powdered juice, lemons, cheese slices, cigars, a little instant cocoa and so on. And above all, write me a lot; you know how important every scrap of information is here, even news about how our lawn is surviving the dry spell. That's all for now; I'll leave room in case I think of anything else.

Kisses, Vašek

P.S. Very important! I bought a beautiful painting from Trinky. We have to send him 5000 crowns.

Tuesday/5

Rain at last! A storm, in fact! It's had no immediate impact on the climate inside, but it's still a relief. I was beginning to think I'd suffocate. Now I'm in high spirits. I will always write you only when I'm in a good mood; if I'm depressed, I'll keep it to myself. I regret that, once again, I didn't manage to get a play written between sessions in prison. It's not writer's block—I still enjoy writing (and I especially want to write here, now that I can't)—it's more like a blockage of ideas. I have the Faust worked out and almost half written, but I'm still not happy with it. Someday I'd like to be able to write something incontestably good again, not something (like *The Mountain Hotel*) that appeals only to oddballs. I'll try to think through the Faust while I'm here. There's a chance I'll be able to study English; that would be marvelous.

As you may already have discovered, we have a new lock on the entrance to our Prague flat. I have two keys here, and I've left one for our tenant with a neighbor; you can have duplicates made from that. They had to change it because the old key wouldn't fit. It wouldn't fit because that same morning the lock had already been changed once. I was told that the Security Forces thought I wasn't answering the door so they broke in and when they didn't find me at home, they had the lock changed and then later, during a house search, it was changed again. I was out knocking around town, taking advantage of my freedom as though I knew I would soon lose it. Later, they found me at someone's flat. I made some remarks when they arrested me, the way Honza Němec used to, which was out of character, but I couldn't think of anything wittier to say. It was an emotional response to feeling so helpless, but their explanation was that I was merely trying to impress a young woman who was listening. Anyway. Wednesday morning—the heat wave continues—a dream about Forman—

2

June 19, 1979

. . . I'm taking this imprisonment neither as tragically as I did the one in 1977 (then, of course, things were a lot worse and I was also new at this and frightened out of my wits), nor as a joke, like last year's. This time I'm being more fatalistic about it, and treating it as something I've long been destined to go through. After those two odd, false starts, it seems that only now—the third time—the inevitable has finally happened. If it hadn't, I'd probably have grown more and more nervous, because I would have been subconsciously expecting it at any moment. When this is over, I may finally be more at ease with myself, and this will have a calming effect on things around me as well. . . .

3

June 24, 1979

. . . Understandably, I can't write to you about any details of my case. I might, however, mention two things: (1) Everything is proceeding with unusual speed and it is not entirely impossible, though I have no direct evidence to support this, that a trial is not too far off. (2) There are indications that this time round I can expect to do several years of "hard time" because—in my case, at least—a wide range of factors is apparently to be taken into account, which means delving rather deeply into my past. The most interesting thing of all is that I am quite unperturbed; I'm reconciled to the prospect, and it neither depresses nor shocks me. If my assumptions are correct, I still have no way of knowing how I'll bear up in subsequent stages; nonetheless, a positive attitude on my part is quite important now because one's elemental emotions can significantly determine one's state of mind later on. . . .

4

July 8, 1979

. . . What else is there to say about my life? I've read a book on the Etruscans, and I'm reading one on Carthage; I'm studying a little English, doing a little yoga, playing some chess (though my partner is too good and I don't enjoy it), and trying to come to terms with the lack of light by day and the lack of darkness at night. My dreams are still colorful and they feature the most incredible characters and scenes from my youth. Recently you appeared as well, but that was an exception because the people I think most about rarely figure in my dreams. I've thought up some things to go into the play on Faust; I rather like it and I'm eager to start writing; in fact I've written a little here, but I'm finding it rather difficult in these circumstances. I feel trammeled somehow, more so than on the outside. . . .

P.S. This letter seems more nostalgic and resigned than I actually feel. But that is clearly the fate of all letters from prison: the fact that you know they will be checked, that one must write legibly (which means in a somewhat childish hand), these and other things have an obvious influence. Regarding the charges against me, I am—if I may put it this way—"politely intractable," sure of my own truth and thus sorry for nothing I've done. . . .

5

July 21, 1979

Dear Olga,

It is Saturday afternoon: I read in the papers that they've raised the price of gasoline, I've just finished feasting on what remained from the first parcel, smoked a cigar and now I'm sitting down to write you because the day on which letters may be sent is drawing near.

First of all: I forgot, as usual, to wish you a happy birthday. I remembered a couple of minutes after I'd handed over my last letter. Forgive me! I don't suppose I'll ever improve. So—belated best wishes. I'll buy you a present when I get out because as I remember, you don't hold much with presents from prison, especially the kind made out of bread.

Did you get my letters 3 and 4? In letter 3 I wrote you a set of guidelines in the event of a trial and in letter 4 there was a parcel voucher. If I don't hear by Wednesday that you received letter 3, then I'll repeat the guidelines, just to make sure. I'll know if you received letter 4 when the second parcel gets here. (I don't know if they'll remove any foodstuffs from the parcel or not. There are some regulations here intended to protect us from jaundice.) It would certainly be a good idea to confirm receipt of each of my letters with a postcard at once so I can keep track. Last time I acknowledged the arrival of your first letter, and since then, two more have come. The first of them thrilled me and made me eager to start writing again (you mentioned that a group of you had read my plays). Many thanks! On the other hand the second one—your third, in fact—made me uneasy. You said you were not sending me a kiss and that I knew why. I don't know why! I do know, however, that you mustn't write such things to me—I felt miserable for several days. These letters are all one has here. You read them a dozen times, turn them over in your mind, every detail is either a delight or a torment and makes you aware of how helpless you are. In other words, you must write me nice letters. And number them, put the date on them and above all, be as exhaustive as you can and write legibly. After all, it's not so difficult to sit down at a typewriter once in a while and write about everything you're up to. . . .

In answer to your questions in the third letter: the boiler is switched on using the second circuit breaker from the door. In the "down" position, the day current is off, in the "up" position, on. If you want to turn off the night current as well when you leave, you put another circuit breaker, the one with "boiler" scratched under it in barely legible letters, in the "down" position. I have the light blue (denim) bag here with various underclothes in it; I also have my leather handbag as well. Everything else, I assume, was confiscated. I'm satisfied with my lawyer. The red paint was for the door, but you can use it for the eaves troughs as well. I'll send you guidelines for the next parcel when the time comes. I've received all your postcards, I think. The money got through; send me more at the end of August.

My questions: Who has been at Hrádeček? Has Mejla been there with Klíma? Will Father be there? Have you arranged to have company throughout the summer? What are your plans? Will you be going to Prague anytime? When you're in Prague, where do you live? How's the car? How are the dogs? Who writes to you? What are our various friends doing? Etc. etc. etc.

As for me, I'm mentally fit, physically as well. I'm afraid I'm putting on weight (what else, when lunch and supper are the only two regular, daily events!). I've read my first English book from beginning to end (*The Triumph*—a look at American foreign policy from behind the scenes.) I understood the general sense of it, even though there were a lot of unfamiliar words in it. A pity I don't have an English-Czech dictionary; the Oxford dictionary Puzuk sent me doesn't answer my practical needs very well because I have no way of knowing whether I've understood the meanings properly. Perhaps when the lawyer comes to see me he might bring a small English-Czech dictionary with him (I have one in Hrádeček). I can borrow English books here. Among the better ones I've read *Lost Illusions* and now I'm reading the *Pickwick Papers*. Otherwise prison is a bore. It's dark, empty and I don't even have the sounds of children shouting outside my window any longer. Occasionally I make notes for the play, but it's hard to come up with ideas in these one-dimensional surroundings.

I've written you something about my case, but I don't know if my letters have got through, so I'll recapitulate: the investigation was wrapped up almost a month ago, so there could be a trial any time now, though not necessarily, of course. In other words, I don't know a lot. But I must be ready for an early trial and a guilty verdict. I think I'm mentally prepared for that; are you? My request to be released was turned down and I filed an official complaint. There was no reply to my request for a visit. My period of detention is up next week and it will clearly be extended, as usual.

I'm surprised that Zdeněk, Landák and other friends haven't sent me postcards. Perhaps they have, but nothing has come through. And postcards, on the whole, do get through. It amused me somewhat to have to sign a statement saying I hadn't received a letter from Jirka Pallas.

Do you miss me? I haven't had a postcard from you, either, for two weeks. Whenever you're in the village, or in town, you can send me a card; it always delights me.

I saw a picture in the paper of the new Nicaraguan government. They look like a group of high-spirited philosophy students and they have my goodwill. I don't know, of course, whether the information I have about them is complete enough.

To be somewhat more concrete about my writing: I've rethought the entire Faust; it has a new setting, new motifs, new characters, a new general structure, etc. All that remains is to write it—and I'm finding that impossible here. My feeling (wrong, perhaps) is that if I were out, I'd certainly be able to write it easily and quickly. Bye for today.

*

It's Sunday and I'm continuing. I read a rather good book: *To Kill a Mockingbird.* Sometimes I have the strangest feeling that I don't really want to leave this place. At least not now. Here you enter a state somewhat akin to hibernation, allow yourself to be swept along by the stereotypical routine of prison life, sink into a kind of sweet mental lethargy and the prospect of going back into the evil world, with its constant demands that you be decisive, becomes somewhat terrifying. On the other hand I'd be happy enough to spend the autumn in Hrádeček again—you know I love the autumn. Well, we shall see. Anything is possible. And I'm glad that I'm mentally prepared for the worst possible outcome. It's a miserable thing to cling to a vague hope, only to be disappointed again and again. If I'm here for a long time, perhaps the troubles we've experienced recently will subside and your life will at least be somewhat calmer.

P.S. I've noticed another odd thing: that in some ways, there is far more truth in this world than in the world outside. Things and people manifest themselves as they really are. Lies and hypocrisy vanish. When I'm out, I'll have some interesting things to tell you about it.

———

Monday, July 23, 1979

Letters are to be handed over tomorrow (Tuesday—an exception), so this is my last chance to finish. I received no mail today either (I know some will arrive the moment I send this letter, and again, I won't be able to respond to practical matters in time). Even so, my mood is good for various reasons. I wanted to repeat my guidelines for the trial: although I expect there to be an appeal afterward, you should still be prepared for my transfer to a regular prison to serve my sentence. The point is I'll need, and be permitted to have, more things there than here, but on the other hand I won't have any money to buy them. So you'll have to ask Magor or someone else who's been there about how it's done, whether it's possible to give me things directly after the trial and what one is allowed to take, etc. Parcels are not permitted as frequently and it would be wonderful if I could take the maximum allowable with me—if only because at first I won't have any money at all. Obviously I'll need some inexpensive shaving gear, a supply of toothpaste, notebooks for writing, letter paper, scissors, a mirror, soap, etc. And mainly a lot of cigarettes. And, if they're allowed, English dictionaries, German language textbooks, English books (Cassirer), etc. Perhaps I'm being prematurely anxious, but my experience of prison—an absolutely fundamental experience—is that it always pays to be prepared well in advance for every eventuality. At the same time, you might perhaps take the things I have here back with you (a bag of laundry). Otherwise, come to the trial of course, and perhaps it would be good if———came as well. I'm writing about this because in theory, the trial could take place any time now.

. . .

I kiss you,
Vašek.

Tuesday morning, July 24

Last night I dreamt about you. We had rented a palazzo in Venice! I'm still in good spirits; write me nice letters and cards, to help me keep them up.

7

August 11, 1979

Dear Olga,

It's Saturday at five o'clock, I've already had supper and I'm drinking juice and wondering what you're doing. Most likely you're sitting in the yard—with some friends, I hope—drinking coffee and thinking about moving into the kitchen to light the stove and make supper. I have to fill in the details of your life like this because I have no authentic news at all: since your third letter, which arrived more than a month ago, I haven't received a single letter from you. Nor from Puzuk or anyone else for that matter—and only yesterday my first letter in a month arrived—from Věra. Almost a third of the text, however, was blacked out with a marker. Sometimes I could make sense of it, sometimes I couldn't; there seemed to be no rationale behind the deletions (sometimes it was only individual words—even unimportant ones). Apart from that, in the past month I've received only your postcard 10 (likewise half deleted) and a rejection of my appeal against the confiscation of my driver's license. Are you getting my letters? You should have received numbers 5 and 6; the latter contained a parcel voucher. Being cut off from all news from home is not a good thing and it might be a good idea to write out all your basic news and send it to Puzuk; he can then ask the lawyer to relay it to me on his next visit.

I've learned that in addition to normal (monthly) parcels one has the right to a fruit parcel every two months. I'll ask for it and if there's another parcel voucher in this letter, then you should be aware that it's extra and send me only fruit for it. (Lemons, apples, peppers, etc. as you see fit.) The letter after that should contain a normal parcel voucher once more.

What can I say about my life here? In recent days I've been bothered by lumbago or rheumatism or whatever it is; it's hard for me to stand up, sit down, etc., and impossible to do yoga. I hope I'll be over it soon; my colleague is giving me massages. I'm now even more introverted than before, if that's possible, since I have a new colleague with whom I can't converse the way I could with the previous one. I have plenty of ideas chasing around in my head, but I find writing impossible—my hands are hopelessly tied by psychological inhibitions (most probably subconscious). I don't brood over my case, nor do I know anything new about it. It's sad and oppressive here, and the people are cold, but don't worry, I'll survive unscathed. After all those earlier experiences, I can experience everything in a reflective manner and I keep a watchful eye on myself, so that I am in no danger, I think, of succumbing to the various forms of prison psychosis. I try to respond to the many subtle warning signs—which is why I am writing to you in my normal hand and not in that neat little chicken-scratch; even such details, it seems to me, are important; there is, in that tight, perfectly legible calligraphy something of an involuntary curtailment, something squelched that naturally influences the way I express myself and thus the way I think as well.

This time I won't give you any tasks; I gave you enough in earlier letters and I reiterated them in the last one. If you manage to get even some of them done, it will be more than enough. Only one thing, perhaps: it would be a good idea to leave my toilet articles, some underwear and clothing with Puzuk; if by any chance they should release me (I'm not counting on it, of course), I'd have something in Prague and I could go to the sauna, for example, and sweat all those prison smells out of my system.

I'm reading my third English book, but there are still too many words I don't know. I read the biography of Villon and remarked that compared to him, I'm still not so badly off. I also read *Holy Week* by Aragon; nothing special. That book by Werfel *(The Forty Days of Musa Dagh)* was wonderful; you should read it.

I'd like to write you something nice but I don't feel much like entrusting it to this paper. You'll have to imagine it for yourself. Meanwhile, I send you kisses, and I'll add something later.

Yours, Vašek

Monday, August 13

My lumbago is on the mend—thanks to the massages. It was probably caused by inactivity, so I'm trying to be more active and tomorrow I'll start doing yoga again. I still think I'm overeating. I'll have to do something about that, too. . . .

P.S. I'm going through a period now when I don't like anything I've ever written and it worries me that I haven't written more and better. There may be a positive side to such doubts—I have a lot of clear ideas about what and how I'd like to write in the future. I wonder what will come of it? Here I will write nothing, that much is clear by now; it's simply impossible. But I can lay plans and make notes. Which is something at least.

*

Tuesday, August 14

Nothing worth remarking on has happened, except perhaps that I have a new colleague—so no more massages. But it doesn't matter; my lumbago is improving and it was obviously nothing serious. I wonder whether I'll get a parcel from you? If everything proceeds normally, it should be here by the end of the week at the very latest. I'm looking forward to it. Greetings to all our friends, acquaintances, relatives—I won't name them, but you know who I mean. Write me as well about how the roses are blooming and how all those special plants we set out are doing.

BE CHEERFUL, LEVELHEADED, HEALTHY AND SOCIABLE, DO YOUR TASKS CONSCIENTIOUSLY, KEEP TRACK OF WHAT GOES ON, DON'T LET TRIVIAL MATTERS UPSET YOU, THINK ABOUT ME AND KEEP YOUR FINGERS CROSSED FOR ME, TRY TO GET ALONG WELL WITH EVERYONE.

Greetings, and I kiss you,
Vašek

9

Saturday, September 8, 1979

Dear Olga,

I was greatly revitalized and strengthened by your visit; afterward, I felt quite exhilarated. Above all, I was glad we share the same opinion about that trip to the USA or rather, that you so unequivocally reinforced my view of the whole business. Here it is genuinely difficult to weigh all the aspects—and so I was faintly nervous about it, but after your visit, all my nervousness vanished—I was reassured that my position on the matter can only be what it is. But in other ways too, talking with you gave me, as they say, a new lease on life. A pity you can't visit more often.

This morning I started making you a trinket. I'll sketch it for you in case I'm unable to send it to you via the lawyer. I had no idea you appreciated such things, otherwise I'd have made something long ago. . . .

Right after your visit, I received the letter you mailed before the fruit parcel. Thank you. There were no deletions and it came in a relatively short time, along with two postcards from you. Could it be that communication between us is improving? But I'm still not receiving anything from anyone else.

There will probably be a parcel voucher along with this letter. The guidelines in my last letter remain in force. I would add only this: (1) Don't send toothpaste (the one you brought me is excellent!). (2) If there is any room left, send me some jam (the kind in the paper containers). I don't get jams anymore here and I've become accustomed to having them. (3) You needn't send cocoa. (4) I would stress vitamins, large amounts of different kinds, enough to last a month. When I have them, I feel better at once. (5) Don't send anything in heavy packaging, so as not to pointlessly use up the weight allowance. I think that's it.

The fruit parcel was great, the apples were delicious, and I even ate the plums with gusto. Needless to say it was all gone in a couple of days.

And now for more instructions:

I approve of your plan to move to Prague at the end of September. You can't spend the winter in Hrádeček alone. Still, you should leave it ready for reoccupation at any time—even for a longer stay. Suppose they release me? In that case I'd spend some time with you in Prague but then I'd like to go to Hrádeček. The problem is, I want to write, and in Prague I won't write a line. Hrádeček, therefore, should be prepared for my possible return (even though my release is unlikely, particularly now, I suppose).

. . .

Take the tape recorder, the amplifier, the tapes and all the relevant cables and accessories to Prague. Perhaps the record player as well, if it's acting up. And my electric typewriter, for repairs. And all the new books and papers and manuscripts. Lock the house and shutter it as best you can. It won't hurt to have T. go out there to take a look at it from time to time. Take Juliana's painting to Prague too. I forgot, again, to ask you how you liked Trinky's picture and if you paid him for it and what he's up to. Has he emigrated yet?

Otherwise, look over the various lists of tasks I've sent you and think about which of them you could manage. And in Prague, be sociable, go to the theater, the movies, visit friends, the shops (antiques—glassware and so on), etc. etc. Keep up with the cultural events, you know the kind I mean. Make notes about them all so you can keep me informed.

So much for instructions.

And now something about my life here. My colleagues are fine on the whole and they like me, but they talk incessantly and I can't read or think, etc. Of course there's no way I can stop them. It's maddening sometimes. But if they let up for ten minutes, my repressed anger immediately dissipates and I'm in a wonderful mood. So for the moment, I'm in no danger of suffering any permanent psychic damage. Except that by the time I'm out, I'll probably have a lifelong aversion to all talk about women.

(continuation—Sunday)

I think the trinket turned out well, but I won't draw it for you—let it be a surprise. I tried to put a touch of art nouveau into it. Let's hope it hardens properly (it's made entirely of bread, the only material I know how to work with). You'll have to add the chain yourself. . . .

I'd like to emphasize again what a beneficial effect your visit had on me. Prison immediately becomes more bearable.

Yesterday evening, using a particular method recommended to me here, I tried to establish telepathic contact with you—but apparently it didn't work. I guess I don't have what it takes (unlike others).

I no longer have lumbago, but my hemorrhoids bother me a lot. I'm doing what I can for them.

Do you know when the premiere in Vienna is? . . . .

Vašek

P.S. Thanks for the money; it arrived safely. But it's almost time to send more, given how long it takes. You needn't send candy—it weighs too much—unless you were able to get those tiny digestive mints; they're light and good. Perfumed Kleenex! I liked it when you said you'd go anywhere with me, even to jail!

(continued—Tuesday evening)

Nothing special has happened. The only significant event in my life was that today I saw a doctor about my painful hemorrhoids; he prescribed five days in bed and warm water for my backside. Lying down for five days will be a very welcome change (sitting continuously on the stools they have here is agony) and besides, I'm hoping for a partial cure at least. Regarding the parcel again: perhaps you should send me a little cocoa after all (I put it on my farina. Your trinket is finished; I don't know if you'll like it and if it isn't too fragile. If you'd like a refund, I'll make something different. For Jana I've made a little anchor. Both look very much like prison products.

Greetings to Puzuk and his family.

I regret that this year I won't be able to see the autumn leaves in Hrádeček. All the best!

Ahoj! V.

P.S. My colleagues here think I'm crazy for my "coolness" toward the proffered exit permit—

I'm not fully satisfied with the trinket after all. Perhaps I'll start a new one. (If only I wasn't always being offered unwanted advice!)

J.-P. Sartre: "Hell is other people." One becomes aware of just how apposite that is here, where people have to live together without interruption in a space six meters square—in intimacy far greater than a man lives with his wife. And there is no escape. Fortunately my nature is such that I get on well with everyone and I'm able to suppress my various emotions. (It's difficult at times—but giving vent to them would make things even more hellish.) I read an article in *RP* [*Rudé právo*] about experiments undertaken by scientists studying the psychological impact on people of living in an enclosed space for long periods of time. I had to smile. They have a laboratory for it right here and may not even be aware of it.

10

Saturday, September 22

Dear Puzuk,

This time I'm writing Olga at your address because she is supposed to be moving to Prague about now and I'm afraid that if I send this to Hrádeček or Dejvice, it could end up being forwarded from Prague to

Vlčice or vice versa, which would only prolong an already lengthy delivery period. Thanks for the letter with photos of the funeral; if you've written me a letter since then, I haven't received it. Perhaps you and Olga could write me together, so that it would be counted as a single letter; it might stand a better chance. You probably know from Olga what's happening with me. There's not a lot of news; life here is hardly what you'd call variegated. I'm reading my fourth English book, but I don't feel any better at it than when I read the first one. On the contrary, the number of words I don't know seems to increase while my ability to remember them diminishes. I'm still at my best reading something I enjoy.

Greetings to Květa and the boys!

Have a happy birthday!

V.

*

Dear Olga,

Once again it's Saturday and I have the chance to spend some time with you like this.

First: indications are that I will soon be tried and convicted and that I should definitely abandon any hopes I may have harbored of being released. At the same time I think I'm beginning to understand that whole business with the USA. It now appears that had I reacted somewhat differently, things might have been better for me today—and it may not have had the detrimental results I feared most. In short, my excessive caution may have been a mistake. Still, I regret nothing I've done; I had good reason for my misgivings, and if they were groundless, I had no way of knowing that and so could not have acted in any other way. I felt it unlikely, rightfully, that such a minor change in my position could so easily have brought about such a fundamental reversal and that no further consequences, or rather demands, would result. As a matter of fact I'm not entirely certain even today that things would have gone as smoothly as they appear to have gone so far. As it is, I can't change anything now and it's pointless to analyze the many "what ifs." I did brood over the matter for about three days, but now I've come to terms with it, because—as you know—I've been prepared for the worst from the start. My position may seem rather absurd now, and to avoid that, there is a step I intend to take, if I can (I've asked my lawyer in for consultation), mainly for the sake of my own feelings; I'd like to think it was I who brought the whole matter to a proper conclusion. Funnily enough, the resolution came at a time when I found myself thinking more and more about America, about how I'd prepare for it and the things I'd do when I got there. Now what I think about is the "work camp" and how I'll come to terms with that. But as I said, I have no regrets, and anyway I've never been very successful at trying to outsmart my own destiny. . . .

My five days in bed seem to have helped—the hemorrhoids have more or less subsided. My colleagues still chatter incessantly (they're doing so even now), but it hasn't driven me crazy yet and I know I'll manage to survive it. For one thing, it's marvelous training in self-control, something I'll still need a lot of, probably. Moreover, it gives me material for a play I've been mulling over for some time now (in addition to my thoughts on the Faust). Otherwise I'm physically and mentally fit, except that I've noticed a marked tendency to laziness and passivity recently, a reluctance to do anything (study, read, write, yoga). It may be my organism's defense against a situation where concentration is impossible. I'm expecting a parcel from you next week (the voucher should have been in my last letter), Friday is my name day and I'm looking forward to having a small feast next Saturday from the things you send me. By the way: a week after that—on my 43rd birthday—I will have been here exactly as long as I was in 1977, i.e., 4 months and a week. And the same day I will have spent ten months in prison altogether. It's interesting that the business about the USA came up the same length of time after my arrest as those complications in 1977(and back then I was even given the same book to read in my cell: Thomas Mann's *Doctor Faustus*). Those days were so much worse for me then than they are now! Then, the skies were beginning to brighten and I was going through hell (I'm beginning to understand how I could have gotten myself in such a mess)—and now it's practically the opposite: the clouds are gathering above me and I'm at peace with myself. As for books, I've read *Aurelien* by Aragon and am astonished at how bad it is, far worse than *Holy Week*. I wasn't expecting much, but I was still taken aback. Otherwise no special literary experiences. Regarding unofficial correspondence, in the last two weeks I've received only your postcard, written after you went back to Hrádeček. Thank you! One request: if you speak to my lawyer, give him a thick, lined notebook to pass on to me; my notebooks will soon be full; perhaps they'll let me have a new one. I've made three trinkets for you; I toiled over them for two days and they're still not right, but it's the best I can do. At least they'll have that prison look. Perhaps I can pass them on to you through the lawyer. (The biggest one will probably be awkward to wear, but you can hang it up somewhere.) . . .

I assume you've finished moving to Prague. Write me in detail about the state of Hrádeček when you left (the heating? the eaves-troughs?), of the Prague flat when you arrived, and in general about everything that's been going on. . . . If you see any nice dark brown corduroy cloth, you should buy it; I'd like to have a natty suit made up from it when I come back.

*

Monday morning—I've been having an irksome time with those trinkets! If you don't like them, give them away or throw them out. . . . I've started eating less and exercising more. Every so often I begin a "new life" here—just as I did when I was free. Monday evening: your postcard with the name-day greetings arrived. Many thanks! (It wasn't clear from the card whether you'd received my last letter with the parcel voucher—but it would seem that postcards travel faster than letters; and if you were to respond to each of my letters the same day with a postcard, I'd get it in time to respond to that in my next letter—and this would make communication between us far quicker and more efficient.) Beside me, a colleague is crying over his first letter from home; I'm trying to make him feel better. By now I'm a hardened old hand.

*

Tuesday—evening. . . . It's raining continuously—what are you doing, I wonder? Did you dry any mushrooms this year? And herbs?

On my birthday, at exactly 7:00 p.m., think of me. I'll think of you too.

Greetings to all the faithful!

I kiss you,

V.

12

[No date; postmarked November 13, 1979]

Dear Olga,

It's Tuesday evening and I've just returned from court a sentenced man. There is so much I'd like to write you about my feelings and experiences and thoughts during the trial, but I'm exhausted and weary—and I also don't know what I'm allowed to write about it. I'm sorting it out in my head and next time I may write more. I can only say now that I'm in good spirits, glad it's over, and not contemplating suicide; on the contrary, I'm looking to the future in good spirits. Depression may come later, but I think not. In my next letter, I'll address the consequences the court decision will have for us—about how you should probably live when I'm not there. It appears you didn't receive letter no. 11. Ask for it at the Municipal Court and if they won't release it to you, they should at least give you the parcel voucher—I have a right to that. But I can't recall having written anything against any regulations. Much of it concerned the flat—I listed about 15 reasons in favor of exchanging flats with the Raceks, but I'm incapable of reiterating them now. Next time. Please send me money—at least a thousand crowns—for my peace of mind. There are always problems with money here. And you should start getting a "camp parcel" ready for me. Magor or someone will advise you on what to include. Best to put EVERYTHING in it, since I won't have anything in the camp, not even money to buy things. Last time I also wrote a letter to Puzuk. Say hello to him. Thanks to both of you for being at the trial. Be courageous and levelheaded. And give my greetings to everyone I'm fond of—you know who I mean.

I kiss you—Vašek

P.S. One-ninth of my sentence is over with—I will try asking for a voucher for a fruit parcel.

Wednesday morning—a few more quick sentences.

I was so tired I slept like a log. Now I'm fresh again.

———

How did you like the things I made? I'm afraid they must have disgusted you, otherwise you might have worn one of them to the trial. If so, give them away. The first day of the trial you smiled at me oddly, as though you were making a face at me. I may have seemed aloof because I wasn't allowed to greet anyone or look at anyone. If you learn that they've shifted me to Pankrác, send me the money there—they say it takes them ages to transfer the money from here. Put at least two or three tubes of toothpaste into the "camp parcel," three after-shave lotions and enough of everything. Also a new toothbrush. No food. You should probably put everything into an old handbag. You can't send me parcels to the camp as often as you can here. Shaving gear, paper, a pen (ballpoint). You might be able to hand me the parcel after the appeal trial. Perhaps they'll allow us to talk afterward. When will I be getting a letter from you? I can't remember when I got the last one. So I know nothing of you. . . . I'm taking my sentence, as they say, philosophically. Perhaps the Lord is punishing me for my pride, and testing me as well. I'm annoyed that I probably won't be able to do any writing—just when I have the play that is constantly on my mind well thought out. (I've changed everything radically again.) All the best; I'll write more next time.

13

Saturday, November 3, 1979

Dear Olga,

I'm still living from the memory of your visit yesterday, which was—as usual— a shot in the arm for me, or a "fet" as they say in prison. This time I must have seemed somewhat absent, awkward, befuddled, if not downright queer. But when they suddenly come down into your hole for you and drag you into the world for half an hour, you can't help feeling a little dazed and not yourself. Only superficially, of course: my real state of mind was unaffected. I heard everything you said, everything interested me, I remembered everything and went over it afterward in my mind and analyzed it. And I was elated by all the good news. If I seemed indifferent to some things, it was only apparent indifference, partly due to my superficial nervousness, partly to my attempt to hide it.

I was delighted by all the gifts you brought me. I haven't had anything from home for a long time and I appreciated all of it.

That same evening I received a pile of backlogged correspondence. Naturally enough after such a long time, it all brought me a great deal of pleasure.

Your letter contained a brief sermon from which I gather you felt, because of what I said in letter 10, that I somehow regretted my decision not to go to the USA and had "again" become tangled up in some inappropriate speculations. Your misunderstanding was probably due to my rather obfuscatory language, since I was attempting to speak through implication. When I wrote it, my impression—based on some improperly understood fragments of information—was that I had misconstrued the whole business with the USA, that I had no real choice in the matter at all, that it was more like a "game" and that I must have seemed like an uncomprehending dolt. Soon afterward, however, I realized that, on the contrary, I had understood the whole business perfectly well from the start, and subsequent events have merely confirmed this. I would never have written about it at all had I known you would draw such broad conclusions. So your reprimands are groundless. During yesterday's visit you raised the question of whether that opportunity—were it to present itself again—wouldn't in fact be worth considering. I was surprised, to say the least. What has changed since the beginning of September? The fact that I now face several years in prison? I knew that at the time, which is the only reason why the decision wasn't entirely straightforward. Even so we made up our minds spontaneously (and independently of one another!) and I see no reason to suddenly change them now. Of course I have no way of knowing how I'll feel in a year or two, but for now I believe we made the right decision. (In court I even said publicly why I want to remain in this country.) So you see: you reprimanded me for harboring doubts (though you only imagined them) and now I'm throwing it back at you. Please understand me: I know you meant well—for my sake—so in fact it's not really a reprimand at all, but rather a clarification. And anyway, the question is rather academic, because no one is offering me anything, nor is this likely in the foreseeable future.

And now about my sentence: I was mentally prepared and neither surprised nor caught off guard by it. Even so, my state of mind changed a lot after the trial: the last traces of uneasiness vanished (which is understandable, since one is made uneasy by uncertainty, not certainty); I was overwhelmed by a great desire to stop thinking about our case and generally, I fell into a state of rather profound numbness. I got no pleasure out of exercising, losing weight, studying, thinking about my play—all these modest activities suddenly seemed to lose their meaning. I wasn't depressed or despairing, I just felt passive and apathetic. So the trial has meant a sudden break after all; I find myself in a radically new existential situation, and the first thing I have to do is learn to live with it, which means finding a completely new structure of values and a new perspective on everything—other hopes, other aims, other interests, other joys. I have to create a new concept of time for myself and ultimately a new concept of life.

This phase of numbness (influenced in part by the fatigue brought on by the nervous strain of the trial) is slowly subsiding and I am learning how to live in the new situation.

I was sentenced to four and a half years. If they add my suspended sentence to that—which is virtually certain—I will be in prison 64 months less a week, i.e., until September 22, 1984. Of course they may release me before then, but we mustn't pin our hopes on it. At the beginning of December, then, I'll have only a tenth of my term behind me.

As I ponder this relatively stiff sentence, I can't help thinking that in fact it's punishment for everything I've done in recent years (though no mention is made of this in the decision). Which compels me to ask myself if I haven't done something wrong. In principle, I think not. Some may feel I put too much into certain projects, that I lacked internal reserves of strength and was not cautious enough. Perhaps, and had it not been the case I might not have ended up like this. Yet a person can't change his nature, and mine is such that when I set out to do something, I have to be completely involved, without leaving myself an emergency exit. Just remember the time and nerves consumed in dealing with petty issues when I was involved with the Theatre on the Balustrade, or those three years I spent fighting on behalf of *Tvář* and reform in the Writers' Union! In the past two years, however, another pattern has emerged: when I came back from prison in 1977 I was so miserable and desperate over all the fuss that I became obsessed with proving that I had not put my own well-being first. This may have made me act excessively, impulsively, at times; I may have lost a healthy perspective on some things and submerged myself in them too deeply. (You once pointed this out to me.) Perhaps I really did "despair," as someone wrote. I hated myself and was continually depressed, and so I escaped into those various activities with a certain pigheadedness. It was not a happy state of affairs and it could not have gone on.

But why am I writing about this? Certainly not to shed tears, nor to reproach myself or to express regret. I'm writing about it because I'm learning to live with this new situation and one of the tasks I've set myself during this long stay in prison will be a kind of "self-consolidation." When I began to write plays, I wasn't as inwardly burdened as I have been in recent years; I had a far more "boyish" fantasy, far more equanimity; I saw most things in proportion; I had a balanced outlook and a sense of humor, without a trace of uptightness, hysteria, bitterness. The positions I took were not absolute; I wasn't constantly brooding over myself, absorbed in my own feelings, etc.—and at the same time I possessed a kind of harmonious inner certitude. Obsessive critical introspection is the other side of "pigheadedness." Anyway, I'd like to renew all that in myself. Jail, of all places, may seem to you a strange instrument of this self-reconstitution, but I truly feel that when I'm cut off from all my former commitments for so long, I might somehow achieve inner freedom and a new mastery over myself. I don't intend to revise my view of the world, of course, but rather to find a better way of fulfilling the demands that the world—as I see it—places on me. I don't want to change myself, but to be myself in a better way. (This is a little like the hopes with which Dostoyevsky's heroes go off to prison. In my case, however, the hopes are neither as dramatic nor as absurd, nor as religiously motivated.) I'd like to return at the age of forty-eight not as an irascible old man—which in some ways I've already become— but rather as the cheerful fellow I once was. Illusory as my plans for the next five years may be, this self-reconstitution will be my main task, one that will determine all the others. And it also seems to me that the only way for someone like me to survive here is to breathe his own meaning into the experience.

If you disapprove of my being "too frank" again, then I must tell you I couldn't care less that others will be reading this. It is important for you to see into my way of thinking—I need communication—and I don't want us to misunderstand each other just because we are too proud to reveal ourselves. You are more principled in these matters than I am, I know, but in this case, I believe openness is of the most vital importance.

Anyway, I'll stop dealing with myself now and try to give some thought to what you are facing.

It seems you are going to be alone for quite some time. The commotion around me so far (my arrest, lawyers, parcels, visits, the trial, etc.) will pass and in its place will come a long stretch of routine, everyday existence, the life of a "grass widow." I think you too should develop some ideas on how to deal with that. Here are some thoughts on the subject:

1. Don't be resentful or let yourself get upset. You won't be a help to anyone that way and you'll only overtax your nerves. It's better to keep active and busy; that will give me the greatest pleasure too.

2. Continue to do everything you've been doing—books, concerts, social contacts, keeping track of events, etc. Save books and texts, tapes, accounts of events, etc.

3. Look after Hrádeček, above all. You'll certainly be there each summer, so tend to its upkeep and don't let it fall into disrepair. You will know best what has to be done and anyway, I've written about it often enough. . . . It will be a marvelous feeling for me to know that things are prospering there.

4. As for the Prague flat, I can see why you don't want to move now. But in time, when life becomes routine again, give it some more thought. The advantages of exchanging it are indisputable. . . .

5. On the whole, life will probably demand that you be more independent in practical areas where I've been active so far (and where, as you've often complained, I've suppressed your initiative). You'll have to look after the car, learn to drive it well, get used to dealing occasionally with officialdom, learn the basics of how some technical things like the electricity, plumbing, heating, the gramophone, tape recorder, typewriter, etc., work.

6. It's clear to me that you have your own worries and problems and that the advice, instructions and assignments reaching you from this burrow of mine may often seem irrelevant, if not downright preposterous and trivial. That's understandable and as time goes by, this irrelevance may become more and more evident. Even so, you shouldn't ignore my suggestions entirely. I don't think my mind has completely turned to mush, and besides, you should give some consideration to my views, if only because it gives me pleasure. As in my previous incarcerations, I firmly believe that I can bear up far

better knowing everything is looked after at home and that I have an influence, however remotely, on our household.

7. Your cultural, domestic and social life should keep you so occupied you won't feel the need for a regular job. In any case, if you're going to devote yourself fully to our affairs, you'll scarcely have time to look for work. But if you do find yourself longing for a job, you should only consider some part-time job during the winter in Prague. I mean something you'd enjoy, the way you enjoyed ushering in the theater.

8. A large bucket of bitterness probably awaits me. Of course I'll have to drink it alone, but I'll manage somehow. Don't let it depress or bother or upset you. Think about me, but not about the bitterness. It's enough that I have to deal with it and it would just make things harder for me if it were to make your life miserable too. What will help me most is knowing that you're coping, that you're cheerful, active, that you know what you want and that you aren't giving in to despair. (During your visit yesterday you seemed to have lost some of your hope, which somehow didn't jibe with the good news you brought. You weren't as cheerful and serene as last time—and also your doubts in the matter of my departure [to the USA] took me aback.

We've survived a lot already and we'll survive this too. We each have our own basket of worries and we'll each have to work through it in our own way. Above all, we must support, not depress, each other. I don't underestimate your worries in the least, and in some regards it will be harder for you than for me.

. . .

By now I've accepted that you're probably not much of a letter writer. Postcards are enough—they always get through and are always appreciated. Still, wouldn't it be possible, once in a while, to send a fuller report of some kind? If you like, you could simply write it out in point form and give it to Puzuk to include in his letters. And while you're at it, it would always be useful to go through my letters and try to respond to my various questions, suggestions, instructions, etc. I don't mind if you react negatively, I only want to know if you've at least taken cognizance of everything.

Thank Puzuk very much for his letter (8) and for the conscientious way he has led our clan and for overseeing my affairs. If he has any financial difficulties (loss of job), please help him out! And by the way, friends owe me a lot of money. I'm not asking for it back right away and in many cases I don't even consider it a loan; still, in about two cases—if they happened to think of returning the money and could manage it—I'd accept repayment: I refer to Pavel who, I assume, has become rich, and—but no. I started to grumble about a friend who I hear is spreading rather nasty remarks, but then I censored it myself and erased the whole passage. Grumbling about a friend, common enough outside, seems inappropriate in a letter from prison.

· · ·

Sunday, November 4

It's a dark and gloomy Sunday morning, too dark to read (and I don't have a good book) and I'm looking forward to two events: an afternoon feast from the things you brought, on the occasion of my roommate's name day, and tomorrow's shower.

Several details that have come to mind:

. . . Rather than calling in my loans, it might be more realistic to gather in books I've lent out. The list is among my things. Some friends have had books that are rather rare for long enough—lest they come to believe such loans are forgivable!

Shouldn't you start making a fuss about the heating oil? Suppose Dr. T. were to help you write a complaint to the head office of the national oil company? As far as I know, this is the first time a commercial enterprise has ever refused to sell something to the family of a jailed citizen. It's not just the heating oil; this could become a monstrous precedent. (Franz Kafka: "Man is an eternal rebel.")

More on the parcel: I need a hard case for my glasses. The one I have here is soft and won't prevent them from breaking. It has to be big enough for my glasses to fit.

I have more plans for my prison term than merely trying to become a "cheerful fellow," but I'll write about that next time.

If they telephone from the theater in Vienna—the premiere should be sometime now—you can wait for the call at Puzuk's and find out how it went. Tell them I'm with them in spirit and that I'm writing another play which I will let them have (when it's done), if they want it. Let me know right away. And by the way: you can send telegrams here as well!

Monday, November 5

I had a good day today: a good bath, a marvelous session of yoga, I ate nothing but healthy things (thanks to you), I was in a fine mood (the sudden intake of vitamins certainly helped). Apparently my despondency is finally over. Greetings to all the faithful and everyone I'm fond of. I'm not going to name them, but say hello to each of them specially as though I had named them all. Even if you weren't as cheerful as the last time, you looked good—you obviously hadn't been out carousing the night before.

BE CALM, SERENE, CHEERFUL, INDUSTRIOUS, SOCIABLE, KIND TO EVERY-ONE, OPTIMISTIC, TAKE CARE OF YOURSELF, DRESS NICELY. SAY ONLY CLEVER THINGS. DON'T PUT OFF UNPLEASANT DUTIES, STUDY MY LETTERS CAREFULLY AND TRY TO CARRY OUT THE TASKS I SET YOU. BE BRAVE, YET PRUDENT. THINK WELL OF ME, FEEL SORRY FOR ME, BUT NOT ENOUGH TO MAKE YOURSELF SAD. DON'T LOSE HOPE AND LOVE ME!

I kiss you, Vašek

P.S. (Monday, at night) I was drifting off nicely when suddenly I recalled our trial, got mad, arose and covered several pages with writing, ate the sweets and smoked three cigarettes and so managed to calm myself. So there it is: water doesn't flow through my veins either.

*

Tuesday, November 6

I've just been informed that restrictions have been placed on the November parcels. You can still send tobacco, juices and sweets, but no other foodstuffs. This means no cheese and no fish. Perhaps this would be the time to send toothpaste, lotions, etc. Apparently the restrictions apply mainly to smoked meats and fish. Perhaps fruit will be allowed. They say their instructions will be included with the parcel vouchers. Parcels already on the way will be given to us as usual.

My lawyer was here again today. I was quite satisfied with him. He's a true professional and very conscientious.

When I receive the verdict, I will write out material for the appeal etc.—and with that, our case will be over as far as I'm concerned. I read about us in *RP* again today. Interesting. From various fragments of chance information you can begin piecing together a picture of the situation.

Goodbye for now, and I kiss you,

V.

14

Saturday, November 17, 1979

Dear Olga,

The main news from my life in the past two weeks is not very cheerful: my damned hemorrhoids have flared up as never before. It's been sheer agony for several days and the pain is unrelieved even at night, so that I can't sleep. It's worse here than it would be outside, one reason being that when you're feeling your worst you can't have a good stiff drink. You're alone with your pain and you have to go through with it. I almost gave up hope. Yesterday I had a checkup in Pankrác and I'm going back the 27th. It's not entirely out of the question that they'll be operating. I'd welcome that, because I don't think I could live with this for five years. I was afraid, as every chronic hemorrhoid sufferer is, that I might have a tumor but it seems not. The only bright spot was a drive through Prague (I saw our apartment building on the embankment).

The other disagreeable thing is that two parcels have still not come—the one for October and the one with the fruit. Two weeks ago we were told they'd been sent, so I don't understand. Did you go to the Municipal Court and try to speed up the vouchers? Those parcels are enormously important; it's the only thing that brightens life up here. By now the third parcel—November's—should be almost on its way. Write me which of my letters you've received and which not.

. . .

I also have some better news: I've started writing a play! That is, I've gone directly from just thinking about it and making notes to writing the text. I consider this a great achievement because I didn't believe I could do it in these circumstances. I've never written like this before: I have very little room, I can't write at night, I mustn't waste paper, I have nothing to stimulate me while I write, etc. The fact is I haven't written much yet—about ten pages. (I had to stop because of the pain.) The main thing is I know I can do it. Theoretically, there should be nothing to prevent me from actually writing a new play here sooner or later. (Of course I don't know what conditions will be like when I'm finally sentenced—I'll certainly have less time then.) I'm delighted by this turnaround because, as you know, for me writing a play is like giving birth (I don't write easily, like most of my colleagues). Of course I don't know how it will turn out—but then I never do. . . .

In my last letter I indulged in a bit of self-analysis. I'll assume it reached you and continue where I left off. I'm thinking over the kind of meaning I should try to breathe into the years in prison that lie ahead. Last time I wrote about how—if I can manage it—it might lead to a kind of general psychological reconstitution on my part. Why do I think this? In recent years I have been living a strange, unnatural, exclusive and somewhat "greenhouse" existence. Now this will change. I will be one of many tiny, helpless ants. I'll be thrown into the world much as I was when I was a lab assistant, a stagehand, a soldier, a student. I will have a number, I'll be one of a multitude and no one will expect anything of me or pay any special attention to me. For some people outside, I may be a kind of "institution"—but I'll be unaware of this, living in a different world surrounded by different worries. This return to an earlier existential situation—one that suited me best and in which I accomplished the most—could help me achieve that planned inner reconstitution I wrote about last time. (Eliminate psychic paralysis, uncertainties, not to see myself through the eyes of those who expect something of me, eliminate nervousness and doubt, etc.) Conceivably, I might begin writing more for the theater again, as an observer of the "theater of the world." It's paradoxical that I find the prospect of such a turnaround in prison, of all places, where I will no doubt find it exceptionally hard to write, but that's not unusual: haven't I always written most when I've had the least time? The mere fact that I've already started writing something is a modest step in the right direction. (I know, I've written letters from prison before that were full of marvelous plans and resolutions that came to nothing, but I always came back too soon. Now it appears I'll have a decent time ahead of me, and that should show.)

Of course I have other plans, too: I'd like to improve my English. I'll never be perfect, I'd only like to learn to read and write it after a fashion. Mainly, though, I'd like to learn German—again, not perfectly; I don't have the disposition for it—but at least as well as I know English. Perhaps a specialist could advise you of a good, complete and wide-ranging textbook and you could put it in my camp gear, which perhaps you'll be allowed to give me. You might add to that a small Czech-German, German-Czech dictionary (there should be one at home)— and if possible a good German book to start with, one I'd enjoy reading (something technical rather than literary). . . .

I would summarize my plans for prison as follows:

1. to remain at least as healthy as I am now (and perhaps cure my hemorrhoids);
2. generally reconstitute myself psychologically;
3. write at least two plays;
4. improve my English;
5. learn German at least as well as I know English;
6. study the entire Bible thoroughly.

If I succeed in fulfilling this plan, the years may not be entirely lost.

*

And now some individual points as they occur to me:

I've received (at last) the verdict. I've written materials on which to base an appeal, I will write a speech (brief) for the trial and that's the end of our case as far as I'm concerned. I'm expecting a visit from the lawyer on Monday.

There's a Mucha exhibition in Roztoky. Are you going to see it?

Puzuk was interested in what books there are in English here: *Treasure Island,* London's stories, a crime novel by Ed McBain, another crime novel, a political book called *The Triumph* (interesting), and *The Financier* by Dreiser. I don't think there are any others. I've had them all and read them, more or less. Now (after the trial) I've given English a rest, but I'll be taking it up again. . . .

By the time you read this, I'll have been in Ruzyně half a year (this time) and exactly a year (in total).

By the way, I learned that the Burgtheater was in Prague. Did you see it? And didn't my friend the dramaturge look you up? Did you find out anything about the new premiere?

.   .   .

Will you write me a letter sometime? Or give Puzuk the information for his letter, including your reaction to my queries and to everything I write about in my letters? I want to know how you spend your days, what the dogs are doing, who you see, where you go, etc. etc. How many books have you managed to get through? Were you in Hrádeček? Is everything okay there?

That's all for today. I will—as usual—add more.

I kiss you, V.

Sunday, November 18, 1979

I spent today in a flurry of fruitful activity—writing official documents. My indisposition seems in retreat, thanks in part to the fact that I now receive warm water on the doctor's orders. I eat a great deal and exercise very little. I am reading George Sand—as much as I can in this darkness. Ahoj!

*

Monday, November 19, 1979

The lawyer didn't come today; perhaps he'll come tomorrow. The parcels didn't come either. This business with the parcels infuriates me. I desperately need the vitamins; I can feel it in my gums and elsewhere, and the hemorrhoids wouldn't bother me so much either. Trifles like this rankle me more than the entire verdict. You must try and get them to send you the vouchers! Correspondence and everything else is harder now than it was when the case was still under investigation. I neither read nor write much so I won't endanger my eyesight. My one delight is the warm water for my backside. Oh well, tomorrow my mood will improve; it doesn't take much to cheer me up and make me suddenly very forgiving. Tell Klaus I thank him very much for the parcel he sent you. Do you happen to know what's become of the gramophone version of *Audience?*

———

P.S. I thought it might be a fine idea if you were to write a nice letter to Vonnegut. Jarda K. would help you with it.

HOPE IS A DIMENSION OF THE SPIRIT. It is not outside us, but within us. When you lose it, you must seek it again WITHIN YOURSELF and in people around you—not in objects or even in events.

. . .

Tuesday, November 20, 1979

The lawyer was here today to discuss the appeal with me; he'll come again tomorrow, but by then this letter will be on its way. I didn't learn much about you and the rest from him, except that my letters 11 and 12 may have finally arrived, which means I might expect those parcels in the foreseeable future after all. (The restrictions on food-stuffs don't come into force until the November parcel, so I ought to receive everything you send.) By rights you should have letter 13 now as well, so a third parcel could be on the way. I'll believe it when I see it. Otherwise, however, you don't seem to be in any kind of regular contact with the lawyer. Puzuk is, and for that I'm grateful. I'm glad you're submitting an appeal as well. We'll see each other next at the hearing, perhaps before Christmas—or in January. If you could, please bring along that bag with all the things I want to take to the camp with me. Perhaps they'll allow us to talk, and you could give it to me then. If not, the lawyer might take it and hand it over in prison or something like that. . . . I'm looking forward to the work camp. At least it will be a change: I'll have more movement and see more people. Everyone here looks forward to it. I have no illusions; there will certainly be hardships but at least it will be different. And this make-shift existence will be over: provisionality is never a good thing. . . . My dear Grumbler, I think of you with tenderness and I even accept with tenderness the fact that you don't write, that you don't do what I ask or respond to my letters (do you at least read them carefully?). (I need to communicate with you and I need your guidance—just as when you used to be my dramaturge.)

Goethe: More light!

I kiss you, V.

Tuesday evening

Good news! I've just received the package of fruit! I've already eaten one orange and I'm overjoyed with the parcel. (I've got warm water, they've turned on a stronger bulb and finally the long-awaited parcel has come—and I feel great, all disgruntlement banished!) . . .

15

Saturday, December 1, 1979

Dear Olga,

I've encountered a certain type of prisoner here who has definitively put me off all the forms of attracting pity to oneself practiced in prisons. Outside, these people are big talkers, powerful bosses, selfish and cynical men who think only of how to get rich at their fellow man's expense—and when they come here, they turn into old maids: weeping, simpering, forever self-pitying, they simulate various illnesses, grovel abjectly and try to pin the blame for everything onto others. I haven't spent a Christmas in prison yet, but I've heard that these fallen bonzos are at their most unbearable then. Out of sheer loathing for that state of mind, I don't intend to concern myself much with Christmas, not even in this letter.

I'll begin, therefore, with a truly unpoetic theme: to wit, my backside. I went to the Pankrác prison surgery again and was told that although my hemorrhoids are ripe for an operation, it was not recommended yet because there is no guarantee that it would make things any better. I'm to treat them as I have been so far, and if they bother me too much during my term—that is, if the treatment fails—I am to request an operation and they will perform it. There is no hidden unwillingness here: I have it in writing in my dossier that they will operate if I insist and it's probably just as they say. In any case, as a naive layman, I must have subconsciously felt this myself, since I've been putting the decision off for twenty years.

. . . It's embarrassing to come back to the subject of what I'll need for the camp, and my going on about it probably seems ludicrous to you, but you must understand how extremely important it is to me. Moreover, I have no idea to what extent you've taken note of my previous instructions. Just to be sure, therefore, I'm adding a new list of things:

A CARTON OF BT CIGARETTES + A CIGARETTE-MAKING DEVICE + PA-PERS + A HARD CASE FOR MY GLASSES + A 1980 POCKET CALENDAR + 5 LINED NOTEBOOKS + A BALL-POINT PEN + REFILLS + A BIBLE + A SMALL CZECH-GERMAN and GERMAN-CZECH DICTIONARY + A GERMAN LAN-GUAGE TEXTBOOK + A LOT OF VITAMINS + TEA + A POCKETKNIFE + A CHEAP RAZOR + A LARGE QUANTITY OF GOOD RAZOR BLADES + 3 TUBES OF ORDINARY SHAVING CREAM + 3 TUBES OF TOOTHPASTE + A NEW (HARD-BRISTLED) TOOTHBRUSH + A SMALL BRUSH FOR WASHING + BROWN SUNTAN LOTION + 3 TUBES OF ALPA + NAIL SCISSORS + A POCKET MIRROR + A NAIL FILE + 2 PAIRS OF WARM SOCKS

. . .

How will you spend Christmas? With your family, I expect. Wish them all a Merry Christmas for me and a Happy New Year. And buy them some presents from me. . . . Buy something for yourself from me—a fancy dress, perhaps; if you decide to put it under a tree some-where, I'll include a tag for you as well. I'll add special Christmas greetings for Jana and Andulka—they'll certainly get a kick out of it, so please give it to them. I hope your first Christmas without me for many years will be a cheerful one. Eat and drink in my stead and don't be sad—when things are in full swing, I'll be long since asleep. I'll think of you intensely at 7 p.m. (just before lights-out). Where are you spend-ing New Year's Eve? Among good friends, I assume. Give them my warmest greetings, naturally, and wish them all the best for the new decade. I don't suppose I need to be explicit about what I wish for you (and myself); the circumstances make it clear enough.

I have an idea for an excellent Christmas gift you might give me: you could write me a long letter at last. Perhaps you could spend one of the holidays writing it. (I'd appreciate it if you would answer at least some of the countless questions I've flooded you with in the last six months. Would it be asking too much, for instance, for you to tell me what state you left Hrádeček in, what work you did, and did not, man-age to get done, how you're living in Prague, what your plans are, etc. etc.?)

In the last while I've read—when I could—a couple of interesting books; among them, a rather interesting one on capital punishment by a Czech author completely unknown to me: Jaroslav Marie *(The Sword and the Scales)*. Perhaps it would interest Zdeněk; it contains, for example, something about T.G.M.'s position on the death penalty.

I've been working on the play—very lightly, and more to keep in shape. After all my illnesses, I've started doing yoga again.

On one postcard, you wrote that much had changed outside and that more and more friends are sending greetings. It should certainly be possible to expand on that—especially to say which of the more distant friends are greeting me.

That's all for today; I'll add more.

Tuesday evening

The parcel didn't come, there's no mail and I don't know what to make of it. This letter will probably reach you in January. If letter 13 hasn't arrived, press them for a parcel voucher. Today I read a long article about us in *RP*. Physically, I'm fit again, mentally also, except that I still feel sluggish and I sleep a lot (afternoon and at night). I also think I'm gaining weight. I finished reading *Lucien Leuwen* by Stendhal. I think a lot, but so far haven't come up with anything special. All the best, Grumbler, and be sociable over Christmas. Think about me, too, but don't be sad. When I write you, I feel very close to you. Write me and you'll see that you'll feel close to me too!

I kiss you, Vašek

. . .

P.S. I often dream about Honza Tříska, Miloš Forman and Pavel K. All of them "foreigners."

16

December 15, 1979

Dear Olga,

In a few days we'll see each other in court and you won't get this letter till later, God knows when. By the time you read it, I'll probably be in some distant camp with a rather different set of worries. Even so—and despite my belief that they'll allow us to talk after the trial—I'll write as though nothing world-shaking were about to happen; at least you'll have, albeit belatedly, a notion of how I'm living.

. . .

Recently, after quite an interval, some correspondence finally arrived: letter 9 from Puzuk, letters 10 and 11 from you, three of your postcards and a postcard from Jana. I was somewhat unjust to scold you for not writing letters at all. So two have come, I was overjoyed by them and I thank you very much. They might have been more detailed about some matters but as it is, I have to be content. I appreciated your saying in one of them that you love me. It's been a long time since you've told me that! . . .

It would seem that you're composed, brave and active. News from Jana confirms this. I'm very glad! It's exactly what I want. Go on being that and more!

I can understand your not wanting to move. But at least you should give some thought to our future living arrangements and explore the possibilities. The thought of being condemned to live with that furniture forever horrifies me. . . . except for the rugs and the pictures—and of course the bed—you could buy something now and again that really appeals to you. Don't go out looking, just wait till you come across something. But that is only one alternative. There are certainly others. I'm only concerned that we not slowly and reluctantly reconcile ourselves to the situation, which will then remain unchanged.

What is there to say about my life? . . . It is very dark here, gloomy and uncongenial. I'm looking forward to the appeal and the changes that will follow. I'm not working on the play much right now, but I am thinking about it and about other literary alternatives; I'll write more about this in good time. When hopelessness comes over me, I do yoga and it helps. It's the trivial details that depress me, never the general situation. I've read a very interesting book by Byrd, the explorer, *Alone*, about how he lived for half a year by himself at the South Pole. Many of his observations about isolation are consistent with my own experience! I read *RP* very closely and analyze everything in it. The day before yesterday, for example, I spent the whole day poring over the state budget for next year. Very interesting! I'm learning to understand what is not written from what is written. I've gotten used to my colleague and I'm sticking him in the play. Only the cigars and the caviar paste are left from the last parcel—I'm saving them both for Christmas. I've used up the vitamins and they did me a great deal of good. I've been here for almost seven months and I find I haven't come up with any decent ideas at all, though I have unlimited time for thinking. It's odd, but mental creativity obviously needs interaction with outside impulses. If the mind is isolated from everything around it, it does not develop, it becomes stunted. (The Buddhist conception of self-perfection in isolation is probably for a different type of person altogether— but it does not lead to visible creative results either; its consequences may be essentially incommunicable, and in any case they are not intended for communication.) I don't feel that my mental growth has become stunted, exactly, but I do feel that a single experience, a single interesting conversation, could stimulate me to incomparably greater mental feats than a week of concentrated thought. In short, the spirit needs the WORLD; without it, it's "running on empty." To my fellow prisoners I seem like an introvert who merely reads, ruminates or writes things down, but essentially I'm not like that at all. What inspires me are experiences of the world, not of my own inner being. Jirka N. could explain this to you from the point of view of phenomenology.

Dear Grumbler, if something else occurs to me, I'll add it. The lawyer might come early in the week (he hasn't been here for some time), and perhaps I'll learn something. . . . Write me about how you spent Christmas and New Year's.

I kiss you, love, V.

*

Sunday morning

The pains in my backside are getting worse and I can only hope they won't peak next week, otherwise I don't know how I could get through the trial. In addition to feeling sluggish from the pain, I think I'm getting the flu again. Under normal circumstances I'd take a pile of vitamins, some aspirins and hot tea—and it would go away. As it is, it will drag on for several days. When will my body ever be well again? THANKS FOR THE PHOTO! Excellent!

. . .

Tuesday evening

Last night I was given two aspirins, I slept well and felt better today. The sun was shining and I could see in the cell. The lawyer came, so I was able to give him messages for you and go over everything with him. You and Puzuk wrote a very fine appeal. I had a good yoga session. And just now, your postcard from December 3 arrived—the last Mucha—with Andrej's poem. Good! That weeping Comenius was appropriate. . . .

Greetings, I kiss you and good-bye until the day after tomorrow.

V.

I hear letter 13 has arrived. After six weeks.

17

New Year's Eve, 1979

Dear Olga,

Your visit left me feeling wonderful and I think it was very successful. You looked pretty (!) and it suited you, you radiated serenity, poise and purposeful energy, told me many important things—in short, I was exceptionally pleased with you. It seems that this time, being a grass widow has been good for you; this temporary emancipation from my domination is allowing you to develop your own identity. But of course I am happiest of all to see that you are living and acting—if I may put it this way—"in my spirit" and that you are effectively standing in for me. (Now if you could only write a new play for me as well.) I may seem somewhat dronelike beside you, a kind of appendage, something that needs looking after like a child or a cripple. I'm becoming more dependent on you than is healthy. Thanks too for bringing all those things; I hope the prison stores accepted such a rich assortment of supplies from you. They also let me take everything you left with me except for the New Year's card, which I don't have yet, though I hope to get it. (I hope you weren't annoyed that I declined the talisman; it wasn't because I didn't care for it, but rather to avoid becoming too dependent on it: I have a tendency to be superstitious.)

This letter—written at the turn of the decade—will probably reach you sooner than has been the custom, and who knows, perhaps it will reach you before some letters written previously: now that I'm sentenced, the correspondence apparently doesn't go by such a complicated route. This is substantiated by the fact that I've now received three

Christmas cards in record time (from Hejdánek's sisters, Honza Schneider and Jarmila—if you talk to them, thank them, and give a special greeting to Jarmila). This letter should contain a voucher for the January parcel, so that three parcels in all should be on the way (December's—letter 15; the fruit package—letter 16 and now January's). Send them all here: I could be moved out any day now, or I could be here another month. If I'm gone when the parcels arrive, I assume they'll be forwarded. The worst they can do is return them to you. The usual stuff: lots of juice, cigars, American cigarettes, oranges, tubes of meat paste, Kleenex, toothpicks, etc. (I don't think you can send regular food just yet.) Could you include a few large envelopes (the largest size); I still have to write something rather bulky for the lawyer.

Christmas was beyond my expectations. I was still delighted by the fresh memory of your visit and the fresh supply of delicacies. On Christmas Eve we put on a big spread; the wall above our little table was decorated with mistletoe, and the table was full of nicely served delicacies (mess tins with caviar, cookies, oranges, a mixture of nuts, chocolates and raisins, cigars, etc.); preparing festive tables, as you know, is a favorite pastime of mine. I spent the rest of the holidays well too; I read Dumas's *Mémoires d'un médicin,* did a bit of yoga, smoked my cigars and thought. And naturally I thought too about all those close to me and friends (including those for whom freedom was a fresh joy at Christmas). I didn't feel at all sentimental; on the contrary, I was mildly euphoric. After Christmas I had my hair cut. They wouldn't let me have it shaved, but it's very short, so I look now the way I did many years ago, which I take as a symbolic prefiguration of my intent to regain some of my former psychic resilience.

Otherwise I'm fine; I'm mentally very calm and composed (my colleague envies me for this), sometimes too much so, and composure becomes indolence. I've interrupted my study of English and I'm not even working on the play (I'll come back to that later); I sleep a lot; I drop off at once and sleep deeply and soundly till morning, and sometimes I doze off during the day as well. I can't remember ever needing so much sleep before. But it's good; the worst of all is not being able to sleep, which is the case with most prisoners. I still have luxurious dreams; today, for example, I dreamed again I was in the USA filming something with Miloš Forman. Miloš has been haunting me in my dreams. (Do you suppose I subconsciously envy him his luck and his success? I know of no other way to explain it, even though my conscious EGO harbors no such feelings.) I'm extremely curious about what it will be like where they put me. Will they let me have all my things, including the books? Will I have any time for myself? Who will be there with me? What will the regime be like? Etc. I doubt I'll be as indolent as I am here; it may be partly the result of living in provisional circumstances. I'm not worried about conflicts; in general I get along with everyone and I can bear indignities with stoic detachment. Self-pity of any kind is utterly foreign to me; I strongly dislike people who are always feeling sorry for themselves. I also cannot stand the exaggeration of ailments that some here indulge in, or in fact any old-womanish attitude to the prison situation. I regret that during my first stay in prison, I allowed myself to get caught in some of the traps, but everything was quite different then, worse in fact; I'm beginning to understand this clearly now; there is simply no comparison with the present. I say this more as a marginal remark—please don't think I'm still brooding over it. Today I see prison as an authentically absurd experience, one that every careful reader of Kafka should understand well. (One day, perhaps, I'll write about it, but my approach will be different than in my earlier efforts.)

In his last letter, Puzuk asked me to write more about the play I'm working on. I've abandoned the original Faustian conception and left only the basic theme, which I have shifted to a different milieu—prison. Yet it is not going to be a play about prison but—in a manner of speaking—about life in general; the prison milieu should serve only as a metaphor of the general human condition (the state of "thrownness" into the world; the existential significance of the past, of recollection, and of the future, the spinning of hopes; the theme of isolation and pseudohope, the discovery of "naked values," etc.). It will be a Beckettian comedy about life; all that remains of Faust is the theme of temptation (the swapping of one's own identity for the "world of entities"). There will only be three people onstage, chatting about trivialities—in other words, everything will be in the subtext. The play is worked out in detail, but I've stopped writing it for the moment. Perhaps when I'm finally relocated, I'll be able (occasionally, at least) to continue. I'm struggling against a number of odd psychological inhibitions; it's not that I have any doubts about the subject itself and the way I've worked it out, it's more that, technically, I'm having trouble writing about prison in prison. It's hard to explain. If I can't overcome this block, I'll set the play aside till later and work on something else, a one-act comedy, perhaps. In short, it's hard to write here. I don't feel entirely free, and without that feeling it can't be done. Many external factors get in the way; even outside, writing for me was a kind of ceremony, and an ecstatic ceremony at that—I had to resort to various complex techniques for breaking through all my inhibitions and my aversion to my own writing etc. and, because I'm an essentially shy person, I had to find different ways of bucking up my courage; and above all, of course, I needed absolute tranquillity, comfort, unlimited time, etc. None of this exists here, of course, and I have to struggle for trivial concessions like a little more light. Still, I have made some progress (I began writing the play) and I continue to hope that all this will somehow be possible. Ideally, I'd like to get some extraordinarily fortuitous and sustaining idea for a one-act play (like the one that gave rise—in a single week—to *Audience*), one that would carry me along with it: then, in all likelihood, I could overcome those obstacles and inhibitions and write something funny, spontaneously. If I could manage that, the rest would follow more easily. So far, however, no such idea has occurred to me. So much for my writing, then, if you can call it that.

*

I've just had a good session of yoga (I'm delighted by the sun, thanks to which I now have light) and I pass to the traditionally more prosaic part of my letter, that is, to suggestions for you:

. . .

I think you should write a longish letter to Klaus (in Czech). Tell him you've spoken to me and that I send him my greeting and best wishes, that I'm well, that you gave me an account of the different productions of my plays and that I thank him very much for everything. I'd also like him to know that now, after the one-act plays, there will obviously be a gap in my writing and that it might be worth trying to fill it with my *The Beggar's Opera*. Tell him I'm fond of the play and that I'm sorry it's so seldom performed. All the same, I'm still hopeful that it might be discovered, as it were. Klaus doesn't offer the plays outside the German-speaking world but tends to wait for interest to be expressed. And that can't happen if no one knows the play; it hasn't been translated and it can't attract any attention as long as it is confined to Germany. (And by the way, I don't know what the German translation is like.) . . . I hate acting as my own agent like this, but I'm not very happy about having only my one-acters performed—it creates the false impression that I only write in a single manner about a single topic. At the same time, I know that *The Beggar's Opera* needs only to be properly translated and understood by someone—in other words, it only needs to be discovered—and then things would take care of themselves. You say they're planning to put it on in France. That's marvelous, but we should find out who is doing it, how and what it's being translated from. The French are notorious for rewriting everything they translate, and they'll even stoop to translating it from German or Italian. That would be a disaster, of course. If necessary, I could write a few notes for the translator and director—I've already done so once; they're at home; I saw them not long ago in Hrádeček among my papers. . . .

When you know more about the response to *Protest* and to Faust, etc., don't forget to write me about it at once. (Now, perhaps, letters will come and go more quickly.)

When you speak with the lawyer, ask him if he's been able to determine whether my letter to Mr. Papp has been forwarded by the court. If not, write him yourself, thank him for his offer and explain to him why I could not accept it. . . .

Don't forget to send me your letter of appeal. (I will need it.) . . .

From time to time I intend to remind you about the question of our flat so it won't be completely forgotten. My subject for today: Jirka G. knows a lot about the conversion of attics. Talk to him about it. Somewhere in Prague, there must be the owner of a nice, cozy attic flat who would love to exchange it for an ordinary flat in Dejvice, especially if we were to throw in the furniture—as a trade-off for the better location. Exchanging one co-op flat for another should be a simpler matter, administratively speaking. That's one alternative. Just look into it as an idea for now—I don't think it can be done right away. But if it could, go ahead without me.

. . .

If you lend anyone the Canadian edition of my plays, don't forget to pin a note to *The Conspirators* saying that I don't wish readers to read it because it was published by mistake in an unauthorized and incorrect version (in progress).

*

This evening my colleague and I are holding a New Year's Eve feast. I'm looking forward to it. At midnight, instead of champagne, we'll drink a toast with Celaskon Effervescens. On New Year's Day we'll eat grapefruit. (In general I eat an enormous amount here and my belly is growing gratifyingly larger. Oddly enough, this doesn't interfere with my yoga. My gluttony will soon be over, though; after I'm moved, I won't be so well off.) I'll think of you at midnight. Don't forget to write me in detail how you spent Christmas and New Year's.

*

Many greetings to my friend Andulka! Tell her I hope she drops her teetotaling, at least for New Year's Eve. In letter 15 I wrote her some lines of poetry; I hope they got through. . . .

I kiss you, Vašek
(green is the color of hope)

New Year's Eve was interesting; I even had two moving experiences. (Alexandre Dumas: "A kind word in prison is worth more than the most expensive gift in freedom.") My colleague and I sang! (I sometimes sing with him, and oddly enough we're on key.) I've resolved that once I'm out, every New Year's Eve I shall think of those in prison. This afternoon my gluttony reached a peak, then I relaxed, washed my almost hairless head (to freshen up), perfumed my handkerchief, drank some fizzy Celaskon, and all of this made me feel good on the threshold of the new decade. What do you suppose it will bring us? (I've begun feeling somewhat skeptical about astrologists—their predictions, it seems to me, too often relate to fundamental alternatives in life that might have come about but didn't.) Incidentally, it was very nice the way you all stood up in the courtroom. Write me how things are regarding the specific matter I talked to you about. I have my reasons for thinking it's important. I'm looking forward to your next visit.

Ahoj V.

. . .

II. Letters 18–86

Heřmanice

January 1980–August 1981

18

January 12, 1980

Dear Olga,

It would be difficult to imagine a more radical CUT than my recent change of habitat: after seven months of solitude, quiet, warmth, indolence—suddenly such a flurry of activity: it reminds me a little of my first days in the army, and a little of those early days in the brewery, but of course it's fundamentally tougher here in every way (this is a prison, after all). My mind has more or less adjusted to the change, my body will likely take longer. Yesterday I came down with what may be the flu; I was utterly exhausted and feverish, they gave me some medicine and I'm allowed to stay in bed today and feeling a good deal better for it. My hemorrhoids are acting up and my skin is raw and slightly chafed (especially where I used to have hair and whiskers), etc. But all that will certainly sort itself out. The change was really too abrupt. It was most helpful, of course, not to have to suffer it alone and to be able to reflect upon the change with others. (Please forgive this scrawl—my fingers seem clumsy.) I was allowed to have everything I brought with me, with the exception of a few small items (lighter, knife, aerosol shaving cream and cologne); you can take them away after your next visit. I have no books as yet, but I am confident they'll let me have them in time as well. (So far I've not needed them, believe me.) While at Pankrác, I managed to read two of the books of Moses. It seems highly unlikely that I'll get a chance to do any writing for now.

We didn't expect to plunge into camp life like this—and so far, we don't know whether it is better or worse than we expected. Time will tell. All that's clear now is that the new circumstances give rise to many odd situations and absurd atmospheres. My main worry so far has been how to find a minute now and then for myself, I mean for my rather complex ablutions (given my hemorrhoids).

While we're on the subject of hygiene: on the basis of this letter, you can send me a parcel of hygienic needs: please include the following items: a soap dish, a facecloth, a body scrub brush, more soap, shaving soap, perhaps some more toothpaste. Otherwise, I'm going to need saccharin or spolarin again (it's more practical than sugar), a calendar for 1980, vitamin C, juices and other things too, but don't put them in the parcel—you can bring them yourself, since it seems that we'll be having a visit on one of the Sundays in February. I'll write you in time which one it will be and give you all the details; meanwhile this is only advance notice. Ask Ivan if he wants to come too; I'm allowed two adult visitors. And write me, so I can give notice in time. Don't come by car, it makes no sense in this weather. Come by train or plane the day before (the visit will take place on a Sunday morning); perhaps you could treat it as an outing and arrange to go together with Kamila and Zuzana. At the time of the visit, you can bring me a parcel weighing 3 kilograms. I'll write you precise instructions. Most of all, I'll probably want cigarettes (there can be 300).

. . .

We're allowed to write once a week from here and the letters travel much faster than from Ruzyně, so communication between us will be much more flexible.

. . .

Will I be able to endure this for five years? Perhaps. In any case, I have no choice. Or maybe I do—but I don't know what would have to happen to make me choose it. I've become hardened in such matters. I'm a Czech hayseed and shall remain so.

I kiss you, Vašek

19

January 27, 1980

Dear Olga,

I've been in Heřmanice three weeks now and I'm gradually becoming acclimatized. My last letter was somewhat of a dud, so there was a hiatus in my correspondence. Thanks for the letter in which you describe how you spent Christmas and New Year's; it arrived not long ago. Two of Ivan's letters were not handed over to me because of something written in English—obviously the usual poetry. I hope it won't discourage either you or Ivan from writing—write me frequently and fully! (Vašek has already had 70 letters from Kamila!) I only ask that you observe certain principles—my getting your letters depends on it: you must (a) maintain the prescribed format; (b) not write my name on the envelope; (c) avoid writing things that could be construed as oblique references, hints, codes or the like. On the positive side, write me about everything you do, what's happening, whom you see regularly, what you're reading, what's come out, etc. etc. in other words, everything that interests me. I'm hungry for all the news, as usual—even more so, given my physical distance from home. Apart from the letter I mentioned, your parcel of hygienic supplies arrived, and two parcels originally sent to Ruzyně—many thanks; your selection was flawless. I'd be interested to know if my letter no. 17 (from Ruzyně) reached you. In it, I told you about my Christmas and New Year's, evaluated your visit and praised you greatly! If not (I sent it two days before my departure) I'll return to those themes in subsequent letters. (Something else about the form of the letters: there is a small change in my prison number; don't overlook it.)

You and Ivan can visit me on February 17 (I don't know, of course, if Ivan can make it or not). You will be officially notified by the administration of this institute. You have to be here at 8 a.m.; you can work out how you'll get here with Zuzana and Kamila. I don't recommend coming by car; the night express would be better, or come a day ahead and stay overnight in a hotel. I'm looking forward to your visit a lot. I'll be shaven and shorn, so don't be alarmed at my appearance. You can bring a 3-kilogram parcel with you; you'll have to choose the contents very carefully and among other things, avoid heavy packaging. . . .

And now something about myself: I've recovered from that cold (or whatever it was) and my body is gradually getting used to it here. Sometimes my teeth, spine, arms, legs, etc. ache but that will pass, especially because mentally, I'm absolutely fit; in fact it might even be said that I'm rather enjoying myself. I certainly can't complain about a lack of interesting experiences and I'm almost surprised at how soon, and how precisely in the spirit of my own expectations, I have been thrown into the kind of experience that, as I wrote you from Ruzyně, might serve as an instrument of my inner, psychic reconstitution and the renewal of my primordial relationship with the world. True, the experience has been rougher than I had anticipated, and it also has many unexpected aspects, but that's all part of it. I won't be able to do any writing but perhaps, in time, I'll manage to study languages. And I might also learn something, some practical skills. I'm terrified by only one thing: I'll be here for such a long time. The atmosphere in the world seems rather stifling and oppressive and of course that does nothing to strengthen my hope that the sentence might be shortened.

. . .

It seems that for a long time to come, I'll be more dependent than ever on your letters. There is no way around it; you will have to get over your aversion and write me long letters, often. Everything interests me. If you're stuck, you can go over my letters from Ruzyně, where you will find a wealth of questions (as yet unanswered) and other matters on which I wanted to hear your opinion.

Jirka and Vašek, who are sitting here beside me writing their families, send you their warmest greetings.

I'd like to write more about myself, my impressions and my thoughts, but it will be better if I stop for now. In any case, the paper is running out and so is the time set aside for writing. I'll be going to bed soon. (With the flood of daily impressions, the colorful dreams I had in Ruzyně have dried up.)

And so I leave you; I'm thinking of you and sending you a kiss—

Vašek

Something else about the letters: WRITE LEGIBLY—ideally on a typewriter—And about the parcel: if it won't put it over the weight limit, you might include two large tins of tea.

20

February 3, 1980

Dear Olga,

Thanks for your first letter to Heřmanice, which arrived safely. As you may have gathered from my last two letters, I can't write you the way I used to from Ruzyně. I have to stick mainly to family matters, I'm not supposed to expatiate on my ideas, and so on. Therefore my response to your questions will be rather truncated: my case officer informed me I'm permitted to tell you that I'm working in the Vítkovice Ironworks, but I can say no more than that, except perhaps that although I don't have to lift anything too heavy for me, I have serious doubts that I'll be able to fulfill my quota. I still believe, however, that my body will get used to it and that I won't always be so tired (the work is not my only activity here—and given my profession and way of life I'm certainly not used to so much movement). Fortunately Saturdays and Sundays are relatively quiet, so I can always recuperate somewhat. It's rather paradoxical: in Ruzyně I longed for the kind of prison regime where I could work, move about and be among people—and now there is so much of it all at once that Ruzyně seems like a sweet dream. I still don't know whether this is better for me than the isolation I expected. It's a fantastic experience and the danger of psychic deformation, which prolonged isolation might cause, is genuinely receding, I think. On the other hand, I can't really imagine, yet, bearing up under this way of life for five years. But I'm not worrying about it yet; as I wrote you last time, I'm mentally fit and trying to be sporting about it all. I eat more than I ever have before, yet I seem to be growing thinner. (To return to the matter of isolation: what you say about Jirka—and how much he's written—merely strengthens my doubts about this being any better. I certainly can't write here. I will be able to read and study a little, but probably only on weekends.) What else can I say about myself? Aside from my exhaustion and fatigue at the end of the working week, I'm healthy. After some minor setbacks, my flu is essentially cured and the hemorrhoids are not acting up. Otherwise I must (and perhaps I may) say that even though there are all sorts here with us, they behave wonderfully toward us and try to help us. From that point of view I can't complain at all; on the contrary, I was surprised and moved by this welcome.

Thanks for the news of yourself. I'd only like to stress again that you should write more often and mainly in more detail. Your letter was sweet, but somewhat telegraphic. Don't worry about style. Is Puzuk going to remain a free-lancer? If it is possible, I'd recommend it—it's better than being employed at something he wouldn't like. How is Otka? I've heard no news of her. How did my former lawyer's legal dispute turn out? Write me in detail about various friends and about your cultural activities. And in general, about how you live. Keep a list of things to tell me when you visit, so you won't forget. (I'm also preparing my questions.) Give my greetings to the crowd at the Slavia Cafe (I'm glad you go there). . . . I'm looking forward to the visit an awful lot—I'll probably have such "anchor points" once every three months. The frost and cold, as you correctly assume, are a genuine bother here; fortunately it has turned warmer now and my next "anchor point" is the approaching spring. Apparently I'll be allowed to have my textbooks in due time; you can probably take the Bible back to Prague with you. There's a relatively well-stocked library here; I've borrowed Herodotus's Histories, but I'm only on page three. I'll have to learn—among other things—how to concentrate amid the turmoil— and that goes not just for reading, but for writing letters as well.

In general, I might add that for now, my mind is fully preoccupied with a single thing: getting to know the new environment, trying to understand its laws and discovering the best way to exist in it. And of course looking after my body and its adaptation. My mind has neither the time nor the inclination to come up with any significant existential or literary thoughts; in the face of this experience, all such attempts seem meaningless or, to be more precise, premature. First I have to digest, experience and understand it all. I'd love to be able to keep a diary, but of course that's out of the question.

I send you kisses and I'm glad I have you—just as you are—which means with all your faults, even your terseness as a letter writer (though it's a fault you should try to correct).

Ahoj—Vašek

· · ·

21

February 8, 1980

Dear Olga,

First a few organizational matters. I've been required to write you the following: "In addition, I must inform you that the appointed time of visits cannot be considered final. I would point out that you must obtain a visiting permit, where a space will be provided for the parcel permit, including the allowable weight." This means there will be no visit this coming weekend (February 17). It will take place later, perhaps in March. You'll be informed in time. Further, my case officer has charged me to write you to arrange that no one except yourself and Ivan write me here, either from inside or outside the country. Mail from other persons will not be turned over to me. . . . I've received nothing from you or Ivan, but I believe that letters are on the way. Write me often! I'm disappointed when friends get letters every week—and I nothing. I know you don't like writing, but I can assure you, letters aren't as hard for you to write as they are for me. . . .

Because I'm only permitted to deal with a narrow range of themes, I'll write you in more detail than I normally would about the state of my health:

1. My hemorrhoids, fortunately, are quiescent; just now they've been bleeding a little, but perhaps nothing will come of it.

2. That cold of mine (or flu or whatever it was) has returned again (I was feverish and trembling, etc.) and this time I was put on the sick list and am taking an antibiotic. So at last, after that first difficult plunge, I can rest a little and physically recuperate. And perhaps I'll also definitively shake the disease.

3. The work and all the rest of it still leaves me considerably exhausted. My lower back and my feet ache from constantly standing. (It's practically impossible to sit down when I work—and standing up has caused me discomfort for as long as I can remember.) Yet I don't think these aches and pains and my constant exhaustion are serious matters—I believe they will go away in time and that I will get used to it. Everyone, I've discovered, experiences such difficulties in the beginning, even younger men more accustomed to physical labor.

. . .

As for work: for a couple of days before taking to my bed, I did something other than what I was originally assigned to do, so I haven't as yet been able to establish whether I'll be able to fulfill the quotas or not. But I'm inclined to believe that ultimately it's an attainable goal, even for me. (I have my own reasons for hoping I succeed.)

And now something about my domestic affairs: in a few days, the supply of cigarettes I brought with me will be exhausted. Then I want to try stuffing those hollow, prerolled papers and smoke them in combination with tailor-mades. I'll probably have enough money, even after I run out of tobacco, to smoke a combination of cheap cigarettes (like Mars) and the hand-stuffed variety, and I may even have some money left over for tea and the occasional sweet. (It's interesting how I yearn for sweet things here.) As for toothpaste and other hygienic needs, I'm well supplied for some time to come.

What else can I say about my life here? The experiences, insights and impressions have been so profuse that so far I haven't been able to sort them out, classify and digest them properly. Still, I'm working on it. And I think the meaning I am trying to give my sojourn in prison might well be accomplished. I watch, I am amazed, I contemplate, I have fun (often at my own expense), and I am careful not to let anything throw me off balance. I am open to the world without exposing myself to it more than absolutely necessary, given my communicative nature. I try to understand everything with unprejudiced detachment. I've not been thrown into this experience alone, and this has helped me enormously. I observe what the experience has done to those who have been here for some time and I try to draw appropriate conclusions from it and not be drawn into any of the minor intellectual or emotional roles that offer themselves. I'm rather curious about how it will all turn out and whether I will really manage to emerge one day, not scarred by the experience, but enriched in the way I'd like.

I see that the circumstances—more complicated than you can probably imagine—have driven me to somewhat Delphian generalities, bordering on banality, and therefore I think I'd better stop.

Stay as well as you can, greet all faithful friends and above all, write me! I know almost nothing about you, about friends and altogether about that other world—and I eagerly await all news.

With kisses, Vašek

23

February 24, 1980

Dear Olga,

Sunday afternoon is coming to an end and I still can't shake this strange, post-visit mood. Again and again, I recall everything you both said, I delight in all the good news, but at the same time, my delight is permeated by a vague despondency and nervousness. I can't say that I'm depressed—the mood is essentially good—I'm just a little derailed, distracted, inattentive, uneasy. The world I live in is utterly different from yours and when you appear here out of the blue and bring with you a piece of that other world, the one you live in and where I belong as well, it is a highly unusual event—exhilarating and elating, yet unsettling too, even irritating. I'll have to get used to this phenomenon as well. It's interesting that the experience is so different from your visits in Ruzyně, when I was awaiting trial. I was cut off from my domestic world there too, but the world I was thrown into was not so radically different; it was more like being temporarily in a "nonworld," a vacuum. The contrast wasn't so sharp.

As far as the visit itself is concerned: even though it was, understandably, somewhat unsettled and thematically chaotic (nor could it be otherwise), I think it was a success and I'm exceptionally pleased. I didn't expect we'd manage to say so much in the hour, and above all, I wasn't expecting so much good news. I took note of everything you both said and now I'm thinking it over and evaluating it. Naturally, I'm glad that my plays are being performed, and that good theaters are doing them; I'm glad that friends are thinking of us; I'm delighted that you're active and that you're even doing something about so thankless a matter as exchanging our flat. But mainly—as ever—I'm glad that everything is as it was, which means okay; in short, that you, Puzuk and all our friends are still the same, just as I've always known you. Fidelity and a kind of constancy are qualities I've always valued above all else and I must say that as the years go by I value them more and more. This is not a conservative love for the status quo, but a respect for human identity and continuity. In any case, I don't suppose it's an accident that all my plays circle around the theme of the breakdown of identity and continuity.

. . .

It's strange, and at this moment almost incomprehensible, that a few hours ago we saw each other and were talking as though nothing had happened. Was it true? I suppose so. One never ceases to be amazed.

So I thank you both for the visit—and again, many greetings to everyone—

Your Vašek

25

March 8, 1980

Dear Olga,

I'm writing you, as chance would have it, very soon after my last letter, so that there isn't much new to relate. I'm well, I read a lot, I rest and think about things. Not that I don't have a lot to write about: in my reading of the Church Fathers and Dostoyevsky, I've been thinking quite a bit about a number of philosophical themes and I would like, for instance, to develop some of my thoughts on the relationship between human identity and immortality—but I'm not certain it would be appropriate because, like it or not, it could hardly be construed as a family matter—at least not in the narrow sense of the word, even though it has often been a subject of family discussions. So I'll leave it for another time and restrict myself to a few more down-to-earth topics.

As you know, I've never been much of a tea drinker (in fact I drank it only when I had a sore throat). It's come all the more as a surprise to me, then, that tea has become virtually a necessity here, apparently because it serves as a substitute for coffee, alcohol, and many other pleasures denied to me. My happiest moment is when I prepare a glass of hot, strong tea, and then sit down with it to read, think or write a letter. I've become a fanatical devotee of Earl Grey, which in England, as everyone knows, is consumed only by little old ladies during afternoon tea parties and which the English tea lover scorns as a perfumed, old-maidish drink. A pity you couldn't get it this time. Check from time to time to see if they have it and if they do, buy a decent supply. It's my only luxury. They have those large tins that hold about four times as much as normal tins—and I think that one, if not two such tins, would fit into a parcel without pushing it over the weight limit. I'd like to have one, not just for what's in it but also for itself—it would be a handy place to keep supplies of tea. If Earl Grey doesn't come in that size, you could take one from another brand and refill it with the Earl Grey.

. . .

To turn to something else: I've discovered that in lengthy prison terms, sensitive people are in danger of becoming embittered, developing grudges against the world, growing dull, indifferent and selfish.

One of my main aims is not to yield an inch to such threats, regardless of how long I'm here. I want to remain open to the world, not to shut myself up against it; I want to retain my interest in other people and my love for them. I have different opinions of different people, but I cannot say that I hate anyone in the world. I have no intention of changing in that regard. If I did, it would mean that I had lost. Hatred has never been either my program, or the point of departure for my actions. And that must not change.

I'm finished for today—give my regards to all our relatives and friends—say hello to Puzuk (have him write me soon) and pass on a special greeting to Andulka. And live cheerfully, harmoniously and actively yourself!

Kisses from your Vašek

27

March 23, 1980

Dear Olga,

I'm delighted to hear you decided to leave Prague for a few days and take a break. I hope the trip didn't coincide with that unpleasant return of winter weather, which up here in the north was particularly bothersome to me.

I've been diligently at work again for a week and my condition now seems definitively cured—otherwise, judging from former experience, it would have recurred by now. I don't find the work as grueling as I did at first, but even so I've asked to be transferred to another workplace more in line with my capabilities. The thing is, I'm expected to keep pace with robust fellows all twenty years or more younger than I am and who, moreover, are used to manual labor and don't have the variety of health problems I do—and though I manage to match their output now and again, I know I haven't got the necessary energy and endurance. . . . My request may not be granted, but this is no place to be excessively reticent and if I've not been shy in speaking out for others, I ought not to be on my own account either.

Otherwise there is nothing particularly new in my life; I've already more or less settled in and apart from trying to survive with dignity and without damage to either body or soul, I manage to do a good turn for others now and again (just as others, now and again, help me). I feel the need to do yoga occasionally, but so far I've found neither the proper space nor the time for it. . . .

The younger Vašek is doing better at his work than I am and he's proud of it; I, of course, never fail to point out that he is younger and has better work. But it's just a kind of banter between ourselves; in fact, he's worked his way into the top nutritional category and I don't want in any way to belittle his efforts.

Conditions aren't very good right now for concentrated letter writing; there's a lively Sunday commotion going on around me (I had no time for writing earlier), so I won't start writing about anything essential. Besides that, I want to add a few lines for Květa, who sent me a nice letter.

Best wishes and kisses to you, and I'm looking forward to news of your trip and altogether about your life.

Ahoj! Vašek

28

April 2, 1980

Dear Olga,

Today I received a letter from Hradec Králové that you must have received as well and which indicates that plans are being hatched against Hrádeček for a change. First of all, Dr. Hrabák should write requesting an extension of the period we have to lodge an appeal, on the grounds that I am serving my sentence and communication with me is difficult. Then he should prepare a persuasive analysis demonstrating that their proceedings against us are groundless. To do that, however, we'll need all the documents on Hrádeček, which probably means a trip there to pick them up. In my view, one important factor is that we had prior approval from the District National Committee to install central heating; it was not, as they claimed, approved after installation. This can be proven by the stamp on the blueprints, and also from the relevant correspondence. . . . I kept all the papers, so it must be among them. Take everything to Prague, Dr. Hrabák will look at them and work something out. What chiefly interests me is what happens if we lose. Will they rip out the central heating? They can't do that, since they gave prior approval. Perhaps they could tear out the boiler—but no, they can't do that either—or the study—but then the house would collapse! The devil knows what's going on. You and Dr. Hrabák (perhaps with Dr. Rychetský's help) will have to mount a defense, but probably without me. If you needed my approval for everything, it would drag on forever. If necessary, I could give you power of attorney to negotiate in my name as well. Otherwise, in official matters like this, the quickest way to get in touch with me is through my lawyer. Let's hope this new round turns out well—just like that earlier one with our Prague flat. . . .

I used to think prison life must be endless boredom and monotony with nothing much to worry about except the basic problem of making the time pass quickly. But now I've discovered it's not like that. You have plenty of worries here all the time, and though they may seem "trivial" to the normal world, they are not at all trivial in the prison context. In fact you're always having to chase after something, arrange something, hunt for something, keep an eye on something, fear for something, hold your ground against something, etc. It's a constant strain on the nerves (someone is always twanging on them), exacerbated by the fact that in many important instances you cannot behave authentically and must keep your real thoughts to yourself. (And as we know, excessive self-control is unhealthy because it generates toxins in the heart.) If we try to accept all this with humor and a sporting sense of detachment, this is not just because we are the way we are, but also because it is, relatively speaking, the best way to deal with such pressures without on the one hand causing pointless damage to ourselves and on the other hand denying and smothering something inside ourselves (the latter way leads to the kind of embitterment I once wrote you about). If I manage to remain cheerful, then, it's a kind of organic self-defense mechanism; you shouldn't simply conclude that something cheerful has happened to me. But I'm sure you don't think this.

Thanks for the card from the Jizera Mountains, which was shown to me and which, unfortunately, is the only news I have had from you in a long time. Is is really impossible to write me more often—even briefly, if not at length?

Tell Puzuk that I'm not against bookshelves as such—I like having books at home and I know they have to be somewhere—I only wrote about the kind of bookshelves I don't want, that is, some monstrosity.

After all, he has bookshelves of stained wood, and not of veneer! Just a comment on his last letter.

I wish you a Happy Easter (even though this won't arrive until it's over). Keep well, be brave and don't get upset over things like that business with Hrádeček. That only belongs to the "world of entities," which one has to take with a smile. . . .

Kisses, Vašek

29

April 6, 1980

Dear Olga,

It's Easter Sunday, the weather is miserable and after extensive effort I've finally managed to find a relatively quiet corner where I am writing you and reading about the Albigensian War. This afternoon, my friends and I are holding a small feast, as is our custom on Sundays and holidays; today, it will consist of tea, egg spread, rolls and cigars (almost the last of our supplies). In the evening, we will watch television. We have a piece of salami laid aside for our dinner tomorrow.

To the various circumstances that make writing difficult must be added the fact that I have nothing to respond to: since the visit six weeks ago I've received only one brief letter (another was not handed over to me), so that my writing resembles a kind of soliloquy. Is it really such a problem to write to me every week?

. . .

I've just remembered the extensive plans I wrote you about from Ruzyně. It seems that except for those that concern my spiritual and mental state, I won't be able to carry out any of them. My notions were somewhat naive and based on conditions in Ruzyně or on the experience of several friends, which are inapplicable to conditions here. What I regret most is that there will be such a long hiatus in my writing; I found it difficult enough to write anyway, and I'm afraid this hiatus might cause me to lose my nerve altogether. In any case, we'll see.

I'm continuing on Easter Monday. Yesterday I watched "The Emperor's Baker" on television, and a crime thriller in which I saw Květuš again after all this time. By now, she's playing heavy mothers. It's always interesting, when I have the occasion to watch television, to see how various friends are aging. Worries about their status, meetings, all-night drinking sessions, official positions, etc.—it is all engraved on their faces. Here, on the contrary, we go to bed early, don't stay up late drinking, are not encumbered by position or official function—and thanks to the military discipline that prevails, we have managed to return to the years of our youth. We have our worries—I wrote about them in my last letter—but they are of a different order somehow, more elemental and thus, perhaps, more natural (even primeval man had his worries).

Everything here is more elemental, somehow: social relationships and mechanisms that are hidden and masked in complex ways outside appear in all their nakedness; everything is bare, as it were, unmediated, transparent; everything can be seen with greater clarity—from that standpoint it is a most instructive experience; you are made aware of many things about life—in general—of which you were not so conscious outside. It is a kind of convex mirror.

Call me a fool, but I still refuse to abandon hope that one day I'll receive a long letter from you in which all the questions in my letters to you will be clearly answered and in which you will respond to my suggestions and thoughts. . . .

Keep well, dress and make yourself up prettily, be cheerful and industrious, think of me and write me!

Kisses, Vašek

30

April 13, 1980

Dear Olga,

This week no letter came from you again, but I'm not angry with you for your inveterate failure to write; on the contrary, I'm thinking of you with tenderness. For the first time in a long time I've had a dream about you. I don't recall the details, I only know we were sitting together in a Malá Strana café and then somewhere—perhaps it was in a railway station—you kissed me publicly. But just because I've forgiven you for not writing because of the dream, it doesn't mean I've released you from future obligations to write me often and in detail.

A letter (no. 15) came from Ivan; thank him, even though it wasn't a very long letter (and on top of that it was shortened by one paragraph, which apparently contained some cultural information).

There is nothing especially new in my life here, except for the fact that life is constantly providing novel experiences and novel insights, all of which, however, are of such a nature that I must leave an account of them for another time. I study the behavior of my tattooed friends, their relationships, the formation of those relationships, etc. Not only is all of this interesting and, for me, new, it is most instructive as well. We are fortunate to have found ourselves in a position that enables us not only to observe it all with a certain detachment, but also to intervene in places, as our conscience dictates. When I say fortunate, I mean that gaining the respect of others in these nasty conditions, where so many vile human qualities dominate, is not just a matter of "merit"—by which I mean how well you acquit yourself in extreme situations—but frequently a matter of fate as well, which means the interplay of accidental factors (such as, for example, what illnesses you have—since some provoke greater disgust than others; obviously it has to do with a herd instinct of sorts in the realm of "natural selection").

There was something new after all: we had a visit from Prague. There seemed to be no particular reason for it, except to see how we were doing. It was a reminder of our former lives and our former world.

On television yesterday I saw "The Good Times Cabaret." It made me extremely uneasy to see acting and singing stars of the 1960s attempting, under Z. Podskalský's slick direction, to evoke something of the humor of those times or to somehow connect with it or to carry on with it at all costs—but in the end it proved utterly impossible. It was all spiritless routine, with lackluster performances, no social resonance, no inner delight. All sham and lies trying to appear authentic at any cost. They meant well. (Horníček is only running off at the mouth. Awful.)

Today, for the first time, after I'd won the time to write this letter, I suddenly discovered that I didn't know what to write. All my life I've been used to writing what I wanted and how I wanted, so it's hard for me to get used to self-censorship. But I must learn. It may even be of some use to me (though I doubt it). Vašek is sitting a short distance away and like a spider making a web, he's spinning out his delicate little handwriting, filling the pages of his letter to Kamila, and I envy him that ease and the fact that even in these conditions, he always knows what to write home, and how.

Kisses, Vašek

31

April 27, 1980

Dear Olga,

I'm writing after a short hiatus. This was not caused—as I'm sure you don't doubt—by idleness on my part, but neither were the reasons serious cause for worry.

I finally received two letters from you (nos. 6 and 7), for which many thanks. Thanks also to Puzuk for his letter (no. 16) and to Květa for her nice postcard. I always confirm receipt of your letters at once (well, not exactly at once, but in my very next letter), so that you can tell from my letters what I've received. It is difficult for me to refer back, because I can't remember what was in which letter, or rather what the number of the letter was, and I can't check on it because I hand the letters in. To give me an idea of what you've received, you should confirm receipt of each of my letters immediately by postcard. A postcard is faster, it's no trouble for you to write, and such a practice would help significantly.

And now, to respond to some of the points in your letters:

(1) I'm rather surprised that my letter no. 24 hasn't reached you, because in its definitive version it met with no objections. In it, I wrote of the complications caused by a sentence of yours—the wording of which I don't know, because the incriminating letter (no. 4) was not given to me—in which you apparently made some inappropriate remarks about officials of the State Correctional Services. I'm sure you didn't mean anything by it; it's just that you must have put it in a somewhat unvarnished manner, as is sometimes your habit. Also, I asked you how often my latest one-acter has been performed and what the response has been—for that wasn't clear either from what you said

during the visit, or from your letters (to be more precise, I seem to recall that what you said and what you wrote were at odds). . . . A general note: when you tell me about things like that, be as precise and concrete as possible, otherwise there is a danger of confusion and misunderstanding. (2) You ask for details of my health. Unfortunately, dear Grumbler, I can't write about that! The only person qualified to answer such queries, I am told, is the prison doctor. But in any case it's not a matter of current concern because my illnesses are, I hope, a thing of the past; apart from occasionally painful hemorrhoids (mainly when I lift heavy objects) I am now, it would seem, generally healthy. (3) I was delighted by the news that my one-acters were a success in France, though I'm a little disappointed that it's always the one-acters that seem to get performed everywhere, while no one remembers *The Beggar's Opera,* not to mention *The Mountain Hotel.* So I was all the more delighted to hear that Magor remembered it. If I have room left, I'll write a couple of comments about that play; if not, I'll write about it next time.

. . .

(5) A general comment on your letters: I have the impression you're not being entirely spontaneous because you're too aware that I'm not the only one who reads them. . . . Try to free yourself of that feeling and write easily and spontaneously; don't worry about word order and things like that. And write as concretely as possible, even about things that seem meaningless. It is only from a mosaic of apparently meaningless things that one can create an approximate picture of the situation and atmosphere around you outside; generalities don't say much. . . . Information like "everything works" and "things are being taken care of," etc. may ease a body's mind, but at the same time they tend to alienate him from his world, because they suggest that everything is proceeding apace, independently of him, that his vital participation is no longer counted on, and that in fact he has no real reason to take an interest in things anymore because things will work out regardless.

There's nothing especially new in my life. I work diligently, in fact you might even say I'm increasingly busy despite the fact that my results, so far, are not too satisfactory. At the same time, my hopes for an assignment more in line with my capabilities have faded somewhat. In this connection, Jirka delivered an especially hard blow by telling me that after forty, one's body can no longer create any new muscles and that therefore I should not expect to return a muscular he-man.

I too am eagerly looking forward to your visit. When it will be I don't know, perhaps in a month or so. I've been told that a parcel with hygienic supplies will not be permitted, and I shall also have to wait until September for socks.

And now, a few improvised remarks about *The Mountain Hotel:* that play—without a story, without characters, without a situation, without action, without psychology, without a plot—is a strange and, I admit, a rather problem-ridden attempt to be a "play about itself," in the sense that the subject of the play is its structure, its mathematical construction and all its structural tricks. It's something like an anthology of dramatic principles. In other words, it is a so-called abstract play. But a word of caution: it was written with a question in mind. Are these principles, I asked myself, in certain circumstances capable in and of themselves (that is, without the traditional dramatic material they are usually applied to) of sustaining meaning? I have in mind a rather fanciful notion of a nostalgic and vaguely unsettling poem about a world with no firm center, no fixed identity, no past and no future, with no coherence or order, a world where all certainties are disintegrating and where, suspended above this disintegration like a melancholy mist, there hangs the memory of a different world, where things were themselves. As a text, the play makes no sense; it could only do so—if at all—in performance: (1) its rhythm, its architecture—spacial and temporal—can only be understood and experienced in a spatiotemporal continuum (it is something like a fugue)—and only such an experience can allow the emptiness and the nothingness that is at issue here to manifest itself in all its horror. (2) The second condition—that it will be a deeply disturbing and scarcely definable experience—is the physical presence of actors to fill this strange vessel. I think it must be played by the best possible actors and that precisely the play's "lack of content," its "abstractness"—by which I mean the absence of any psychology, etc.—could make room for the full "presentation" of living, physical, biological mankind (in the person of the actors). And the play's unnerving impact should derive from the contrast between the endless merry-go-round represented by the swapping of roles, situations and banal speeches on the one hand, and living people—living humanity—on the other.

There is no more paper—I kiss you and I love you—Vašek.

32

May 10, 1980

Dear Olga,

I've already written this letter once, over a week ago, on May Day, but because I mistakenly wrote about something I wasn't supposed to, I'm writing it to you again—as a matter of fact at the moment when I've just finished writing letter 33. This minor mixup is an advantage in this case, because I've just received a letter from you and I can respond to it without having to rewrite letter 33.

So first, to answer your letter: . . . I'm delighted, not only that you are reading diligently and that you are taking seriously all the work that has to be done at Hrádeček (even though you may wring your hands over it), but also that you are gradually learning to write me. Your letter was lively and spontaneous, thanks to which your presence has been vividly evoked, along with something of the atmosphere of the life around you, which is what I've been constantly crying out for. That your letter might have been longer and more detailed is another matter—that is something you still have to learn.

In my letter of May 1, . . . I responded to Ivan's promise (as yet unfulfilled, by the way) to write me something—as much as possible—about present-day physics. My layman's knowledge of physics is probably frozen somewhere in the early sixties (when a Czech book popularizing Heisenberg and Weizsäcker came out). Today, everything must be different.

. . .

In my last letter, I wrote you a few remarks on *The Mountain Hotel.* In my letter of May 1, I made some comments on *The Beggar's Opera* (by the way, when you write about my plays, write the title out in full). Jirka told me an interesting thing a while ago: he said that some people had not been enthusiastic after reading the play, but when they saw it, they changed their minds completely. I've run into the same thing myself. It's understandable: most people don't know how to read plays—and why should they? A play is written such that only performance can impart meaning to it. If plays were written to be read, they would be written differently. As you know, I am fond of *The Beggar's Opera* and I'm sorry it's so seldom performed. All it needs is one decent production and the situation could change. Therefore I'd appreciate it if you could, should the occasion arise, remind people of its existence. . . . I bring this up not because I think I'm being neglected, but because when only my one-act plays are performed, it distorts me somewhat as an author—it may seem (especially to anyone unfamiliar with my earlier plays) that I am merely documenting my own experience and not concerned with other matters as well.

I was pleased by Ivan's reminder that I wrote most prolifically after getting out of the army. I realize that he's right, but more than that: while I was in the army, just like here, I had no idea how I would write once I got out. And as soon as I returned, I began to write *The Memorandum.* Of course, there's no reason why this should happen again, but it was certainly an encouraging reminder.

. . .

Your faithful, lifelong fellow traveler—

Vašek

33

May 24, 1980

Dear Olga,

First, my attempt to go somewhat beyond the framework of practical everyday themes and develop certain psychological ideas about myself didn't work out; then, conditions for letter writing were not good and my letter was delayed another week or so. If this sometimes happens, don't panic; there's nothing sinister behind it. By now I've completely lost track of what I've written you in the various versions of my letters, and of which were sent, so it will be better if I don't try to recapitulate anything, especially since the visit is approaching and we'll be able to deal with it all in person.

First about the visit: as you probably know already from the official notification, it will take place on Sunday, June 8 at 9:00 a.m. Ivan may come as well—whether he actually does or not will depend only on whether he can. If so, I'll be happy; if not, I won't mind, knowing that he had a good reason not to. If by any chance—which I hope won't happen—some last minute hitch should prevent you from coming, write a request for a new visit at once to the Institute of Correctional Services here. Since you will be doing most of the talking during the visit, please prepare a kind of synopsis—a list of everything you want to say to me. Go over my letters and refresh your memory on all the things I asked you about. I know that in a brief hour you can't say everything; nevertheless I'd be glad if you could be as precise as possible in what you say, so that I won't have to ask you a lot of supplementary questions in my letters. You know that I'm an inveterate bureaucrat and I like concreteness, clarity and precision. . . . Don't bring me anything; as you know, I have no right to a parcel and I won't be permitted to receive anything at all. So let's try and avoid awkward situations. That's all as far as instructions go. To conclude: I'm looking forward tremendously; your visit (with Ivan) will be a bright spot in my existence here. And there is something else: (1) wouldn't it be better to come a day before and spend the night in a hotel? (2) be prepared to see me with the shortest prison haircut I've ever had; I look pretty silly (or so I seem to myself).

For the sake of order, let me recapitulate the correspondence received: I received your letters nos. 7 and 9, I've been shown substantial parts of letter 10; only letter 8 didn't arrive. All of Ivan's letters up to no. 17 have arrived, and three from Květa. Thanks to them both, and I send Květa a tender family kiss for her sweet letters (it might interest her to know that they showed the film *Gypsies Go to Heaven* here, but my efforts to see it failed). Further, I received an official decision to the effect that after all these years, the building inspectors' approval of our cottage has been disapproved. I don't know whether to laugh or cry at the thought of how many bureaucrats are constantly occupied with us. Your worries are still not over. If I understand correctly, there is to be a new inspection. It could go a number of ways; the best possible outcome, relatively speaking, would be for them to approve it with the proviso that Hrádeček be reclassified as a first-class dwelling and therefore must become our primary residence. This would mean losing our flat in Prague, but it would save Hrádeček. Then of course the local officials might refuse us permission to live there on the grounds of a "citizen's complaint." Or can they not do that? I don't know. Obviously now you'll have to request permission to live there temporarily. If they won't grant you that, you can live at the neighbors' over the summer. But these are just a layman's guesses; our lawyers will certainly know what to do and how to go about it.

In conclusion, a small ecological observation: when they brought us here in January, I paid close attention to the areas we traveled through and discovered that about a third were ordinary fields and woods, another third city streets, towns and villages, and almost all the remaining third consisted of ugly, nondescript areas essentially like rubbish dumps. There were variously oversized factory yards, full of litter, filth and unused areas, muddy access roads leading God knows where, garages, warehouses, stockpiles of abandoned construction material and other things, etc. etc. Unsightly byways, chaos and squalor, garbage and refuse everywhere, areas with no visible purpose or logic. Conclusion: we don't appreciate place, space, land. But not to be so critical all the time, something good is going on in Ostrava: they are reclaiming the slag heaps. (Thanks to this, I too can see a bit of green.)

Greetings to everyone; I kiss you and I'm looking forward, looking forward—

Vašek

35

June 8, 1980

Dear Olga,

First of all, I'm grateful to you and Ivan for the visit. It was very successful, I'm still under its beneficial influence and I realize once more what an enormous significance even such a brief encounter has for someone here: suddenly, you realize that your "other," normal world is not just a dream or a memory, but that it physically exists. And suddenly, even the world in which you must move appears in an entirely different perspective. It's not just that you have the chance to talk to those nearest to you, but also that you can talk with someone cut, as it were, from a different cloth, someone who—in the moral sense of the word—has nothing in common with any of this. For about an hour after the visit, I retreated into myself and meditated, and only then did I return to what are now my everyday affairs. Some remarks on the visit:
1. The fact that it was almost idyllic, both in tone and atmosphere, should not be allowed to create the false impression that not a lot is happening and that everything is fine. Nothing is fine, but you must know that and I'm sure you have no illusions about it. Nor have

I, and I am forced to admit that even in our world, not everything is as harmonious and fine as one would like, and that you too were unable to tell me everything, though understandably you don't have to censor yourselves as much as I do.

2. I forgot to tell you I loved the way you looked. You were smartly dressed and very chic. Even your hair looks good that way—of course if you look after it (it has, as you know, a tendency to look like spikes or straw—but it didn't during the visit—and I hope you wear your hair that elegantly all the time). Puzuk too looked very natty.

3. I think we told each other all the essential bits of information, and if we forgot some details, it's not a tragedy. We might have told each other a thousand times more of our thoughts, reflections, observations and experiences, etc.—but we didn't expect to accomplish anything like that in a one-hour visit after a quarter of a year. Under the circumstances, we told each other more than I would have thought possible.

So much for the visit.

It made me almost euphoric and only now (it's afternoon) is the euphoria slowly becoming painful nostalgia. This is not so much because the visit is already over and the next one won't be till Lord knows when, but rather because of the contrast between the life I was reminded of during the visit and the life I have returned to. (Just a while ago, for example, I listened to a short lecture delivered by one of my fellow prisoners about how wretched people are, how you mustn't believe anyone and how it makes no sense to help anyone. I hear lectures on this theme daily, but in the context of today it took on a rather different coloring.)

*

I'm continuing after a brief interruption. The nostalgia is gone now and the euphoria has returned. Whatever caused the turnabout, it must have been trifling: it takes so little to improve one's mood here—a kind word, some slight interest of neighbor for neighbor, the sight of a tree. The utter lack of anything beautiful, exalting, of positive emotional experiences, gives one a special thirst that frequently expresses itself in the ease with which one can be moved or transported—as Vašek has correctly pointed out—even by a television drama that reason tells one ought to be condemned for its mendacity. *Libuše* can't be called mendacious—it's just a fairy tale—and so I was understandably all the more moved when I saw it on May 9. Involuntarily, I found myself conjuring up—somewhat in the manner of Libuše's final vision—the great variety of historical contexts in which the opera has been performed (and it usually creates the greatest resonance and moves audiences most profoundly when the nation is furthest from its own mythological self-image)—and all of this, moreover, in the quite special context in which I was able to see it.

But to return to the realities: I'm sending this to Hrádeček now, as I will all subsequent letters. So I'll be there in spirit, rather than in Prague, and I won't be able to resist giving instructions about what needs to be done. But I'll be listing the tasks more for my own satisfaction than any hope that you'll act upon them. I think I'll devote my next letter to this—if no more pressing theme comes up. (When I'm allowed to receive a parcel sometime, you'll have to try and find me those fat Chinese refills for my ball-point pen. These standard ones you gave me—as you can see—write too broadly and badly.)

Thank you once again for the visit. . . .

Your Vašek

37

June 22, 1980

Dear Olga,

As you know, I've never written with a ball-point pen and therefore I knew nothing about them, nor did I need to. It's only here that I've come to understand there are ballpoints and ballpoints. I'm writing this letter with a (borrowed) Chinese pen, a highly treasured item because it is so different from a normal ballpoint, whose main feature is the ability to secrete a disgusting, sticky substance that gets smeared all over everything. I'm looking forward to becoming the owner of a "China pen" too. (I probably had a lot of them at home, without ever being aware of their hidden virtues.)

I have promised to try writing a meditative letter, because I don't want to be writing all the time about what you should be doing, but now my promise has put me in an awkward position: after the failure of those earlier meditative letters, I feel blocked and nervous. On the other hand, I'm too ambitious simply to accept the fact that while Vašek sends a pretty theological tract out of here each week, I am merely flooding the outside world with directives about what should be bought and what should be given a coat of paint. But I'm not about to wring my hands—lest this period of relative quiet be over before I start—and I shall resort to the method of "spontaneous confession" that Jirka uses, successfully, in his letters.

I've received nothing from you since your letter no. 13, written before your visit, and I'm waiting impatiently. For the moment, I'm in good health except for a constant numbness in my arms, probably related to my work. When I manage to scrounge a minute, I read Pitaval's *Famous Court Cases* (most interesting reading). Before that, I read a popular book on modern physics *(Crazy Ideas)* which provides me with a theme for a minor meditation: when I wrote you about *The Mountain Hotel* I forgot to stress that in this play time and space are bent and distorted in several ways (time leaps forward and backward, drags on slowly or surges ahead, characters enter opposite to where they made their exits—as though they had gone round the entire globe in the meantime, or the whole curved universe, etc.). All of this can be understood simply as something with no purpose beyond itself, i.e., as an expression of pure playfulness on the author's part, and I have no objections to such an interpretation. But these things may also be understood rather differently, as a natural component of the play's semantic structure. All my plays, as I have said several times already, deal in one way or another with the theme of human identity and the state of crisis in which it finds itself. . . . The disintegration of human identity also means (psychologically) the disintegration of existential continuity and therefore (philosophically) the disintegration of time (as an intensely experienced dimension of Being). I first tried to indicate this specifically in *The Increased Difficulty of Concentration* and it is presented consistently (nonthematically, or rather not as a "subject") in *The Mountain Hotel,* where various "poetic" tableaux of the crisis of identity (the interchangeability of characters, etc.) are linked—again, "poetically"—to the disintegration not only of time, but of the whole space-time continuum. And now, coming back to the book I've read: it seems to me (is this true, Ivan?), that modern physics is demonstrating with increasing clarity that space and time are merely attributes of what physics refers to as matter, and that without matter, space and time cannot exist. Moreover: everything that, in man's mesocosmic view, raises problems about matter (in other words: about the identity of Being), necessarily also raises problems about these attributes. Concretely: the identity of matter is, from our point of view, made extremely problematic within the dimensions of the atomic nucleus (the particles become mysteriously transformed into different particles or they lose all the classical characteristics of matter, etc. etc.) and parallel with that, space and time are made problematic in this world (they become relative, disconnected, random quanta). I am not attempting to define a causal connection between "physical" and "human" reality (a task more appropriate for a phenomenologist than a playwright), but what interests me about it (at least as a writer) is first of all the "poetic" connection between them (as something that lies in between the causal and metaphorical connections). The paper is coming to an end, others are waiting to use the Chinese ballpoint, and therefore I conclude with a promise, occasion permitting, to continue (even though it may be in a fragmentary, aphoristic way)—most probably with reflections on a theme that may well be the most important of all: "identity and immortality."

. . .

Kisses, Vašek

38

July 15, 1980

Dear Olga,

As you've no doubt noticed, there has been a three-week hiatus in my writing. There are various reasons for this, among them the fact that I'm still not quite able to write the way I should, that is, exclusively about family matters. After letter 37, for example, I was seized by a slight anxiety because in the "meditative" part I broached a theme without being able properly to formulate, develop and carry it through to a meaningful conclusion. And so, in sheer terror that I was forgetting how to write, I made a special effort on the next letter, until it turned into a short essay on the metaphysical roots of human responsibility. A sense of responsibility should be—as I am persuaded here daily—the foundation of family life; nevertheless I must confess that my reflections were too abstract to be classified as "family matters." Consequently, the letter never went to you, nor did the following one, which I spoiled by being too specific for a change. Anyway, I'm not giving up the hope that I can teach myself to write you letters that you will receive, which is, after all, the most important thing.

As far as letters from outside go, I've received your letter no. 14, which naturally made me happy. But it's the only letter from you—and from outside altogether—that I've received since the visit! You must admit that a single page in six weeks is hardly enough. Obviously you still don't realize how important letters from home are. The more you write about yourself, the more details you provide, the more I am outside in spirit, with you in our normal world—and the less I have to be here. But as it is, "our world" remains just a cloud of fog behind which I imagine things that may fail entirely to mesh with reality. I admire all you've been doing during my imprisonment; this is the only point on which you need to improve. Don't treat your letters to me as an unavoidable duty, but simply as a source of amusement. Take a glass of wine into the study and pound out anything that comes into your head, what you've been going through, etc. Any specific information—even if it is apparently insignificant—means something to me.

Ivan's letter on physics was not given to me because it was too highly specialized. I asked him to write it and I apologize—it's my fault. Perhaps Ivan has a copy that I can read someday. Let's hope physics won't have progressed so far by then that the letter will be out of date. Likewise, I didn't receive one of Ivan's postcards (I did get yours). And finally, I very much regret not being given a letter from Květa—because of some quotations and verses. Ask her to write me again, but without the quotations and poetry.

Before turning to tasks for you, some brief news of myself: I've just realized that a quarter of my sentence is over. If it were a journey from Hrádeček to Prague, I'd be somewhere just outside of Jičín. If the comparison could be extended, it would mean that I'd have all the treacherous hills and curves behind me, while before me would lie a stretch of straight road, in places almost like a superhighway. So far, however, there's little evidence that this is so. Psychologically, I'm fit; sometimes I feel depressed and sometimes my good humor borders on mild euphoria—just like at home, in fact. With this difference: the petty details that upset me or cheer me up are different here. On the whole, I can't complain about my health—apart from hemorrhoids, numbness in my arms, pain in my legs (from standing), and similar minor ailments that I've already become inured to, I'm healthy—the fevers and shivers have, it seems, definitely disappeared.

. . .

And now I must try to squeeze in a few questions to help you write me: are Věra, Jiří and Toby still at Hrádeček? How are you getting along together? Are Andrej and Andulka there? What are their children doing? Do you have the car with you? Do you drive alone to do the shopping? What work have you managed to get done? What about the fence? The heating? The other tasks? Who has been visiting you? Have you had any good parties? What did you talk about? What records do you play most? Does Andulka come to see you and do you get along with each other? How do the neighbors treat you? Whom do you see most often and who, on the contrary, has dropped out of sight? Has Grossman, for example, got in touch? What about Mirek and his construction job? What about Landák, Trinky, Pavel, Jarda? Couldn't Pavel write to say what's going on in world theater and drama? Have you had any arguments with anyone? Do you occasionally talk about me? Do you miss me? What do you miss most about me? Do you ever have crises? Etc. etc. etc. etc. etc.

. . .

Thinking of you and kissing you,
Your Vašek

P.S. I read in the papers that a great horned owl has put in a rare appearance near Vlčice.

P.P.S. Re the parcel: medium thick, heavy-duty socks.

39

July 20, 1980

Dear Olga,

Because five days ago I wrote you letter 38 in which I went on at length about various practical matters (tasks, suggestions, questions, information, etc.), and because I wish to respect a suggestion that I not complicate communication with home by pointlessly giving too free a rein to my writer's fantasy, I will limit myself today to several haphazard and heterogeneous themes, as they occur to me.

My life: condition stable, rather overcast, no special communicable news except perhaps that I've had my head shaved, thus realizing an ancient plan of mine. Behind this act lies the hope that my hair will grow back in bushier and healthier than before this radical intervention. The last time I was shaved bald I was a six-year-old kid, but I must have looked essentially better back then. I don't think this hairstyle suits me very well today, since it highlights my age and my general decrepitude (because of the contrast between my smooth skull and my wrinkled face). Some say I look like Fantomas; others say I remind them of a real American gangster. Whatever the case, don't worry about being unpleasantly surprised on the next visit—by that time, I assume I'll have a handsome brush-cut.

Not long ago I had the chance and the time to think a little—in peace and quiet—about myself. Memories, reflections, plans, dreams, etc. swirled about in a kind of endless vortex that went nowhere and from which nothing emerged. It was really just a kind of recapitulation of fundamental certainties and also fundamental questions, hopes and doubts. I can only come up with new ideas when I'm working on some specific task, when there's an outside stimulus, when I'm inspired by dialogue, by a project, and so on. I've already remarked during my pretrial detention, I think, that I'm incapable of thinking or even creating "just for the hell of it." I'm a social creature pure and simple, wedged into the world and inspired by the world, not an introvert like Věra Linhartová, for instance, or Pepík Topol (even though he's not quite an introvert, at least not as much as it would seem at first sight). And so I have tried to form, in my mind, at least a kind of basic alphabet.

Before that, I had the chance to watch television occasionally and once more I realized an odd thing: how distorted one's perspective on everything is here. I am constantly and disproportionately moved, excited and uplifted by television (and film). The beautiful, positive emotions one sees there, the gentleness, the kindness, the wisdom, the courtesy, the way people do not humiliate and insult each other, the meaningful ways they behave—in short everything, perceived against this horizon here—provide a tremendous release. Yesterday, for example, I saw a Polish film, *Con Amore,* that I enjoyed a lot. It was essentially about how there are times when an artist must put his art aside in order to do something positive in life, something modest that may not earn him a place in history but which is the expression of a moral imperative or simply a love for people. At the same time, this film put forward the rather optimistic notion that the artist who is capable of subordinating his art to life—temporarily at least—is ultimately more interesting than the artist who sacrifices everything to his art. The latter will end up sacrificing his art as well, because he strips it of meaning. In short, the film excited me, moved me and in addition, there were very pretty girls in it, something else one doesn't see much of here.

I return in my thoughts to you, to Hrádeček, to its guests, to Andulka, to Puzuk's family and to numerous friends—to all of you, more often than my letters can make clear. In short, I'm with you, though you may not be aware of it, perhaps because you think I have troubles enough of my own. I do, but these excursions into our world help me not only to shake off those troubles but—oddly enough—to resolve them as well. Sometimes I focus on one thing, sometimes on another; God knows what it depends on. Recently, for example, I've thought a lot about Charlie. Once, in a letter from pretrial detention, I asked you (or did I merely intend to do it? I don't know anymore) to arrange for a high-quality live recording of all his songs—with an audience. (Charlie without that live atmosphere is merely a pale shadow of himself); I'm sure you didn't manage to get it done. I think sometimes of Zdena and Jula and feel sad because I don't suppose I'll ever see them again. When Vladimír Kafka died, Günter Grass said to me after the funeral: the older you get, the harder it is to find new friends and the harder you take it when you lose old ones. Is that true? I don't know; in the last few years I—and you too—have found many new young friends—perhaps better than some of our old ones—but all the same, this depopulation is hard to bear. Just remember the summer of '67: Tříska, Koblasa, Věra, Honza Němec, Pavel Juráček—and of course Landák—and later Pavel and Jarda and others—if it weren't for new friends, Hrádeček would be almost empty in the summer. Zdeněk would be there with us, though. Give him a kiss. Was this passage too sentimental? Don't take it too seriously—after all, I did say I was going to write whatever came into my mind—

40

July 27, 1980

Dear Olga,

So I've finally got another little letter from you (no. 15). It gave me great pleasure, naturally (who would not appreciate so rare a commodity), and I got special pleasure from the description of your birthday party. You certainly assembled a colorful collection of people there, which stirred my feelings because—as you know—I've always loved bringing people together and mixing them in various ways (just as I have always enjoyed concocting unlikely soups and sauces and salads; clearly, you're following honorably in my footsteps). . . .

Almost at the same time as your letter another communication came from the Ministry of Construction, which you must have received as well. Frankly I haven't been able to bring myself to study it in detail yet—I've just skimmed it, but that was enough for me to gather that it's another attack on us. The whole affair is gradually becoming incomprehensible and, what is worse, I realize that I'm becoming less capable of defending myself for one simple reason: slowly but surely, I'm forgetting how it all was. I know only one thing: that we had a verbal (and therefore virtually unverifiable) approval of the changes from the District National Committee and in particular, in the matter of the heating, I had a lively, ongoing correspondence and negotiations with the DNC (after all, they approved both the plans and the planner!). So I'm somewhat confused by it all. I have no idea what should happen next and how this dispute is likely to turn out. I can only hope you won't be driven out of Hrádeček and that we won't have to tear the place down.

Otherwise, it seems that things are quite eventful out there. But don't get the wrong idea, this is no island of tranquillity either. I was harboring grand illusions when I thought I'd be able to give my nerves a rest in prison. It's a kind of paradox—as I think I mentioned during your last visit—that I of all people, who loves harmony and wants people to like and respect each other, must live my entire life in conflict, tension and stress. And yet I've never got used to it: today, as much or more so than twenty years ago, I still tend to fret and worry and experience things with excessive intensity, and it will clearly always be that way. Strange. Very strange. Ask Jirka what he thinks about it.

Today I realized that my mood depends not only on the weather, but also on the kind of dreams I have, or to be more precise, on the mood of my dreams (which is far more important than their thematic content). Today, for example, I dreamed you gave birth to twins after a sixteen-month pregnancy. You didn't have them with me, but with some American professor. The professor didn't bother me at all, I only regretted that the twins weren't mine (it was interesting how strictly I was able to separate the professor as such from my nonpaternity). At the same time, Jirka and Dana had twins too, but one got hopelessly lost in their flat in Ječná Street and they never found him again. The mood of the dream was extremely oppressive, and thus I was depressed after reveille. But I'm not depressed now—now I'm with you in Hrádeček and I feel fine.

Vašek

41

[Postmarked: August 8, 1980]

Dear Olga,

As you probably know by now, the visit is set for Saturday, September 6 at 9:00 a.m. I'm glad we know about it further in advance this time, so you can plan your summer movements better and I have before me a fixed point on which to pin my anticipation. I was given permission for neither a parcel of hygienic supplies nor a fruit package, so that in addition to what I ordered (see letter 38), you'll have to squeeze into the parcel's weight limit my most up-to-date razor with a supply of blades that fit, a good (stiff) toothbrush, two large (or four small) tubes of toothpaste and, if there is room, some medium thick, heavy-duty socks (they can be knee-length). And if possible some cream or skin lotion. But nothing at the expense of cigarettes, tea and chocolate.

· · ·

Now, what might I write about myself? That I'm having various difficulties and that I'm dealing with them in the usual way: legal self-defense. That I'm healthy, oddly enough (even my hemorrhoids are giving me a rest), though I'm exhausted all the time (the worst thing is the pain in my legs from having to stand at work). As for my mental disposition, what I wrote you last time—I think—is still true: my moods are changeable, depressions alternate with good spirits. Some unpleasant triviality, some uncertainty, fear or danger, some minor vexation (for example someone swipes my butts—you see how my vocabulary has expanded?) can suddenly evoke despondency, nervousness, anxiety and alarm, a feeling of futility and despair. But this may last only a few hours—until something equally trivial occurs and fills me with such sudden delight that former feelings are utterly forgotten, things regain their meaning and I become an incredible optimist once more, full of élan and the will to live. Failing such a triviality, I can overcome the depression myself, perhaps by telling myself I got what I deserve, as punishment for not being a better person, and that it all has a deeper meaning (Jirka the inveterate atheist, however, makes great fun of this method). Not long ago, I couldn't sleep for the first half of the night (to make matters worse, it was just before a morning shift) because I had several unbelievable things to think over; suddenly, my thinking led me to the subject for a play, and the second half of the night I couldn't sleep because I was thinking that through. (Of course I was impossible at work next day.) It was the first time in a long while that I'd had such an idea—something that adequately reflected my new experience of life; it's too early to say whether this idea will survive or be thrown out like all the rest. But I didn't intend to write about that; I was only describing my moodiness. Anyway, I guess I'm what they call high-strung, and in fact I always have been: remember how in Hrádeček I could never concentrate on anything until the mail arrived? It's like that here: whenever I hear my name shouted in the corridor or somewhere, my heart begins pounding, and once I leaped to my feet in such a panic that I opened a gash on my shorn noggin. But you mustn't draw any far-reaching conclusions from my behavior; it means nothing, except what it is: I seem to experience everything more intensely, and in a way, pay more intensely for it.

Once you're here, however, whether you want to or not, you have to ask the question: does all of this have a meaning, and if so, what? The more I think about it, the more I realize that the final and decisive answer is not to be found in external factors that rely on so-called information, for no mere information can give me an answer to that question. Ultimately, I can only find an answer—a positive answer—

within myself, in my general faith in the meaning of things, in my hope. What, in fact, is man responsible to? What does he relate to? What is the final horizon of his actions, the absolute vanishing point of everything he does, the undeceivable "memory of Being," the conscience of the world and the final "court of appeal"? What is the decisive standard of measurement, the background or the field of each of his existential experiences? And likewise, what is the most important witness or the secret sharer in his daily conversations with himself, the thing that— regardless of what situation he is thrown into—he incessantly inquires after, depends upon and toward which his actions are directed, the thing that, in its omniscience and its incorruptibility, both haunts and saves him, the only thing he can trust in and strive for?

Ever since childhood, I have felt that I would not be myself—a human being—if I did not live in a permanent and manifold tension with this "horizon" of mine, the source of meaning and hope—and ever since my youth, I've never been certain whether this is an "experience of God" or not. Whatever it is, I'm certainly not a proper Christian and Catholic (as so many of my good friends are) and there are many reasons for this. For instance, I do not worship this god of mine and I don't see why I should. What he is—a horizon without which nothing would have meaning and without which I would not, in fact, exist—he is by virtue of his essence, and not thanks to some strong-arm tactics that command respect. By worshiping him in some model fashion, I don't think I could improve either the world or myself, and it seems quite absurd to me that this "intimate-universal" partner of mine—who is sometimes my conscience, sometimes my hope, sometimes my freedom and sometimes the mystery of the world—might demand to be worshiped or might even judge me according to the degree to which I worship him. Related to this is my constant compulsion to reconsider things—originally, authentically, from the beginning—that is, in an unmediated dialogue with this god of mine; I refuse to simplify matters by referring to some respected, more material authority, even if it were the Holy Writ itself. (I accept the Gospel of Jesus as a challenge to go my own way.) When it gets right down to it, I am a child of the age of conceptual, rather than mystical, thought and therefore my god as well—if I am compelled to speak of him (which I do very unwillingly)— must appear as something terribly abstract, vague and unattractive (all the more so since my relationship to him is so difficult to pin down). But it appears so only to someone I try to tell about him—the experience itself is quite vivid, intimate and particular, perhaps (thanks to its constantly astonishing diversity) more lively than for someone whose "normal" God is provided with all the appropriate attributes (which oddly enough can alienate more often than drawing one closer). And something else that is typical of my god: he is a master of waiting, and in doing so he frequently unnerves me. It is as though he set up various possibilities around me and then waited silently to see what I would do. If I fail, he punishes me, and of course he uses me as the agent of that punishment (pangs of conscience, for example); if I don't fail, he rewards me (through my own relief and joy)—and frequently, he leaves me in uncertainty. (By the way, when my conscience bothers me, why does it bother me? And when I rejoice, why do I rejoice? Is it not again because of him?) His Last Judgment is taking place now, continuously, always—and yet it is always the last: nothing that has happened can ever un-happen, everything remains in the "memory of Being"—and I too remain there—condemned to be with myself till the end of time—just as I am and just as I make myself.

But I began with something quite different: with the question of whether it all had a meaning. That I can only find the final answer within myself does not mean, of course, that I'm not interested in what the "external world" thinks of it, or that this external world does not interest me. After all, I live in it, it shapes my possibilities, my own alternatives in life are structured from its materials and it is only through the world that I relate to that "higher" horizon. So: I'd be grateful to you if you could prepare a few words on that theme for the visit as well. You know my positions; they have not changed. But hasn't the world around us changed? Haven't meanings shifted in it? Why, for instance, are so many friends suddenly leaving the country?

Last time I forgot to thank you for the reproduction of Slavík's painting. I wasn't allowed to keep it, but I examined it thoroughly. And I liked it a lot—that is, if it is the way I imagine it to be as I study the photograph. (I'd like to see a painting by Juliana as well.) . . .

Greetings to everyone—as usual; I think of everyone and I often talk with you: whenever something crosses my mind or happens to me, I think immediately about what I'll write to you about it. So that the "memory of Being," among other things, contains a lot of unwritten letters to you. Is it the same with you, too?

44

Dear Olga,

While I'm assuming that during your visit we'll be speaking about the problems of our correspondence as well, I'm not assuming that we'll be able to talk about it in much detail, so this may be an appropriate theme for today's letter—which is unfortunately a week late and will reach you only after the visit.

*

First something about my letters to you: writing them is always the most important event of the week for me and it's a small ceremony: I usually write you on Saturday, sometimes on Sunday. First I discharge all my weekend duties, such as washing my socks, etc. (so my writing won't be interrupted by thoughts of what remains to be done or seen to), then I wait for the moment that is relatively the quietest. I try, if possible, to attain a state of inner harmony (as a matter of principle I never write when I am sad, nervous or angry about something)—in this, as in everything, tea is a great help—and then I seek out the quietest corner where I set up my writing camp and once there I leave only in cases of direst need.

There are several reasons why letter writing is so important to me: (1) first and foremost, my home, you, my close friends and our world become vividly present in my mind when I write; (2) it's my only chance to write here (over the years, I've discovered that writing has become almost a biological necessity); (3) it's my only chance for some kind of intellectual self-fulfillment; (4) I clarify some things for myself in the act of writing; (5) it's my only line of communication with you and our world (during the week, I catch myself thinking of all the things I'd like to or should write you about, and how I should write it; this need for communication is all the more tormenting because it is so hard to satisfy). The writing itself, however, is difficult because I'm never sure whether I've gone beyond some predetermined framework—which unfortunately happens far too often—so that my most important letters for the most part never reached you. Obviously, all these things do not create the most favorable climate for writing; that is why my letters seem rather cramped and impersonal. In other words, I don't like them very much. And yet I always look forward to writing them and I continue to hope that someday I'll succeed in finding a mode of expression that is completely authentic and at the same time, does not continually cause me problems.

*

And now something about your letters: last week, letters 17 and 18 arrived in quick succession and both of them, understandably, brought me great delight. I won't try to deny that their sometimes confusing telegraphic style, their lack of organization and compositional logic and their considerable laxness in matters syntactical, grammatical and graphical is somewhat bothersome to my annoyingly pedantic nature. At the same time, I'm well aware that all of this is just the surface and the only important thing is what lies beneath it. And there—particularly in your most recent letters—I find a great deal, perhaps more than you know: important information (though it may concern only the "atmosphere"), substantial and significant insights and many worthwhile ideas. Above all, beneath this surface I sense you, or rather I hear you. Perhaps this is because you're not hamstrung by an excessive respect for external form, expression and organization. Your letters are authentic and probably fuller, in essential ways, than mine, which have been cobbled together with such diligence and anxiety. So: don't try to improve your letters, don't rewrite them and don't correct them; go ahead and make mistakes—I'll be happy with errors and objects not agreeing with subjects or getting left out altogether, I'll be happy to guess at the missing component. What is essential for me is the spirit and, to be somewhat overblown about it, the inner "gospel" of your letters.

But to be more concrete: two passages in letter 18 had a beneficial and stimulating effect on me: the one about new friendships taking the place of the old, and then your brief reflection on yourself. Insofar as my "love letter" provoked you to write the latter passage, then I don't regret having written it and I thank Kamila for inadvertently goading me into it. Otherwise, however, I can't tell whether that letter appealed to you or put you off. My guess would be it put you off, which goes to show that one really shouldn't force oneself to write about things that don't come naturally. Besides that, I think you missed what the letter was really about: it was an attempt briefly (and therefore in a necessarily simplified way) to say what you mean to me, or what our relationship means to me; I was certainly not trying to write your portrait, and if I mentioned some of your qualities, it was only superficially and haphazardly (such as examples of how our personalities differ and therefore complement each other). So it would be unjust to criticize me for overlooking or failing to mention other qualities. As you know, I've been thinking for some years now of writing a collection of essays about you—and someday, when it's done, that will be the appropriate time to discuss the question of how well or how badly I represented you. This relates to the theme of sentimentality which you raised: of course I'm not confusing sentimentality with sentiment and emotional warmth, but I don't believe either that sentimentality is necessarily a suspect quality pertaining only to tyrants. Someone with a good heart may well be as sentimental as someone evil, and on the contrary, neither need necessarily be sentimental at all. True, I tend to be sentimental and you don't—but that doesn't mean I consider you insensitive or doubt your need for emotional warmth, just as it doesn't follow that I'm a villain. But I only say this for the sake of accuracy; it doesn't touch the essence of things, and what you wrote about yourself, your forbearance, your love of people, about new friendships, your ability to correct and forgive yourself—I not only liked all of that, it gave me enormous pleasure as well. Moreover, it confirms our two-in-oneness: I feel that—not just here, but in the last few years, and in my own way, of course—I have been going through an evolution like the one you observe in yourself. But more than that, I think we help each other in this evolution and, in this sense (unconscious though it may be), influence each other.

Otherwise, about some individual points in your letters: I'm glad to hear you have a lithography from Mr. Stritzko; please thank him for praying for me. Likewise I'm delighted that *The Mountain Hotel* is gaining supporters and I'm breathlessly awaiting some quotations from Magor's essay. I praise and admire your decision to start working on the windows (its probably too late now, but if I'd known sooner, I would have suggested you use an epoxy-based paint, which I understand will last for ages). I don't quite understand why your dream pushed me into bed with Marketa, of all people, when she is one of the few beings with whom I have not only in all politeness avoided such a possibility, but absolutely forbidden it to myself, even for the future.

*

I'm looking forward to the visit and I will try to commit to memory everything I want to talk to you about. Oh, dear—

I kiss you, Vašek

45

September 6, 1980

Dear Olga,

It's just after the visit and this time—unlike previous visits, after which I have felt euphoric and filled with élan and optimism—I feel considerable anxiety. It's because the visit itself had a somewhat anxious atmosphere, for several reasons. First, I wasn't entirely well, I had a slight headache and I was somewhat out of sorts; secondly, you caught me off guard at the beginning by saying how badly I looked and making related comments that I was unprepared for. I was so rattled that I wasn't quite up to form for the rest of the visit, I probably expressed myself badly and felt rather unsure of myself. I simply didn't have the spark, as they say. It's not a tragedy, of course, but it does give pause for thought: in the first place, you obviously meant well, and my friends obviously mean well, when they worry about me and about my health, my nerves, etc. But the point is I've already come to accept that it's entirely up to me to decide how best to get through all this without damage to body and soul. At the same time, this daily effort derives from the obvious assumption that I have simply got to go through with it, that it has a meaning and that it is my duty. Given this, the one possible form of help I have come to expect from the outside—and it is a supremely important form of help—is reassurance that this is so, in other words, that I really must carry through with it, that it really does have a meaning and that I'm not toiling and moiling away here for nothing. And suddenly you cast doubts—if only for a moment—on the whole enterprise and you raise the question that I do not and cannot permit myself to ask if I'm to survive with honor: is it all worth it? And that was what rattled me; without really meaning to, you gave me the precise opposite of what I expected and needed. I don't mean that it was a mistake on your part: for one thing, you were expressing a sincere and deep concern for my fate, and this naturally pleased and moved me; for another thing, it told me something about the atmosphere outside; for no matter what one decides (and one ultimately discovers the decision inside oneself and not in any external atmosphere) one should, after all, make one's choice in the light of a somewhat objective knowledge of the context in which and for which the decision is made; and even though a decision may seem pigheaded or absurd, one should at the very least know that it can or does appear that way. In other words, the situation outside is changing, the significance of things is shifting, I can't follow that development from here and it's right that I know as much about it as possible. It certainly makes no sense to keep alive any illusions or any falsely idyllic or optimistic picture I may have of the situation just to satisfy my expectations. Thus I don't hold it against you for speaking as you did; on the contrary, I welcome it. I'm merely explaining here why it took me by surprise and upset me. (I'm continuing on Sunday, with a new pen from you, because my old refill ran out on the very day of the visit. I feel much better than yesterday; a pity the visit wasn't today, I would have been in better form.) But it is instructive: I see now, in practice, what I'd known before only theoretically, that one of the dangers here is the tendency to create a fixed notion of the situation (based on conditions as they were when one came here, gradually idealized over time) without understanding that this situation might develop or change. On the other hand, however, I must say that much of what you told me subsequently seemed—to me at least—in sharp contradiction to the early part of our conversation; it confirmed my inner hope, my sense of the significance of it all, and my good faith.

Otherwise, just a few more comments on the visit. . . . For the first time I realized that there are areas in which being cut off from each other is slowly making communication more difficult, not so much because of what is going on outside but rather because of how I live here. If, for example, I were to tell you—without first explaining the wider context— what raises or dampens my spirits in these conditions, what I consider success and what is normal, what role I must play in which situations, etc. etc., you'd perhaps have great difficulty understanding any of it, and many things that have now become routine for me would probably make your hair stand on end. I'm looking forward to telling you all this one day. I expect you'll laugh a lot and cry a lot and above all, there will be many things you simply won't believe. It's interesting that this first occurred to me during our conversation. . . .

So the visit is over; thank you for it and I'm already looking forward to the next one. I'll do all I can to look better and not to depress you with my appearance; perhaps some of my hair will have grown back by then.

And now on to another subject: you mentioned the upcoming production of *The Mountain Hotel.* I've already written you something about it, but I'd like to return to it for a moment, because I still worry that those who are putting it on won't have the proper notion of how to go about it. When thinking of how best to convey my own idea of the play,

I realize that it is, in fact, a fugue. If they think about the staging while listening to *The Art of the Fugue* or the *Brandenburg Concertos,* they will certainly see what I have in mind: up to a certain point, the constant variation and permutation of the same motifs may seem to be an end in itself, boring and stereotypical, but if you persist, either as author or "consumer," and are not afraid of going further with it, then eventually there comes a moment when boredom ceases and everything takes on meaning. Like a fugue, which because it is consistently "about nothing," is ultimately "about everything," so this play—thanks to its structure and the persistence of its combinatory logic—aspires to be "about nothing," yes, but at the same time, "about everything." In other words its most important elements are its rhythm, its structure, its spatiotemporal architecture. At the same time, however, these elements must not obtrude in any banal way—in the form of some biomechanical, rhythmic movements by the actors or something of that nature; they must be concealed behind completely straightforward, suggestively realistic acting. Perhaps the denouement could allow for a certain degree of sensitive stylization. It might be of some help to pass on these notes of mine to the friends who have something to do with the upcoming production. On the other hand, perhaps I'm just carrying wood into the forest, in which case so much the better.

I kiss you and I'm looking forward to the time around St. Nicholas's Day when I will see you again! Ahoj—

Vašek

46

September 13, 1980

Dear Olga,

I suspect there are only three kinds of letters that I know, more or less, how to write: (1) official letters to institutions; (2) letters that are a free and cheerful stream of foolish things; (3) letters resembling what might be called microessays. In the present situation, however, I find it hard to apply this limited letter-writing ability because the above-mentioned genres are ruled out either by their very nature or because they don't make the grade, as it were. Well, what's to be done? I have to accept the fact that my letters are not going to leave their mark on the world, and anyway that's not their purpose, so it doesn't really matter. So much, then—as an appendix to letter 44—for my letters in general. And now concretely about this letter: it will be a mosaic of subjects, separated by a yellow asterisk.

*

Regarding my wretched appearance, which caused you so much concern during the visit: it seems that it did not herald my general decline but was rather the result of a short-term indisposition. On Sunday—a day after the visit and shortly after I'd finished writing letter 45—I fell ill, was sick for two days and am now convalescing. When the visit took place, the illness was just launching an attack on me and that's why I wasn't myself, which in any case, I wrote you right afterward, that is, before I knew I was falling ill. Perhaps this news will ease your mind.

. . .

Despite the tenser atmosphere of our visit this time (I detailed my thoughts in letter 45), I must say I've been in a positive frame of mind and constant good spirits for several days. Obviously there is a panoply of reasons for this, both serious and trivial, many of which I may not even be aware of. For example these factors (chosen at random): (a) thanks to my illness, I've been able to rest and find a way to concentrate and meditate in the middle of the hubbub around me; (b) I don't know exactly why, but I have a vague feeling that my future—in the long run, of course—is not as bleak as it might seem at first glance; (c) the hopeful fact that—as I told you (if you noticed)—I may be shifted to better work, also has a certain influence; (d) last but not least, there is the fact that I am not merely a depressive psychopath, as an old diagnosis would have it, but a bit of a die-hard as well who, when he is feeling particularly miserable, can always find—Lord knows where—a new source of vitality and joy of life. In other words: for the time being, you really have no need to be worried about me.

. . .

I'm delighted with the parcel; I make tea for myself every day, stirring it with that long spoon, and occasionally I nibble on a piece of chocolate, and once in a while I smoke a good cigarette—mostly on

Saturdays and Sundays. Again, I must praise you for your perfect choice of items.

*

As you probably know, my lawyer came to visit and we had a nice chat for two hours, though it was only about legal matters.

. . .

Greetings and kisses for all faithful and close friends—

Your, Vašek

47

September 21, 1980

Dear Olga,

I'm slowly getting used to not writing you about fundamental topics of general import, and coming to accept that the talk of Prague will not be what fine, clever letters I'm writing from prison. Today's letter is no exception; I intend to devote it to a number of petty details from my life, only those I'm permitted to write about, of course. But even that may be of some use; judging from my experience with your letters, every scrap of information about your life—even apparently meaningless bits—has enormous value for me since it brings your—or rather our—world and its climate close to me.

A new and important thing in my life here is the fact that I have started a course in welding, which means I'm going to be a welder and you are about to become a welder's wife. This is important mainly because after nine months I am finally going to be doing work that is incomparably better than what I've done till now.

. . .

Partly influenced by the poor impression my appearance made on you—I have increased the care I devote to the various aspects of my earthly existence. Some random examples: I am trying—as far as I can here—to eat properly, which means a maximum of the healthy and nutritious food available and a minimum of what serves only to fill the stomach. I try to get as much sleep as I can and to facilitate this I'm taking steps to rationalize my regime (without of course interfering with my daily duties and routines, etc.). Thirdly: I contrive to satisfy the whims that give me inner comfort (tea drinking, for example, or eating chocolate, etc.) according to a carefully devised plan. Fourthly: I devote a lot of intellectual energy to the precise scheduling of various private functions, to the rational economizing of my strength and my free time (the latter is in short supply, however) and to establishing proper hierarchies for various activities and nonactivities from the point of view of psychic, neurological and biological harmony. I give careful thought to what I can allow myself and when, so that I won't squander my strength in daydreaming, in pointless and vain pursuits. Sometimes, for example, it is essential not to do anything at all and to rest, physically and mentally, as completely as I can. At other times it is more important to concentrate fully on a particular thing and not let myself be distracted by anything random, like the idle chatter of my fellow inmates. At still other times, it is important to let myself be caught up—as an interested observer—in precisely such random occurrences, including the idle chatter, and to get as much as possible out of it. . . . Sometimes I am ridiculed (in a friendly way) for planning and thinking everything out carefully, but I don't mind because I always have a cogent response: I can demonstrate how, given my "style of prison living" and my attitude, I am mentally and neurologically better off than someone whose behavior—despite a swaggering, tough-guy exterior—is in fact hopelessly aimless. (But not many ridicule me, and if they do, it's all part of the camaraderie.) Altogether, I must say—and this may sound pompous, but why shouldn't I say something good about myself once in a while—that when I look around me, many of these "tough guys," who brag about themselves and are ready to fight at the drop of a hat, are from a certain point of view really just doormats and old maids beside me—which is pretty funny, given my "exterior" (awkwardness, politeness, courtesy, overanxiety, etc.). My tough-guy neighbors must feel this in some way, judging by how even the biggest of the "kings," as they're called here, don't take even a tenth of the liberties with me they take with others, including some of the even bigger kings. Magor will certainly confirm for you how deceptive a thing one's position in the social structures here can be, and how important, and I—who have so little faith in myself—must say that in this regard I'm not having the slightest problem and that among my fellow prisoners, my position is more than just good, and I sometimes wonder if I deserve such respect. But enough self-glorification. In any case, I see I've got completely sidetracked from my original theme. . . .

Another subject I could write many pages about is my moods. Here, too, the situation is slowly but steadily improving: my feelings of depression, hopelessness and futility are becoming less frequent and different sorts of good moods are on the increase. Quite frequently, I have something I lacked during your visit, something like a "spark": I feel supremely confident, I have a cogent response for everything, I'm bristling with wit and I can even be sharp-tongued and "politely mouthy." At other times I'm taciturn, silent, introverted—but still I smile absentmindedly, because my mind is "wandering," as they say. Yet again, I'm fearless and feel that nothing can unnerve me and no one can outdo me. And at still other times, I take childish delight in small achievements like darning a hole in my sock or finding the time and space for a little yoga, or simply not allowing myself to be depressed by some accident, insult, the loss of important things, etc.

One of the more frequent themes of my meditations and daydreams are the friends that have left the country. Initially, I feel a slight nostalgia and even some envy (of their artistic achievements) and a slight anxiety (they are doing what they enjoy at last, they are involved in their work, free from endless complications, no doubt viewing our toiling and moiling as pointless now, while I on the other hand am deprived of all that, without the slightest chance of working in a theater and reveling in the ideas that theater has always inspired in me). That is how such meditations begin, and they always end with a peculiar sensation of inner joy that I am where I should be, that I have not turned away from myself, that I have not bolted for the emergency exit and that for all the privations, I am rid of the worst privation of all (one that I have known myself too): the feeling that I could not measure up to my task, though I may not have set it myself—at least not in this form and to this degree—but merely accepted it from the hand of fate, accident and history.

I kiss you, Vašek

48

September 27, 1980

Dear Olga,

Obviously there is an expectation, from various sides, that once I return from here I will write something about it all. The more I think about it, the less sure I feel of fulfilling that expectation. Not because I don't somehow feel the need to communicate everything I see and live through here; on the contrary, time and again I find myself spinning my impressions, experiences, insights and meditations into a kind of imaginary text, but it is only a kind of free and unregulated, spontaneous stream of thought and I'm not sure I'd really be capable of writing it down, especially when it's all over. It's an endless poem of sorts in the style of Egon Bondy—and therein lies the problem: I have a different disposition altogether. I lack his marvelous temerity to write down everything that occurs to him; I am too hesitant, too self-controlled, I must carefully weigh, construct, cut, etch, chisel and redo everything many times. I have never written spontaneously and I doubt that I ever could, yet I know of no other way to deal with this experience directly and authentically. And so most probably I won't do any more than construct plays again as I used to do, and my new experience will be projected into them, if at all, indirectly. . . .

In my last letter, I wrote you a little about how I am trying to bring a certain order into my outer life in the form of a deliberate program of "self-care," aimed at promoting physical health and steadiness of nerve. Today, I'm going to continue that theme with a short essay on tea. When I was outside, I didn't understand the cult of tea that exists in prison, but I wasn't here long before grasping its significance and succumbing to it myself (I, who used to drink tea, if at all, only once a year, when I had the flu) or more precisely, including it as an inseparable aspect of my "self-care" program. I'll try to indicate briefly some of the functions tea assumes in these circumstances. (1) First of all, it cures: one always tries tea first to head off a whole range of minor indispositions such as headaches, sluggishness, chills, the inability to concentrate, sore throat, incipient colds, etc. etc.—and it often works. (2) It warms: ten fur coats will not get rid of occasional numbness better than a glass of hot tea. (3) Stimulation: it is only here, where one has no alcohol, coffee and all the other means of excitation common on the outside, that one appreciates how powerful a stimulant tea, or rather, the caffeine it contains, is. It is a real pick-me-up; it reduces weariness, nervousness, bad moods, apathy, sleepiness, etc., and restores one's freshness, alertness, ability to concentrate, energy, strength and appetite for life. (I now know precisely how much tea I can drink during the day and when I should take my last drink if I want to fall sleep at a certain hour.) (4) Last but not least—in fact most important of all, perhaps—is tea's peculiar uplifting function. Tea, it seems to me, becomes a kind of material symbol of freedom here: (a) it is in effect the only fare that one can prepare oneself, and thus freely: when and how I make it is entirely up to me. In the preparation of it, I realize myself as a free being, as it were, capable of looking after myself. (b) Tea—as a sign of private relaxation, of a brief pause in the midst of the hubbub, of rumination and private contemplation—functions as the external, material attribute of a certain unbridling of the spirit and thus as a companion in moments of focused inner freedom. (c) The world of freedom considered as leisure time is represented by tea in the opposite—in the extroverted and therefore the social—sense: sitting down to a cup of tea here is a substitute for the world of bars, wine rooms, parties, binges, social life, in other words again, something you choose yourself and in which you realize your freedom in social terms. In short: tea here has a rich panoply of functions, it's become a habit, I drink it every day, preparing it is one of my small daily ceremonies (and even such small ceremonies help to hold one together—it is something like a salutary straitjacket), I look forward to it, and consuming it (which I schedule carefully, so it does not become a formless and random activity) is an extremely important component in my daily "self-care" program.

*

I'm continuing this on my name day, which began very pleasantly: the clocks were turned back, so we slept an hour longer.

Thanks for the postcard announcing your move to Prague and your intention to write a letter. It hasn't arrived yet, but I firmly believe that it is on its way at least and that it will reach me in time for my birthday. I got a letter from my sweet sister-in-law and as I read it, it took me back vividly to my last days of freedom. Once again I realized that the rather hectic pace of those days, culminating in that "last supper" at the Fregata restaurant, seemed directly influenced by an intimation that the end was approaching. Whether that is true or not, the fact is I had been living for some time with a vague feeling that my fate was unavoidable and I made no secret of it. Please thank her and pass on to her a tender in-law's kiss. (She mentioned complications with a distant relative whose actions seem to me—particularly from here—very pitiful; my fellow prisoners would say he was "máčo.")

I've finished the course and begun to work on a machine like Jirka's. No doubt I'll make a few blunders before getting used to it, but that's to be expected. In any case, this move to a different kind of work is an important change for the better in my life.

I saw one episode of Dietl's "Odyssey of an Engineer" and even I, having recently come to appreciate, relatively speaking, certain aspects of Dietl's adroitness, had to admit that it was sheer nonsense. (I'm told it happened to be the weakest episode.) Yesterday, however, I made up for it to my complete satisfaction by spending several moments with Chaplin.

.   .   .

Hugs and kisses, Vašek

49

October 4, 1980

Dear Olga,

Thank you for both your name-day greetings, the first of which I still have with me for the time being, and I'm using it, successfully, to aromatize my locker. It was a good idea to put that perfume on it, and I think you should do it with every letter. (What perfume is it, anyway? Jasmine? It evokes my stay in Ruzyně, all my stays there; you must have used it on your letters to me there.) Your letter finally came too, but unfortunately it was considered objectionable and not given to me; I was only apprised of the contents of several unobjectionable paragraphs. It's a shame to wait a month for a letter and then not receive it. The moral of this is that you really should write more often. I don't know what was in the objectionable parts (it may have been messages from various people and news about them) but I believe that if you write me more frequently, your letters won't contain such a concentration of information and they won't cause problems. The list of productions and performances of my plays wasn't given to me either, but I was informed of its contents and of course was very pleased. It was a good idea to send it. Your photo of the fence and Ajda was original, but it made me think you might occasionally send me other photos as well with a greater potential of information, so I might study them and perhaps even keep them with me (in exchange for some photos I have here now—your portrait, and three photographs from my father's funeral, which mean a lot to me because all those closest to me are in them (including myself with a more civilian visage, hair and a mustache) but which otherwise do not exactly inspire joy; it's not the best idea to have photos from one's father's funeral as the only memento of home). About your letter, or rather the parts I was told about: I can't sun myself here, of course, but I occasionally find myself in the sun, if only for brief periods. This year, however, there hasn't been much sun at all. I don't have scurvy, nor am I likely to get it, but I welcome vitamins—the rose-hip tea would be a good idea; I'd add it to regular tea as a medicine. I can't buy garlic so you can put some in the parcel too; I haven't asked for it so far because it's too heavy and gets used up right away. Which is a problem with many other healthy and delicious things you could send me, things I would love to have. There is still lots of time to think about what will go into the parcel—I'll write my instructions in due time. I'm glad you drew the conclusion you mentioned from the book you read.

*

Not much new has happened in my life. I'm working at the new machine, I still spoil some work occasionally, but on the whole I can handle it. The main thing is I enjoy it; it helps pass the time, the work is varied (at least compared to what I was doing before) and not arduous. One significant event last week was a visit to the dentist. He seems excellent; he doesn't shy away from obstacles, works sensitively and has a good habit, which I miss in other doctors, of explaining clearly what's wrong with you, what he's doing about it and why. He cleaned tartar deposits from my teeth, and even got rid of an ugly fracture on one of my front teeth that I thought was permanent, and now he's trying to do something about my cervical caries (again, something most other dentists consider almost fatally incurable). As you can see, I'm developing my "self-care" program in the area of stomatology as well.

As for cultural experiences: on television, I saw the first part of a very good American film on Martin Luther King (whom I greatly admired, as you know) and some more episodes in that Dietl serial, no longer as idiotic as the episode I mentioned last time, but still typical Dietl with all that that entails. I'd like to write an essay about the phenomenon. As for reading, I didn't finish *The Green Hills of Africa;* hunting reminiscences is a genre that has always bored me to death. I've started reading Hemingway's novel *To Have and Have Not* and a biography of Mohammed. I regularly read *Melodie* magazine, rather thoroughly in fact, from cover to cover, and the fact that it's swarming with concepts I don't understand and people I know nothing about doesn't bother me at all. . . .

Tomorrow is my birthday and because I'm in the same room as a prisoner who was born the same year and the same day as I was, we're preparing a minor celebration. The high point will be an attempt to make a cake from available materials; I'm very curious about how it will turn out, and above all, I'm on edge about its final consistency; perhaps consistency isn't the right word, but physical state—and every state except gas is possible. The first course will consist of canned pork.

*

Once again, I'm going through a period of colorful dreams. The action is always most curious; I was much taken, for example, by a dream that revolved entirely around Terezka Kohoutová's getting married to General Bastian of the Bundeswehr, if you know who he is. (They retired him because he came out publicly against an increase in NATO armaments.) I didn't learn about the wedding plans from Terezka, but from the general, who paid me a visit. It's interesting that in most of my dreams I move about in the world as though I were free, yet at the same time I know I'm an inmate—so that formally, they are excursions (temporary) into the outside world, something like what they refer to here as "an interruption of the sentence."

*

I kiss you and all close friends and implore you: write me more often!

51

October 19, 1980

Dear Olga,

I was informed about your postcard, which didn't give me much joy. First of all, I was rather badly shaken by the news that Mrs. Koníčková had died. Write me more about it, and tell me whether it was illness or an accident. Mrs. Koníčková—among others—was the last person I talked to outside—when they were taking me away. Convey my condolences to her family. The news that you've been "bad" also disturbed me—I hope that by now you're "good" again. In the third place, I was surprised by your complaint that you haven't had a letter from me for a long time. That is odd, because I write you every week with unshakable regularity and all my recent letters—i.e., since your visit—were almost certainly sent off, otherwise I would have been told. Perhaps the mail has been held up. (Is it still impossible to lock our mailbox? You should do something about it, otherwise anyone could take anything they wanted.)

I was delighted to get the vitamins from abroad, the receipt of which I confirmed in a special letter. As I gathered from the label, they contain every possible substance required by the human body and then some, which particularly pleases me because, as you know, given my mania for amalgamation I like everything to be neatly in one place. I began taking them according to a precise plan to make them last as long as possible. They arrived at just the right time, because November is coming, the worst month for all manner of things, including hemorrhoids. Perhaps they will help my body to adjust to winter.

Nothing world-shaking has taken place in my life; the most important experience of recent days has been my rereading of Camus's *The Stranger.* As you know, it's not a cheerful book and yet I'm indebted to it for a few moments of great joy, that special and elevating kind of joy I always feel on encountering a supreme work of art. Part of it is the sensation that it is "just right," exactly as it should be; in other words, a feeling that I too might have written it, or even that I did write it myself. It may sound silly to put it so baldly, but I'm sure you understand what I mean. It's simply an inner identification that you can feel equally well when looking at a painting or listening to a piece of music, even though you are not a painter or composer yourself. Moreover this book has many dimensions and it merged, in an interesting way, with my own thoughts on responsibility. The stranger is not a man without responsibilities, he is merely a man who refuses to conform to conventional order, i.e., to the conventional structure of duties, and he feels obligated to accept only those duties that are an authentic expression of his own sense of responsibility. He is not executed for what he did, but for refusing to conform. Of course that is only one level of the book; its meaning is broader, richer, and seems to oscillate uneasily or remain just out of focus—but that is as it should be: given the utter clarity and transparency of the work itself, its so-called meaning is not completely spelled out nor can this be done: yet that is precisely what draws the reader in and arouses his enthusiasm. *The Fall* is in the same volume as *The Stranger;* I'm looking forward to reading that again and I'll mention it in a future letter.

.   .   .

I kiss you, Vašek

52

October 27, 1980

Dear Olga,

.   .   .

Of all the philosophy I have read since my youth, existentialism, and thus phenomenology as well, were always what stimulated and attracted me most. I enjoyed reading works by those authors, yet my knowledge in that regard was always rather superficial. I was influenced more by the atmosphere of their thinking than I was by particular theses, concepts, conclusions, etc. I read them for the delight and excitement I found in them, rather than to learn, study or commit details to memory. For some time, therefore, I approached philosophy somewhat the way we approach art. In one sense, though, I still feel there is a deeper connection: the aesthetics of my plays—to simplify it somewhat—were based on a particular kind of foregrounding (as Shklovský analyzes it), i.e., on a viewpoint that removes the obfuscations of conventional perception from phenomena, tears them out of their habitual and automatic interpretational contexts and attempts to perceive them—as Ivan writes—"without glasses." Among other things, that means perceiving their absurdity as an insufficiently clear dimension of reality (because it is obscured by conventional interpretations). Ridding phenomena of false meaning. Manifesting them as absurd, and thus opening the question of their true meaning. The absurdity of entities as an invitation to inquire after the nature of Being.

A theme I wanted to write about: what is home? A certain concrete horizon to which one relates. (Patočka analyzes the phenomenon of "home.") The hiddenness of that horizon. The more urgently one relates to it as a result. The outline of this horizon changes (sometimes it is created by mountains, at other times by an urban skyline), the arrangement of people, relationships, milieus, traditions, etc. changes, but the horizon "as such" remains. As something absolute. Something that merely assumes different concrete forms. The paper has run out—

I kiss you, Vašek

53

November 1, 1980

Dear Olga,

I have the impression that my recent letters have been rather chaotic and hopelessly rushed thanks to the combination of unfavorable circumstances in which I wrote them; perhaps this time I will improve somewhat—for I have Saturday and Sunday ahead of me when presumably I should have time enough to write a letter.

First briefly about the news of the week. . . . I have new glasses, or rather new lenses in my glasses, a half a diopter stronger. I've been considering this step for some time and I'm glad it could be taken quickly and without complications. It's a normal, gradual worsening of the eyesight, consistent with my age; there are no other factors hidden behind it.

Among general events, I was affected most by yesterday's news of Werich's death. As you know, I have him to thank for having got me into theater twenty-one years ago (he took me on at Theatre ABC at a time when I had no prospects whatsoever), and that despite some mutual reservations, I have always thought highly of him. He had one exceptionally important influence on me: he helped me realize (among other things) that theater can be something incomparably more than just a play, a director, actors, audience and an auditorium: it is a special focus of social and intellectual life, helping to create the "spirit of the times" and embodying and manifesting its fantasy and humor; it is a living instrument of social self-awareness, one that is, in an unrepeatable way, lodged in its own time. On the other hand, as far as I know, he rather liked me and respected what I was doing as well. I know he had been seriously ill for some time, but my impression is that the blame for his death can be laid in equal measure on his illness and on his psychological and mental disposition in recent years. From several recent conversations with him, I gathered he was afflicted by a deep skepticism and resignation, an isolated, sad, bitter and disaffected man, without faith and without hope. For someone who loved living so much and who in a way was the embodiment of love for the world and everything good in it, this development must have radically (though perhaps subconsciously) undermined his zest for living—and this, as we know, is one of the most destructive of diseases. Werich's death really means, at last, the definitive end of an era in Czech intellectual history. Please convey my condolences to Jana. You remember what Vladimír Holan and my visits to his place on Kampa Island once meant to me. How odd that both these frequently so contradictory tenants of the same house passed away so soon one after the other; they were two extreme poles of essentially the same intellectual world and it seems that with them, that world really is finally passing away. Today, the truth of the human spirit seems to have less and less need of Holan's artful wizardry with words and metaphors, or something as deceptively simple as Werich's freedom of spirit. It is as though one were personally required to pay a far more painful and universal price for those qualities than the humanistic traditions of the First Republic assumed. That avant-garde, with its wonderfully brash self-confidence and messianism, now belongs irrevocably to the memory of our national culture, regardless of how much those memories influenced, and still influence us.

*

Today, however, I wanted to write about rather different, more abstract things. . . .

As you must certainly have observed from some of my letters, I often return in my thoughts (though only in a fragmentary, disorderly and simplified way—the only way possible, in fact) to various aspects of my inquiry into the question of responsibility as that which makes one a person and forms the basis of one's identity. (Of course I've long ago lost track of which remarks on that theme were sent to you and which were not.) There are perfectly good reasons why I return to this theme here and now: after all, I have been torn out of my world, my home, my matrix, which somehow "automatically," directly and spontaneously—with a living, everyday particularity—imparted meaning to everything I did. But because this background is now concealed and distant from me, the question of how I "relate" to this "concealed" world, or rather my responsibility to it, precisely because it is concealed, has begun to emerge from subconsciousness into consciousness as an actual, living theme. Consequently, I'm beginning to understand a lot of things with a new urgency, above all that in everything he does, man—usually without being aware of it, or far more than he knows—relates to something outside himself, something like his own, personal existential horizon. All his actions, in fact, take place against the background of this horizon, which defines and gives meaning to those actions somewhat in the way the heavens make the stars what they are. And even things apparently trivial, and apparently meant to fulfill personal needs, conceal somewhere in their depths this sense of "relating." For instance when I drink my obligatory tea and attempt to invoke the most harmonious frame of mind possible, I am not—strictly speaking—doing it for myself alone: if my wish is to survive with as little harm as possible and with my nerves intact, then I am undoubtedly doing this for someone or something, for you, for those near and dear to me, for my friends and acquaintances, for a community and—if you like—a "public," for an assembly of relationships, values, and ideals that give meaning to my life. I do it for my world, or simply, for the world. The idea of chemically pure egoism is absurd; when the last bit of concern for the world dies—concern for the fact that we live in and for the world and that only in the context of some "non-I" are things like happiness, freedom, etc. possible or even thinkable—then all our reasons for anything whatever will die with it, even reasons for what are apparently the most private pleasures, like drinking tea in a quiet corner.

This horizon, however, has several layers: first of all there is the horizon that is physically the closest, that is, the strange horizon of the environment into which I have, for the moment, been thrown but in which I am also learning how to live and where I also wish, somehow, to be myself. And even if it is only a tiny walled-in space, I accept it and

I must accept it and I cannot disregard it (if only because one cannot, in fact, disregard anything). Nevertheless its walls conceal the infinitely more important real horizon of my existence—though it be distant, invisible and evocable "only" in memory and imagination. Beyond the walls of my pseudohome is hidden the horizon of my genuine home; in any case, even the way I relate to that pseudohome is determined and given meaning by how I relate to my hidden but real home on the outside, to the unseen but nevertheless very concrete horizon of my life. This horizon, important though it is, is still not the final and absolute horizon. Just as, to the traveler, the physical horizon gradually changes (mountains give way to plains, to other mountains, to city skylines, etc. etc.), so too this concrete existential horizon, or rather the structure of our existential home, changes: the importance of various people, relationships, environments, obligations, values, loves and fears develops and is transformed over time. Today, for example, the people with whom I consider intellectual and moral communication important are different from those who were part of my horizon ten or even five years ago (a word of caution: physical change of place plays no role here; the operative factor is a redirection of personality, which need not be, though often is, connected with a change of place). But just as beyond the traveler's changing (and sometimes hidden) particular horizon there always remains, permanently present (or intimated?) a kind of (imaginary?) "horizon as such," "horizon in itself" (no landscape, after all, is without a horizon)—the outline of the horizon may conceal or reveal itself and change in all kinds of ways, but the horizon as such abides—so, too, beyond that particular existential horizon (temporarily concealed by walls but all the more vividly experienced) is hidden another—in fact a "third"—horizon. It is the most imaginary, the most abstract, the most concealed and the most difficult of all to grasp, but at the same time, paradoxically, the most certain (it endures though everything concrete disintegrates), the most lasting. It is final and absolute (as the absolute horizon of all of life's relativities); it is the horizon about which I began to write some time ago in a letter, the horizon which—as the metaphysical vanishing-point of life, defining its meaning—many experience as God. The paper is coming to an end, and I will finish (more precisely: interrupt) my meditation and when I have the opportunity, I will continue by writing about what I should have (as phenomenologists might point out) begun with: that is, with some thoughts about how, in concrete terms, I experience my relationship to the "concealed" horizon of my home, what destinies it contains in my imagination—or to put it more simply, what I miss, what I think and reminisce about, what I imagine, and what I long for.

*

Greetings and kisses to all (old and new) inhabitants of my horizon—and most of all, to you.

Vašek

54

November 8, 1980

Dear Olga,

As you probably already know, our visit is scheduled for Saturday, December 6. First, then, some peripheral remarks:

1. I've already written you about what I'd like to be included in the parcel; essentially, it should be the same as the one before (basic items: a kilo of tea, 300 good cigarettes, chocolates, perhaps some other Christmas sweets). Particular items: 3 spolarins, two pairs of warm socks, one large toothpaste. You needn't bring lotion with you (a friend gave me some); if there's some room left for hygienic items, all I need is another soap dish (I have one already, but need another for work) and a stiff sponge for my body. Otherwise, I have everything I need.

2. Please go over some of my earlier letters, which contain a lot of unanswered questions, and prepare replies to compensate for the verbal parsimony of your letters. You should have a systematic report ready and shouldn't rely on my questions—I can't have notes with me, and knowing myself, I am bound to forget many things. The basic thematic areas that interest me are: (a) a detailed description of your life: I have only a very hazy impression of many things— from your movements between Hrádeček and Prague (about who spends time with you at Hrádeček and when; who visits, and how often, who drives you there, etc.) to your life in Prague (how you actually spend your days, whom you see and how frequently, what you are working on, what you think about and how you feel, what cultural events you attend, etc.) (b) Hrádeček—the condition it's in,

how it looks, work completed and incompleted, the legal situation. (c) The Prague flat—are you getting rid of the furniture or has it remained only an intention or half-completed? If exchanging the flat isn't an immediate issue (though there's nothing to prevent you from working on it—regardless of the problems surrounding the building inspector's approval of Hrádeček), then it should at least be quickly cleared of those veneered monstrosities and left empty, or rather furnished only provisionally or with what comes to hand. (As I've written you more than once, that middle-class furniture is a burden on my spirit even here and while I'm only condemned to a few years in Heřmanice, I'm horrified at the prospect of a life sentence with that furniture.) d) Social life: I lack news of many friends, those who've emigrated and those who've remained; the outlines of that "particular horizon" I devoted my last letter to are even more shrouded in fog than necessary. (Among many other things, I'd be most interested to know, for instance, how the outside world seems to Otka now that she is out of prison—that might well make some things more vivid to me than information provided by those who have lived continuously in that external world.) e) The outcome of my plays and news about how they were received. . . .

The last visit was almost too improvised; there were clearly many things we wanted to say but time and again we fell silent out of sheer uncertainty as to what we should actually talk about and in what order, how much detail we should go into on various matters, etc. When the visit is only an hour long, you are constantly anxious about wasting precious minutes on less important subjects at the expense of more important ones. In fact you can scarcely say which are more important and which less; occasionally you may even be subconsciously influenced by the feeling that you must rush to get everything in (that applies mainly to me—whence the impression of a certain lack of focus or inadequate attention to particular subjects). I think such dangers can be avoided by taking two measures: (1) we will both try, beforehand, to get ourselves into the most balanced and harmonious frame of mind; (2) prepare yourself well and be somewhat systematic in what you say (you know how I appreciate that), so it won't just be a fountain of individual facts lacking a context (later, one often attributes inappropriate and distorted meanings to those separate bits).

Will Ivan come as well? Naturally I'd be delighted if he could maintain the tradition by coming—perhaps it could be coordinated somehow with the St. Nicholas celebrations. (You'd probably not leave until night, so you could celebrate, in the tradition of my own St. Nicholas Eve two years ago, when—if you remember—I played the angel for a number of families and then, at night, set out on a certain adventurous journey. And by the way: how did you get to Ostrava last time? Weren't you overdoing it just a little, not wanting to tell me anything about it?)

I don't suppose I have to emphasize how much I'm looking forward to the visit and how I cling to the prospect; in any case, it should be clear enough from the above instructions.

*

The main new thing in my life: I'm reading Brod's biography of Kafka; it's very good (I don't know why I haven't read it before, perhaps because of a certain mistrust of Brod on my part) and especially interesting for me personally. I'm delighted by each new thing I learn about Kafka because of how precisely it corresponds to what I have assumed and imagined to be true. I've always harbored a feeling (hidden, since it might raise suspicions of arrogance) that I somehow understand Kafka better than others, not because I can claim a deeper intellectual insight into his work, but because of an intensely personal and existential understanding of experience that borders on spiritual kinship, if I may put it that way. (I have never much held with theoretical "interpretations" of Kafka; immensely more important for me was the quite trivial and "pretheoretical" certainty, as it were, that he was "right" and that what he writes is "exactly how it is.") As far as culture goes, I also saw Kachyňa's film *July Encounter*. It lacked Kachyňa's usual semierudite "artistic" ambitions, banal poeticity and mendacious sentimentality, and therefore was the best thing by him I've ever seen. It's a "heartwarming" summer holiday idyll, a tasteful, sweet and unprepossessing "fairy tale of love," which is appropriate (or inappropriate, depending on how you look at it) for a prison cinema, since it shows life on the outside as something so colorful, kind and beautiful that even the hardest soul cannot remain unaffected.

Otherwise, concerning myself: I don't know what effect those imported vitamins are having on me, but the fact is that the sudden arrival of real winter with subzero temperatures and snow (combined with unwholesome, overcast November weather) left my body indifferent (in other words, I didn't get sick at once, as I expected)—and it's quite possible, even probable, that this is due to the vitamins.

As I promised in my last letter, this letter should have been devoted to the question of how I experience being torn out of my home, what I miss most and how, etc. As you can see, there were so many specific things to relate that there's no more room for my intended subject, and frankly I'm just as glad: the more I thought about it during the week, the more the whole thing seemed too complex and difficult to describe. The phenomenon of loss of freedom, as I am only now beginning to realize, is more concealed from direct perception and more mysterious in its structure and consequences than may be apparent on the outside. In some ways the whole experience is better—compared to conventional expectations—in some ways worse; but in any case, it is different and immensely more complicated. With some relief, therefore, I will set the whole subject aside until I've thought it over more carefully.

. . .

Vašek

55

November 15, 1980

Dear Olga,

Two of your letters (22 and 23) finally reached me and of course I was pleased. A brief response, at least, to them:

I promise to complain no more about your meager and infrequent letters; I wouldn't want my continual reproaches to traumatize you so deeply you'd stop writing me altogether. Only one (final!) remark (in fact I may already have made it): don't think about your letters, don't treat them as a burdensome duty, don't plan them or mull them over in advance; whenever you feel like it and have the time and are in a good mood, just sit down and write me whatever comes into your head—what you're doing, what you're thinking about, etc. I don't expect essays, I just want to hear from you.

It's unfortunate that the fence hasn't been painted; perhaps it will last till spring. For me it's the work of a lifetime and if it rots, I'll never make another like it.

It seems you're always having teeth pulled; are you getting new ones to replace them? You mustn't be remiss in such matters. Follow my example: I am trying, in far more complicated circumstances, to do what I can to keep up my appearance (of course I can't do anything about the ugly haircuts, but hair, unlike teeth, grows back in again).

. . .

Your recommendation to eat a lot of cheese brought a tender smile to my face.

*

I can't say there's anything remarkably new in my life. I live in relative tranquillity, I have no aches and pains (thanks to better work) and in other ways, too, I'm healthy. I'm still reading Brod on Kafka and to make it last longer, I broke off and read de Maupassant's "The Darling," a nice way to relax. On television I saw a dismal Czech drama about how some boys stole a stamp collection valued at 40,000 crowns and were not punished for it because when they discovered they'd been found out, they returned the stamps. If real life were like that, there'd be a lot fewer of us here.

*

For some time now I've been preparing to write about the way in which I feel the loss of freedom and normal life. As I mentioned in my last letter, it's a complex theme and I still don't know the most accurate way to describe the whole matter. Today's remarks, then, are provisional, and relate only to some of the simpler aspects of the theme so that, far from exhausting the subject, they merely broach it.

In those first weeks of detention (as in my earlier periods in detention) I felt a powerful homesickness for everything imaginable, most of all, of course, for those closest to me, but not just for them: I longed for many specific things, atmospheres, milieus, relationships, situations, experiences, etc. And I thought a lot about what I would do if they let me go. I called to mind those close to me, my friends and acquaintances, and my head was constantly aswirl with all the things I wanted to talk to them about (and with self-reproach for not having done so while still free). More than that: I imagined myself sweating in the sauna, swimming in the public pool, walking about Malá Strana, sleeping in my own bed in my own pajamas, eating steak, crab cocktail or cake with whipped cream in one restaurant or another, barbecuing chicken at Hrádeček and making the tartar sauce to go with it while sipping white wine and listening to some of my favorite records, sunning myself on the lawn, drinking strong coffee in the morning, visiting galleries and bars, going to good movies and visiting artist friends in their studios—etc. etc. etc.

As the months went by, however, these particular memories, nagging desires and intense, recurring images and plans began to fade into the background. I don't think this was because I was slowly forgetting the horizon of my home; it just seemed as though its particular outlines and the maddening urgency of particular aspects of it were beginning to fade. Various details seemed to merge gradually into a more coalescent image—already veiled in translucent tulle—of my home as something like a distant "paradise lost" which at one time had simply existed but which was no longer and perhaps one day—Lord knows when—would in some form exist again (considerably altered, no doubt). This whole world—in one of my earlier letters I called it my "particular horizon"—simply lost its physical presence and the urgency of its absence, and shifted from the sphere of specific, pleasurably painful sensory memories, longings, desires and physically tormenting prospects into some deeper sphere of my soul where it is still present, but in quite a different way. It seems more mediated, less immediate and physically urgent, more spiritual somehow—but for this very reason more essential, in its own way: as a hidden set of life's parameters, the measure and the vanishing point of its meaning. I no longer experience the absence of that world in a particularly physical way (for some time now, for example, I've felt that if I were suddenly given the chicken with tartar sauce and white wine I had once longed for, I'd probably vomit), but this makes me all the more alive to that world as something—a unity, a set of values—that is a source of hope, a reason for my sacrifices (as they are so nobly called), a repository for the true meaning of my actions. And the less materially tormented I am by its material absence, the stronger and the more essentially present that absence becomes in my daily life, but in a more abstracted form, as a "blurred" but omnipresent backdrop to that hope, helping me again and again to see everything in the proper light, in outlines of pristine sharpness.

Among other things this shift is an existential self-defense mechanism: if you were to spend several years brooding constantly over whom you might be with, where you might be, what you might be doing, eating, etc. if you were free, it would probably drive you mad. Increasingly, therefore, you focus on values that are within reach: a moment's peace and quiet, time to read something good, a good night's sleep, steering clear of some pointless annoyance, keeping your things clean and neat, satisfaction with your work, etc. While the comparison is not precise (I won't be here for life, I hope), in some ways it's like the condition of the man who loses a leg: as time goes by, he will focus more and more on the best way to walk painlessly with an artificial limb, and less and less on what he might have done if he still had both legs. Yet "two-leggedness" is still a presence in his life, though in a form somewhat different from what it would be in people who actually have two legs. From a fact he takes for granted, it becomes something at once more abstract and more on his mind, the measure of everything he does—but chiefly the measure of his effort to live with an artificial leg.

Again, I'm writing only about some aspects, those more easily describable, of this theme. This should properly be followed by a consideration of how one experiences loss of freedom, what that loss actually consists in, what it really is that one misses most fundamentally. For I miss far more than just my home, with all the people and the values that are a part of it. That is just part of a wider and more complex loss. After all, our "existential" home is in one sense "only" the specific outcome of what we have chosen—but here, more than just the outcome is missing; one lacks the very opportunity to choose. For the time being, however, I don't have the temerity to write about these more complex matters; I'm not sufficiently clear about it all yet.

*

And now at last, back to my "one-legged" present. Some small additional remarks about the parcel: if you have the chance to buy toothpaste of a different brand than I've had so far, do it. The rosehip tea you wrote about (particularly if it really contains vitamins), you can include, a good amount of it but not at the expense of that kilo of ordinary tea. Don't forget that small spolarin; buy three or four boxes—two, it turns out, don't last a quarter of a year.

I'll say good-bye for today. Be of cheerful mind, be active and optimistic and think well of me!

Kisses from your Vašek

56

November 22, 1980

Dear Olga,

. . .

Rereading my last letter, I was slightly taken aback to realize that I wrote nothing about what would seem to be the most important loss of all—my opportunity to write. This compelled me to think about myself a little. I shall try, succinctly (and as usual, in a very simplified way), to communicate the results of my thinking to you.

First, although I've been writing ever since I was about six, or rather since I first learned the alphabet, I have never (unlike many other writers) felt writing in itself as a physical craving so intense I couldn't live without satisfying it. In my case, the whole matter is somewhat more complicated: as silly as it may sound, I would say that I simply enjoy creating, that I enjoy inventing things (mostly what are called works of art, but not them alone, and if so, then not because they are called art but because that is what the ways of seeing, looking at things and thinking that are nearest to mine are called). If I could have freely chosen my education when I was young, I might well have become a film director instead of a writer; my longing to invent and create and thus to say something about the world and myself might have found a more appropriate outlet in the directing of films. There are several reasons for this, including the fact that I am a sociable creature and the less solitary genres suit me more; and since I've already taken up something as solitary as writing, then at least I write plays, which bring me close to the theater, a "nonsolitary" institution.

Naturally, I'm used to making notes and lists and dealing with all kinds of things in writing (as you know, I'd even note down such banalities as my intention to have a haircut or buy peppers) and with this possibility denied I feel almost as though I'd lost an arm (to pick up on the simile of the one-legged man in my last letter). So I do miss that aspect of writing, every day and almost biologically, but of course it's not the main thing. Literary creation as such, the actual writing of plays—and this may surprise some—is not something I miss very acutely. Even on the outside, after all, I could go for long periods without writing.

There are several reasons for this, one of which is the following: I enjoy writing only when I know it's just right, when it flows, when I have a decent idea (which seldom happens in my case, because very little seems to suit my rather special approach), when the thing "writes itself," as they say. At such times I enjoy writing perhaps more than anything else. When it doesn't flow, or when I feel it isn't exactly right—that is, when it doesn't precisely suit my poetics—then not only do I not enjoy writing, it actually repels me. (I am not the kind of author who can write on demand or on commission, in any style, about anything at all; or rather I might find it possible, but only by constantly suppressing myself.) In other words: "writing per se," any kind of writing at all, is not something I miss nor could I, since I don't need it in the slightest. I would probably miss play-writing very badly only if I had a surefire idea and someone were preventing me from realizing it.

In my case, however, such ideas usually come to me in the act of writing (I think something up and write it down, or in fact, think about it by making notes or thinking about my notes). If I don't have a specific and sufficiently attractive idea and moreover, if my opportunities to work out such an idea are severely limited, there is no reason why I should miss writing.

.   .   .

This doesn't mean, of course, that I don't miss what for me is the main aspect of writing, the concrete expression of "thinking and creating." Naturally I feel that loss a great deal. But the need—if it can be called a "need" at all—is so abstract, so vague, so lacking in particular roots (in one or another sphere of the body or soul), that for the most part I don't tangibly suffer from the lack of it—as something definite and nameable—and I am scarcely aware of it in any precise or permanent sense (for instance I can hardly imagine myself sitting unhappily in the corner of the room because I'd suddenly been overwhelmed by a longing for lost creativity). At the most, one feels that one has been living a long time without a sense of hearing, without substance, without meaning (hence, too, that constant speculation about the "meaning" of it all!), but one would feel that anyway, even without being a writer. That specific lack has been so "absorbed" into the general joylessness of being here that without some finely tuned skills in self-awareness, one would scarcely be aware of it at all. Moreover, precisely because of this abstractness (inventing and creating relate to everything, but to nothing in particular; you realize yourself through them, and in general they elevate you as a person, but satisfy no particular impulse), the lack of opportunity to write cannot be directly associated with any part of the "particular horizon." Self-realization "as a creator," or rather, the potential for such self-realization, is something diffused throughout the entire horizon, an integral part of it, though it can never be seen there as a visible object. You may miss actresses or ballet dancers, the atmosphere backstage, the chance to address a public, etc., but it would be hard (consciously) to miss something as indefinite as "inventing and creating." Of course I'm used to the occasional twinge of longing to write for the theater (I'd lost that possibility long before coming here, after all), and it would therefore be illogical to write about that in relation to my stay here; and the second and more essential thing—which, though curtailed, I had not really lost until coming here—cannot very well be related to any particular aspect of my lost home. In any case, it's not something "over and done with," something I had once and now have no longer. It is rather something from the realm of possibility, of what I might do or a way I might be (not in the sense of a profession, or of reputation, but in the existential sense). That is, from a realm I deliberately avoided getting into in my last letter (as I made clear) because I had not yet sufficiently recognized or understood my position in it, or because I was simply unable, thus far, to define it notionally. The point is that creation is related to freedom, and the loss of either is similar: for the most part we do not feel a general lack of freedom directly and tangibly, what we feel is only a lack of particular things, which we would choose if we had the freedom to do so.

. . .

Kisses, Vašek

December 6, 1980

Dear Olga,

Because I'm officially ill, I have more time and I'm just sitting down, as promised, shortly after our visit (I have only had a small break in the meantime: bread with margarine and garlic, some good tea, a cigar) to write you.

*

First, understandably, a few words about the visit: on my side it was preceded by several long and complicated measures designed to get myself into optimum physical and mental shape, so I would look healthy, converse wittily, show some spark, etc., in short, so that the visit would turn out better than the last one. I was able to put all the measures into effect as planned, yet the desired result was far from being achieved, perhaps because excessive preparations are always detrimental to the outcome and also because I was made slightly groggy by the pills (probably the antibiotics, which I must be consistent about taking if they are to work properly). If I didn't manage to be as I would have liked, it doesn't mean that I was nervous, depressed, not myself. On the contrary: I worked so thoroughly to avert the danger of nervousness and lack of focus that I was (or so I seemed to myself) almost too apathetic, indifferent, cold. I didn't express myself well, not because I was uneasy this time, but rather because I was too calm (my tongue and some parts of my brain even seemed unresponsive and muted). My critical dissatisfaction with myself (during the entire visit I never uttered a single clever idea, a single interesting fact, a single remark to make you laugh) does not mean, of course, that I consider the visit a failure. It might have seemed so to someone who doesn't know us, but I know us and I'm more than satisfied: the mild, muted state I (or rather several external layers of my "I") was in (in other words, not the inner essence of my "I"), which might have struck you as apathy, got transferred—or so I felt—to you as well and consequently the whole visit took on a kind of easygoing, sporting, civilized and entirely untragic quality. Perhaps that is the best approach—to ignore the exceptional nature of the situation and behave as if we'd just seen each other that morning and met again at the car, after doing some shopping, so we could drive home together. The excitement, the nervousness, the rush, the anxiety, the feeling of responsibility, the seriousness and uniqueness of the moment, all fall away (in this case the pitfall of Christmas sentimentality understandably fell away too), and as a result, not only can more be said in tranquillity but we can also be together, at that moment, in an entirely authentic way. The lack of warmth, of holiday spirit, excitement and heartrending emotion could be deplored only by one who, out of ignorance, might mistake the easygoing tone for a sign of shallowness in the relationship, the spirit and the heart. But we should be glad the visit was normal, straightforward, unemotional, because that, after all, is the best way to maintain my connection with you, Ivan and my entire home. Anything out of the ordinary, unnatural or forced, any playacting or heightening of significance, would merely confirm our enforced separation, unintentionally increase the distance between ourselves, undermine authenticity and transform the physical distance between us into a spiritual and mental distance. In short: I'm entirely satisfied with the visit and I have no self-reproach for its blandness. I hope you take it in that spirit as well and that you don't mind leaving Ostrava with no emotionally charged experiences, or any scintillating comments by me that you could quote when friends ask you about the visit. For me, there's a single lesson to be drawn from the visit: that it's wrong to anticipate it too intensely. Not only does this undermine my spontaneity, but it lends to the visit a kind of fateful significance which ultimately makes the anticipation of it more important than the visit itself; the visit can then only mean the end of anticipation, and thus, in fact, it becomes something undesirable.

*

You asked about the fate of Stoppard's *Rosencrantz and Guildenstern Are Dead* in the Theatre on the Balustrade. Well, we once did, in fact, try to put it on at the Balustrade. On the basis of a reader's report by Zdeněk, we chose Kořán's translation over Kusín's (which was later published by Orbis). If I remember correctly, I was the main proponent of the play, but despite the manic energy with which I virtually imposed it on the theater (as I can do, when I take it into my head), it was ultimately not produced. It's hard to say precisely why it wasn't; perhaps there were objective reasons (not enough time, too many plays in the season already), perhaps there were some fears on Vodička's part that it wouldn't be popular enough, perhaps Grossman's support for it was rather somnolent (you know, don't you, Grossman's typically somnolent way of agreeing to something?); I can't remember any longer exactly why. It's not impossible that my own vehement support might have had something to do with it (Vodička opposed most of my ideas on principle), and also the fact that Honza Kačer, from the Činoherní Klub, was supposed to direct it. (At the time, the Činoherní Klub was our only rival; the star of the Theatre on the Balustrade was slowly setting, the Činoherní Klub's star was rising, and someone may have been afraid of creating the impression that we needed rescuing by the competition; or perhaps—and this may have been subconscious—there were fears that a guest director might depart too radically from the house style and his production overshadow the rest of our season.) Using Kačer was, I think, my idea as well and I had a good reason for it: I felt it might be interesting to confront the somewhat intellectual tradition of our own theater (including the acting style) and this apparently (to Czech eyes at least) intellectual play with the way of using actors developed by the Činoherní Klub, which included a vigorous opening out of the actors' personalities and the themes hidden within them. I felt that this might give an interesting shot in the arm to our own troupe, and also that it would be very good for the play. (I've always believed that such "significational," highly constructed, "deductive," "model" plays would be best served by actors with vigorous personalities, full of physical existence, as it were—and in any case, wasn't this confirmed in our theater by Libíček, for example?) My idea was that this version would make a good companion piece for our own production of *Waiting for Godot,* which has something in common with Stoppard's play, particularly its debt to the theatrical tradition of the two-handed curtain raiser, with two clowns who in a sense play (with words and otherwise) but whose play in fact points far beyond itself (I would say they "juggle with the world"). My idea was that Rosencrantz and Guildenstern would be played by the same actors who played Estragon and Vladimir in *Godot* and our audience could then view two variations on the same principle. I felt that Stoppard's play was close to our theater not only in its intellectual sophistication and its clever multilayered meaning, but also because it pointed (more than Beckett the metaphysician did, of course) to the moral and social dimension of human existence (the theme of betrayal). After all, my plays, too, gave our theater that general direction—and it's no accident that in the Czech intellectual context, this comes up again and again. Later, I saw *Rosencrantz and Guildenstern* in a large theater on Broadway; it was marvelously acted and the audience was lively and responsive, yet I still think the play belongs more properly in a small, "high profile" theater and that a touch of nightclub or cabaret atmosphere in the performance setting would not hurt it a bit. Everything in that play is properly turned on its head, everything is paradoxical, and so I think that its "high" meanings would resonate well in a somewhat obscure, "low" setting, the kind of atmosphere that the Balustrade worked with (mainly before the renovations) and the kind that probably best serves the plays of Ionesco and Beckett as well.

.   .   .

Thank you for the visit and for everything!

Kisses, Vašek

MERRY CHRISTMAS!

60

December 21, 1980

Dear Olga,

Our efforts to come to an understanding on the matter of our flat are like the dialogue in some obscure farce, because shortly after I devoted almost all of letter 59 to the question (and the relevant jobs to be done), your letter 24 arrived, in which you explain the whole matter clearly, so that in response, you will receive a list of things to do that apparently ignores your explanation entirely. Anyway, it might be best if I were to drop the subject and leave it entirely up to you. You already know what we want, and obviously only you can decide when and how and what you can accomplish. At this distance, knowing as little as I do, and given this comic means of communication, I'm in no position to advise you, so I humbly await your occasional reports in the belief that you will take my expectations into account in ways that are appropriate to the real situation.

.   .   .

I was informed last night that another letter from you had arrived (obviously written after the visit) but that it would not be given to me, because there are greetings from various friends in it, and I am allowed to receive messages and greetings only from relatives. I wasn't even given the photos you included. A pity. It's the third time this has happened.

*

You mention that almost every day you speak about me with someone and thus I am, in some small way, present at home; Ivan also wrote to me about my relative presence—and that leads me to a theme I sometimes ponder, the question of what human existence really is, viewed in space and time.

Unlike other living creatures, man has the power to represent to himself things he cannot directly see or perceive. When I close my eyes and so desire, I can see Hradčany, a Prague streetcar or the inside of the Rotisserie with a Parma cutlet, tartar sauce and a glass of white wine in front of me. Similarly, we can easily call to mind an absent person; in our minds, we may delight in his gestures, his smile, his manner of speech, etc. But instead of exhausting the matter, this may well be just the beginning: the personality of the other person is far more than just a closed set of recollections about individual phenomena or events relating to him or characterizing him, as the Parma cutlet is characterized by a certain aroma and taste; nor is he, in our minds, merely the sum of what he has done or undertaken. He is that too, of course, but at the same time he is primarily a broad range of "potentialities": what he might do or think, how he might behave or react in certain circumstances, etc. etc. Human personality is therefore (among other things) a large set of possibilities, potentials, perspectives, relationships, demands, opinions and anticipated responses; it is something open, always actual; not merely a phenomenon, but a source of thinkable phenomena as well; not merely a concretely lived life, but a way of life itself and a living alternative, something that speaks to us and provokes us again and again. Human personality is a particular view of the world, an image of the world, an aspect of the world's Being, a challenge to the world. Not only that: when we call to mind someone who is absent, we regret that he is not here to experience something, or on the contrary, we are relieved that he doesn't have to be here; we imagine, with joy or sadness, how he might respond to something when he finds out; we are apprehensive about what he might do were he present; we long to have him experience a situation with us so we can talk it over with him, or on the contrary we worry lest he be compelled to experience it, etc. We therefore imagine the other person not merely as someone we know from the past, someone we revitalize in our memory; he does not even represent, for us, merely that "aspect of the world's Being," something outside us and something in and of itself; but we know him and experience him as an integral part of our own present and future and our own potentialities. We "know" him and surmise him, but above all, we somehow always relate to him anew. We act with regard to him, as though he were with us and knew everything (or, on the contrary, in such a way that he will never find out about something, which is merely a negative form of the same thing). Obviously, then, his personality is a particular state as well, a dimension or aspect of our own existence. As a certain "aspect of the world's Being" which we depend upon in our own actions and which thus belongs to our "particular horizon," he is ultimately—whether we want him to be or not—a part of that aspect of the world's being which is our own "I."

The personality of the other, or rather his human existence (at least as we experience it), goes far beyond the physical person of its "bearer" and is not identical with it (even though, of course, it has its origin or center of gravity within it). We may still experience that personality vividly even when we are completely out of touch with its bearer. The other person continues to exist for us (i.e., in us), even when he leaves the room, or the city, or the country, or when he is imprisoned. Our relationship to him is in no way directly bound to his physical presence. We may even have a living experience of his personality when we do not know him personally and have never actually met him. (In the same way, however, it is possible to be in close physical proximity with someone without ever experiencing his personality, as though that person were, for us, a piece of furniture.)

Just as our experience of another includes within itself the broad horizon of "the possible," that experience itself is, of course, an aspect of "the possible" as well: someone's human personality does not cease to exist the moment we are not actually experiencing it, nor does it even cease to exist when no one is actually experiencing it. If nothing else, it has a continuing existence in the sphere of "the possible," as the possibility of such an experience. Thus human existence not only extends beyond the physical existence of its bearer, it clearly goes even beyond the physical existence of the experience of it by others. Nothing that has once happened can un-happen; everything that once was, in whatever form, still is—forever lodged in the "memory of Being." And everything we consider real, actual, present, is only a small and vaguely defined island in the ocean of "imaginary," "potential" or "past" Being. It is from this matrix alone that it draws its substance and its meaning; only against this background can we experience it in the way we do. Along with everything that ever happened in whatever way (or could or should have happened) and what can now no longer un-happen, human personality, human existence too will endure, once and for all, in the "memory of Being." In other words, not only will it not cease to exist when its "owner" goes into another room, or is impris-oned, or when everyone else has forgotten about him, but it will not cease to exist even when he dies, nor even when the last man who ever knew him or knew that someone like him ever existed, forgets about him, or dies. Nothing can ever erase from the history of Being a human personality that once was; it exists in that history forever.

But it exists there—and this is the most important aspect of the whole matter—in a radically different way from everything else, from my Parma cutlet in the Rotisserie, for example, which is indubitably a part of that history as well. The point is that human existence, as I have tried to indicate, is not just something that has simply hap-pened; it is an "image of the world," "an aspect of the world's Being," a "challenge to the world," and as such—it seems to me—it necessarily forms a very special node in the tissue of Being. It is not merely something separate and individual, enclosed within itself and limited to itself, but it is, repeatedly, the whole world. It is as if it were a light constantly reilluminating the world; a crystal in which the world is constantly being reflected; a point upon which all of Being's lines of force constantly appear to converge, centripetally, as it were. Human existence, I would say, is not just a particular fact or datum, but a kind of gospel as well, pointing to the absolute and, in a way that has no precedent, manifesting the mystery of the world and the question of its meaning.

You have often wondered where I, such a rational man, come by my conviction that the human soul is immortal. In time, I'll try to write something longer and more fundamental about it; but if you like, you may take what I've written today as a small contribution to the subject. I haven't explained the real root of my faith in immortality, I've merely indicated a way in which modern man can conceive of immortality or how he might include it in his picture of the world. But by now it's part of the tradition of these epistolary essays of mine that they are some-what "fitful": what should come later precedes what should come first; linking material is frequently lacking; many subjects are merely broached or simplified. Perhaps all this may be excused by the circumstances.

*

The foregoing meditation, as well as the clear, parsimonious hand in which it is written, has so exhausted me (I remind you that I'm surrounded by noise, which always makes it difficult for me to concentrate on writing) that I'm not sure I'll have the strength to fill the rest of the paper.

Here are a few brief scraps of information about me:

1. I'm still on the sick list, thanks to which I've gained considerable weight; I got used to eating more here than on the outside, which was necessary considering I expend more energy; I'm not expending it now, but the habit has persisted, and if they were to let me go home for Christmas (so far this seems improbable), I wouldn't be able to get into my civilian trousers.
2. I feel well and I'm assuming I'll be declared fit after Christmas.
3. I'm trying to sleep a lot and read a lot.
4. Over Christmas I'm probably going to watch a little television and I'll be enjoying various delicacies that are available here at Christmastime, among them substances I haven't tasted for a year and a half, such as cake and butter.
5. I'm saving the sweets from the parcel for Christmas as well (so far I haven't touched them); otherwise, I'm making careful and economic use of the things from the parcel and I'm delighted with them, something I may have not stressed enough in earlier letters.

*

This letter will probably reach you sometime around the New Year and so some New Year's wishes would be in order. The more I think about it, the more I incline to the opinion that the most important thing of all is not to lose hope and faith in life itself. Anyone who does so is lost, regardless of what good fortune may befall him. On the other hand, those who do not lose it can never come to a bad end. This doesn't mean closing one's eyes to the horrors of the world—quite the contrary, in fact: only those who have not lost faith and hope can see the horrors of the world with genuine clarity. Which may sound like a paradox and probably requires explanation, but that would mean writing a new letter, so for the time being you'll have to accept it as an axiom or an invitation to thought. And so, from the bottom of my heart, my New Year's wish is that you not lose your hope, faith and ability to delight in the world—even if the world is the way it is. If you can manage that, everything else will come; if you give in, nothing can help you—and what then (among other things) would become of me?

Kiss all our dear, close friends and wish them for me the same as I have wished you.

Kisses, Vašek

61

December 26, 1980

Dear Olga,

In my last letter I outdid myself and produced some rather abstract thoughts, so this letter will be in an exclusively restful mode.

First of all, a brief report on how I spent Christmas, or rather the part of Christmas that is past. On Christmas Eve, I ate too much, as one should. After the institutional supper (breaded cutlet with potato salad) I took part in a small banquet (sandwiches, cookies, cake), which finished me off, the more so since I had previously fasted for about 30 hours. The table was decorated with Christmas paper from you, with that Christmas chain and that little tree. (Who drew it? You told me, but I've forgotten.) Then I watched television, where I saw a bit of Suk's "Serenade," Karel Gott's Christmas concert (nothing special) and a rather good play by M. Poledňáková—which unfortunately I didn't see right through. On Christmas Day, too, I watched a lot of television, and was compelled (as often happens) to sit through some heavy-handed variety shows and listen to a lot of mindless pop-songs; better things were to be seen on the other channel, but my efforts to persuade fellow prisoners of this were, as usual, in vain. So today, instead of watching Victor Hugo, I'll probably be looking at "Televarieté." Still, I managed to see an interesting thing yesterday (everyone else thought it was idiotic)—a Soviet television film based on a play about Baron Prášil (I know the author by name, but I can't remember it now). In it, Baron Prášil is presented as a kind of poet of life, a dreamer, a man of fantasies who refuses to adapt to the conventional world and repudiate his own truth; he has simply decided to butt heads with the system and thus is very upsetting to the drowsy majority, whose "philosophical credo" goes "You can't break down a wall with your head." He can be honored and celebrated only after his death, when he is no longer dangerous. In a way, it was a celebration of all Russian dreamers, idealists and revolutionaries who were persecuted in their lifetimes and later had monuments erected to them. Well thought out, and above all well acted and produced (it won a prize). So much for my experiences in front of the TV set. Otherwise, I've borrowed *The History of Diplomacy* (also Soviet) and I'm reading it in my spare time. I'm healthy (I'll be going back to work after the holidays) and mentally on an even keel. I'm not suffering from Christmas depression and if I feel homesick, I don't let on, for I can keep it under control. (By the way: I'm beginning to see self-control as something extremely important; it's an ability which, I believe, is part of being a real man, and I'm glad I have it; I can even practice and train it systematically. I've been goaded into this, among other things, by the sight of so many of my fellow prisoners playing the tough guy without being tough in the least.) . . .

*

It's Sunday already, and the holidays are almost over. Yesterday I had a rather successful day, because I got through an interesting book by a Soviet journalist on the assassination of Kennedy, and on television I managed to see the second part of an English series on Shakespeare. . . . Several times during the holidays I've been in an unusually positive, happy mood, and several times (such as now) I've sunk into my "Sunday despondency." I'm looking forward to working again; I don't feel the despondency then. Apart from this "Sunday despondency" (when the occasion arises, I shall attempt to analyze it) I sometimes feel that I'm growing stupider: I seem to forget a lot, to express myself badly, to be doing nothing to improve my mind and widen my horizons, and even to have forgotten how to write. This feeling may be deceptive, and when I return to the normal world it may well quickly disappear, but it's unpleasant all the same. And it could also be dangerous, because it could be one of the ways in which NOTHINGNESS, the chief enemy of life, might take hold of one. But nothingness is not taking hold of me, or rather, I am triumphing over it, and I mention it only for the sake of completeness.

I forgot to mention that in the program "A Chair for the Guest," I saw Lada Fialka for the first time in a long while. He came across well, and spoke to the point, rather sensibly and compellingly. I was somewhat taken aback to hear him speak of the Balustrade as "his" theater, i.e., as a theater of pantomime, as though drama had never been a part of it. But that might not have been deliberate.

While I'm going on about television: people here are always asking me which actors I know personally, what they're like in everyday life, how they live, who they go out with, etc. The fact that I know almost all of them and that many are or were my friends never fails to arouse surprise and respect; equal surprise, however, is aroused by the fact that I don't gossip about them. In fact, however, I don't know much gossip, and if I do, I'm loath to talk about it. So I end up saying "He's a nice guy" or something like that. They could easily think I'm a phony and don't know these people at all. But no one thinks that.

In two days, the year in which I will enter the second half of my sentence begins. Not bad, is it?

I think about you and all those close and dear—

Kisses, Vašek

62

January 2–6, 1981

Dear Olga,

I had no hopes that a letter would come over the holidays and lo!—two came, one from you (26) and one from Ivan (27). Besides that, I read both of your postcards and your nice New Year's greeting; thanks so much for everything. Please give my greetings to your mother; I'm sorry for her trouble and I'm glad you're looking after her. At first I felt a little ashamed that while you were alone on Christmas Eve, fasting and contemplating, I was stuffing myself here and passing the time in front of the television, but then I concluded that had you been here with me and been able to see into my situation, you'd certainly have approved. Many thanks to Ivan for his letter as well.

*

It's customary at New Year's for people to give some thought to what they went through during the preceding year; I do so now, giving some thought as well to things I thought about over the past year. . . .

The problem of human identity remains at the center of my thinking about human affairs. If I use the word "identity," it is not because I believe it explains anything about the secret of human existence; I began using it when I was developing my plays, or thinking about them later, because it helped me clarify the ramifications of the theme that most attracted me: "the crisis of human identity." All my plays in fact are variations on this theme, the disintegration of man's oneness with himself and the loss of everything that gives human existence a meaningful order, continuity and its unique outline.

At the same time, as you must have noticed from my letters, the importance of the notion of human responsibility has grown in my meditations. It has begun to appear, with increasing clarity, as that fundamental point from which all identity grows and by which it stands or falls; it is the foundation, the root, the center of gravity, the constructional principle or axis of identity, something like the "idea" that determines its degree and type. It is the mortar binding it together, and when the mortar dries out, identity too begins irreversibly to crumble and fall apart. (That is why I wrote you that the secret of man is the secret of his responsibility.)

In other words: the degree and type of human identity provides me with a vantage point from which the various questions of human existence may be mapped out, and the question of responsibility then becomes the key to the problem of identity. Naturally this does not explain the mystery, it merely shifts it into an increasingly "narrower," or rather more specific, area.

But what, in fact, is human responsibility? And what does it relate to? It is, after all, a relationship and thus assumes the existence of two poles: a person who is responsible, and someone, or something, for whom or for which he is responsible.

Modern man, to the extent that he is not a believer and does not understand responsibility as a relationship to God, has many more or less concrete answers to this question. For some, responsibility is a relationship man has with other people, and with society, and they seek its roots (with varying degrees of emphasis) in education, in the social order, in social and cultural traditions, in the instinct for self-preservation, in subconscious calculation or, on the contrary, in love and sacrifice, that is, in the various psychological potentialities of man. For some, the source of responsibility is simply conscience, a part of the biological equipment of our species (something like Freud's "super-ego"). For others, it is ultimately a chimera left over from the times when people still feared the gods.

Responsibility is certainly all of these things, or rather, they are particular expressions of it, or ways in which it may be described. But is that the end of it? Do these answers really answer the question?

I'm convinced they do not. At least I am not at all satisfied by these answers because I don't believe they touch the heart of the matter. They tell us as much about responsibility as the model of an atom tells us about the essence of matter, or a tachometer about the essence of motion.

This opinion of mine, however, is more than just an opinion: it is directly rooted in my "experience of the world," that is, in the experience I, as an actual person, have had over the years. All attempts to brush aside the mystery by localizing it in a particular region of the scientifically describable world (or more precisely, of the world as reconstructed by science) go directly against the grain of that experience. Such attempts, it seems to me, are self-deceiving and lazy, nothing more than one of the "ideological" manifestations of the crisis of human identity: man surrenders his humanity by turning it over to the offices of an expert.

For me, the fundamental flaw in the many different positivistic "explanations" lies in the fact that it reduces human responsibility—as it does everything else—to a mere relationship of something relative, transitory and finite to something else relative, transitory and finite (for example, the relationship of a citizen to the legal code, or of the unconscious to the "superego"). By its very nature, however, such an understanding hides, and must hide, what is most important and, in my opinion, as clear as day: what we have here is not the mutual relationship of two relativities to each other, but the relationship of relativity to "non-relativity," the relationship of finiteness to "infinity," of a unique existence to the totality of Being. It is true that responsibility usually finds expression as the relationship of something in us to something around us or something else in us, but essentially it is always a relationship between us, as a "relativity"—and our only genuine antithesis, that which alone permits us to experience our relativity as relativity: that is, to an omnipresent, absolute horizon as the "final instance" that lies behind everything and above everything, which as it were provides everything with a framework, a measure and a background and which ultimately qualifies and defines everything relative. This superabstract and superimaginary horizon is, at the same time, something confoundedly concrete—for do we not experience it today and every day, through all our particular experiences of the world of relativities, as a constantly present limiting element, and in fact as a dimension that touches us most compellingly? (It is altogether questionable which—as an existential experience—is in fact more compelling: the "particular horizon" and the transitory landscapes and human silhouettes that line the road along which our life leads, or that "other," permanent horizon we feel behind it or rather, that continually breathes on us through it, as an invisible source of its meaning.)

In other words, as an ability or a determination or a perceived duty of man to vouch for himself completely, absolutely and in all circumstances (in other words, as the only true creator of freedom), human responsibility is precisely the agent by which one first defines oneself as a person vis-à-vis the universe, that is, as the miracle of Being that one is. On the one hand, it is only thus that one defines and so infuses meaning into one's dependency on the world; on the other hand, it is only thus that one definitively separates oneself from the world as a sovereign and independent being; it is only thus that one, as it were, stands on one's own two feet. I would say that responsibility for oneself is a knife we use to carve out our own inimitable features in the panorama of Being; it is the pen with which we write into the history of Being that story of the fresh creation of the world that each new human existence always is.

In short, it seems to me that just as there can be no matter without space, and no space without matter, their can be no transitory human existence without the horizon of permanence against which it develops and to which—whether it knows this or not—it constantly relates. At the same time the mark human existence leaves on this background every instant makes that existence, in a sense, permanent as well—not only as a dead image of life, but as that which it really is, in other words, its subject. But I see I've opened up an entirely new theme.

A concluding remark, therefore: you mustn't take these and similar meditations too literally; they are only attempts to capture something from the flow of my feelings and inner thought processes; sometimes I map it out with these formulations, at other times I may use completely different ones. I'm no philosopher and it is not my ambition to construct a conceptually fixed system; anyone who tries to understand it that way will soon discover that I am perpetually contradicting myself, that I leave many things unexplained or explain them differently each time, etc.

*

And now something from my external existence: I have made it through the holidays without mishap; New Year's was not too jolly an occasion; now we're back to everyday life and I am well and working.

Give a kiss to everyone who—as you wrote—is fond of me; give an especially emphatic kiss to Andulka.

I think of you, and am your
Vašek

63

January 11, 1981

Dear Olga,

Since my New Year's letter was of a somewhat more abstract nature, I shall deal today, for a change, with down-to-earth realities.

*

In my free time over the New Year holidays I watched television, wrote you a letter and read *The History of Diplomacy*. In the cinema I saw a rather interesting Hungarian film, *Who Is the Law For?* The day before New Year's Eve I enjoyed myself immensely (unlike the majority) watching Smoljak and Svěrák's *Fireball*. . . .

*

The state of my health: so far, my lungs have successfully withstood the freezing cold, the discomfort and other difficulties of life here; I hope this will continue to be so. On the other hand, I'm bothered by pains in my elbows and I'm going to have them looked at next week. I'm in good spirits. Not long ago, I made an interesting discovery: the human body requires (thanks to adrenaline or whatever) that one get angry occasionally and objectify that anger (usually by giving someone a tongue-lashing). This happened to me (I scolded one of my fellow prisoners at work) and I was astonished at how good I felt afterward.

For the entire shift, I was cheerful, hardworking, and I didn't even feel the cold. It's not in my nature, but I can see that for the sake of my health, I'll have to bawl someone out occasionally.

*

A word of caution, lest it seem that prison has awakened an aggressive streak in me: it's nonsense, of course. I'm as pacific as I ever was and the more new things I experience, the less willing I am to come to any premature conclusions. If prison has influenced my relationship to the world at all, then perhaps only in this way: while on the one hand considerably broadening the circle of things I am capable of understanding, it has, on the other hand, considerably narrowed the circle of things I can respect.

*

I've realized an interesting thing: that of all the deaths in the last while, I find myself thinking most often about the death of John Lennon. (Yesterday I finally discovered some details about it in the Sunday supplement of *Mlada fronta.*) This may be because his death so compellingly reaches beyond itself, as though there were latent in it more tragic connections, problems and aspects pointing to the present world crisis than in any other event. It might even be called "the death of the century" (perhaps more so than the deaths of Kennedy or King). Is that how it strikes people on the outside too—or is it merely the cock-eyed impression of someone torn from the context? However it is, you should certainly try to get, from friends, the last record he released, at least—

. . .

Your New Year's card and your New Year's wishes were very nice; a pity I couldn't have kept them with me for a little while, at least. When you write me something more substantial, always write it as a normal letter, for I can keep that (until the next letter arrives) and I can thus study it at my leisure. As for postcards, don't send me those beautiful reproductions of old paintings—postcards are thrown out as soon as they are read, and it pains my heart needlessly.

*

Four days ago was the first anniversary of our arrival in Heřmanice. In retrospect, the year seems to have come and gone quickly. For the anniversary, I've made an important discovery (to be precise: it's the most obvious and banal thing, and it seems important to me only in an entirely specific psychoneural context), and that is, that everything passes; every crisis, depression, failure, every complex and apparently insoluble situation—everything bad, in short—has ultimately one good quality; it is of finite duration and somehow it always—no matter how unlikely it seems at the time—comes to an end and must come to an end. This applies, I hope, to my stay in prison as a whole.

I kiss you, Vašek

64

January 17, 1981

Dear Olga,

. . .

For the New Year, I wrote that the most important thing of all is for you not to lose faith and hope. As promised, I'd like to return briefly to that subject.

First of all: when I speak of faith and hope, I'm not thinking of optimism in the conventional sense, by which we usually mean the belief that "everything will turn out well." I don't share such a belief and consider it—when expressed in that general way—a dangerous illusion. I don't know how "everything" will turn out and therefore I have to admit the possibility that everything—or at least most things—will turn out badly. Faith, however, does not depend on prognoses about possible outcome. One may imagine a man with no faith who believes everything will turn out well, and a man with faith who expects everything to turn out badly. Optimism as I understand it here is therefore not unequivocally positive and life-giving, but may well be the opposite: I have met many people who were full of euphoria and élan, most of it overblown, when they felt things would turn out well, but when they came round to the opposite point of view—usually at the first opportunity—they suddenly became profoundly skeptical. Their skepticism (often expressed in catastrophic visions) was of course just as emotive, superficial and selective as their previous enthusiasm had been; it was merely the other side of the same coin. In short, the need for illusions in order to live one's life is not an expression of strength, but of weakness, and the consequences of such a life are just what one would expect.

Genuine faith is something far more profound and mysterious, and it certainly doesn't depend on how reality appears to one at a given moment. For this reason, too, only someone with faith in the deeper sense of the word will be able to see things as they really are (or rather be open to reality, i.e., to phenomena), and not distort them in one way or another, since he has no personal, emotive reasons for so doing. This, of course, is not true of the man who lacks faith: he has no reason whatever to try to get to the bottom of reality, for such an effort— perhaps more than any other—requires faith, and is unthinkable without it. The faithless man simply tries to survive with the least possible pain and discomfort and is indifferent to everything else. Any claims he makes about reality will usually, in one way or another, serve his "conception" of life—in other words, again, merely what suits him. He is not open without prejudice to all the dimensions of reality.

But what, in fact, is this genuine faith? Where does it come from, what does it consist in and what is it directed toward? I don't have an exhaustive answer, of course, so I shall try to indicate only a couple of obvious things. Faith in this sense can, and usually does, assume specific forms, that is, it is usually "faith in something," but that "something" is not the decisive factor, it is not, that is, a fetish of some kind, a challenge to which would either shake the faith or require a rapid change of fetish. Genuine faith is original, primal and discrete; it precedes its object (if it has one). In other words, it is faith that animates its object, not the other way around. (Naturally an opposite, "reciprocal" tendency exists as well, but I think it is always secondary, a reflex caused by the main factor.) This is one of the ways in which genuine faith differs from the optimist's enthusiasm: it does not draw its energy from some particular reality or assumption, on whose existence it is utterly dependent and with whose loss it would collapse like a pricked balloon. It is not a state of enchantment, induced by the narcotic of an evocative object, but rather an intrinsic "state of the spirit," a profound "existential dimension," an inner direction that you either have or don't have, and which—if you have it—raises your entire existence onto a kind of higher level of Being. At the same time, it is not important at all how, and to what extent, you think about your faith, or whether you are aware of it at all; the only thing that matters is how profoundly the assumption of meaning, or the longing for it, lies dormant in the very bowels of your relationship to the world and of all your actions. I mean both the meaning of individual entities and "meaning altogether" (as the unique and ultimate source of the meaning of individual entities), meaning that transcends the relative limits of space, time or utilitarian (i.e. relativistic) human calculation. (For it is only in the light of the eternal, absolute "memory of Being," that most of the good things one does can be explained.) And so, just as that meaning transcends the relative world whose meaning it constitutes, so faith in meaning transcends all relative utility, and is therefore independent of how things turn out: everything—even what turns out badly—has its own admittedly obscure meaning in relation to faith. Without this assumption of meaning or a longing for it, the experience of nonsense—absence of meaning—would be unthinkable. (That is the case with so-called absurd art which, more than anything else—because it is a desperate cry against loss of meaning—contains faith; the only art that may be able to get along without faith is strictly commercial art.) In any case faith, with its profound assumption of meaning, has its natural antithesis in the experience of nothingness; they are interrelated and human life is in fact a constant struggle for our souls waged by these two powers. If nothingness wins out, dramatic tension vanishes, man surrenders to apathy, and faith and meaning exist only as a backdrop against which others become aware of his fall.

Even though faith can assume the shape of particular human moods, states, loves or other psychological characteristics and expressions, it goes considerably further, pointing man—like responsibility, with which it is closely linked—toward something that is both beyond things and within them: their "absolute horizon." This horizon, as the originator, the bearer and the giver of meaning, far from being a cold, abstract astronomical and metaphysical quantum is, as it turns out, the source of those vital forces that exalt man, humanity and history. It might be put thus: if man is a kind of concentrated reprise of the general miracle of Being, then all visible expressions of his miraculousness have their origin in what primordially and uniquely binds him to the miracle of Being, that is, in his faith in the meaning of that miracle. To be sure, it is a "carte blanche faith," but it is precisely this endless tension between the living experience of meaning on the one hand, and its unknowableness on the other, that gives real inner tension to all the actions by which man represents himself as man.

———

In my last letter, I wrote you in some connection that the circle of what I can respect had somewhat "narrowed." Afterward, I realized that this formulation can be misleading; I should have written that this circle has merely become more clearly defined, because I have, for myself, made more precise the standards by which I am guided in such matters.

*

And now a practical matter: sometime in March or April 1979, they took away my driver's license for half a year; that period is long since up and I've discovered that it's necessary to let them know I'm alive and residing in a Correctional Institute and that when I return, I'll want the license back (no doubt they'll want to test my knowledge of the regulations beforehand). If you neither pick up your license nor tell them where you are, there's a danger they'll declare it null and void—and then I'd have to go right back to the beginning again at driving school! I don't know if they have it at the Transportation Office in Trutnov or in Prague; I don't even remember the details. Perhaps it would be best if you were to look after it for me—

. . .

Kisses, Vašek

65

January 24, 1981

Dear Olga,

This week, I received letter 28 from you and 29 from Ivan. This proves that it is within your powers to write more often—and I feel happier at once. I hope you can both keep it up. . . .

*

I have one very good piece of news: the warden has given me permission to have language textbooks. . . . I can have four books altogether: (1) an English textbook; (2) a German textbook; (3) a small Czech-English, English-Czech dictionary; (4) a small Czech-German, German-Czech dictionary. . . . The dictionaries may only be the pocket-sized variety, if slightly larger bidirectional ones are not to be had, that is. I hope you manage to get something good, either in the stores or from acquaintances; the quality and interest level of these texts are very important, for that will determine, to a considerable extent, how deeply I get involved in the study of languages and whether I'll be able to carry out, in that regard at least, the extensive plans with which I went off to serve my sentence.

*

While I'm on practical matters: the next visit is slowly drawing closer (I expect it will be sometime around the beginning of March) and perhaps it's appropriate to express my wishes concerning the parcel. Essentially, it should contain the same things as last time, with only slight deviations. That means: (1) one kilo of Earl Grey tea; (2) 300 cigarettes; this time, they needn't all be Stuyvesants, you could include some other foreign brands as well (stronger, but only with filter tips); (3) a large tube of toothpaste (or two smaller ones); (4) a set of razor blades for my razor; (5) a large quantity of vitamins; (6) chocolates; (7) several needles; (8) if any of the weight allowance remains, then perhaps some dehydrated juices. That's everything; thanks in advance.

*

As for my health: (1) since my pre-Christmas illness my lungs have (so far) not acted up; (2) pains in my joints have been about eighty percent eliminated by injections and other medicines; (3) a piece of iron fell on my foot, but nothing was either broken or cracked; it is merely bruised, but still rather painful (and will probably be so for some time) and I have a ridiculous limp. I've been exempted from some things, but I still go to work. I'm applying compresses and ointments. Otherwise I'm healthy and feel well.

*

And now to Ivan's letter: as I recently pointed out to you, the meditations in my letters can't be taken too literally; if it didn't sound too immodest, I would say that in terms of genre, they belong more to art or poetry than philosophy, and they certainly can't be treated as though they were a new theory in physics. But Ivan is an inveterate logician and can't help but pose his questions, so I have no choice but to respond, though to tell you the truth I'm somewhat reluctant to, given the nature of my meditations. . . .

The essence of Ivan's questions, if I understand them properly, lies in his concern about the mode of our "immortality" in the "memory of Being." In other words, in what "version" of ourselves do we exist "there"? I think it is part of the essence of things (that is, of the absoluteness of that type of "existence") that we are present there totally and completely, that is, as everything we are and were, to ourselves and to others (including the most distant person who may have heard something distorted about us and forgotten it at once); and ultimately, as everything we "genuinely" are and have ever been. . . . At the same time, everything in the "memory of Being" is absolutely what it is; that means that a person is a person and a character in a novel is a character in a novel (along with everything that appertains to him, including the way other people experience him).

In general then: I exist in the "memory of Being" as the person I am today, and also as the person I am to others, i.e., both for those I am with at present, and for those I've been cut off from (and it is debatable which of them knows me better). Moreover, I exist there, too, as the tension between all my "versions," for that tension, too (and perhaps that above all), is me. Not only that, I am ultimately there both as a summation of all those versions and, at the same time, something that goes infinitely beyond them; in other words, as that which I "genuinely" am (which I cannot know, obviously, because I am not God). But that is, understandably, only "there."

*

And now—on what's left of the sheet of paper—one remark on my meditations: you or Ivan may ask where, in my opinion, do such things as the "absolute horizon," the "memory of Being," etc. exist. Or are they a kind of immaterial component of so-called objective reality, independent, as they say, of our, or of my, consciousness? Or are they merely human fictions, or even my own personal fictions? I think that modern philosophy (and mainly phenomenology) has surpassed that entire mode of inquiry. In any case, I'm not bothered by such questions; in fact they even seem to me scholastic, artificial, superfluous, out of place and trifling, because they are essentially unanswerable (that is: unanswerable in any exact way and essentially dependent for their answers on conviction as a concrete form of faith—God, for example, is a reality to the Christian and a fiction to the Marxist). For me, categories like the "absolute horizon" are nothing more and nothing less than the object and the outcome of my "experience with the world," and more than that I cannot say: whether they exist beyond me or beyond us, and how, technically, they do so, is something I obviously don't know and will never discover, so I see no reason to worry over such matters.

. . .

Kisses, Vašek

66

January 31, 1981

Dear Olga,

From time to time, I fear something will happen to you. It's like the fear your mother used to feel when she wrote us not to cross the railway tracks. In my case, however, it is brought on by enforced separation and the feeling of helplessness that comes from it. And now something really has happened to you (as you can see, your letter 29 arrived); it's exactly the kind of injury that proves danger is lurking everywhere and that my mother was quite right when she'd say she could never completely relax until we were safe at home in bed. I hope you've been getting medical attention and that you're feeling better. As for the second bit of bad news, the damage to our car, my first reaction was one of delight—that I'm not home and don't have to look after the repairs. I've always loathed from the bottom of my heart the bother around fixing the car. Make sure the insurance company pays for all the damages, and when the car is fixed, sell it as soon as possible. I've nothing against your buying another Russian car, but do give some thought to a Niva this time (if they're available) instead of a Lada; from what I know of the Niva, it would be suitable for the terrain in the Krkonoše Mountains. . . .

*

The kind of meditations that have been appearing in my letters in recent months won't be appearing anymore (not because I don't have enough to say about such matters). I mention it because you wrote me that I don't seem, from my letters, to be growing stupid—and I wouldn't want this new situation to make you change your mind. I do sometimes feel I'm growing stupid but justified or not, it would be wrong to form an impression of my state of mind from my letters (they are not really written in the kind of internal and external conditions I've been used to writing in; the difference is perhaps greater than you can imagine). . . .

*

I've been told I'm to write only about myself, and so today I turn my attention in that direction. . . . When I wrote you not long ago that my standards of judgment in what I can respect had become more precise, I was thinking, among other things, of self-control. Not to covet at any cost what one sees in someone else; not to let oneself be dragged along by unsatisfied hankerings and not to try satisfying them at the expense of one's dignity; not to lose one's temper at every opportunity and not to think just of oneself all the time; not to break down and fall into despair whenever the situation becomes serious, or at least keep one's hopelessness to oneself and not burden those around one with it and above all, not to let it affect one's actions; to accept the natural consequences of one's own behavior, to suppress the tendency to hate and the desire for revenge and to know how to forgive; not to bemoan oneself and one's fate (as though it were at the center of all human misfortune); not to unleash suppressed energy in empty and unjust ways and not to compensate for one's suffering by making others suffer, etc.—all these are expressions of self-control that impress me as signs of genuine manliness, so different from that false, superficial and put-on manliness whose chief expression is a lot of crude words, threats and even physical blows (usually delivered, of course, to someone unlikely to return them), the manliness of the "roughneck" that frequently hides a cringing, cowardly nature. The sphere of what I understand has considerably widened here—and so I understand this "roughneckism" and all the strange and varied expressions of it far better than before; I understand it, but it does not enjoy my respect.

. . .

I'm done, and as usual my greetings to everyone, with special stress today on my greetings to Andulka. She is a rare creature, full of love and incapable of hatred, and I'm glad that you—as I understand from your letters—are friends.

Ahoj, kissing you and looking forward—

Vašek

67

February 13, 1981

Dear Olga,

Well, it seems I was somewhat overeffusive in my praise of your letter writing: again, no letter has come for more than two weeks, though yesterday I was shown your postcard in which you confirm receipt of the textbook voucher and ask what kind of vitamins you can bring. I think any kind will do (of course it must be in the original packaging). On the other hand, you needn't bring razor blades; I have enough. My playing the drums, which you mention on the postcard, is memorable because that snapshot was taken about three hours before my arrest.

*

I'm not having much luck so far either in writing about myself, which I began in the last letter, as you can observe for yourself from the fact that this letter will reach you a week later than it should have, probably along with letter 68, which I'll write the day after tomorrow. Nevertheless, I'll continue writing about myself (as instructed), despite the fact that I'm basically not very happy doing it. Which suggests an appropriate starting point: some of the reasons for this aversion of mine.

First and foremost, it is neither my nature nor my habit to concern myself seriously, and out loud, with myself. My chief inhibition is probably diffidence (which I will write about when the occasion arises). My aversion to "disrobing in public" was a factor in my decision to stop writing poetry and start writing plays, a genre in which the persona of the author is best concealed, since in drama, he speaks only through the mouths of others and his work, therefore, is about as objectified as it can get. When I tried just now to recall the times I had spoken about myself, my mind, my problems, etc. I realized that I usually did so only over wine in the company of sweet ladies (or babbling into their ears, something you never approved of); but such talk usually had overtones of irony and mystification in it, and I did so in the awareness that these overtones were audible and understood. But my writing from prison has no such context and it cannot have such overtones, and for this reason I must quell not only my diffidence (more so in this case than when writing about other matters) but also the aversion I feel toward my own circumspect gravity (a product of circumstances) and my somewhat heavy-handed mentoring (I sometimes feel like Sally, who writes the agony column in *Mladý svět*).

Writing about a particular person—and especially about oneself—in the hope that the written statement will be at least somewhat accurate—not only assumes an ability to shuck various inhibitions, it also requires a special skill. The point is that man is essentially indescribable, that is, if a precise and exhaustive account is required. Man can only—and with only relative success—be transformed into a kind of literary abbreviation or exaggeration, and at the cost of enormous oversimplification (which is not to say that sometimes precisely such oversimplification may not produce—in good literature, for example—a miracle: a re-creation of the world that is "more real than real:" in other words, a world in which—precisely because of this "simplification"—something from the sphere of the "meaning" of phenomena, something which in normal "unsimplified" reality is hopelessly submerged in their depths, swims to the surface. The ability to choose the proper means of abbreviation, the kind that, through simplification, does not eclipse but truly clarifies, is precisely the skill required to utter a meaningful statement about someone, and of course this skill is three times as necessary if the subject of the statement is the author of it himself. (How, when one looks at oneself, can one reject subjective self-evaluation yet remain oneself? What is worse: how can one deal with the fact that one knows so much about oneself? How much easier it is to write of those we know less well!) I don't think I'm particularly gifted in that regard or, if so, then only in a very limited sense. To put it more simply, psychology or character description is not my forte as an author.

Certainly: one could quite easily—indirectly perhaps, but with essentially more truth—write about oneself simply by writing about the particular things and situations one comes in contact with, but in my case this is impossible, so I must digress down the treacherous path of self-characterization by way of generalizations. (And incidentally, how else do the best literary characters emerge except from a background of specific situations and actions which—paradoxically—bring the fictional character to life more richly, and therefore more vividly than even the most accomplished of conceptual descriptions?)

Before I conclude these comments on my reluctance to write about myself, there is at least one more thing I must mention: I have written you about myself a couple of times already (not everything was sent) and each time, I realized one thing: just as, according to Heisenberg's research, the nature and relationships of physical particles change merely by virtue of being observed, so each of our traits changes— subtly but inevitably, though we describe them with the greatest of precision—simply because we describe them, because they enter our field of vision. Just as a quality reflected upon in a particular way is no longer quite what it was before it was reflected upon, so a person with a particular trait is not quite the same person after he reports on that trait. The consequences of this shift are varied, but the most frequent is an increase in self-stylization. When a person describes himself, it is as though he were not merely saying that he is a certain way, but that he is consciously so and that in fact (though he claim the opposite) that is how he wishes to be. By declaring his own view of himself, he is in effect announcing to the world that he would welcome it if the world saw him in the same way (or on the contrary, he may be challenging the world to refute his interpretation). In other words, in describing oneself, one is already somehow stylizing oneself. Of course being aware of this accursed fact does not encourage one to try it.

.   .   .

In the space that's left, a brief remark about my letters in general: despite a great many complications I don't want to give up my habit of writing you a four-page letter every week. (I have good reasons for this; among them this: there are certain things that one need not do, but wants to, even though they complicate rather than simplify life, and in this place it is not good to give such things up, for it could be the imperceptible beginning of a disintegration that might lead, for in- stance, to not reading the newspaper or not cleaning one's teeth twice a day, or not caring whether one has buttons on one's shirts, until at last, one would not care about anything at all.) Still, there may be some weeks when I simply don't write you—perhaps only because I want to take a proper rest, or because at the time allotted to letter writing, I may only be capable of writing something inane. So if from time to time you don't get a letter, don't panic—just as I do not panic when I haven't heard from you in a long time.

Kisses, Vašek

68

February 15, 1981

Dear Olga,

The day before yesterday, I finished my belated letter 67, which was given almost entirely over to an explanation of why I don't like writing about myself, and what the hidden pitfalls in that kind of writing are. Having prepared the ground, I can begin in earnest today. I'll try to write about myself now, that is, as I appear to myself at this point in time, during my imprisonment. Were I to be thorough, it would provide material for a long series of letters. Whether this will happen, of course, I don't know, for I may at any time, for whatever reason, abandon my commentary in favor of other subjects, or I may simply put it off for a while. Whatever happens, I will return to writing about myself in some form sooner or later; in the given situation, it is a theme around which one always circles, either closely or more freely.

*

I'll start off with a list and a description of the various moods that I have here, and I'll begin with an account of my fundamental physical states which, understandably, significantly influence my moods.

I would say that I experience three basic physical states here:

1. I feel well, i.e., normal. There is nothing wrong with me, I have no aches and pains, and I am unaware of my body. This state is scarcely capable in itself of producing a good mood in me, but it is an important condition for that mood. In other words: feeling well physically doesn't necessarily guarantee good spirits, but I can hardly be in good spirits if I don't feel physically well.

2. The second state is one of sickness, when I have a specific, localizable illness or a physiological disorder such as a cold, the flu, a fever, an injured foot, diarrhea, constipation, hemorrhoids or aching

joints. This state is in no way intolerable because it is understandable, describable and can be got rid of or at least cured (as you know, I can't complain about the medical care here; given the possibilities of the place, it is as good as it can be). It does not automatically produce a bad mood; in some regards, it may even be pleasant (it is common knowledge, for instance, that fever can sometimes cause mild euphoria).

3. The worst physical state is when I don't feel well and yet I'm not sick in any definite way. I find it hard to concentrate, I'm absentminded and nervous, I constantly feel the cold, I have a slight headache, I have slight chills, my eyes water, I seem tired, groggy and weak (yet I have no immediate reason to feel tired and I've slept well), my entire body aches (but not so much that it could be considered a definite illness); I am simply out of sorts, nothing seems to go right, nothing gives me pleasure, I can't express myself properly or make up my mind, I think slowly, my hands tremble slightly, I seem to be looking "through" people and things, I feel hollow and dull; everything is unsteady, including my voice—in short, I'm not myself. . . . It is a most unpleasant state, first because I don't know how to get rid of it (it would be ridiculous to see the doctor every time, and tea—the only expedient that is always available—works only sometimes and only when the condition is very mild), secondly because it complicates prison life (mainly work) considerably, and finally because when I feel this way, the only possible mood I can have is a rotten one. . . . At home, I would put together a combination of pills (Algena, Acylpyrin, etc.), wash them down with hot grog, collapse under the duvet and in three hours I'd be fit. No such solution, of course, is available here so you drag yourself through the world in this state all day long or even for several days running. As you will certainly appreciate, this puts the whole matter in quite a different perspective.

So much, then, for my physical states.

*

And now for my moods. I made myself a little chart which indicated that I can roughly cover my many different moods—with an appropriate degree of schematization, of course—by describing eight bad moods and seven good ones (the number may change as I write). Should I begin with the bad ones or the good ones? The bad ones, I think, since my list will then unfold in a positive direction and climax with a happy ending. But on the other hand, so this letter won't be unnecessarily gloomy, I will begin with one of my rather pleasant bad moods:

1. It is a state of melancholy. It can be brought about by an external circumstance or it can come on suddenly, out of the blue. Usually, however, it is brought on by external circumstances—chiefly cultural experiences, and particularly television or movies. In them, one sees nature, trees, meadows, colors, the bustle of cities, affable, gentle people dressed in civilian clothing, nice surroundings and nice things. In short, one sees life "on the outside" (whether it is an accurate representation of that life in its essentials is another question; the fact is, however, it contains all the external signs by which that life differs from this one)—and one is somehow "sadly elated" by all this. . . . One smiles and is charmed and transported, moved by the silliest things—and then the lights come on in the mess hall, we line up to leave and suddenly—after that brief diversion—I am brought down to earth with unusual force and pointed emphasis and once again I am given to understand where I am. It is at this point that the melancholy takes hold of me—a strange mixture of delight in pretty things and sadness that they are so far away. It contains a touch—no more—of sentimental self-pity, a bit (or a lot) of absurdity, a sense of enormous and irreversible loss (as though one were going to be here for life), but also an odd, harmonious reconciliation with that loss. Because of that touch of self-pity, it is a somewhat egocentric state, yet it contains the shadow of a gently pathetic self-effacement: you are glad that, inaccessible though these nice things may be, others at least can experience them. The fact that they exist somewhere at all, and that someone is experiencing them, is, oddly enough, a source of joy, elation and stimulation, even though it has nothing to do with you. At bottom it is probably a negative and destructive state (which is why I include it among my "bad" moods), but there is something oddly pleasurable about it too, something like the smell of flowers in the cemetery on All Souls' Day.

(More about other moods next time.)

*

Greetings to all close friends, among whom today I'd like to mention Otka—there aren't many women who are as devoted and at the same time courageous as she is, and I'm glad I have had the opportunity of knowing her—

Kisses, Vašek

69

February 22, 1981

Dear Olga,

Finally (after more than three weeks!) a letter from home (yours, no. 30). I'm glad you've recovered. . . . I read about the film *Oblomov* and the review gave me the impression it might be good. Perhaps it will come here someday. (By the way, I've long been interested in the absurd figure of Stolz as someone even more hopeless than Oblomov, and once I even had it in mind to dramatize Oblomov.)

*

The textbooks have arrived, and I thank you very much for them. I haven't got them with me yet, but I've seen them. I think both will be excellent, exactly what I wanted, and I'm glad that they're part of the same series: perhaps that will make a parallel study of both languages easier. The German dictionary, however, causes me some worry: not just because it's not in one volume, as I wanted, but mainly because it's too big; I'm going to have problems finding a place for it and I won't even need so detailed a dictionary. I believe you when you say a smaller one isn't available in the stores, but I think someone might have one—I'm thinking concretely of that pocket-sized one from that colored series, you know the one I mean. I know I once had it in Prague; perhaps you'll still manage to find it somewhere. That would suit me perfectly and solve the problem of where to put it. If you can find it or get it somewhere, bring it with you on the visit—I'll try to arrange to take it from you and return you the large, two-volume set.

. . .

And now to continue the survey of some of my moods:

2. The second of my bad moods is a state of nervousness, fear and anxiety. Earlier, I had this mood quite often; now it occurs relatively rarely. It begins as a feeling of insecurity and vague danger—the vaguer the feeling, the worse the mood. Of course I used to experience this mood when I was free as well, but then I was, or felt, threatened by essentially different things. The common factor is that initial sense of insecurity. . . . What upsets me is not knowing what to expect, the sensation that something unknown to me is hanging over my head or being hatched against me behind my back. This makes me nervous and

inattentive; I imagine catastrophes and can't think sensibly or deal with anything except my own uncertainty. This psychophysical uncertainty grows to become fear of the potential and unknown threat, of not being prepared for it, able to stand up to it, or even of making matters worse by doing something inappropriate. Sometimes, the fear can become a general existential anxiety. It is typical of this mood that I am less terrified by what, objectively, might happen to me than by whether I will be able to respond appropriately. That is, I fear the decisions other people make less than the decisions I might be expected to make myself. In this regard, it's remarkably like stage fright, and I've always been prone to that. I was always a bundle of nerves before an opening, a test in school, a public appearance, whenever something was expected of me and I doubted my ability to meet that expectation. But when matters were out of my hands, and I could no longer influence them for better or worse, I was relatively calm, regardless of how miserable a fate was awaiting me. This mood is frequently induced by meaningless trifles or utter chimeras—which I won't describe—and they can keep me there, despite rational arguments to the contrary. The mood can vanish as suddenly as it came; any superficial factor may expel it, turn it completely around (usually with a sense of euphoric relief). Nowadays, as I say, I have this mood rather rarely, partly because I may have learned some self-control, and partly because to a certain extent, I suppose I've become accustomed to my new environment. I understand its laws of "motion" (a few, at least), I have learned to anticipate some things and consequently it is no longer such a source of mysteries, imponderables and uncertainties as it must have been in the early phases. Despite its rare appearances, however, the mood belongs in my survey because, among other things, it has wider implications. I've occasionally found, for instance, that I strike some people as a timid and frightened man, and they have been unable to reconcile that impression with the fact that my behavior betrayed none of the concrete consequences of timidity. . . .

3. Another one of my bad moods is the precise opposite of this nervousness—that is, a state of mutedness and apathy, when I don't care about anything, when nothing surprises, upsets, angers or excites me. Everything goes right by me, or bounces off a kind of armor of indifference that I put round myself and which suddenly makes me feel like a hundred-and-seventy-pound lump of organic matter with no human responses and no interest in human affairs. In the germinal phase of this mood there is something rather healthy—a mechanism of

self-defense or self-preservation: if one were constantly required to notice, experience and participate in everything with the same intensity, one would quickly go mad or else be swept away in the essentially accidental and unstructured tide of things. Obviously there is a psychic device that protects you by automatically turning off in moments of excessive stress. Properly, you must always give full and responsible consideration to when—in the given situation—it is appropriate to be fully involved in things, when it is enough to be a concerned observer and when, on the contrary, it is best simply not to take any notice. I tolerate my own apathy as long as it remains within limits, that is, as long as it is only the temporary reaction of one whose spirit is exhausted by the constant effort of making distinctions and simply needs a rest. It would be more serious, however, if something of the indifference I sometimes feel were to leave its mark on my character. Indifference and resignation, I believe, are the most serious forms of human decline into nothingness (I once wrote a letter on this theme but for some reason it wasn't sent; I'll certainly return to it again in some connection). I hope that no such decline threatens me, and therefore I treat my occasional apathy as no more than a way of resting the nervous system which, in certain environments, may well be essential.

*

As usual, I'm looking forward enormously to the visit; I kiss you and send my greetings to all close friends, with a special kindredly kiss today for Kamila and Zuzana—

Your Vašek

70

March 1, 1981

Dear Olga,

And here it is again—once every three months—the "dead" letter, the one I write before the visit which you won't get till after it. For the occasion, I've chosen a theme that seemed somewhat in harmony with the letter's "deadness," that is, my worst mood. As an inveterate systematizer, I would eventually find the theme unavoidable anyway, so I thought it appropriate to get it over with now, when its somewhat gloomy nature can be lightened or cut short by the joyful atmosphere of anticipating the visit, the visit itself and fresh recollections of it. Yet scarcely had I sat down to write the letter, than we had to fall in for a movie, after which I'm in no mood to write about my worst mood; so first, a minor digression.

I once wrote about the particular significance I feel in the death of John Lennon. Yesterday I read an interesting article on Lennon's death by Jiří Černý in *Melodie,* and I realized that what I feel is obviously widespread. When a reactionary underworld decides to shoot a progressive president, that act has in itself—on its primary level, as it were—a determinable meaning, and therefore such a death does not cry out so powerfully for an investigation of its deeper, symbolic sense. Lennon's murder, however, is so nonsensical at that primary level that it is quite impossible to think about it other than as a symbol. And you can't help feeling that the shot was fired by the reality of the eighties at one of the departing dreams—the dream of the sixties for peace, freedom and brotherhood, the dream of the flower children, the communes, the LSD trips and "making love not war," a shot as it were in the face of that existential revolution of the "third consciousness" and "the greening of America." As a symbol, Lennon's death has of course more aspects to it, and more complex ones at that, but this is the first one, the one that suggests itself most acutely. I do not believe that certain values and ideals of the sixties have been discredited as empty illusions and mistakes; certain things can never be called into question, either by time or by history, because they are simply an indivisible dimension of the Being of humanity and therefore of history as well, which, though it is a history of repressions, murders, stupidities, wars and violence, is at the same time a history of magnificent dreams, longings and ideals. I only think that everything today is somehow harder and rougher, that one has to pay more dearly for things and that the dream of a freer, more meaningful life is no longer just a matter of running away from Mommy, as it were, but of a tough-minded, everyday confrontation with the dark powers of the new age. The fact that Lennon was shot by a psychopathic victim, of sorts, of the modern pop-cult created by the mass media, is also not without symbolic meaning: passive identification with an idol, replacing "active faith," finds its obscure climax in the schizophrenia of a man who shoots his idol to regain his own identity (like something out of a cheap psychoanalytical detective thriller).

On my list of bad moods (the sequence of which has its own logic) my worst mood occupies eighth place, but it will be quite in keeping with the style of my letters if I write about it now—since I'm always, in fact, jumping backward and forward so that many things begin to make sense only long after they are written.

8. Essentially, it involves falling into a state of utter and complete self-doubt. I call to mind everything I ever wrote (of a theoretical nature) and all the errors, the inaccuracies, the clumsiness. As for my plays, I seem to have written so terribly few of them and all their faults file by me on parade. Comparing myself to others, I am compelled to realize again and again how much better and more meaningfully they have acted in various situations, and how much they managed to achieve. I fault myself for lacking ideas and energy, and I question whether I will ever again write anything worthwhile (there is so much I would like to say—but will I be capable of saying it?); I admonish myself for not having a proper education, for knowing nothing (I can't even write a nice letter home every week like Vašík); I am physically repugnant to myself (a double chin, bags under my eyes, and so on); my habits, my politeness (inappropriate in this setting) and my tendency to embarrass easily disgust me; I seem to lack strength, decisiveness and good humor and in general, I'm good for nothing and can expect nothing positive in life (I've long since given everything there was in me to give) and it is fitting that I should rot here for the rest of my life, because what would I do on the outside?

Oddly enough, these occasional fits of utter self-doubt and self-loathing are not unpleasant. I don't torture or torment myself (ordinary fits of helpless rage are far more unpleasant and usually make one physically miserable); I humbly accept my general feeling of worthlessness as the outcome of some predetermined will. (Unlike someone with an inferiority complex, I am quite free of the need to compensate for this inferiority by persuading myself and the world of my own importance; in fact, I tend the opposite way.) Still, I consider this my worst mood. The reason is simple: just as states of mind after taking LSD, they say, are models of potential psychosis (they demonstrate how one would go mad if one were eventually to do so), I see this mood of mine as a cautionary model: if I were once to cease being myself and my identity, as it has been hitherto, were to disintegrate, then perhaps this particular mood indicates how it would happen: I would probably cease to believe in myself once and for all, and become utterly paralyzed by self-doubt.

Fortunately, there is no such danger and my mood of self-doubt is really nothing more than that—a mood. Everyone knows this mood to a greater or lesser extent and I have always had it off and on; it's just that now, in my present situation, conditions are more conducive to it. The essence of this mood is that the healthy, necessary and probably unavoidable doubts that haunt every creative person (and which may be the other face of ambition—those who wish to do things best are the first to doubt the value of what they do) begin to run rampant and take on a life of their own, and what began as critical self-assessment ceases to be critical and ends up serving an obsessive self-flagellation.

This strange combination—of a profound and almost indestructible faith in self with a frequent lack of self-confidence—is simply an inseparable part of my nature, something I've given a good deal of thought to and have well mapped out in my head. In time, I'd like to devote a letter to it (if I'm not utterly fed up by then with writing about myself all the time). But that would be out of place here, because it concerns— in a manner of speaking—the essence of my nature and so it goes far beyond the framework of today's theme—my eighth bad mood.

I'd like to forestall any misunderstanding and stress again that, though I may occasionally succumb to this mood, it is never serious enough to have a destructive effect on my ability to make decisions, on my behavior or my actions. I am enough the master of my moods to be careful, when under the influence of those moods, to do only what I must. The point is I can't let my moods decide what I should do: that is exclusively a matter for the rather mysterious sense of responsibility that I have pondered over more than once in earlier letters.

Your Vašek

71

March 13, 1981

Dear Olga,

I was unusually satisfied with the visit; I'd even say it was one of the best so far. We were all obviously well rested and fit and able to talk about everything with good humor, but not to the point of depriving serious matters of their seriousness. And instead of being depressed after the visit, I was exhilarated, almost as though I had taken a drug or a "hit," as they say here. So thank you very much for the visit and also, of course, for the parcel, it was perfect as usual and precisely according to my instructions. Thank you also for your letter, no. 31, which has just arrived, a good complement to your oral report.

*

A brief marginal note about my letters and what Ivan said about them: the diverse meditations that have been appearing in my letters since sometime last summer until recently actually do form a loose entity, in which there are about three logical gaps (Ivan put his finger on one of them), but perhaps it's not so important and I may be able to make up for it in time. The present phase of my "writing about myself," which will occupy a few more letters and which—to avoid monotony—I will occasionally intersperse with other subjects, is something of a recreational period, but perhaps it won't be entirely without interest for you. Then I have some other themes in mind for later; what will ultimately come of all this remains to be seen. Nevertheless, whether my drive to write about anything—serious or unimportant—comes from inside me, or from external circumstances, it will all cohere, if only because it will always be me writing it; even in letters from prison, I cannot very well become someone I am not.

*

Your news about the upcoming production of *Mountain Hotel* in Vienna not only pleased me, but provoked me as well into giving a little more thought to that play. If I repeat anything I've already written about it, bear with me.

I'm not very fond of so-called symbols in art, or to be more precise, a certain type of symbol in which one level of phenomena is simply replaced by another and all you need to know is how to operate a simple switch to relate what is said on the second level back to the first and, by this process of "translation," practically exhaust the entire meaning of the work. On the contrary, I like it when a work can be interpreted in different ways, when it is something of an enigma and when its meaning, though it may transcend the work itself, does so by radiating in all directions, when it cannot be reduced to a straightforward conceptual formula. Art in general is a little like playing with fire;

the artist deals with something without knowing precisely what it is; he creates something without knowing precisely what it will "mean." The work, it seems to me, should always be somehow "cleverer" than its author and he should ultimately be able to stand before it filled with the same sense of awe and with the same questions in his mind as someone seeing or reading it for the first time. . . .

Having said that, I can perhaps now add something to what I've already written about *The Mountain Hotel:* if I wanted to express the "meaning" of that play in the simplest and most accessible formulation (hopefully without, I repeat, either capturing nor completely exhausting that meaning), then I might say, for instance, that the hotel is in fact the human world. We have all come into it not knowing why, we can't move to another hotel, yet we enjoy relative freedom on its premises, and if that freedom is limited in any way, then only to the extent that we, as inhabitants of the "hotel," limit each other. And all of us sooner or later leave it. At the same time, most of us cannot find, either inside or outside this "hotel," any firm point to which we can unambiguously, enduringly and unproblematically relate, a point which in our eyes would lend to everything—and above all to our sojourn, our existence, in the "hotel"—a kind of central meaning from which would radiate, in a comprehensible way, all its other coherences and meanings. Yet though we live, find pleasure, think, suffer, meet, part, pass each other by in various ways, that fatal lack of focus or perspective makes everything around us and within us somehow unstable, disconnected, confused. Things contradict each other, they lack order, continuity, logic, meaning and purpose; life in this hotel has a distressing restlessness to it. Again and again, we latch onto illusory values as substitutes for that missing firm point; we know all this, more or less, yet we cannot come to terms with it; on the contrary, we sink deeper and deeper into it.

. . . I repeat that the purpose of the play is not to have the viewer leave with this, or any other, exclusive conceptually clarified awareness of its "meaning"; if we can explain and name anything too well, we come to terms with it too quickly, our interpretation soothes us, the work ceases to tantalize and irritate us and we quickly forget it. . . . I would rather the play disturbed them in some indeterminable way; I would rather their experience of it were ambivalent and full of contradictions. On the one hand they should be delighted to some extent by its artful construction, by having understood its rhythm and allowing themselves to be swept along by it. On the other hand, they should feel that it all has something compelling to do with the most serious questions of their own existence; they should even experience it as a strange and provocative "probe" into their own existence, but without dismissing it too quickly by explaining that "probe" away. Of course I have no way of knowing whether my play is capable of evoking that kind of ambivalent response, but if it were, I would be completely satisfied. I've never believed that a playwright is any cleverer than his audience or that he has a right to instruct them in anything at all. I have always seen the meaning of my work simply in "thrusting the viewer into his own situation," "opening him up" to thoughts about it and provoking him into experiencing it more deeply. And no matter what he realizes after having been thus provoked, no matter what conclusions he comes to within himself, or what he ultimately decides, it is always, in my view, more valuable than the profoundest words of wisdom accepted passively from the playwright.

By the way, I tried to describe *The Mountain Hotel* to a perceptive fellow prisoner here; he listened to me with great interest and astonishment, and when at last I asked him what he would think if he hadn't known me and for some reason had to see the play, he replied quite candidly that he'd think I was a fake who was trying to make a fool out of him and he would be royally offended. When I say I'd be happy if the play could unsettle the audience and somehow "shake them up" existentially, I certainly don't mean I think it should happen in that particular way. Still, if it did, I would have only myself to blame for not being able to realize my fine intentions in a meaningful way, or simply for trying to do something that couldn't be done.

*

There is a little space left, so here are some more marginal remarks on the visit and your letter.

Do you recall that during the March visit last year I was also being treated in the clinic? Everything was so like now that it seemed to be a mere continuation—as though a whole long, hard year had not gone by in the meantime!

Not only do I approve of your diversified cultural and social activities and high jinks, I welcome them; still, I think that here and there they might be combined with more down to earth duties (in any case, you shouldn't treat them too much like duties, otherwise you'll grow to hate them).

Those in the know tell me that most of the spare parts for the Niva are the same as those for the Lada, so if you buy a Lada again, you won't be much better off. Have you done something about my driver's license? . . .

The vitamins will last precisely until the next visit, and if I manage one English and one German lesson a month, the textbooks will last exactly until the end of my sentence.

It is truly unbelievable how long we've been together and how many different loops and curves our life has gone through in that time. Everything passes and perhaps this present aberration will pass too.

Kisses, Vašek

P.S. A detailed study of the parcel inspired much delight, but even so, I found two small faults:

1. To make room for ten short cigars you put in 40 fewer cigarettes—which is, I think, a bit overdoing it—
2. There should have been three, not two, tubes of toothpaste— (But those are really mere trifles—)

72

March 14, 1981

Dear Olga,

My stay in the clinic is coming to an end; I'm well and wonderfully rested, I'm in good spirits and it's hardly appropriate, therefore, to write about my bad moods. My sense of order, however, demands that I continue with what's begun.

*

4. My fourth bad mood—I call it Sunday depression—is not specifically a prison mood either; it undoubtedly existed, even when I was free, in a full range of prefigurations. Here, however, it has ripened into a particular form that is closely related to local conditions. During the week, life is a treadmill and I look forward to the weekend when I'll have more free time, write home, see a movie, watch television, rest, perhaps even read something, etc. Then the much anticipated weekend arrives and no matter how efficient I try to be, I invariably feel that it

goes by just too quickly for me to do all the things I was so looking forward to. Nevertheless, the moment eventually arrives when all my private weekend tasks are done, the letter is written, my things are in order, the movie is seen and suddenly—usually late Sunday afternoon—I have something that might be called absolute free time. And the question arises: what now? Read? Make some tea and simply rest? Watch an old movie? Chat with someone? The atmosphere around me is strange; there are people everywhere, talking; someone strumming a guitar; there are no quiet corners; it's impossible to leave the designated area and, out of sheer inability to decide how best to spend the precious time, I essentially just wander about aimlessly or rather, regardless of what I do, I always feel I could be doing something more pleasant and more significant. Inextricably mixed with it is the awareness that time is slipping away and that, for all my plans and resolutions—I am wasting it, whether for subjective or objective reasons. It is interesting that at such times I am aware of being in prison more urgently than I am during the weekly rat race. And at this point, a strange, vague depression begins to creep into my mind and eventually occupies it, and I start looking forward, oddly enough, to work and the rest of the weekly treadmill. I can't put my finger precisely on what this Sunday depression consists in; I don't think, for instance, that I feel more homesick or a greater longing to be free than at any other time, and even less do I long for anything specific. It's simply that a hopelessness descends on me. It comes from how time passes, from how everyone around me is passing it, from how I am passing it—and last but not least, from how dreary and desolate is the space I live in (though on this point, too, I'd be unable to specify exactly what I lack so urgently: it's clean, with running water and a normal toilet, I have my own bed—all the basic requirements of life are there). And the occasional reminders of what is missing, oddly enough, induce a regretful longing rather than joy. (For instance, the rather pleasant music they play for us at certain times, when most of my fellow prisoners stand under the loudspeakers and squirm about happily, merely deepens my depression.) My one modest source of self-satisfaction, writing home, is over with and after that "performance" I suddenly feel unusually empty (added to which I'm usually dissatisfied with my "performance"). Sometimes the sensation of emptiness expands until things appear to lose their meaning and everything seems pointless, petty, vain, hopeless and desperately sad. And then at last comes the evening television news, bringing liberation, in fact.

Much has been written about the hopeless, desolate atmosphere of Sundays in large cities, and there are many evocative cabaret songs about it. Essentially, it is what sociologists call the problem of leisure time; modern man has lost touch with the original, mythical significance and substance of festive occasions, and all that remains is emptiness. Perhaps my Sunday depression in prison is merely an extreme form or a distorted echo of a common problem of civilization called Sunday. I personally see this mood as one of the typical fissures through which nothingness, that modern face of the devil, seeps into people's lives.

*

5. When things don't turn out as I had planned, when I'm having difficulty with something, when I experience minor failures, waste time pointlessly, etc., in short, when everything conspires against me, as it were, and this "conspiracy" reaches a certain pitch, my (otherwise widely admired) composure leaves me and I fall into a foul mood. The final drop that makes my cup of patience run over is usually something trivial (for instance, someone tries to push in to wash at the same tap I happen to be using) and—thanks to the buildup of other unpleasant trivialities before it—I lose control of my emotions and my sense of proportion and am swept away in a kind of angry negation: I accuse people wrongly, I am unjust, cranky and irascible. It's typical, however, that even in this state I can usually stifle the mood and if I let it seep out at all, then only in a somewhat filtered form. I keep myself under control, however, not because I fear the consequences of an explosion, but simply because of my deeply rooted, indestructible and profoundly unhealthy politeness. (Unhealthy because, among other things, an honest outburst of anger provides marvelous relief—I wrote you about one of my outbursts—whereas suppressing it can only make one a nervous wreck. One consequence of my reticence is that I usually let off steam out loud, but in the wrong place; I simply unload on a neutral bystander or friend a whole bucket of sarcasm, unjust accusations, grotesque exaggerations and cheap generalizations—addressed to anyone at all, guilty or innocent, with the possible exception of the person I'm telling it all to. I don't often have such fits of anger, but they occur more frequently than on the outside. This does not mean I've turned into a bilious old man, it's just that life here, which is collective in every respect, provides infinitely more occasion for this kind of irascibility to thrive. It's a bad mood not just for me personally, but also because of

its objective consequences. My position among my fellow prisoners depends on one positive thing—they see me as an open person, one who listens gladly and talks sympathetically to everyone and snubs no one (though he may not agree with them), but who is that way mainly because he is essentially above things and observes the mad whirl with interest and compassion without having a particular little ax of his own to grind. But if the position that brings me respect and protects me depends on a calm, analytical attitude to things, then obviously every angry, undignified reaction on my part can jeopardize that position. Still, I have such moods from time to time and when I do, I couldn't care less about loss of dignity. On the other hand they usually last no more than a few minutes and frequently—again, because of a random event or simply because my quantum of anger has subsided—they turn into their exact opposite when, almost before the echoes of my former exasperation have died out, I must laugh heartily at myself.

For some time now I haven't written you about what I'm reading. There hasn't been much—a little book on the Watergate affair by Borovička, something else that slips my mind right now, and yesterday I read *Foolish Wisdom* by Feuchtwanger and borrowed Malaparte—*Kaput.*

Greetings to my male friends, kisses to my female friends, and of course to you—

Vašek

73

March 21, 1981

Dear Olga,

Thank you for letter 32 (the first post-visit letter). You are slowly learning how to write me and your letters always make me happy and tell me a lot. If only you could manage to write more often! . . .

*

It's the first day of spring, a beautiful day, so perhaps it's appropriate to conclude my list of bad moods.

7. One of the essential aspects of every good mood is a sense of

identification with something outside oneself, whether it be delight in meeting and establishing a rapport with someone, or delight in personal achievement (i.e., we have intervened in the world and the world responded as we intended it to) or finally, delight in some kind of work or action. Things seem to have a perceivable meaning and thus we seem to be in a kind of harmony with the world. If I include feelings of alienation and absurdity among my bad moods, it's chiefly because this sense of identification is lacking in them. Indeed, the impression that I'm deeply alienated from what goes on around me, that I don't understand its logic and meaning, the belief that it will remain, probably forever, distant, alien and incompatible with everything I think and feel—this is neither pleasant nor uplifting. On the contrary, it is chilling and sometimes even terrifying. Of course one may experience absurdity in many ways: through individual insight, or in conversation; it may be an intense but ephemeral mood, or a profound and dominant feeling in one's life. Though I wouldn't say that a sense of absurdity is my strongest, deepest and most fundamental feeling, yet I think I have always had an amplified tendency to see the absurd dimensions of the world, and thus I may be more susceptible to this mood than many others, especially here, where I'm cut off from all the bonds that are natural and meaningful to me and placed in an utterly alien and essentially remote environment. Still, I don't necessarily consider it a thoroughly negative mood.

First of all, the sensation of absurdity is never—at least not as I understand it—the expression of a loss of faith in the meaning of life. Quite the opposite: only someone whose very being thirsts after meaning, for whom "meaning" is an integral dimension of his own existence, can experience the absence of meaning as something painful, or more precisely, can perceive it at all. In its tormenting absence, meaning may have a more urgent presence than when it is simply taken for granted, no questions asked—somewhat in the way one who is sick may better understand what it means to be well than one who is healthy. I believe that genuine absence of meaning and genuine unbelief manifest themselves differently; as indifference, apathy, resignation and the decline of existence to the vegetative level. In other words: the experience of absurdity is inseparable from the experience of meaning; it is merely, in a manner of speaking, its "obverse," just as meaningfulness is the "reverse" of absurdity. Absurdity, therefore, cannot be thought of as something a priori negative or even reprehensible.

Moreover, I would even say that on some levels, the experience of absurdity may seem to move things forward. In many cases, it is precisely this sensation of distance and alienation from the world, of having abandoned the conventional stereotypes of experience on which the superficial and mystified meaning of the world is based, that opens the door to genuinely fresh, sharp and penetrating vision—vision that particularizes; and this particularizing vision is precisely what can put us face-to-face with truth and therefore—through its "capacity for doubt"—can uncover as well the real weight that "meaning" has. (Some may have wondered—to return to myself—at the apparent contradiction between my "absurd" writing and my "idealism" in other things; perhaps this explanation will be illuminating.)

My seventh mood, however unpleasant, has yet another (rather practical) positive side: by creating a gap between me and my surroundings, it protects me in a sense. When I observe my surroundings in this way, I am less superficially vulnerable than someone who is fully "involved," caught up in the turbulence of random events and his immediate response to them. In short, I am less submerged, and so can manage to keep my head above water, which enables me to see better and—perhaps—to bear witness more effectively.

*

. . . Most of the time I don't have any of the fifteen moods I have written or will write about; they are only some obvious—and terribly simplified—"outcroppings" of my general existence in the world. The vast majority of my moods, however, remain undescribed because they are not outstanding or obvious in any way. I simply am, I move through space and time, I tend to my affairs while thoughts of all kinds chase about in my mind—and that's the end of it. As with my general meditations—and perhaps even more so—these reflections must be treated with reserve: everything I write applies, but at the same time it doesn't apply; everything is as I say it is, yet it is also quite different, and in describing one of my traits, I suppress twenty others. If I persist, it is only because I hope what I write may interest you, though it may provide only the occasional flash of insight into the atmosphere of my present life.

Kisses, Vašek

74

April 4, 1981

Dear Olga,

I'm in a fine mood because I've received three nice letters (from you, from Ivan and from Květa—thanks to you all!), because I can feel spring outside, and because I am physically well (due also to the vitamins you brought—bring them again next time!). And so I am trying to see signs of good rather than bad in other things as well. There was a brief hiatus in my writing, but I may return to my moods again, because when I start something, I like to finish it. Today, however, I'm going to jump somewhere else.

*

I've already mentioned in various contexts a certain sphere of traits that I have always had but which have become far clearer and more obvious to me here: I mean my courtesy, my extravagant politeness, my timidity, my tendency to embarrass easily, my anxiety, my frequently inappropriate thoughtfulness, my respect for those in authority and my apprehensiveness in dealing with them, etc. In a way all these qualities derive from my instinctive lack of self-confidence and my continuing uncertainty as to whether I am accepted by those around me, and they appear to be in sharp contrast to many other traits no less characteristic, and even with my entire life so far. (I will explain this apparent contradiction later.)

None of us knows, of course, how much of his temperament can be attributed to heredity and how much to environment. Still, I'm more and more convinced that two determinable things, at least, had an important influence on the development of those traits—and in fact on my entire relationship with the world. As a "gentleman's son" I had a rather privileged childhood—particularly when we lived in Moravia. I enjoyed many advantages that other children did not have, and greater care was lavished on me at home than is usual or even possible in other circumstances, such care being chiefly administered by people of a so-called lower social standing. I have no intention of playing the poor little rich boy and portraying my childhood in a wealthy family as more difficult than that of children in poor families; I only want to describe the influence this pampering really had on me. The impact was precisely the opposite of what one might expect. The social divide separating me both from the other children and from the grown-ups in my world not only failed to instill in me a feeling of superiority, I actually felt it as a handicap, a wrong, an injustice. It made me constantly feel inferior. Without wanting to be, I was thrust into a position that excluded me from my surroundings, isolated me behind an invisible wall and alienated me from people; it caused the world, quite rightly, to mistrust me, and very likely to ridicule me behind my back. No one ever let me know these things directly, but that made it all the worse: I had an unarticulated feeling that there was some carefully concealed conspiracy against me and what was more, I felt it was justified. After all, why should I, of all people, have more than anyone else? Children are surprisingly perceptive and sensitive to such things, without of course understanding them or being able to express them. (I remember fighting tooth and nail to put an end to some minor privilege—yet I was unable to explain why I felt so strongly about it.) It may seem paradoxical, but I think that because of those early experiences I have always had a heightened sensitivity and aversion to various manifestations of social inequality, and to privilege in general.

The second significant circumstance was the fact that I was fat. It's well known that a community of children, whose behavior is somehow closer to nature and therefore guided more by primitive instincts than moral awareness, has a tendency—like some animal packs—to exclude individuals who are less physically fit or otherwise handicapped in some way. I was not handicapped, I was just a well-fed piglet who had difficulty not only climbing (I still can't climb to this day), but even jumping across a creek or turning a somersault. This gave the other children a welcome opportunity to tease me endlessly, and sometimes to engage in various forms of persecution, regarded by all but me as mere pranks. I recall, for instance, that at one point it was a favorite pastime in our class to slap my chubby thighs. Two factors complemented each other well: instinctual mistrust of a classmate from a rich family found in my chubbiness a marvelous opportunity for unwitting "social revenge." (I don't blame my parents for this; they always did what they thought best and if they did anything wrong, it was quite unintentional. They too were prisoners of their social milieu and its customs and had no way of knowing that their excessive concern for my welfare would have such an outcome.)

As the years go by, it becomes clearer to me that these ancient experiences caused me to feel—vaguely, somewhat subconsciously and not particularly tragically, yet irradicably and in everything that I do—that I am, in a fundamental and essential way, a little bit "outside the order of the world," that in fact I'm always running along (like that well-fed piglet) a short distance behind my marching classmates, trying to catch up and take my place with the others as a fully fledged and equal member of that moving body, and that I am powerless to do otherwise. Along with this goes a deeply rooted feeling that however indisputable the places I do have in the "order of the world" may seem, they are still essentially uncertain and problematic. It's as though I were never quite sure that my inclusion in the world won't turn out to be illusory, fraudulent and temporary, as though I were still secretly expecting, sooner or later, to be exposed as an interloper and driven out in ridicule. It's as though in a tiny corner of my mind, I still suspected the world of suspecting me of something, of not completely believing in me and quietly making fun of me behind my back, as though I needed to persuade the world of my good intentions, to justify my existence and protest my innocence. Yet with it goes a gnawing question: have I not, in the final analysis, been rightly excluded (or rather, not excluded by mistake) and do I not in fact have a fatal flaw that prevents me from merging wholly with the order of things?

This explanation, I realize, may well puzzle those who know me, and invite polemics, counterarguments or doubts, and may easily be seen as a pose or a form of self-stylization, but this is only because it is incomplete. It deals with a single side of the matter and refers to qualities outside their wider context. Someday, perhaps, I will manage to correct that impression and explain, among other things, why this feeling of being "outside the order" has not just been a lifelong source of self-doubts, but also a lifelong wellspring of energy directed at continually improving my self-definition. It is more, therefore, than just the root of many of my inadequacies; it is also a decisive force behind everything worthwhile I have managed to accomplish. Just as my sense of the absurd both distances me from the world and also compels me to enter into it to an ever-increasing degree, so my uncertainty about myself compels me—often in a rather breakneck fashion—to prove myself over and over again.

*

And now for something I thought of while writing this letter and that concerns you: not only was our marriage (a hundred years ago) an act, among other things, signifying my definitive emancipation from dependence on my mother and through her, on the social milieu of my family, but when we began to "go out" together (two hundred years ago) it marked the moment when I (perhaps) overcame the "fat boy" stereotype. Such things may be superficial, but they symbolize far more.

Kisses, Vašek

75

April 12, 1981

Dear Olga,

Thanks for your letter of April 2. I feel better at once when I get a letter every week; in any case, I've been meaning to write you for some time now to make weekly letter writing a rule—it's truly important for me and I believe it's within your powers. . . .

*

From what I wrote last time, one might well conclude that I see myself as thoroughly unsteady, uncertain, hesitant, endlessly doubting everything and inclined to believe anything that casts doubt on myself. Such an impression, as you well know, would be quite wrong. Though it may seem paradoxical at first, just the opposite is true. Oddly enough, in some ways I am extremely steadfast, persevering, tenacious, purposeful, I'd even be so bold as to say indestructible. (You know very well how obstinate I can be; it used to upset you, especially when that obstinacy was fixed on something of marginal importance.) True, there are many things that do not amuse or interest me and I can be pretty ignorant about them; but when my mind is made up or I get fired up about something, I am capable of giving over my entire being to it, regardless of personal cost, and I follow it through to the end. I don't like things begun and not finished, I don't like halfheartedness or evasive maneuvering, I can't stand disorder. Certainly my life has taken many strange twists and turns; I may not always have invested in the right things and in the right way; in the positions I have taken and the things I have said many contradictions, excesses or naivetés can no doubt be found, and I'm more acutely aware of them, understandably, than anyone else. Yet when I think about it, two things about me can't be denied: that somewhere behind those twists and turns there is a clear, lifelong continuity; and secondly—even though sometimes, for whatever reason, I've found myself on the wrong path, I've always managed to extricate myself and end up once more where I should have been in the first place.

Different factors have obviously had an influence here. In my youth, for example, I was never given anything for nothing and much of what others took for granted (an education, for instance) I achieved only through great defiance and obstinacy. That, I think, was an important schooling of my will and perseverance. And to give some credit to my bourgeois origins, which all my life have brought me nothing but complications (it was precisely these obstacles which proved of benefit, but that, of course, is another matter), even when—paradoxically—I was in a state of vehement inner revolt against everything bourgeois around me, I cannot rule out the fact that my own "relentlessness," my "indestructibility," my unshakable (because entirely anti-illusionary) faith that things have a meaning, and finally my special ability to extricate myself, somehow, from hopeless situations (and even to profit from them) are related to that traditional quality of middle-classness (particularly in the era of liberalism), which is the ability to take risks, the courage to start all over again from nothing, the ever vital hope and élan to begin new enterprises.

But this still does not answer the main question: how can such contradictory qualities exist in a single person?

Naturally I can't provide an exhaustive answer (if only because no human personality can be converted to a clear mathematical model or equation, in which everything is brought into logical concord), nevertheless I still feel strongly that these are merely two sides of the same coin. In other words: my constant uncertainty about my place in the "order of things" may be precisely what compels me, with more determination than someone who is sure of his place, to define, develop and strengthen my position, to defend and bear witness to my truth, to stand up for myself and my cause. It would seem that the more one doubts oneself, one's involvement in the world and everything one does, the more energy one must put into overcoming those doubts and defending oneself and one's cause before their judgment.

Put this way it may seem rather schematic, but let's not forget some of my other more concrete qualities, inclinations and interests, where the connection is clearer. For instance, is not my well-known passion for bringing people together, reconciling them and functioning as a "social binding agent" an obvious expression of a heightened longing for harmony and for a creative role in it? And does not the same apply to many of my other eccentricities, from my pedantic fondness for rational structures (obvious, for instance, in the architecture of my plays) to my delight in giving dinner parties for my friends? Or, is not another of my faces (somewhat hidden today, to be sure)—that of a "merry drinking companion," a carouser, a bit of a high-stepper, even, some suspect, with inclinations to Don Juanism—also just an expression of my unconscious need to confirm and strengthen my sense of "inclusion"? And is not, ultimately, my lifelong steadfastness in my relationship with you only another consequence of the same thing, or (to draw from a different barrel) my sometimes rather dubious attempt to be on the good side of everyone and my enduring inability to come to terms with the fact that it simply can't be done? And I could go on and on.

It seems, then, that my problematic relationship to "order" is thoroughly dialectic: it is, to the same degree, a source of depression, fits of self-flagellation and negative lapses, and the source of an unceasing effort to help create that "order" in one way or another and to share in it in enduring and meaningful ways. The final effect of this dialectic is that my life is bound up in paradoxes, one of the greatest of which is that I am continually flinging myself with a passion into undertakings I know will cause me difficulties that I will bear with greater hardship than most of those who would never dream of attempting such a thing in the first place. But more than that: the greater these hardships, the more determined I am, oddly enough, not to try to avoid them or ease their burden in some inappropriate way. And if the past two years have definitively put me off any kind of moralizing and made me loath to pass judgment on anyone, then my aversion has deepened in roughly the same degree to the thought that I myself should, in anything essential, ever behave like a coward.

*

The situation I face these days is—as you must know—rather unclear (at least for me) and conceals within itself, to the same degree, both the possibility that my life will be essentially tougher than it has been so far, and the possibility that it will take a turn for the better. As a matter of course, I always reckon with the worse alternative, without losing any of my faith. . . .

Your, Vašek

76

April 16, 1981

Dear Olga,

Due to the lack of reliable information I still don't know if I should consider my new situation as an auspicious development or not. It has had one tangibly unpleasant effect for me in the sense that I have been "orphaned," but evaluating it generally, that is not the essential thing; under certain circumstances I could even bear the burden of my "orphanhood" gladly and in good spirits. But whatever the situation is, one thing is clear now: it is three times as important, and almost vitally essential, that you write me more often, which means at least one letter full of detail a week.

*

In recent letters I have used the notion of "order" several times (the order of the world, the order of things, etc.). As I was sewing my trousers today, it occurred to me that I should explain, to you and myself, a little of what that notion means to me.

The meaning of an abstract notion like order understandably changes and shifts with each new context, and at the same time, it relies on such subtle matters as the tone and coloration of that context (the more so when the context is a series of epistolary reflections of a literary nature and not the conceptually rigorous constructions of a philosopher). Still, I would say that the notion of order has—for me personally at least—four main and clearly distinguishable meanings. In other words, we can talk about something like "the four orders."

Behind all phenomena and discrete entities in the world, we may observe, intimate or experience existentially in various ways something like a general "order of Being." The essence and meaning of this order are veiled in mystery; it is as much an enigma as the Sphinx, it always speaks to us differently and always, I suppose, in ways that we ourselves are open to, in ways, to put it simply, that we can hear.

Alongside the general miracle of Being—both as a part of that miracle and as its protagonist, as a special reiteration of it and a rebellious attempt to know, understand, control and transcend it—stands the miracle of the human spirit, of human existence. Into the infinite silence of the omnipresent order of Being, then, there sounds the impassioned voice of the order of human freedom, of life, of spirit. The subtly structured world of meaningful and hopeful human life, opening new vistas of freedom and carrying man to a deeper experience of Being, the countless remarkable intellectual (mystical, religious, scientific) and moral systems, that special way in which the order of Being both re-creates and, at the same time, lends its own meaning to mythology (in earlier times) and artistic creation (today, i.e., in the historical period), in short the way in which man becomes man in the finest sense of the word—all of this constitutes the "order of life," "the order of the spirit," "the order of human work." Together, it all constitutes an objectivized expression of that "second creation of the world," which is human existence.

I would say that this "order of life" is a kind of "legitimate son" of "the order of Being," because it grows out of an indestructible faith in the latter's meaning and a fearless confrontation with its mystery.

Over and against this passionate order, which is the work of people created "in God's image," there constantly recurs its evil caricature and misshapen protagonist, "the bastard son of Being," the offspring of indifference to the meaning of Being and vindictive fear of its mystery: the chilling work of man as "the image of the devil": the order of homogenization by violence, perfectly organized impotence and centrally directed desolation and boredom, in which man is conceived as a cybernetic unit without free will, without the power to reason for himself, without a unique life of his own, and where that monstrous ideal, order, is a euphemism for the graveyard. (I refer you to Fromm's excellent analysis of fascism.)

Thus against "the order of life," sustained by a longing for meaning and an experience of the mystery of Being, there stands this "order of death," a monument to non-sense, an executioner of mystery, a materialization of nothingness.

The fourth and final order is the one I had in mind during my recent reflections on myself. It is nothing more and nothing less than the real order of things, of human things above all, the reality around us, its rules, customs, circumstances, relationships—just as they are, which means full of variety, contradictions, complexities, with everything that is good and bad, pretty and ugly, meaningful and absurd. It is simply the "mishmash of everything" that we call life. It includes not only the sphere of established practices, customs, conventions, prejudices and habits, etc., but also the sphere of natural and healthy demands and reasonable expectations. It is a certain system of activity into which one may enter responsibly or irresponsibly, to fulfill the best in oneself or to realize the worst; to change that order for the better or to develop everything in it that is base, distorted and alienating. But regardless of how he does it or of the quality of his intentions, man may enter and find a place in this order easily, authentically, spontaneously and with supreme confidence, or on the contrary, he may find his efforts from start to finish accompanied by degrees of uncertainty, doubts or a gnawing sensation of his own strangeness.

To return to myself: some might understand my notorious love of order and my fondness for harmonic structures as a kind of necrophilic love for "the order of death." I would protest, of course: my heightened need to include myself in the "order of things" (in the fourth sense of the word, that is) expresses itself in an intensifying effort to participate in "the order of life" and at the same time, to challenge what threatens it most, that is, "the order of death."

*

Well, there's room left over, so I'll add some concrete details of my life (it's been quite a while since I've done that): it's Easter now and once again I'm battling a cold (though the worst of it, apparently, is over). I'm treating myself, mainly with tea, which reminds me of an important thing: I've discovered that over time my tea loses its characteristic aroma and taste—obviously because it's only in that bag—so that after a month it scarcely differs from any of its less exotic counterparts. You might think, therefore, about putting the tea in some appropriate containers, perhaps those large tins they sometimes sell it in (I think they hold half a kilo, so two would do). This time, unfortunately, it would increase the weight, but next time you could bring me the tea in a bag again and I would transfer it to the tins. . . .

I read Malaparte's *Kaput* and liked it a lot, among other things for the odd way it manipulates space and time: it is a kind of anatomy of the crisis of European moral consciousness and it takes place at various times during the war and at various—vastly different—places in Europe. I've always been excited by the mystery of time and space; one of my ancient collections of poems, written some twenty-six years ago, was called *Spaces and Times*. Since then it has continued to fascinate me—right down to *The Mountain Hotel*. By freely manipulating space and time, you can create very special atmospheres, tones, coherences, feelings and impressions—which, by the way, is one of the thousands of ways in which the "order of the spirit" tests its strength, as it were, with the "order of Being." Otherwise I've read a biography of K. H. Franke (which confirmed for me again that cruelty and cowardice are natural sisters), and now I'm reading a biography of Toulouse-Lautrec. At the same time I'm trying—for at least an hour every other day—to work on my English and German.

*

I've just realized an odd thing: because I don't fight with anyone, avoid pushing and shoving in crowded situations, and because no one shakes hands here, my only physical contact with people (not counting accidentally bumping into someone, and dreams, of course) has, for two years now, been our greetings and farewells during visits. I suppose one begins to realize such things only after some time.

I kiss you, Your Vašek

77

April 26, 1981

Dear Olga,

A brief addendum to my last letter: a natural scientist might object (with typical blindness) that what I call "the order of death" is not an entirely illegitimate progeny of the "order of Being" because in fact it is only an application of the second law of thermodynamics, that is, a reflection of the tendency in the universe toward entropic death. That objection would completely miss the point for several reasons, the main one being that we don't know at all whether this tendency we ascribe to the whole universe may not just be some hopelessly superficial "microaspect"—accessible to modern physics in its present state—of quite different processes, infinitely more complex and general, which may only apply in some spatiotemporal and material-structural fraction of the universe. But even so, man—and the entire biosphere—is heading in essentially the opposite direction: toward greater uniqueness, variety and more complex and refined structures that constantly disrupt and surpass particular systemic levels to establish newer and higher levels of "order" (in which each higher order gives meaning to the order below it). Every attempt by man, therefore, to oppose that tendency is a negation of his own essence, a betrayal of consciousness and a destructive act of self-denial. (To this hypothetical objection of the natural scientist, I have merely reacted in a way comprehensible to natural scientists, that is, superficially.) (Ivan, forgive me, I don't think of you as a natural scientist, but a normal person with an interest in natural science.)

. . .

78

May 1, 1981

Dear Olga,

. . .

It's May Day, and I'm celebrating it by the kind of work I enjoy most, that is, continuing to write about myself.

While one's persuasions do not automatically give an exact or exhaustive picture of what one is (on the contrary, the picture may often be somewhat misleading and distorted), they are nevertheless an integral part of human identity (being always related, somehow, to one's general makeup, character, experiences, etc.), and therefore, under-standably, they also reveal something about a person, though only in the context of everything else he is, or rather, of how he lives and acts. My account of myself, therefore, would be incomplete without a simplified, abbreviated account of what is understood by my "persuasions."

To begin with: I have never created, or accepted, any comprehensive "worldview," let alone any complete, unified, integrated and self-contained philosophical, ideological or other system of beliefs which, with no further adjustments, I could then identify with and which would provide answers to all my questions. This was certainly not out of apathy (it is not difficult to take refuge beneath the protective wing of a ready-made system, and it may even simplify one's life considerably), nor on the contrary, out of any overanxious desire to take my stand, come what may, outside all currents of thought. It was simply because something very deep inside me has always resisted such an approach; I simply don't seem to have the internal capacity for it.

The origin of this "inability" is obviously something in my constitution, in how I am internally structured, as it were. I have already written you about what faith means to me: it is simply a particular state of mind, that is, a state of persistent and productive openness, of persistent questioning, a need to "experience the world," again and again, in as direct and unmediated a way as possible, and it does not, therefore, flow into me from some concretely defined outside object. For me, perseverance and continuity do not come from fixating on unchanging "convictions" but rather from a ceaseless process of searching, demystification and penetration beneath the surface of phenomena in ways that do not depend on allegiance to given, ready-made methodology. My entire "experience of the world" has persuaded me of the mysterious multiformity and infinite "elusiveness" of the order of Being, which—by its very nature and by the very nature of the human mind—simply cannot be grasped and described by a consistent system of knowledge. By this I don't mean to denigrate the significance of philosophical concepts; many I find fascinating for their penetrating insights and even their capacity to speak personally to me. Still, I can't bring myself to accept them if it means closing the door to other concepts, or reinterpreting other concepts to conform to what I had already accepted. The order of Being has many facets; it can be regarded from many different points of view and experienced on many different levels;

it is not within the powers of the "order of the spirit" to grasp it entirely—that is, to reveal its secrets. To do that would require, de facto, an act of absolute merging, and that would mean the end of the "order of the spirit," if not of the "order of Being" as well—total death. All one can do—and in any case, this is what creates the essence and the beauty of the whole adventure of the spirit—is to touch, for better or for worse, a particular level of reality, and apply and develop a particular way of looking at it and experiencing it.

But to be more specific: it seems to me foolish, impossible and utterly pointless, for instance, to try to reconcile Darwin with Christ, or Marx with Heidegger, or Plato with Buddha. Each of them represents a certain level of Being and human experience and each bears witness to the world in his own particular way; each of them, to some extent and in some way, speaks to me, explains many things to me, and even helps me to live, and I simply don't see why, for the sake of one, I should be denied an authentic experience of whatever another can show me, even more so because we are not talking here about different opinions on the same thing, but different ways of talking about very different things. I am simply advocating a kind of "parallelism" or "pluralism" in knowledge. So-called contradictions between different systems of thought do not bother me in the least, and it doesn't seem at all perverse to conduct oneself quite "situationally" in that regard. If a certain term, or terminology or theory seems apt in a given situation or context, I have no compunctions whatsoever about exploiting it to the full (and I don't mind if it makes me seem like an epigone). At the same time, however, I don't feel the least bit bound by any "allegiance," and in a different situation or context, I will use, just as brazenly, something entirely different, something that seems more precise and appropriate. I would say this is more an artistic than a scientific approach. Of eclecticism I have no fear whatever; such fears can only bother someone who is unsure of himself, who does not believe in the steadfastness of his standards of plausibility or precision, in his own reason and its natural continuity, quite simply, in his own identity. (The uncertainties of my own that I've written you about belong to a different tribe: they have more to do with my social anchoring.)

The more slavishly and dogmatically a person falls for a ready-made ideological system or "worldview," the more certainly he will bury all chances of thinking, of freedom, of being clear about what he knows, the more certainly he will deaden the adventure of the mind and the more certainly—in practice—he will begin to serve the "order of death." In any case, the moment when any system of thought culminates and declares itself complete, when it is brought to perfection and universality, has more than once been described as that deceptive moment when the system ceases to live, collapses in upon itself (like the material collapse of a white dwarf star) and reality eludes its grasp once and for all.

Of course: knowledge and convictions, as they are called, do not come from detached observation alone, but from lively involvement and inner experience as well; in other words, they are existential and unique. Therefore I, and anyone else, will always find certain opinions and clusters of opinion and ways of thinking and seeing closer to our own than others: but that, obviously, is quite different from mere identification with a fixed system.

In short: a great many thinkers appeal to me and speak to me, some more, some less—from Klíma to Husserl, from Kant to Camus, from Hegel to Šafařík. The more or less of it is not accidental, of course, and if it made any sense to do so (which on the whole it does not), it could probably be determined with relative precision why I feel closer to some ideas than to others, why I have a clear opinion on some things and none at all on others, and why some things leave me completely cold. Such an analysis would reveal something general about my persuasions and certainly about my "identity," but it would hardly prove that I belong to or even acknowledge the flag of any "worldview," or that I belong in any pigeonhole.

My distaste for ready-made structures of opinion (or rather for passive acceptance of them) goes so far that if, in some context, I choose or borrow a certain term or category, I try the next time to avoid it if at all possible—that's how much I fear that some meaningful and useful concept might gradually become a mere incantation that would only end up obscuring reality.

Kisses, Vašek

P.S. A record by the Bee Gees has come out; you should certainly buy it!!

79

Dear Olga,

For two long weeks now I've had no letter from you (the last one I received was written almost a month ago!). A fine way to exacerbate my sentence! I'm wallowing in a mire of ignorance, which of course only deepens my "orphanhood" and increases my worry about what is happening at home. This joyless situation has determined the theme of today's letter.

*

I once wrote you about what my home means to me, about the ways I miss it, and how the role played for me by the world I've been torn out of is changing. A counterpart of sorts to that theme is the question of what my imprisonment means to me, and what role it plays in my life.

I have learned to pay no more attention than is necessary and normal to prison and the fact that I am here: I take an interest in it only to the degree that—first—is indispensable to living here without unnecessary problems and—secondly—derives from my natural curiosity about my human and social milieu, a curiosity I would feel anywhere, at any time. Still, the questions I posed above have led me to a surprising discovery: the fact of my imprisonment—not as a phenomenon in itself, but in its various concrete manifestations, consequences and related factors—affects my life far more than I would have assumed at first sight. To begin with, it permeates every aspect of my everyday life: it establishes my daily schedule with great exactness, and from morning till evening influences to a greater or lesser extent all my activities, their intentions, the conditions under which they take place, their scope; it affects my demeanor and behavior, it shapes my habits and routines, the conduct of my life, how I obtain what I need, do my personal chores—in short, it penetrates into everything that would normally be the province of one's personal responsibility for himself and his involvement in the world around him. Nor is that all: it more or less determines the character, the motifs, the circumstances and the expression of all my moods; it establishes my perspective on space and time; it gives a concrete aspect to my joys, hopes, aims, fears and afflictions, and to all the complications I have to contend with each day; it colors the criteria I apply in judging the many different phenomena and events that surround me; it gives concrete form to a large part of what sociologists call one's "value system." This ubiquitous, pervasive influence penetrates to the minutest details of what I do; for instance—to choose an illustration from one sphere of my life that touches you as well—it affects not only the content, scope and significance of my letters home, but also their style and even the handwriting. (You have certainly noticed that I try to write legibly.)

Understandably, one's surroundings always have an influence on one's daily life—but in very few places does this happen in as complex a way as it does here.

But the effects I describe here are far from exhausting the matter: oddly enough, my imprisonment is present as well in something apparently removed from all external factors, that is, in my inner life: what I think about and what gives that inner life sustenance. Regardless of what I reflect upon, traces of the fact of my imprisonment can always be found in the perspective of those reflections and in the shading of my emotions; it is always there, a particular dimension or aspect of them, trapped inside them as if by a spell. I can't escape it even in my sleep: bizarre resonances of it filter into almost all my dreams. Nor can I escape it even when I am carried away by some cultural experience, a good movie or book; a subtle analysis of these experiences would be conclusive.

The concrete consequences and aspects of my imprisonment provide—of necessity—a self-evident, inevitable framework, background or "system of coordinates" for the whole of my present sojourn in the world, for my entire existence—regardless of whether the focus happens to be on the problems of my immediate life in this place or on various aspects of my life or standing "in general." This framework, of course, does not change me, my mind, my character or my "identity" in any remarkable way. It merely forms that peculiar terrain through which I am destined to go, adjusting my step to every change in topography. This does not make me someone else, it just means that I have to move in a rather special way, metaphorically speaking. And indeed: apart from a few marginal indications of an internal shift that has deepened the way I think (and my awe) of various human matters, and except for a few generally negligible details (such as, for instance, my growing distaste for all sexual and erotic banter, or my tendency to forget certain facts), I have not observed any marked changes in myself. Perhaps I am beginning to take certain values more seriously, responsibly, thoughtfully—but I can't be sure, and I won't know until I'm free again. Judging by my letters, you may think I've grown serious and lost my sense of irony and humor, but that is an optical illusion that comes from the natural limitations of how I express myself.

In many ways, of course, prison life is incomparably harder than anything I have ever experienced before. (If I say "in many ways," it means of course not in every way!) Even so, I feel no more generally and persistently despondent, sorrowful, hopeless than anywhere else; I still seem the same; it's just that the range of what can bring me joy and what depresses me has radically altered. A kind word, a letter from home, a cigarette smoked in peace and quiet, an uninterrupted hour of interesting reading—such things, in my present circumstances, can delight me as only the richest and fullest experiences can outside.

If the fact of my imprisonment has so fully permeated my present life in its details, then as such—i.e., as a complete and self-contained "phenomenon in and of itself"—it comes near me only in a single solitary instance: when I am overpowered (this happens only rarely and it never becomes especially drastic) by a general apprehensiveness at being closed away and cut off from "real activity" and "the real world." It seems that only when I am in this mood (a bad mood, of course, the final one I wanted to write about) do I experience, in a direct and existential way, the fact of having been deprived of my freedom and surrounded by wire; in other words, it is my only pure and specific prison mood. And yet what bothers me is not so much the fact that I can't (at this very moment) go for a walk, arrange something, go somewhere, but the fact that even if I desperately needed to, I couldn't. That is logically connected to the sensation of helplessness and my amplified fear that something inauspicious is happening in my world—to you or around you or to others close to me—and I can't be there to assess the situation and share it, face it and try to ward off its ill effects. Suddenly, I feel dumb, crippled or bound in some way. It is not simple claustrophobia (I didn't even suffer from that while I was awaiting trial), it is a deeper and more intrinsic sensation, rooted in my spirit and not merely in my nervous system.

I repeat, I'm not in this mood often and so far it has only appeared in very weak, gentle forms. But if I receive no news from home, there is, naturally, a danger that it will get worse. Thus saying, I have cleverly come round, toward the end of my letter, to where I began. Perhaps this will move you—

―――――――

A small addendum to the last letter: it may do no harm, after all, to illustrate my too general remarks with an example: Claude Tresmontant, in his book *The Bible and the Classical Tradition* (we have it at home), presents a very lucid exposition of how the Judeo-Christian way of thinking and biblical metaphysics differ from the thinking and the metaphysics of antiquity and the whole tradition of European philosophy that grew out of classical philosophy. If I had to say which of these two ways is nearer to my own, I would reply without hesitation that it is the Judeo-Christian way, with its concreteness and its respect for the world of the senses; but I would add at once that I do not feel bound to identify with it entirely or that nothing from the classical tradition (which includes the great German systems like Kant's, Hegel's and Marx's) has anything to say to me. These different approaches, it seems to me, have simply grown out of different experiences of the world and perspectives on it and capture different aspects of Being. I feel open to both. . . .

*

Despite your aversion to writing, I kiss you.
Your Vašek

80

May 16, 1981

Dear Olga,

Well, a letter from you finally arrived but unfortunately it wasn't given to me (because, as I was informed, you went beyond family matters and included various greetings). So I can only go on waiting. Never mind, please don't take it as a reprimand, but merely a sigh, for lack of news and worry about you. I wouldn't want my letters to seem like an endless rebuke; I know your life is not easy and I appreciate more than I've let on that you have not only accepted the circumstances I've brought upon you, with all the personal sacrifice involved, but also that you are constant and faithful in the deeper sense as well, that is, that you are not looking out only for yourself, to survive with dignity in this situation—a respectable enough aim in itself—but on the contrary that you are trying to help others and be useful. I think about you and Ivan a lot now and I firmly believe that some of the strange and unsettling things you are encountering—because you belong with me—will not develop into anything more serious. In short, the tender joy I feel because of your bravery is joined to a constant fear for your safety. The former feeling commands me to be gentle with you and refrain from rebuking you; the latter feeling, on the contrary, compels me to demand constantly that you write more often. Please take it in that spirit and bear with me—

*

Perhaps because I've been rather nervous recently, it would be best if I were to write about my good moods.

My most frequent (and somehow fundamental) good mood occurs when things go my way. I suppose this is true of everyone, and not just in prison. It happens most often when the work I do is going well (which is not always the case; it depends on a lot of external factors too, but also, of course, on the condition I'm in). It need not, however, concern only work. As you know, I'm an inveterate planner and I need to be able to think things out in advance as much as possible and to "proceed" according to some conception. There is an enormous opportunity to satisfy this need here because successfully attending to one's many minor obligations, necessities and pleasures is of course far more complicated here than on the outside (especially for me, since I'm bound by many personal habits, phobias and unusual hygienic obligations, and since every trifle is practically a ceremony). So if I am to arrange such things successfully, with as little fuss and loss of time and energy as possible, I have to work out well in advance what has to be done and how and when to do it. If I can manage this and perhaps even go beyond my plan, then that in itself is usually the guarantee of a good mood.

*

Yes, I know: those are precisely the traits that might lead some to suspect I really belong to the "order of death," that I am a fanatical supporter of system, of bureaucratic clarity, of maximum intelligibility, in short, of the kind of moribund "nonactivity" that would slam the door on all chance occurrence, all diversity and exception, all surprise, all mystery and all freedom—in other words, everything that displays some novelty, evolution, life. Now, it would be an utter misconception to believe that all forms of order are automatically manifestations of the "order of death." The mere fact that something is structured is not the essential thing here, but rather why and how it is structured. If the structure is an end in itself, or rather, if its only meaning is to be most consistently what it is, itself, which means endlessly augmenting and strengthening the type of order proper to it, then it is in fact more than a phenomenal manifestation of the "order of death." If, however, it is a means, a visible face, a phase or an aspect of something else, something more, something beyond and above itself, that is, if it refers not just to itself but beyond itself as well (for instance, by throwing open the question of its own meaning), then on the contrary, it is a manifestation of the "order of life," or rather the "order of Being" itself. After all, it is only from something structured to some degree that the evidence—sometimes legible only "between the lines"—of higher structures may appear or germinate. Only reality that is somehow structured can form the backdrop or be the external manifestation of a higher structure, one that can in turn give it meaning. And after all, we can only identify the otherwise incomprehensible signs of the higher meta-structure against the backdrop of the lower structure's comprehensibility. In short, mystery would be unthinkable without some kind of order, because how else do mysteries and miracles declare themselves, except by deviating from a given order, thus providing a disturbing insight into the unknown territory of the "higher structures"?

But to be specific: if, for example, conventions and structures are characteristic of my plays (e.g., the mechanical and geometric patterns that occur in the dialogue), then this was only because I was attempting, through them and against the backdrop they provided, to give dramatic shape to a particular question, surprise, mystery or shock—either by developing those patterns ad absurdum or, on the contrary, by gradually breaking them down. In any case, I've often said that where everything is permitted, nothing can surprise, that conventions can only be challenged or broken down when they already exist, that mystery has the power to disturb only on the carefully constructed terrain of transparency. Transcendence can only take place when there is something to transcend; chaos and caprice make nothing possible and point nowhere, unless to indicate the way down, to lower levels of structuredness, to greater "sameness," in other words—again—the way to death. I don't suppose I'm explaining this very well, though perhaps what I'm trying to say is clear: that there's simply no order like order.

Of course my basic good mood can be brought on by more than just a combination of successfully executed plans. Often it's enough not to come up against anything bad, not to have some of my forebodings confirmed, or to have the ground that is laid by relative calm, the absence of complications and good health suddenly fertilized by an auspicious microevent. If this good mood comes over me, I suddenly become very active and enterprising, I am full of élan, enthusiasm and energy, even for the kind of activities I normally avoid or at least try to put off. Gone is my awkwardness, my distaste for dealing with things, asking for things or explaining things and even my occasional muted states in which I find it hard to express myself coherently and well. To my surprise, I become supremely confident, bold, eloquent and perhaps even witty (though that is not for me to judge), I have a ready response to everything, I can deftly deflect a jocular attack, comment aptly on things around me, that is, in a way that does not demean myself, yet such that those around me can accept what I say, gratefully, even though it may not flatter them. In short, I can take things the way I would like to take them always: spontaneously, maintaining the proper balance between interest and sportsmanlike objectivity, between humane compassion and a particularizing distance, between personal involvement and the analytical viewpoint of a spectator.

Somewhere in the background of all this, however, is a feeling that I would say is the most profound source of any good mood, for anyone, at any time: that is, the feeling that one's life is fundamentally meaningful and the hope that is implicit within that. It is a joyous identification with life. And everything that a short while ago had still upset, angered or filled me with longing suddenly upsets me no longer. Even my sentence doesn't seem as endless as before, and I am almost persuaded (quite falsely, unfortunately, but at the same time, in an extraordinarily healthy way) that only a few more happy events stand between me and my release. (Incidentally, I have discovered a new way to "shorten" my sentence: I simply imagine that the time I've already served never was, that I've just been sentenced, and only to what time actually remains—which at this point is two and a half years. That, of course, is not a long sentence at all and so I have a reason to be happy.)

I think of you more than I ever have before, I'm looking forward to seeing you and I kiss you—

Your, Vašek

81

May 23, 1981

Dear Olga,

Finally (after a month!) I've received news from you. The gap in your writing is of course fully excused, even though its cause was exactly what made me so impatient and therefore such a nag. If you can paint the flat, you would seem to be well in spite of everything, which understandably delights me. There must be some truth in what they say, that women—contrary to what one would expect—can take some things better than men.

. . . I got your letter on the 19th and so the news that I had a world premiere on the 20th came just in time for me to work myself into a proper state of opening-night nerves. When I came back from the afternoon shift that day and assumed that the performance would already be over, I celebrated it (not knowing, of course, if there was anything to celebrate) with hot milk (powdered) and an American cigarette. . . .

*

I have one additional piece of good news: I received notification that the criminal proceedings brought against me in 1970 for subversion have been withdrawn. I'd long since forgotten all about it, and then recently I suddenly remembered it and wondered if they'd perhaps drop them. A day later the notification arrived! Otherwise there's nothing particularly new in my life; try as I might, I can't make the time go any faster, even though—on the whole—I shouldn't try too hard, given that I'll be forty-five this year! . . .

*

But now, back to the theme already broached: I was not being quite precise to speak of my good moods in the plural, for what they are, rather, is a variety of colorations, aspects or tendencies of a single, basic mood. I devoted the last letter to its most frequent variation. Next, I'd like to mention a complementary pair of moods defined chiefly by their opposing orientation in time: what might be called a "retrospective" and a "prospective" good mood.

In the first of these moods, I submerge myself—often for some time and rather deeply—in memories. I recall to mind different stages of my life and many specific experiences (chiefly the good ones, of course). What comes back most vividly is not a precise sequence of events, but the different atmospheres of those times, their spatial, intellectual, social and "period" dimensions. The specific memories are very vivid, of course, but they usually lack a correspondingly specific context; instead, they seem to emerge from a light haze and vanish into it again. Reminiscing in this way is not just indulging in sentimental self-intoxication with memories of better times. It has a strongly positive significance: it allows me to submit my life, which—it seems to me now—I had lived in a somewhat rushed and cavalier manner, to an "existential assessment" by reexperiencing it in a somewhat calmer and more focused way. It permits me—since I've found myself at this compulsory way station anyway—to examine the landscapes my life has taken me through, to get a better perspective on them, and to draw conclusions that will be useful when I continue my journey. One aspect—marginal, though rather peculiar—of these reminiscences: I occasionally have what might be called "olfactory quasi-hallucinations." Suddenly, my machine, my belongings, my fellow cell-mate or anything else seems to emit a smell that arouses, from a sleep of long years, the memory of something once associated with a similar odor; the muddy aroma of the Labe River when I was at boarding school in Poděbrady, or the smell of Ajda when she shakes the water from her fur after a swim in the pond, or the fragrance of the garden in my grandfather's villa in Zlín or the ozone emanations of the woods around Žďár after a storm, or the musty smell of old theatrical textiles mingled with make-up powder from my first years in the Theatre on the Balustrade, etc.

The "prospective" variation of my good mood is apparently an inevitable phenomenon in prison life and I suspect that everyone who has been here knows it: a daydream, inexhaustible and unfailingly fresh, about what those first few days after one's release will be like. I know it's a little foolish, utterly premature (in my case at least) and impractical; still, in normal people it is irrepressible, and it is, after all,

a natural, understandable, completely harmless and rather healthy phenomenon. It shows that one has not ceased to look forward to the
pleasures of life in freedom, in other words, that one hasn't become
bitter, indifferent or more adapted to life in prison than is healthy—in
short, that one hasn't lost one's vital connection with the outside world.
Essentially, it is only one of the faces of faith and hope in life—albeit
the most primitive, banal and superficial one—and that, I think, is
enough to fully justify this activity. And so for the million and first time
I imagine how we'll greet each other when I show up at home one day
and I'll talk a blue streak and you will deferentially (for the first few
hours, at least) tend to my every whim; and how, the first chance I get,
I'll sweat it all out of my system in the sauna and go for a swim in the
pool at Podolí (I hope that after all this time I won't sink to the bottom),
how my closest friends will welcome me back and we'll go somewhere
for a good dinner; how I'll embrace Zdeněk and drop in on Ivan and
regale you all with fascinating and witty stories and you'll all be wonderfully amazed and laugh heartily and perhaps even cry a little; how
I'll give a party for some friends, and another party for other friends;
how I'll waltz with Andulka to the theme song from *Dr. Zhivago;* how
amused I'll be that some of my successful cronies won't know which
way to look when we meet; how I'll sleep in for as long as I want in the
morning, have good coffee and rum for breakfast and then soak in the
bath and have you tell me all the news, how I'll listen to all my tapes
and records, drinking whiskey as I do, and read everything that (I hope)
you're carefully piling on my writing desk, and go on walks through
Malá Strana and on Petřín Hill (with the dogs) and visit my favorite bars
and shoot the breeze with Jirka Němec, Ivan Jirous, Honza Lopatka and
all my other faithful companions, and I'll go to The Two Suns for a beer
and pay my respects to Mr. Bondy, and I'll finally have an elegant suit
of clothes made to measure (all I have left are jeans), etc. These fantasies keep recurring whether you want them to or not, and they are
always exciting; I imagine them down to the finest detail, unperturbed
by the justifiable suspicion that everything will be different in the end
and not nearly as wonderful, because meanwhile "my" world is inevitably changing and because it has and will continue to have a thousand
things to do besides waiting for me and preparing the kind of welcome
I so preposterously dream of here, cut off from the reality of history,
as it were. But so as not to appear entirely foolish: I do think about
more serious matters now and again, of course—my position, my
plans, my writing, etc., but those are just normal, serious subjects of

normal, serious thinking; the real, infallible source of hopeful joy and endless anticipation really lies in this utterly down-to-earth prison day-dream about the first steps and the first days of freedom. What do you think? Will it be November 29, 1983? Or sooner, perhaps? Or later?

Kisses, Your Vašek

82

May 30, 1981

Dear Olga,

Your last letter and Ivan's last letter were not given to me, so all I can do is hope we can say all we have to say—especially the things that immediately concern us—during the visit. Today isn't the first, and it certainly won't be the last time I'll write about matters quite different from what I'd like to write about (it seems we both lead colorful lives); I've always found it difficult to push myself in a given direction; still, it should be easier this time—theoretically, at least—because in addition to the usual reasons, there is another one no less important: this is the last letter you'll receive before the visit, so to a certain extent it will influence the atmosphere of the visit, and since despite everything I'd like a good mood to prevail, it is appropriate that I continue writing, despite everything, about my good moods.

*

There are many books, television programs and films that, for a variety of reasons, catch my interest. Infrequently, however, something not only catches my interest, but thrills me as well (interestingly enough, it needn't always be a work of art; a good essay may do the same); in short, I have a supreme artistic experience. When it happens, though, it's certainly worth it: suddenly, I feel moved to tears, not emotionally, or not only that (I can be moved by the silliest things, as you can)—it's more like sudden happiness. My tears are oddly mingled with laughter and they have a common source: a delight in the truth, in the supremacy and authenticity of communication; a sensation of great joy has nothing to do with whether the work is sad or gay. Part of this, of course, is a physiological abreaction to constant stress and tension, yet at the same time, it is an experience purely "in and of itself," supremely spiritual and meaningful on its own terms. Even the delight it brings is pure, that is, independent of any particular interest, purpose or circumstance. The joy comes from total inner identification; one has been smiled upon, unexpectedly, by something from the mysterious essence of the "order of the spirit" and "the order of Being." More than that, one has actually been called upon to partake in a "feast": in short, one has shared in something crucially important, been totally involved in it. Characteristically, this "cultural" good mood can make many bothersome, exhausting or at least preoccupying matters suddenly seem unimportant and trivial.

Another kind of good mood can be brought about by what I would call a "human encounter." Now and again, I establish an understanding with someone. He may understand me better, or I him, or he helps me somehow—perhaps with no more than a kind word, or I help him—perhaps by dissuading him from a foolish act or by persuading him to exercise better self-control. Perhaps I simply have a good talk with someone or, in a kind of cheerfully creative dialogue, we experience a small event together. Such things are common enough on the outside, but they have a special value here and it is no surprise that they unfailingly produce a good mood.

Directly related to my "retrospective" and "prospective" moods, both of which are somewhat introspective, is what might be called "contemplation." It is a kind of higher degree of introspection, when I no longer allow myself to be carried along so freely by memories or dreams of returning from prison, but rather I think to a purpose— about everything possible: myself and my life, my writing, the things that relate to my situation at the moment and of course—above all, perhaps—about many general themes. I once wrote you about how, in the first weeks and months of my imprisonment I imagined, very vividly and almost physically, all the things, now denied to me, that constituted my life outside, how I missed things so intensely and looked forward to them in a very sensual way. Now—with the passage of time—these experiences are not nearly as immediate and urgent and instead my home (my "particular horizon") operates inside me, with increasing clarity of meaning, moral content, demands and hopes, in other words, in terms of what lies beneath its sensory surface. For this reason too, "contemplation"—as the manifestation of a deeper, more spiritual relationship to the values of the world and my life—is gradually coming to prevail over those two more "down-to-earth" levels—remembering the past and imagining the future. . . . It may be a slow process; something worthwhile is going on inside me—perhaps. Many things are becoming imperceptibly clearer, silently firmer, or are being discarded and classified. Much that is superficial and impulsive is falling by the wayside, while the value of other things is being recognized more deeply.

The highest phase, as it were, of this "contemplation" is my final and best mood. It is difficult to characterize concisely and accurately; it is a state of general and fundamental joy that I am alive, that I am, that my life—in spite of everything—has meaning, that I have done some good, that there are people who know me, understand me, share with me—though it may only be at a distance and in general terms—my fate. They know what I want and why I do what I do, they think about me, worry about me, wish me well and—perhaps the most important and wonderful thing of all—they are fond of me. It is an experience of the manifestation—the vivid presence—of an otherwise hidden, yet all-determining dimension of the spirit, that is, the presence of faith, hope and the profound conviction that there is a "meaning." . . . I don't have this mood often at all, but it is very useful: it fills me with strength and energy and courage, substances I need desperately.

*

Last time, when I described to you all the things I was looking forward to, I recalled my first stay in prison in 1977 when I wrote you a long list of wonderful resolutions about how I would live when I returned: how I would treasure my freedom, my time and all the joys of life in an entirely new way, how I would try to live better (something like that wonderful and ineffectual resolve of Chekhov's characters, which has always fascinated me and which I have semiparodied in my plays; I say "semiparodied" because I feel that in Chekhov, these things are partial parodies already), how I would cherish nature, good people and good books and fill every minute of my life with them, etc. Thinking back on that now, with time and a somewhat fuller prison experience behind me, I blush to realize how overblown it all was, how commonplace an expression of a rather commonplace bit of prison psychosis. My aim now is far more modest: to return as unscarred by the experience as possible, which means, much as I went in. If I can manage that, I'll be completely satisfied. If I can accomplish anything more I'll be happy, of course, but I now know that such things simply can't be planned. Change for the better somehow happens "by itself," from the essence of one's spirit and one's life, under pressure from experience, and not because one planned it. In any case, you can't tell until later whether anything of the sort really happened at all.

*

Yesterday was the second anniversary of my arrest; so you can read my preceding lines as a small, marginal comment on that.

I kiss you, I'm thinking about you and looking forward an awful lot—

Your Vašek

83

June 10, 1981

Dear Olga,

And once again, the "dead letter" is here, that is, the one written in the happy atmosphere that goes with waiting for a visit and which will reach you when the visit is only a memory. I'm devoting it to formulating questions I would like to address in several future letters. . . .

*

No living creature has ever appeared in the world of his own free will, yet each one clings to life and does so, as far as possible, in a way proper to itself. Biologists call this the survival instinct and man—like every animal—possesses it too. It is integral to his animal nature, and it permeates his entire existence. Yet the manner in which it is present in man differs in one subtle yet immensely important way from how it is present in all other living creatures. At any time, man can call that instinct into question and repudiate it by asking himself something the rest of the animal kingdom cannot, the simple question as to whether he really ought to live and if so, then why.

Because I am less concerned with what defines us as animal beings than I am with what makes us human, I will leave the survival instinct as such to the experts and begin where this instinct leaves off, as it were: at the moment we ask ourselves the question "to be or not to be." If the capacity to ask that question is what makes us human—that is, if it lays the foundation for our human existence—then how we respond to it will lay the foundation for our human identity—and will indicate who we are.

*

If we were to ask most people why they choose to live, they would probably answer something to the effect that they enjoy life, that it's not bad enough to make them feel the need to end it, and that—all things considered—it does provide pleasures they would not want to forgo. And though they are not entirely happy, they still continue to hope that life will bring them a few happy moments, the kind that make it worth living. If this does not satisfy us and we demand more specific reasons, we would find a panoply of things laid before us: beer, love, the joys of work, good food, the family, sports, a house of one's own, culture, the joy of freely questing after truth, the delight a sense of human community brings, and serving others, etc.

To a greater or lesser degree, we may find these various notions about what makes life meaningful appealing; some may seem rather earthbound, others very noble. Nevertheless their intrinsic "value" (from a more or less moralistic, positivistic point of view) interests me far less than something else: in what way and how deeply are they rooted in man? Is there something in their structure that enables them to impart meaning? What is their authentic meaning, weight and context? In short, what is their deeper existential background and context? After all, seen from the viewpoint of why one has decided to live, it is genuinely more important to discover why the "objects" appealed to (which in any case are frequently interchangeable and not intrinsic to the person involved) sometimes turn one toward life and sometimes not, than it is to classify and evaluate them. For it would seem that none of them—from good food to serving the truth, for instance—can in themselves guarantee anything. Anything may give meaning to one's life or take it away; anything (or almost anything) can raise one above one's animal nature or drive one back to it; almost anything can be a source of either hope or despair, a reason for living or a reason for dying.

———

If, therefore, the question "why live" defines the outer limits of the theme I will hover around in my letters, then the way I intend to hover should be evident from the preceding paragraph: I'm less concerned about what is commonly said in conversations on the subject, that is, about the different specific values and ideals in life, than I am about human existence as the subject of those values and ideals.

I'm looking forward to seeing you, and I kiss you—

Vašek

P.S. Written in haste this time, therefore in a less elegant hand—

86

July 26, 1981

Dear Olga,

On Monday, July 20, I actually left Heřmanice and on Tuesday arrived safely at the Pankrác hospital, where I am writing you now. Originally it appeared I'd be here for some time and that instead of going back to Heřmanice I would go directly to a new location. Now, of course, the situation has changed and it looks as though in the next few days I will either go back to Heřmanice, which is more likely, or somewhere else. In any case I will definitely not be staying here: all the relevant diagnostic tests are done and though the results indicate I should probably have an operation, this won't happen right away, at least not while I'm here (as it seemed at first), and if it is done, then not until the first half of September, when I am to come back for another checkup and the final decision about the operation will be made. So during August, I will still be in a Correctional Institute, probably Heřmanice.

*

And now, perhaps, some more specific details about the state of my health: I was given a proctoscope (it wasn't as bad as I had imagined), a bowel X-ray and various general examinations along with it, such as an ECG and so on. It was confirmed that apart from rather large external hemorrhoids I have something else unwholesome inside and it would be best to remove everything, especially since I have more than two years of my sentence left to go and in prison I can obviously never enjoy the conditions that allowed me to live with my hemorrhoids for years. On the contrary, the constant problems with my backside would probably only get worse. I was assured that I don't have a malignant tumor, and even though patients have an understandable tendency not to believe doctors in such matters, I do believe them and I don't think things are any worse than I've been told. (This is corroborated by the fact that I am gaining, not losing weight, as I discovered again when I donned my civilian trousers for the trip.) I must say that the way I've been examined and treated has inspired my complete confidence in this hospital, and this has also caused my original fear of an operation to subside. On the contrary, I am coming round to the belief that an operation is the best solution. . . .

*

My stay in the hospital has been a strange and mostly wonderful experience: after nineteen months of constant rush and confusion I'm enjoying peace and quiet again, for a while; after twenty-six months without privacy I've been by myself for days on end (I'm alone in the cell; it's magnificent!); and those I do have contact with are normal, affable people; I'm in Prague, my home; I can see the Prague rooftops from my window and the sounds of my mother tongue reach me once more—in short, everything is new and exciting. If the change is not entirely ideal, it's only because I haven't smoked for a week, which after thirty years of smoking is rather unpleasant. (I especially miss cigarettes during certain intimate moments—I have to take a laxative instead, and it's not the same.) So I'm resting, sleeping a lot, gaining weight (unfortunately), reading a lot, thinking, occasionally looking out the window—in short, I have whole days to myself, something I haven't had for a long time.

. . .

As far as newspapers are concerned: I can't, in fact, get them here and I miss them. Don't send them to me now; I'll be gone before they arrive, but after the beginning of September, just to be sure, don't throw the papers out—and when I'm here again, i.e., for a longer time, you could send them to me (about once a week, as printed matter, and only the page in each one that has news from home and abroad). . . .

*

Forgive my rather sloppy (actually my increasingly sloppy) handwriting—but I'm writing in bed and finding it difficult.

And so I'd rather close. Greetings and kisses to you,

Your Vašek

III. Letters 87–128

Plzeň-Bory

August 1, 1981–May 15, 1982

87

August 1, 1981

Dear Olga,

As you've no doubt already been officially informed, the possibility I had been less prepared for has happened—in other words, instead of returning to Heřmanice, I've left Pankrác and gone directly to my new domicile, Bory, where I've been since Thursday, July 30. Of course it's a little too early to evaluate the change; a lot depends, for instance, on what kind of workplace I'll be assigned to, yet I must say that so far I think the change is absolutely terrific, beyond all my expectations. It appears to me infinitely better in every way here than in Heřmanice, and I'm in a constant state of mild euphoria. I've been here a couple of times before, once about thirty years ago to visit my uncle, and later to bring the wives of some friends here on the odd visit; it always depressed me and I never thought I'd see the day I'd be so delighted to be here myself. Paradoxes indeed!

*

Thanks to my movements, our correspondence may well be in a muddle for a while. . . . I'd be glad if, as soon as you get this letter, you'd write me here and recapitulate everything essential from all the letters whose receipt I haven't yet confirmed. (Knowing you, there won't be many of them; two at the most.)

. . .

Unlike Heřmanice, here relatives can prepay subscriptions to various magazines, which of course is marvelous. I'll pay for *Rudé právo* myself out of my pocket money, but it would be very good if you could have some magazines sent to me. I have in mind *100 + 1, Melodie, Kino, Záběr*); you can decide for yourself about *Scéna,* or even a theatrical or film review (I have no idea what's coming out these days). If you know of any other interesting cultural or cultural/political magazine, go right ahead and subscribe too; Zuzana or other friends will certainly advise you and undoubtedly will know which magazines you are allowed to send here and which not. (Don't order *Mladý svět,* I've gone off it completely.) The sooner they begin to arrive, the happier I'll be.

*

As you know, on August 29 the first half of my sentence will be over. On the same day, I'll be sending a request for parole to the District Court of the City of Plzeň, Fourth Department. It would be fine if at the same time (or somewhat later) you and Ivan could send a letter to the same court supporting my request. My lawyer will certainly be glad to help you write it; I'll leave what to write entirely up to you. (I will limit myself to a brief official request.) Sometime later the court will decide the matter, the hearing will be public and I would naturally welcome it if you and perhaps some others could be there, my lawyer as well. God knows when it will be, but the notification may come suddenly, which is why I'm writing about it now, so you'll have time to prepare for it.

*

The workplace I've been assigned to is not the one that attracted me most, but it's a very good one all the same. So far, I have not had to alter anything in my extremely favorable impression of this prison (especially compared to Heřmanice). I don't know when our visit will be, but I'll find out as soon as I can. Ivan's holiday letter reached me from Heřmanice; thank him for it. Perhaps Ivan could write me some more about modern physics when the chance arises—

Greetings and kisses, Vašek

89

August 15, 1981

Dear Olga,

I'm sitting on a bench in the local micropark, in a good mood and doing what I like best, that is, thinking about what I will do once I'm free again. Therefore I would like to devote today's letter to several marginal observations about my daydreams of what I assume will be a happier future.

   As you know, I'm an inveterate planner and master of ceremonies, and so you can imagine in what incredible detail I construct my sweet fantasies, such as how I'll go to the sauna, combine it with swimming in the pool and sunbathing, then go home for a snooze, then in the evening put on some nice clothes and go with you to a good restaurant, and I imagine all the things we'll eat and drink there etc. etc. When I think about it, all such daydreams have one thing in common: sooner or later, a disturbing question always arises: what then? What next? For the time must come, after all, when—figuratively speaking—I will have swum enough, preened myself enough, eaten enough, slept enough; when I will no longer want to indulge in those delights any more, yet my life will clearly be far from over, and it will be high time—especially after all that—to breathe some meaning and substance into it. All the joys of life—the kind we cling to and look forward to and which ulti-mately make our lives worth living—occur in time and have a dramatic sequence of their own, from exposition to "catastrophe." And thus not only do they come to an end, but they do so "catastrophically": once they are over, one is inevitably overwhelmed by a sensation of vacancy and barrenness; there no longer seems to be anything to look forward to, to cling to, to hope for and therefore, in fact, to live for.

   Just to clarify my point: when I mentioned a sauna and a good dinner, I deliberately chose the most trivial example, i.e. a truly ephem-eral pleasure, in no way lavishly structured, either existentially or intel-lectually (though to be truthful, such pleasure is all there is to the meaning of life for many). But the same applies to all the other more substantial joys in life. For example, if I imagine that rare and wonder-ful moment when I get an idea for a play, an idea so fine and so gratifying that it practically knocks me off my chair, and if, in a kind of joyful trance, I imagine actually turning the idea into a play I'm happy with, then having it neatly typed out, reading it to some friends who like it, and even finding theaters that express an interest in putting it on—imagining all that, I must also necessarily imagine the moment when it's all over and the awful question comes up again: "Well?" "Is that all?" "What next?" I would even venture to say that the more "serious" and time-consuming the activity that lends meaning to life, the more terrifying the emptiness that follows it.

   Most people's lives, it seems to me, are fragmented into individual pleasures (both mundane and exalted, wretched and admirable, but most often a rich mixture of everything imaginable), and it is precisely these individual pleasures that give people the elementary and essentially spontaneous feeling that life has meaning. To put it another way, such pleasures ensure that the question of what life actually means never comes up. The first, or rather the most frequent occasion for posing this all-important question, only arises, I believe, when one first suffers or experiences, existentially, the "gap," the abyss that separates the pleasures in life from one another. That, at least, is how I feel it. I have thrown myself enthusiastically into all kinds of things, from serving good dinners to working for a "suprapersonal" cause, yet these joyful activities were always restricted to particular temporal compartments of my life relating to a particular event or constellation of events, and thus I have always experienced them as mere "islands of meaningfulness" floating in an ocean of nothingness.

Of course: even in those intervals or gaps one knew and felt the meaning of what one had devoted oneself to in periods when life was full, otherwise one would have no sense of personal continuity; still, this awareness was always very slight, like a feather adrift on that ocean of nothingness. And conversely, a memory of the "intervals"—those periods of emptiness—is present even in the most meaningful moments. It can never be eliminated entirely. Thus the experience of meaning is always more or less scarred or disrupted by the perspective of nothingness. It may well be that this warning thought comes through most clearly at the climax of a particular joy, not only tainting it but intensifying it as well. Even if one is standing firmly on solid ground, then, one can never forget that the ground is just an island, or lose sight of the "sea horizon" surrounding it.

My description of all this may be rather primitive but perhaps what I'm trying to say is clear: one usually begins to pose the question of the meaning of life and reflect on it in a fundamental way when one is suddenly ambushed and overpowered by a painful question: "and what next?" A question essentially the same as the question, "So what?" It asks not simply what will follow when a certain pleasure is over, but also what meaning a finite pleasure can have. In other words, what is the meaning of that which gives our lives meaning, or, what is the "meta-meaning" of the meaningful? It is only when all those thousands of things that impart meaning (spontaneously) to our lives—that seem to make life worth living, or for which we have simply lived—are thus challenged, that the stage is set for us to pose, in all seriousness, the question about what our lives mean.

Posing it then means, among other things, asking whether those "islands" are really so isolated, so randomly adrift on the ocean as they appear in moments of despair, or are they in fact merely the visible peaks of some coherent undersea mountain range?

*

Anyway, my sojourn on the park bench has long since ended, I'm back again in my fortress dwelling and so I ought to return to my present reality.

. . .

About my letters: theoretically, I have more time for them here than I did in Heřmanice; in practice, however, I find them harder to write because of tight spatial restrictions and my loquacious fellow prisoners.

On Tuesday I have an appointment with the neurologist, who let's hope will give me the injections I've been so longing for. The pain in my elbows is becoming quite unbearable.

For now, I have the chance to watch television every evening. Yesterday I saw a Czech film *Wrath* (Karel Valtera and Zbyněk Brynych); it was an incredible thing. Before that I saw, in the local cinema, Kačer's film *I Am Heaven* based on a story by Iva Herčíková. Pretty bad, I suppose, though very ambitious. The only undisputable thing was Lenka Machoninová's performance. If you meet her, give her my regards.

Thinking of you and kissing you, Vašek

90

August 23, 1981

Dear Olga,

. . .

I've decided, after appropriate consultations and mature reflection, that I will go along with the doctors' advice and if they recommend it, I will agree to an operation. I can't alter this decision, or rather I could, theoretically, but it would be very embarrassing, all the more so because I would have no persuasive reason for changing my mind. Your desire for me to hold off not only came too late (I might well have had the operation over with by now) but also your concern, though I'm pleased and touched by it, is, I think, immaterial. I would have to have the operation sooner or later anyway, and it's better to get it over with before I become an old man. . . .

Otherwise, I missed in your letter a more systematic account of all that's gone on in Hrádeček, who's been there, when, and for how long, what the atmosphere was like, how different work is progressing and what shape the house is in, when you're going to Prague and when you'll be moving back there (don't forget I have to know all this so I can address the letters far in advance!), how the new car is working and whether you drive it by yourself, etc. And this is not to mention the total lack of news about the development of yours and Ivan's case, or rather about your impressions of the results of the investigation (you needn't hesitate to write about it; it's a family matter par excellence, after all!). . . .

Important information for both of you: on the envelope, above the name of the institution, write my name and the date of my birth as well; Ivan did not do this, probably because on letters to Heřmanice the name was not required on the envolope. Above the salutation write my relationship to you, my date of birth, the number of the section and the address of the institution (indicate your relationship to me as well). Unlike Heřmanice, don't title me "The Convicted V.H." Speed of delivery depends on following these rules!

Otherwise, my life has got on the rails and is proceeding at its own pace; in fact it seems to be going faster than before. The neurologist didn't give me injections, so I'm looking forward, hopefully, to being given them in Pankrác. Meanwhile I'm trying to ease the pain in my elbows with elbow warmers I made myself. My elbows are the only thing bothering me now, otherwise my body is behaving satisfactorily, my hemorrhoids are on the whole quiescent and the main thing is I feel generally better; those strange periods of sluggishness, the trembling and the temperatures that plagued me in Heřmanice have almost vanished.

.   .   .

But now I'll pick up what I was talking about in my last letter and try to make my views somewhat more precise.

To begin with: spleen, melancholy, anxiety, a sense of futility, etc.

are normal human feelings and a spell of them certainly doesn't mean that we are experiencing the deep sense of nothingness I had in mind when I wrote about the "gaps" and the "abysses" between separate "islands of meaning." Such an experience, I think, is quite rare; most people don't brood over these matters, nor do they feel them deeply; they simply live, do what they enjoy doing, experience a kind of elementary sensation of meaningfulness and if they don't happen to feel that way at a given moment, they need only arrange their lives properly or recall the time when they used to have it, and the feeling soon returns.

For such people, the question of what life means is, in a sense, answered before they ask it. They simply respond to it through their lives, by being alive, by living for something or for someone, by caring for something, by delighting in something, or, on the contrary, being bothered by something, by striving for something and perhaps even dedicating themselves to a cause. But it is all existentially (axiomatically, as it were) given, obvious, something they do simply because they "must," without ever asking why. Such people may believe in God, but they can just as easily be atheists. They might claim to support a certain ideology or none, but whatever their opinions, what joins them is the fact that they are—unconsciously perhaps—believers: they believe in life, in its meaning and the meaning of life's values and ideals. Their belief, however, is unreflected, spontaneous. It is not something in and of itself, because they have never seriously stepped outside it in order to try and grasp it and understand it as a metaphysical problem. It would seem to be an intrinsic part of their nature, their characters, their instinctive orientation, their natural human inclinations, interests and affinities, their archetypal behavioral models, influenced of course by education, the historical and social environment, the intellectual climate, etc.

The values that constitute this elementary meaningfulness of life are, of course, manifold and they have as well a manifold moral dimension: for among such "believers" are to be found, side by side, those who devote themselves unselfishly to supremely human causes, and those who behave with brutal violence to their surroundings in the name of some thoroughly dubious ideal; those who are full of love and generosity and those who are selfish, out for their own profit, evil, hypocritical, cowardly, willing participants in any form of duplicity, who change their colors as a matter of course, and even those who are utterly degenerate. The point is that this general and spontaneous "faith" is not, as yet, morally unambiguous; it is simply a kind of "natural" persuasion that some things matter.

But even that is not entirely accurate: some sense of responsibility—be it ever so twisted and concealed—is the backbone of all human identity and thus of the trajectory one's life, driven by that spontaneous faith, takes. A certain residue of moral awareness, therefore, clings to every human tendency, including the most dubious ones—though in a thoroughly evil person, it may only manifest itself as the need (if he is aware of it at all) to make excuses for his evil in some way, or to lie to himself about it. Why would he bother at all if he did not feel a vague and slender moral imperative somewhere inside him or above him? Why would he need to polemicize and come to terms with something that for him simply did not exist?

All this notwithstanding, such unreflected faith is not in itself an automatic guarantee of anything either good or bad: it can just as easily lead to the highest and most beautiful moral undertakings as it can to the most pitiful pursuit of the most banal forms of personal gratification. Although infinitely more diverse and structured in its diverse manifestations than any purely biological need to live, this faith is, nevertheless, essentially only a "human extension" of what joins us to the other animals, that is, the instinct for self-preservation.

The order of the spirit does not genuinely emancipate itself from this foundation and fulfill itself as a real miracle of "the re-creation of Being" until later—that is, until the human spirit poses, in all seriousness—in its metaphysical dimension, that is—the question of the meaning of life and the meaning of its meaningful activities, the meaning and essence of its own responsibility, of its mysteriousness and the mystery of its moral content.

*

Without altering my generally quite positive impressions of this prison, I must say that some things are worse here than in Heřmanice (though they are an insignificant minority beside the things that are better). Among them is the fact that there is a limited choice of books. It is all the more important, therefore, that you subscribe to those magazines for me. While I haven't got my case-officer's permission for them yet, I believe I will get it. . . .

Kisses, Your Vašek

91

August 29, 1981

Dear Olga,

. . .

Today I have served half my sentence and so I've written a request for parole, and also a letter to my lawyer in which I've asked him, among other things, to visit me sometime. Please let him know about any eventual moves I may have to make.

*

When I was still in Heřmanice, something happened to me that superficially was in no way remarkable, but was nevertheless very profoundly important to me internally: I had an afternoon shift, it was wonderful summer weather, I was sitting on a pile of iron, resting, thinking over my own affairs and at the same time, gazing at the crown of a single tree some distance beyond the fence. The sky was a dark blue, cloudless, the air was hot and still, the leaves of the tree shimmered and trembled slightly. And slowly but surely, I found myself in a very strange and wonderful state of mind: I imagined I was lying somewhere in the grass beneath a tree, doing nothing, expecting nothing, worrying about nothing, simply letting the intoxication of a hot summer day possess me. Suddenly, it seemed to me that all the beautiful summer days I had ever experienced and would yet experience were present in that moment; I had direct, physical memories of the summers I spent in Žďárec as a child; I could smell the hay, the pond and I don't know what else (as I write this, it seems like a parody of a passage from one of my plays—but what can I do? And anyway, isn't parody often merely an attempt at self-control by stepping back a little from oneself and one's secret emotions?). I seemed to be experiencing, in my mind, a moment of supreme bliss, of infinite joy (all the other important joys, such as the presence of those I love, seemed latent in that moment), and though I felt physically intoxicated by it, there was far more to it than that: it was a moment of supreme self-awareness, a supremely elevating state of the soul, a total and totally harmonic merging of existence with itself and with the entire world.

So far, there was nothing especially unusual about this. The important thing was that because this experience, which contrasted so entirely with my prison-house/ironworks reality, was more sudden and urgent than usual, I realized more clearly something I had felt only dimly in such moments before, which is that this state of supreme bliss inevitably contains the hint of a vaguely constricting anxiety, the faint echo of an infinite yearning, the strange undertone of a deep and inconsolable sense of futility. One is exhilarated, one has everything imaginable, one neither needs nor wants anything any longer—and yet simultaneously, it seems as though one had nothing, that one's happiness were no more than a tragic mirage, with no purpose and leading nowhere. In short, the more wonderful the moment, the more clearly that telltale question arises: and then what? What more? What else? What next? What is to be done with it and what will come of it? It is, I would say, an experience of the limits of the finite; one has approached the outermost limits of the meaning that his finite, worldly existence can offer him (that "spontaneous" and "unmetaphysical" meaning) and for this very reason, he is suddenly given a glimpse into the abyss of the infinite, of uncertainty, of mystery. There is simply nowhere else to go—except into emptiness, into the abyss itself.

This is the familiar dialectic of life and death. The more intensely and fully one lives and is aware of one's life, the more powerfully there comes to meet him, from the bowels of his experience, that which makes Being, life and meaning what they are, their opposite: non-Being, death and nothingness, the only background against which they can be measured and defined. I think everyone must have experienced this at some time: in a moment of supreme happiness, it suddenly occurs to you that there is nothing left now but death (a feeling, by the way, that has entered into common speech, for we say, "I love you to death," "See Naples and die," etc.).

This vague anxiety, this breath of infinite nonfulfillment emanating from an experience of the greatest fulfillment, this sensation of terrifying incomprehensibility that blooms in a moment of firmest comprehension, can always be brushed aside like a bothersome piece of fluff. You may wait till the cloud temporarily covering the sun passes by, and go on living in peace and delight without asking troublesome questions. But you may also do the opposite: forget about all the "spontaneous meaningfulness" that gave you such supreme pleasure, forget about the answer given before the question was posed and stop precisely at the point where the cold air from the abyss struck you most powerfully—when you felt most intensely that in fact you have nothing, know nothing and worst of all, do not even know what you want—and bravely confront the question that comes to mind in such moments. That is, the genuine, profound and essentially metaphysical question of the meaning of life.

There it is: I'm trying to write about the meaning of life and so far, I've done no more than make repeated efforts to define the questions more precisely, or rather the existential circumstances in which it takes hold of one.

But there's no hurry—I still have quite enough prison Saturdays and Sundays ahead of me (at least as many before me as behind me).

*

Today I watched a variety show put on by prisoners for other prisoners. I enjoyed it a lot, and was even quite moved. It's hard to explain why, but these things moved me a lot back in Heřmanice too; its entire human context makes it something strange and unrepeatable, something scarcely to be found on any stage "outside." I don't suppose many playwrights have had this experience; it's difficult to know what to make of it. I've long since put out of my mind any thought of what I'll write once I'm free.

*

Looking forward to seeing you, and kisses—

Vašek

92

September 6, 1981

Dear Olga,

I'm sure you remember the end of Ionesco's *The Chairs,* when the Orator comes on to give the assembled public an extremely important message, amounting to the sum total of what the Old Man and the Old Woman have learned during their lifetime, for they cannot abide the idea of leaving the world without passing this knowledge on, knowledge that is expected to reveal some fundamental truth and explain "how it all is." The suggestion is that the Orator will acquaint his invited guests with the meaning of life. The long-awaited speech, however, is mere gibberish.

Many have interpreted this to express the author's conviction that communication is impossible, that two people can never come to an understanding about anything, much less the "meaning of life," because life in fact has no meaning, all is vanity and man is hopelessly submerged in total meaninglessness, particularly that of his own existence. Ionesco is therefore considered by many to be the dramatist of absolute skepticism and nihilism.

What Ionesco meant is his own business, and it is any interpreter's business how he interprets it. I mention it now not because I want to impose my own explanation on it, but because the motif of the Orator seems a useful starting point for further thought on the matter.

Notice: the Old Man and the Old Woman—aware of the significance of what they have to say and the importance of giving it to the world in a comprehensible form—decide not to deliver the message themselves but to hire a professional communicator.

If the Orator's purpose was really to inform the public of the meaning of life, then it seems to me that his attempt failed because, among other things, the meaning of life is not, as people often think, just an item of unfamiliar information that can be communicated by someone who knows it to someone who doesn't, somewhat the way an astronomer would tell us how many planets the solar system has, or a statistician how many of us are alcoholics. The mystery of Being and the meaning of life are not "data" and people cannot be separated into two groups, those who know the data and those who don't. None of us becomes greater than anyone else simply by virtue of having learned something the others have not, or rather by coming into the possession of some fundamental "truth" that the others, to their misfortune, have not discovered. Šafařík correctly distinguishes between truth and information: information is portable and transmissible, whereas it is by no means as simple with truth. (In any case, history has adequately demonstrated that the more people who succumb to the illusion that truth is a commodity that may readily be passed on, the greater the horrors that follow, since that illusion inevitably leads to the conviction that the world can be improved simply by spreading the truth as quickly as possible. And what quicker way to spread it than by violence?)

What I understand by "the meaning of life" is that it is not only unlike information or a commodity that can be freely passed on, it isn't even "objectively" knowable or graspable as a concept. It is in no way finite or complete, an existence in itself. Any attempt to grasp the meaning of life as if it were knowable in this way merely raises questions about what exactly is being offered as the alleged meaning of life. The would-be response thus merely becomes a better way of obfuscating the question, in which case it really becomes remarkably like the Orator's speech in *The Chairs*.

For me, the notion of some complete and finite knowledge that explains everything and raises no further questions is clearly related to the notion of an end—an end to the spirit, to life, to time and to Being. Anything meaningful that has ever been said in this matter (including every religious gospel), is on the contrary remarkable for its dramatic openness, its incompleteness. It is not a confirmation so much as a challenge or an appeal; something that is, in the highest sense, "taking place," living, something that overwhelms us or speaks to us, obliges or excites us, something that is in concord with our innermost experience and which may even change our entire life from the ground up but which never, of course, attempts to answer, unambiguously, the unanswerable question of meaning (answer in the sense of "settling the matter" or "sweeping it off the table"). It always tends rather to suggest a certain way of living with the question.

Is that too little? I don't think so at all. Living with the question means nothing more than constantly "responding" to it, or rather, being in some form of living "contact" with that "meaning," or constantly hearing a faint echo of it. It does not mean an end to the problem, but an ever closer coexistence with it. Though we cannot "respond" to it in the traditional sense of that word, nevertheless, by longing for it and seeking after it, we in fact indirectly confront it over and over again. In this regard, we are a little like a blind man touching the woman he loves, whom he has never seen and never will. The question of the meaning of life, then, is not a full stop at the end of life, but the beginning of a deeper experience of life. It is like a light whose source we cannot see, but in whose illumination we nevertheless live— whether we delight in its incomprehensible abundance or suffer from its incomprehensible dearth.

It is being in constant touch with this mystery that ultimately makes us genuinely human. Man is the only creature who is both a part of Being (and thus a bearer of its mystery), and aware of that mystery as a mystery. He is both the question and the questioner, and cannot help being so. It might even be said (and I believe someone already has), that man is "questioning Being," or Being that can inquire after itself, or rather the one through whom Being can inquire after itself.

Thus one's first serious confrontation with the question of meaning does not occur only when one first feels that life has lost its meaning, it also happens at the moment when meaning first seriously touches one, as a result of one's own reflections on it. The moment this happens is also the beginning of man's history as man, the history of culture, the history of the "order of the spirit."

This history is not a history of "responding," but one of "questioning"; it does not begin with a life whose meaning is already known, but with a life which understands that it does not know what its meaning is and that it must constantly come to terms with this hard fact.

This process of "coming to terms with meaning" is the most complex, the most obscure and at the same time the most important metaphysical-existential experience that one can go through in life.

I don't know any other way of dealing with the question of "the meaning of life" except by undergoing the experience personally and attempting to report on it. In one way or another, I've been trying to do this in my letters from the start and I intend to continue, in the hope that whatever I manage to squeeze out of myself in these difficult circumstances will be taken neither literally nor too seriously, but understood as a stream of improvised attempts to articulate my unarticulated "inner life." The point is, I would not want to sound like Ionesco's Orator.

. . .

I can't wait for the visit!

Kisses, Vašek

93

September 12, 1981

Dear Olga,

What a strange visit that was! Essentially it was good—you brought me no earthshakingly bad news, nor did I have any bad news for you.

You and Ivan are both in good physical and mental condition; so am I. We said all the important things we had to say. We're fond of each other, and yet why deny it, from the external point of view the visit was a mess! I take the main blame for it, not because self-blame is an old habit of mine, but because it really was my fault. Instead of coherent, witty and cordial talk I only managed to stammer something out now and then in an off-putting way, and this created a tension that ultimately infected the two of you as well.

There were several reasons for my unsatisfactory behavior: in the first place, I was extremely cold (I waited for you three and a half hours, and I didn't move in all that time) and as soon as the visit began, the brittle chill that had slowly accumulated suddenly broke to the surface and I was afraid to speak because I felt my teeth would start chattering. (Added to that was my strange "weekend sickness," which afflicted me in Heřmanice but is even worse here: I'm physically fit the whole week and then on Saturday morning, I invariably begin to feel odd; the change in my daily rhythms, the more cramped quarters, the cold—it all has an effect on this "disease.") The newness of my surroundings has to be taken into account too, and various marginal factors and creatures that have a strangely chilling effect on the space, and of course there's that queer mutedness which is the inevitable result—if conditions are even slightly unfavorable—of week after week of mounting nervous tension before the visit. You prepare yourself so extensively, rehearsing what to say and how to say it a thousand times in your head—and in the end, you say nothing at all, but sit there like a block of wood (the more so because you've entirely lost the ability to judge what may and may not be said). Anyway, it makes no sense to dwell on it; I merely wanted to apologize for making it, against my own will, such a negative experience, and at the same time I'd like to assure you that otherwise I'm quite normal, just the way you know me, and that you must blame my dullness entirely on the unusual external circumstances, which always have a terrible effect on me (I know myself and I know that I can be in the best possible frame of mind, bristling with paradoxes and brilliant repartee, and all it takes is a minor hitch—someone laughing maliciously in the background or dropping comments that make me nervous—and suddenly, I collapse like a pricked balloon and I'm reduced to awkward stammering). And in any case, my initial feeling of depression about the visit (and my anger with myself because of it) was soon relegated to the background when a deeper, beneficial significance began to surface, and even the visit's unsuccessful aspect began to appear in a positive light. I realized that among people who really belong together, there can be no embarrassment. They know each other so well and are so familiar with how things really are, that such accidental external circumstances can't touch them in any way, let alone throw them off.

To complete my commentary on the visit, however, I must mention a feeling that, while not strong, adverse or depressing, was nevertheless more noticeable than at other times (of course the external anxiety surrounding this visit may have been partly to blame): it is a feeling, a subconscious illusion that, though reason deny it a hundred times, the external world is waiting for one's return and is concerned with one more than it is or can be. I know that in general I can't complain of lack of interest in my case; yet not even I, an inveterate realist and anti-illusionary, could help painting a rosy pictures about some things, only to be slightly disappointed to discover that life goes on without me: people get married, divorced, leave the country, vanish over the horizon, grow accustomed to things and forget—and above all everyone has a thousand worries about things that concern them far more immediately than the imprisonment of a friend. And the longer the sentence, the more it becomes just another aspect of their "concrete horizon" and thus ceases to be a preoccupation. In fact there is nothing to be preoccupied with: it can't be changed and one must go on living, all the more so because the matter has long ceased to be anything out of the ordinary. All this is as it should be, and it is only fitting that one should constantly remind oneself of this as part of one's daily mental ablutions. This is not a negative feeling, and I don't mean to be self-pitying, but I have come to realize that the fewer foolish illusions you have in prison, the easier it will be to return one day to normal life.

This time I haven't the slightest criticism of the parcel; everything was quite wonderful. It is too bad I wasn't able to take it all with me; that was the result of unforeseen circumstances and I take it in a sporting spirit. (Though I do feel badly about the juices; they would be especially welcome in the hospital, because for a while they'll probably be all I can consume.)

*

I'm glad you've taken up photography; you've always complained that you felt my presence stifled your initiative—and indeed, they had to lock me up for you to realize some of your old ambitions! The main thing is to stick with it.

*

Each time you visit, you tell me about more friends who have left the country. I understand them, particularly the young people who want to know the world, study, see something, and who don't feel bound to this place by a sense of responsibility to work already begun, or by a feeling that there are some things a man does not walk away from. And yet when I think about it, it seems to me that a decision to leave is always appropriate when (to return to my last letter) someone conceives of study chiefly as gathering of information. If one is after truth, however, one had better look for it in oneself and the world fate has thrown one into. If you don't make the effort here, you'll scarcely find it elsewhere. Aren't some of these departures an escape from truth instead of a journey in search of it?

> I kiss you,
> Your faithful Vašek

94

September 19, 1981

Dear Olga,

I've been in the hospital again since Thursday, I'm alone again (this is good), I'm not smoking (this is not good, but I was prepared for it) and I can neither read nor study (a new thing that caught me off guard). And so most of the time I just lie here, staring at the ceiling. I'm bored and sometimes depressed, partly because my hemorrhoids are frequently painful (every time I'm moved) and partly because my elbows hurt more and more (or rather my whole arms, which are slowly beginning to behave as though they were crippled). I'll probably have the operation on Wednesday, Sept. 23, and then remain here for another two weeks at least. Write me something encouraging soon!

Several times in my letters, I've mentioned my belief that the assumption of something stable to which everything fleeting relates in one way or another, of a kind of "absolute horizon" against which everything ephemeral transpires, is very deeply built into the way we look at things and how we behave. If not consciously, then at least subconsciously, we always assume—figuratively speaking—the existence of a kind of tablet on which everything is drawn or written down, and we reject the notion that it might merely be drawn or written "on the wind," and thus that everything is condemned to vanish without a trace. In any case the very categories of change, motion, relativity, impermanence, etc. would not exist, or rather could not be contemplated, if their polar opposites did not exist and were not always contemplated along with them, forming a background against which they become thinkable and possible at all: I mean the notions of permanence, stability, absoluteness. Of course there is more to it than a rule of logic: our responsibility—that is, what makes us human in the first place—is also unthinkable without the assumption of some stable background to which it relates and which defines it. This assumption, therefore, has a moral dimension as well (but I wish to return to this elsewhere).

When we begin inquiring seriously after the meaning of life and Being, there usually begins to emerge, sooner or later, from the dimness of our unconsciousness the emotional assumption of this "absolute horizon," this "tablet" on which everything transitory is inscribed, this point of stability from which the entire order of Being grows and which makes that order an order in the first place.

It emerges for understandable reasons: to long for meaning and seek after it is essentially to long for certitude, for something lasting, valid, steadfast. We are awash in transience, and if we do not wish to surrender to it entirely—that is, to give up on our journey (and thus on ourselves)—we must feel that "everything is to some purpose," that it has a direction, that it will not simply perish of itself, that it is not simply enclosed in its own temporary fortuitousness. We will never learn, of course, what its purpose or direction is, but it's enough for us to feel that just as Being has its own secret order that has a direction, that signifies something and therefore has a meaning, so too our lives mean something and have a direction, are "known about," valued and ascribed a significance somewhere, and are not—from "the cosmic point of view," as it were—overlooked or forgotten. What else is such a feeling—such a hope, such a faith—but a kind of "petition" to the "absolute horizon" as the one true background guaranteeing that nothing ultimately vanishes and that therefore nothing is ultimately pointless?

The assumption of an "absolute horizon," naturally, "explains" nothing. It is, however, the only source of our hope, the only "reason" for faith as a (consciously reflected) state of mind, the only existential metaexperience (i.e., an experience concealed within all other experiences) which—without explaining the meaning of life—evokes the hope that it actually does have meaning, encourages one to live, helps one resist the feeling that all is vanity and futility, the pressure of nothingness.

That experience, therefore, is an inseparable part of our dramatic coexistence with the question of meaning. And it is indubitably a "positive element" in that drama.

. . .

I've discovered that when I can't smoke I'm practically incapable of writing, let alone thinking; what's more, my body is numb because I still can't find the proper position in bed for writing (and there's nowhere else to write); and my right tennis elbow is slowly making matters worse. (Perhaps they'll finally give me the injection I've been longing for.) And so I think it's better to bring the letter to a close.

The operation, I've just learned, will take place Thursday, not Wednesday.

I'm waiting impatiently to see if the newspapers you sent reach me here, or any mail at all.

Greetings to all my friends, kisses to my girlfriends (if I still have any), and I think of you tenderly as my "point of stability" (I've realized that whenever something nice, or on the contrary, something absurd, happens to me and I mull it over in my mind, the immediate, unconscious result is always a report addressed to you—I'm obviously influenced by the fact that for almost two and a half years you've been the only addressee of my communication with the normal world).

Kisses,
Your Vašek

95

September 26, 1981

Dear Olga,

Why is it that when we are traveling alone (a single stop) in the second car of a conductorless streetcar, so that obviously no one could catch us not paying, we still usually—though perhaps after an inner tussle—drop our fare in the box? Why do we do good at all even when there is clearly no personal advantage in doing so (for instance when no one knows about it and never will)? And if we fail to do good, why do we apologize to ourselves? Why do we sometimes tend to behave the way we all should, even though we know that no one ever behaves that way all the time?

I am not interested in why man commits evil; I want to know why he does good (here and there) or at least feels that he ought to. The usual answer is conscience. What is conscience? Psychologically, it is a feeling that he ought to do something and that if he doesn't he will reproach and torment himself for it. But why should he?

It seems to me that even when no one is watching, and even when he is certain no one will ever find out about his behavior, there is something in man that compels him to behave (to a degree, at least) as though someone were constantly observing him. And if he does something he shouldn't in such a situation, he may even engage in a kind of "dialogue" with this "observer," pleading his own case and attempting, in all manner of ways, to explain and apologize for his own behavior.

I don't know, of course, how it all is. One thing, however, can hardly be denied: human behavior always carries within it—more or less clearly—traces of an emotional assumption or inner experience of "the total integrity of Being." It is as though we were internally persuaded (and as though Being itself were confirming us in this) that "everything somehow is," that everything has its roots, its reasons, its explanation, its coherence and its meaning; that somewhere, everything "is known" completely; that everything, beneath the approximate and transitory aspect of it with which we communicate, is anchored in solid ground—the "ground of Being"; that everything is indestructibly present in the "absolute horizon of Being."

Responsibility means vouching for ourselves, and doing so even in the wider perspective of "what everyone should do." It means vouching for ourselves in time, knowing everything we have ever done and why, what we are doing and why, and what we have decided to do. It means standing behind everything we do and being prepared to defend our position or existentially bear witness to it anywhere and at any time. (That is why responsibility is also the main key to human identity.) But to whom are we responsible? I don't know "to whom," but it is certainly not, in the final instance, to any of the transitory things of this world. It follows that I am convinced that the primary source of all responsibility, or better still, the final reason for it, is the assumption of an absolute horizon. It is precisely responsibility— as the bearer of continuity and thus of identity, that is the clearest existential "reflection" or "pledge" in man of the permanence and absoluteness of the absolute horizon of Being. It might be said, therefore, that this absolute horizon is present in us not only as an assumption, but also as a source of humanity and as a challenge (Kant talks about "the moral law within me" and the "categorical imperative," but he understands it, I think, too exclusively as an a priori and not enough as a concrete experience of existence, or rather as a "meta-experience").

This means, of course, that there is something more essential here than just the assumption of a "memory of Being" (what is done cannot be undone), a kind of total registration of everything. It is as though man assumed not only that everything is known "somewhere," but that in this "somewhere," everything is evaluated, consummated, draws its final validity and therefore is given meaning; that it is not, therefore, just a passive, "optical" backdrop but chiefly a moral one, including standards of judgment and expectation, an assumption of "absolute justice", the conferring of absolute meaning.

Clearly this is a supremely spiritual experience, or rather an experience of something supremely spiritual. Nevertheless, I confess I still can't talk of God in this connection: God, after all, is one who rejoices, rages, loves, desires to be worshiped: in short, he behaves too much like a person for me. Yet I'm aware of a paradox here: if God does not occupy the place I am trying to define here, it will all appear to be no more than some abstract shilly-shallying. But what am I to do?

Whatever the case may be, the most profound and solid "experience of meaningfulness"—as a state of joyous, confirmed and reflected faith in the meaning of the universe and of one's own life—has its source precisely here: in the vital experience of being in touch with the absolute horizon of Being. I think that this experience, and this experience alone, is the "suboceanic mountain range" that gives coherence and integrity to all those isolated "islands of meaning" adrift on the ocean of Nothingness, the only effective defense against that Nothingness. Though it reveals nothing of the secret of Being, nor responds in any way to the question of meaning, it is still the most essential way of coexisting with it.

*

I have undergone the postoperational ordeal so far without complaint (I'm a MAN, after all), including catheterization, if you know what that is. Now I have only the final act to go through, the moment when my born-again backside must once more face the necessity of fulfilling its mission in life. My assumption that twenty-five years of coexistence with hemorrhoids and countless incidents of inflammation would stand me in good stead for the operation has been confirmed.

Since, however, I don't wish to create the impression that there is no reason to admire and sympathize with me, I must add at once that today, the third day after the operation, I feel particularly miserable, I have a temperature (38.7 C), an obstructed bladder, my entire body is stiff—and thanks to all that, this letter has been squeezed out with great difficulty and enormous self-control. I've just been given an injection, so perhaps things will improve. (I'll continue tomorrow morning.)

. . .

I went through a terrifying night in the world of Ladislav Klíma—I must have had a temperature of at least 40 degrees. It's better now, 38.5. Fevers in themselves don't bother me—I'm even fond of them— I'm only worried lest they signal complications. Perhaps not. Ah, those juices you brought me, I could certainly use them now! Please forgive the unevenness of my expression and handwriting; I don't know if it was wise to start in on my meditations in this state. But I've done it, I haven't the energy to rewrite and so I'll send it just as it is.

Kisses, Vašek

96

October 3, 1981

Dear Olga,

In recent years I've met several intelligent and decent people who were very clearly and to my mind, very tragically, marked by their fate: they became bitter, misanthropic world-haters who lost faith in everything. Quite separately, they managed to persuade themselves that people are selfish, evil and untrustworthy, that it makes no sense to help anyone, to try to achieve anything or rectify anything, that all moral principles, higher aims and suprapersonal ideals are naively utopian and that one must accept the world "as it is"—which is to say unalterably bad—and behave accordingly. And that means looking out for no one but oneself and and living the rest of one's life as quietly and inconspicuously as possible.

In certain extreme circumstances it is by no means difficult to succumb to this philosophy of life. Nevertheless I think that giving up on life—and this philosophy is an expression of that attitude—is one of the saddest forms of human downfall. Because it is a descent into regions where life really does lose its meaning.

Indeed, it is not the authors of absurd plays or pessimistic poems, nor the suicides, nor people constantly afflicted by anger, boredom, anxiety and despair, nor the alcoholics and drug addicts, who have, in the deepest sense, lost their grip on the meaning of life and become "nonbelievers": it is people who are apathetic. (By the way, in the last couple of years I've met a lot of eccentrics, miserable and desperate men, adventurers, perverts, Pollyannas and of course a wide assortment of greater and lesser scoundrels, but not many who are apathetic in the sense I mean. Such men do not remain for long in places like this. Still, some here are making a successful bid to join those ranks— men with a more intellectual bent, or who are "decent men who have tripped up.")

Resignation, like faith, can be deliberate or unpremeditated. If it is deliberate, then the tinge of bad conscience that customarily clings to it requires it to be justified and defended extensively (before whom? why?) by referring to the evil of the world and the incorrigibility of that evil. The important thing to note here, of course, is that it was not the evil of the world that ultimately led the person to give up, but rather his own resignation that led him to the theory about the evil of the world. However "unbelievers" may deny it, the existential choice always comes first, and only then is it followed by the dead-end, pessimistic picture of the world that is meant to justify that choice. And the more resolutely one is determined to say to hell with everything, the more ferociously one clings to apocalyptic theories. To put it even less charitably: "unbelievers" insist on the incorrigible evil of the world so obstinately chiefly to justify committing some of those evils themselves. (Notice that whenever someone starts carrying on about how corrupt everything around him is, it is usually a clear signal that he is preparing to do something rather nasty himself.)

On a certain level, of course, we may observe yet another process: if this "evil world" is described first as something unfortunate but given, as a regrettable status quo, as a "reality" that we have no choice but to come to terms with, then gradually—while the "unbeliever" is learning to live in this evil world, as he grows accustomed to it and establishes himself in it—the reality that was originally regrettable begins, as he conceives it, to change imperceptibly into one that is "not as bad as it could be," certainly better than the eventual state of uncertainty created by "utopian" efforts to transform it, until at last the status quo he once condemned becomes, in essence, an ideal. And thus we arrive at the sad state of affairs wherein the ruthless critic of the world is indiscernibly transformed into its defender, the "uncommitted" theoretician of its immutability becomes an active opponent of changing it, the skeptical outsider becomes a common reactionary.

Today I understand, perhaps better than I ever did before, that one can become embittered. The temptation of Nothingness is enormous and omnipresent, and it has more and more to rest its case on, more to appeal to. Against it, man stands alone, weak and poorly armed, his position worse than ever before in history. And yet I am convinced that there is nothing in this vale of tears that, of itself, can rob man of hope, faith and the meaning of life. He loses these things only when he himself falters, when he yields to the temptations of Nothingness.

To sum up: I think that resignation, indifference, the hardening of the heart and laziness of the spirit are dimensions of a genuine "unbelief" and a genuine "loss of meaning." The person who has fallen into that state not only ceases to ask himself what meaning life has, he no longer even spontaneously responds to the question existentially by living for something—simply because he must, because it won't let him alone, because he is the way he is. The person who has completely lost all sense of the meaning of life is merely vegetating and doesn't mind it; he lives like a parasite and doesn't mind it; he is entirely absorbed in the problem of his own metabolism and essentially nothing beyond that interests him: other people, society, the world, Being—for him they are all simply things to be either consumed or avoided, or turned into a comfortable place to make his bed.

Everything meaningful in life, though it may assume the most dramatic form of questioning and doubting, is distinguished by a certain transcendence of individual human existence—beyond the limits of mere "self-care"—toward other people, toward society, toward the world. Only by looking "outward," by caring for things that, in terms of pure survival, he needn't bother with at all, by constantly asking himself all sorts of questions, and by throwing himself over and over again into the tumult of the world, with the intention of making his voice count—only thus does one really become a person, a creator of the "order of the spirit," a being capable of a miracle: the re-creation of the world. To give up on any form of transcending oneself means, de facto, to give up on one's own human existence and to be contented with belonging to the animal kingdom.

The tragedy of modern man is not that he knows less and less about the meaning of his own life, but that it bothers him less and less.

*

When my suffering reached a peak yesterday (I don't mean the pain in my backside, but in my soul) and my decision to write you a letter full of bitter reproaches ripened (for more than two weeks I had not had a single line, from you or anyone else), the good Lord clearly couldn't bear it any longer, he relented and brought down upon my bed a whole armful of correspondence and newspapers. . . . I'm grateful to Ivan for both his letters about physics. I don't completely understand everything on first reading, but I understand the general sense of his explanation. (I may return to this in my next letter, but for the time being a brief remark: I understand that it is possible to refute the different ways in which something can be explained, and I'm always delighted when it happens. But I don't see how you can refute the conviction that "everything is, somehow," that Being has an order. The realism of that conviction is something so general and vague that it must be utterly immune to criticism! Every proof that Being does not behave as expected can be dismissed by referring to a higher law, inaccessible to us in the same way that our world is inaccessible to two-dimensional beings. And such an assumption can neither be confirmed, nor refuted!) . . .

*

What can I say about my state? The high temperatures are over, I'm slowly healing; so far, it still hurts a lot; I suffer especially when I have to use my backside. I think it will be sometime yet before I'm completely well.

Greetings to all friends and those close to me.

I kiss you, Vašek

WRITE MORE OFTEN!
WRITE MORE DETAILS!
WRITE MORE!

BUY HOFMANNSTHAL!

97

October 10, 1981

Dear Olga,

We all know, of course, that we can die at any time and that one day die we must; still we try to think about it as little as possible. If we manage to drive thoughts of death from the center of our awareness, however, this does not mean that we have driven it from our lives. That is truly beyond our capacities, for death is an intrinsic dimension and an inseparable part of our existence, a hidden presence in everything we do, in every moment of our lives, in every step we take, in every decision, in every thought. If something compels us not to think about death, then, it is obviously not its distance and our fateful inability to influence it, but on the contrary, its constant and active presence in every aspect of our lives.

Even as animal beings, we confront death from morning to night, for is not the care we take of ourselves each day—from breakfast, through keeping a watchful eye on traffic lights, to going to bed at night—essentially a single, uninterrupted war with death? What links us to all other creatures—the instinct for self-preservation—is nothing more, after all, than an all-out effort to resist death and postpone it for as long as possible. And the second instinct we share with the other animals, the reproductive instinct, is again only another way of confronting death: we resist it not only as individuals but as a species (in preserving the species we are trying to defend something of ourselves as well against death). Can anything be more emphatically and integrally present in our lives than something we struggle against every second, something we constantly defy in our most ordinary actions, something we deny daily with the full weight of our existence?

Death in us (as animal beings) is not, of course, present only as a constant threat, but from our first moments of life, it permeates our lives primarily as destiny—that is, as that toward which we are inevitably headed and that for which every moment of our lives secretly prepares, brings closer and thus in fact brings about.

More important (in this context at least) than the presence of death in us as animals is, of course, its presence in us as human beings. For unlike all other creatures, we know death not only as a threat, we also know that it is our destiny: we know we will die and therefore we also know that everything our animal nature compels us to do in defiance of death is to no avail. We will inevitably lose our battle. At the most, we may fend it off for a few more minutes, days or years—but to what purpose? To fill the time with yet another struggle against death. It might be expected that our human awareness, bearing as it does the cruel truth about the certitude of our death and the essential futility of all our "self-care," would rise up against our animal instincts and cripple them entirely.

As we know, it doesn't happen that way: man desires to live just like any other living creature.

Might it be because we are able to drive the thought of death so effectively from our minds that it has lost any influence over our lives? Or is it because human consciousness is too "fresh," in terms of evolution, and therefore too uninfluential an element of our organism to shake pillars as firm as our basic animal instincts?

I think that consciousness is a devilishly influential "element of the organism" and that our "desire to live" does not derive at all from our ability to put death out of our minds, but quite the contrary: the awareness of death is the most essential starting point for any genuinely human, i.e., conscious and deliberate, will to life. True, it need not be, and usually isn't, an awareness of death in the sense of a "thematic" reflection on the subject, but rather an awareness—or rather the existential acceptance—of death as something "dissolved" in our entire existence, latently present in every sphere of human behavior, a firm component in what we consciously decide to be. On the existential level, too, death is present in us not as something with which we must identify, but which must be defied, overcome, spanned, denied. We might say that in the structure of human existence, the awareness of death is something like a challenge, a gauntlet flung down, an appeal, a provocation, in short, something that has the power to mobilize and arouse.

What does death, the awareness of death, awaken within us? Precisely what makes human existence a miracle of re-creation: that special belief that breathes significance, i.e., a sense of meaning, into our lives—without our necessarily perceiving a metaphysical dimension to it; in other words, the belief that despite everything, human life has a meaning and that therefore every authentic human act of "transcendence" has meaning as well. I would put it even more forcefully: without the awareness of death, nothing like the "meaning of life" could exist, and human life would therefore have nothing human in it: it would remain on the animal level.

Perhaps it is clear now what I mean: that which (on the surface) makes one human, that is to say, one's "transcendence" beyond the limits of mere "self-care" (knowledge, love, morality, art, etc.—in short, the "order of the spirit"), can be understood essentially as a way of overcoming death—not the mere instinctual overcoming of death as an instinctually felt threat, but an existential overcoming of death as existentially accepted fate. So the "transcendence" that is the foundation for all meaningfulness in life is first and foremost a "transcendence of death," wherein death is transcended only through and by virtue of an existential metaexperience of the "absolute horizon." Only the deeply held belief that "nothing that is done can be undone," that "everything is, somehow," that "everything is known somewhere, somehow" and that everything, therefore, is completely evaluated and assigned a meaning "somewhere"—only this conviction enables one to live with the awareness of death and to overcome it (this aspect of belief in life can also be understood as a latent belief in immortality). And indeed: all human activity within that "transcendence," that is, everything that only man can do (from the smallest of good deeds, like traditional almsgiving, to the greatest labor of the creative spirit, to the supreme sacrifice for so-called transpersonal values), contains locked deep inside it the assumption of immortality—that is, of an "absolute horizon." Without this central assumption (though it remain unthought and be denied a hundred times) none of those human actions is either explicable, thinkable or even possible; without it, it is even impossible to explain how "the meaning of life" and "belief" can defy the awareness of death in man, and therefore, how man can live with this awareness.

In other words: if we go on living despite the knowledge that our death is inevitable, and if we even live like human beings, that is, meaningfully and with dignity, then we can do so only thanks to an unshakable inner experience of the absolute horizon of Being, aroused in us precisely by this awareness of death.

*

This week I received two more bundles of newspapers (the fourth and the fifth) and a birthday telegram from my sister-in-law, which naturally pleased me. Give her my thanks and tell her I am thinking about her more intensely in this October time. No letter from you came, so that my freshest idea about your life is 18 days old (ah, me). I learn about world events more quickly—I always get the newspapers a week after they come out—so that, for instance, in six days I knew it was true that three days before, Sadat had been assassinated. My backside is healing, the doctors are satisfied (they say it was a mess) and so my sojourn here is probably coming to an end. If I don't leave this week, then it will certainly be next week. I have to confess I'm looking forward most of all to a smoke. A message for Ivan: have him write me again soon about physics, perhaps about the neutrino and the antineutrino which are, I'm told, the trendy particles these days.

Kisses, Vašek

P.S. In letter 94, please add the green lines and asterisks. I can't stand the thought of one letter differing from the others. I didn't have a marker.

99

October 24, 1981

Dear Olga,

The moment one first thinks of asking "So what?" of an event once felt to be supremely meaningful, an exceedingly important experience, one proper only to man, is germinated, though we may scarcely notice it: the experience of absurdity. This question has a special infectiousness or power to expand: as soon as you admit it in a single case, it can easily be raised again in a thousand other cases; as soon as doubt is cast on a single hitherto indisputable value in life, there is no more reason not to cast doubt on everything. At the end of all this doubting, however, there can only be the dispiriting impression that everything is hopelessly senseless, trivial, empty and futile. Suddenly, life seems no more than a game, an imitation, a mock-up of itself. It seems that no matter how much things resemble what they present themselves as, in reality they are not that at all. Speech becomes sounds that only sound like speech. Creation becomes a set of functions that only look like creation. Love or human community becomes an empty sequence of habitual functions, gestures and phrases, phrases about love and human community. Life manifests itself as mere vegetating. Gone is the feeling of truth, authenticity and ultimately of reality; they are all reduced to shadows and apparitions, dead outlines, forms without content, the mechanics of convention and routine. The last "islands of meaningfulness" have sunk irrevocably beneath the ocean of Nothingness. In this existential state of mind, "meaning" is present only by virtue of its total absence; it becomes that which man desperately lacks, what he thirsts after and whose absence he painfully suffers.

But what does man lack? What, in fact, is this "meaning"?

I would say that the meaning of any phenomenon lies in its being anchored in something outside itself, and thus in its belonging to some higher or wider context, in its illumination by a more universal perspective; in its being "hung," like a picture, within a higher order, placed against the background of a horizon. As a consequence, the "higher context"—what is "outside it," is projected, as it were, "back" into the phenomenon to which it lends meaning, so that it appears not only to permeate and animate it, but to provide an immediate foundation for its "intrinsic determination," its identity. That is why it seems that everything from which meaning has vanished is nothing but a dead imitation of what it was when it still meant something.

If we feel that different, separate aspects of life—experiences, events, things, achievements—are meaningful, this is precisely because we have found them to be rooted in the wider contexts of life. If, however, we fall to doubting, then calling in doubt these "signifying circumstances" must sooner or later lead to questioning the meaning of "life itself," that is, the meaning of the very circumstances that impart meaning. The answer, of course, cannot logically be sought "inside" the entities whose meaning we seek, that is, in the world of those relative and ephemeral contexts, but only inside "life itself": in the context of the absolute, against the absolute horizon. Which of course ultimately means that all those partial "signifying circumstances" are themselves given meaning by this "deepest of anchorings," which through them provides a basis for the identity of all things. The hidden backbone and the deepest source of everything that has meaning is always—whether we realize it or not—this "anchoredness in the absolute."

A search for the meaning of life, then, is in fact a search for the absolute horizon. It is as though we were constantly striving for something beyond us and above us, something firm, something we wish to grasp and hold on to and which we in fact—or so it seems to us—do grasp and hold on to. It is, of course, a troublesome and paradoxical process: we know we must hold on in order not to fall, yet not only do we not know, nor will we ever find out, what we are holding on to or what is holding on to us, but we are never certain that we are holding on to anything at all: there is no way to confirm it, and in such matters, we have no choice but to believe in our own belief.

We do not know the meaning of life—just as we do not know the mystery of Being—and yet in some way we "possess" it—as our own, immediate version of that "anchoredness" or as our own way of longing for it. There is no direct answer to the question of what life means, but indirectly, each of us answers and must answer it anew every moment of his life. It is the darkest and the most distressing mystery—yet it is our final hope, the only firm point in life and the only reason for it: were we in some way not to "possess" it, search for it or at least feel its lack, we couldn't begin to live as what we are, that is, as creators of the "order of the spirit," as "re-creators" of the world, as dignified beings, capable of stepping beyond ourselves, that is, beyond the shadow of our animal foundations.

I'm still in the clinic and am to remain here until the end of the month. My right tennis elbow caused the inflammation of a tendon on my forearm, so my arm is in a splint. (I've taken it off to write; I was hopeless with my left hand.) I'm not badly off here, though I'll be glad enough to get the convalescence over with.

*

Thank you for letter 47! Take your pains to Dr. Rejholc; he's one of our top experts in such things. If you speak with Klaus, give him many greetings, of course, and stress that I'm having trouble with my elbows too and ask him to have Mr. Laub check the translation of *The Beggar's Opera* (if he hasn't done so already). Paravan looks very good— and so do you! I'm still waiting for your birthday greetings and your photo. I don't need socks for the time being. I'm really sorry you feel depressions coming on. But you can't afford to have depressions now— wait till I come home! Be cheerful, sociable, active, brave and prudent (but mainly prudent). I welcome your intention to write me more often. . . .

Kisses, Vašek

100

October 30, 1981

Dear Olga,

I've just moved from the clinic and because I'm here alone (my colleagues are at work), I'm sitting down to write a letter, though it's only Friday: still, it's not likely anything that could radically influence my letter will come by tomorrow.

*

When, on the occasion of the round figure numbering today's letter, I think back on my letters as a whole, I realize, among other things, that I am in fact constantly writing about the same thing. I have no copies of my letters, nor is my memory very good, so I have no overview of what I've written. But the main reason for this phenomenon consists in something else: in the sphere of questions I address in my letters, expression does not follow insight. Far from it, they are inseparable. It is only in the struggle to give them a definite expression that I recognize my actual themes. Language is the most proper medium of self-awareness and quite often it is not until you have formulated something that you realize what it is really about, or how you feel about it; thus one's view of many subtle questions is only made precise and in some cases, only established at all, in the renewed effort to give it the best possible expression. This, of course, is no great discovery and I emphasize it only to justify myself somewhat: by repeatedly writing about the same things, each time in a slightly different context or from a different perspective and in slightly different words—I gradually clarify these matters for myself and what I actually think about them.

In other circumstances I would proceed differently: I would cover a mountain of paper with writing, recasting my reflections a thousand times, striking out, rearranging, improving, never letting anything out of my hands that I knew was merely the unfinished record of a single moment or phase of my struggle. When all this exhausting labor was over, one of two things could happen: either I would conclude that it all held together, that it could never be improved and that I could release it to the world—or, more probably, I would throw it all out and start working on something else. In these circumstances, of course, I can't do it that way, so my only choice is to serve you up something like a "work in gestation." My letters are, after all, essentially only the tentative steps of one who, by trial and error—in the dark, as it were—is looking for the right way. . . .

So there may be something good, after all, in this enforced way of writing: it compels me to compromise, something which—plagued as I am by a longing for perfection—I would be loath to do under other circumstances and which would probably mean I would never write about such matters at all.

These remarks would not be complete if I did not, once more, point out that the meditations I squeeze out of myself here are by no means easy to squeeze out. As you know, writing has never come easily to me, and now there are impediments that, in civilian life, were entirely unforeseen: I can't choose the time, so I frequently have to write when I'm in a highly inappropriate mood; I never have enough time for writing; and—perhaps worst of all—I never have the solitude and tranquillity: someone is always talking to me, time and again I have to interrupt my writing for this or that reason, I haven't enough room, etc.

Still, I enjoy writing my letters. After all, it's the only creative activity I have here; at least it helps me shake off the miserable feeling that I'm doing nothing at all; and last but not least, I'm actually managing to clarify a few things for myself, and in some areas—in a roundabout way—I'm strengthening myself and learning. True, I would rather be reading books of philosophy by real philosophers, but since that's impossible, my only recourse is to philosophize myself.

. . .

For the time being, I've finished with the series of letters on the meaning of life (without, of course, being satisfied with it); now for a change I would like to write on some less abstract subjects (chiefly, but not exclusively, on the theater and drama)—and then we'll see. But although the circle of things I can write about is considerably constricted (a whole huge area which I would love to address—my new insights and experiences—is entirely out of bounds), I'm certainly not worried that I won't have anything to write about—and it also seems more than likely that I'll be able to return, sooner or later, to more general existential, moral and metaphysical questions.

*

Have you sent me the vitamins? So far I've received nothing. The newspapers are still being forwarded (from Pankrác); I hope that Ivan knows I'm here now and that I won't need newspapers from home. Write me more often, even briefly: I'm worried about you! Don't walk over bridges alone at night, and don't go anywhere alone, if possible.

Kisses, Vašek

P.S. I'm jealous of Landák! I want to be performed with Stoppard too!

102

November 14, 1981

Dear Olga,

It was an entirely superficial thing—reading a book from the theater world—that caused me, for the first time in a long while, to think back on the theater. And so in the next few letters, I will try to recapitulate a few of my elementary experiences with theater and some of my opinions—entirely personal—about it.

Though I've been writing for the theater for twenty years, though I worked in theater for ten years and though my university education in a sense predetermined that I work in it, I still don't feel theater to be my personal "destiny" and I can't say, as theater people frequently do, that I couldn't live without it. I am no fonder of reading plays or books on theater than anything else; I scarcely go to the theater; most seminars and conferences on theater don't interest me; I feel quite out of place in theater clubs or dressing rooms and I am shy in the presence of famous actresses (paradoxically, this sometimes made them think I was arrogant). The whole world of so-called professional theater, Czech theater in particular with its obsessive penchant for egghead theorizing and its everlasting personal conflicts and gossip, is deeply alien to me; I don't miss it and I have never sought it out. (I was once invited to a congress of theater artists and after an hour or so of crushing boredom, I fled.) My attitude does not come from any feeling of superiority; the reasons for it are quite different: I devoted myself to theater as long as I was able to do something I enjoyed and as long as my work seemed to have some meaning, and it interested me only to the extent that it had something to say to me. Had anything else provided greater opportunities in that regard, I would not have hesitated to take it up, and would have left the theater without regrets. Anything, in fact, that can speak to me in any way—and it needn't be theater—interests me as much as theater does. I do not pay more attention to something just because it is theater, nor do I pay less attention to something just because it is not. For me, the decisive factor is simply whether the matter is intrinsically fascinating enough or not. So my motto is certainly not theater of any kind, at any price, theater for theater's sake. (Once, in The Academy of Dramatic Arts in Prague, I had an assignment to write program notes for a play in the DISK Theater which meant absolutely nothing to me. With the best will in the world, I could not do it, and finally, in desperation, I proposed that the audience be given a blank piece of paper on which they could write whatever they wanted. My professors understood this as some kind of Dadaist joke, but it only seemed that way: in fact, it was an almost symbolically pure expression of my utter inability to get involved in something I don't enjoy.) In short: I am definitely not what we call a "divadelník"—a professional theater person, someone for whom theater is the only imaginable vocation. When I was involved in theater it was always with a specific theater, and when I write for theater, I do so in a way specific to myself—and if no one were interested in my way, I'd prefer to write only for myself or stop writing plays altogether, rather than try to do it differently just because someone asked me to, as playwright. I'll come back later to what kind of "specific theater" I enjoy, and to the question of my specific way of writing and why its appropriate locus is drama. For now, I merely want to say that if I was relatively quick to find myself in theater, as opposed to something else, luck had a lot to do with it. . . .

At first it really was just a series of coincidences: after my stint in the army (I was not allowed to go to university) and with no special interest in theater (I wrote poetry at the time), I happened to become a stagehand under Werich, who at the time was involved in practically the only theater in Prague that, for all one's reservations, displayed something of the special social atmosphere that interests me most in theater. It was my first encounter with anything like it, that is, with the hidden potential of theater. Equally fortuitous was my meeting, shortly after that, with Ivan Vyskočil, who brought me into the Theatre on the Balustrade, which at the time was just getting off the ground. Not only did this provide the opportunities I mentioned to a degree unprecedented at the time, it also gave me a chance to do more than shift the scenery around. It was also by accident that not long before, I had discovered the dramatic world of Samuel Beckett, Eugene Ionesco and other more or less "absurd" playwrights. I was tremendously excited, inspired and drawn to them, or rather I found them extremely close to my own temperament and sensibility, and it was they who stimulated me to try to communicate everything I wanted to say through drama. At that time, my long-standing efforts to get into film had come to nothing (the only way to do it then was to get into the Film Academy— and an earlier attempt to transfer from the technical university to FAMU landed me in the army, as a sapper). And finally, it was a coincidence that Jan Grossman, whom I had greatly admired long before that and who was already a friend at the time—though I was considerably younger—was asked to join the Theatre on the Balustrade shortly after I was. He became head of drama and gave me the chance, along with him, to do something I really enjoyed, without compelling me to fit into an alien mold or do any kind of violence to myself.

Had it not been for that lucky combination of circumstances I don't know what I would have done, or whether I'd have had anything to do with theater at all. I might have begun writing plays sooner or later anyway; then again I might not have.

But all that is long past; what the Theatre on the Balustrade was for those few years can neither be represented nor explained; that whole phenomenon was an integral part of its time and that time is over. But writing plays, in a sense, has remained with me to this day. If I ask why, I realize that it is not just because of the events that shaped my destiny, nor is it (I hope) the outcome of complacency or inertia on my part. As for starting something different, either I haven't had the opportunity or the courage, or (so far, at least) I haven't been able to; and anyway, I have no reason to. I don't think I've written myself out as a playwright. I have a lot of vague but therefore all the more exciting ideas about what I could and would still like to do on that territory, so I can still torment myself with that. As you know, I'm a man of obsessions, and I hate giving something up before I've exhausted all (my) possibilities. And so, in fact—though at a distance—I remain with the theater. At the same time, I feel entirely free: I know that I can give it up at any time and start something else, without too painful a "transition."

Kisses, Vašek

103

November 21, 1981

Dear Olga,

. . .

There's nothing particularly new in my life; I had the flu, and traces of it remain, so I'm not myself, which will undoubtedly have an unfavorable effect on today's letter (as will the fact that this time, I have particularly little time for writing).

*

Writing is a supremely solitary activity and so it is somewhat of a paradox that I, of all people, should have taken it up. The thing is, I'm basically a social person, even politically-minded (not that I would like a career in politics, but in the sense that I take an interest in public matters, i.e., in matters of the polis—the community). I was probably attracted to theater (among other things) because, of all the artistic disciplines, it has the greatest potential to be a social phenomenon in the true sense.

I say "potential" deliberately, for it is far from true that every theater is automatically a social phenomenon—as I understand it, at least. The fact that a theatrical performance is the collective product of a group of creative artists and that it can only happen in the physical presence of another group (the audience) is not in itself enough to make it social in the sense I mean. In most cases, it is probably no more than a formal, mechanical, superficial collectivity, defined simply by the fact that any form of theater requires the participation of a number of people. A theater that is content to leave it at that, a theater that considers this semblance of socialness to be genuine, does not interest me in the least, of course—just as nothing does that merely pretends to be something, or lies to itself about what it is. That's why I wrote, in my last letter, that theater as such doesn't attract me. What I loosely refer to as the "socialness" of theater and what I find primarily interesting and enjoyable in theater, derives from something incomparably more subtle and complex. The first embryonic appearance of genuine socialness happens the moment those participating in the theater cease to be a mere group of people and become a community. It is that special moment when their mutual presence becomes mutual participation; when their encounter in a single space and time becomes an existential encounter; when their common existence in this world is suddenly enveloped by a very specific and unrepeatable atmosphere; when a shared experience, mutually understood, evokes the wonderful elation that makes all the sacrifices worthwhile. It is a moment when a common participation in a particular adventure of the mind, the imagination and the sense of humor, and a common experience of truth or a flash of insight into the "life in truth" suddenly establishes new relationships between the participants. Halfhearted coexistence suddenly blossoms into a feeling of mutual solidarity or brotherhood, even of brotherly love, despite the fact that many of the participants may not have known or seen each other before. This electrifying atmosphere of "alliance" and "fellowship" is a central aspect of the "socialness" of the theater I am talking about. It is hard to investigate its causes and consequences theoretically, because it is supremely difficult to investigate existential reality theoretically. Still, I will try to sketch in some of its most general outlines.

But not till next time—I'm really not in the proper mood for it now, not to mention the external circumstances.

*

Kisses, Vašek

104

November 29, 1981

Dear Olga,

Thanks for letter 51. You responded very nicely to what I wrote about death; I was encouraged, and your thoughts on sickness are very good as well. I'll probably come back to them in time; the thing is, my stay in prison has really given me a new perspective on the theme of "sickness and health." I was also pleased by the stylistic polish of your letter. (If it was influenced by a debate with Zdeněk or any other friend, it is certainly all to the good! Those who know what they want to say not only need not worry about borrowing expressions from others, they in fact must do it, because therein lies the essence of mutual understanding!) . . .

*

I'd like to return to the theme already broached and to circle awhile longer around what I call the "socialness" of the theater.

What is it, in fact, that creates the special atmosphere on which this "socialness" is based? As I understand it, it is something slightly differ-ent—or, more precisely, something more special—than mere success as such. All kinds of things may enjoy theatrical success: a magnificent performance of a classical tragedy, a charming operetta, a clever con-temporary psychodrama, a good mystery, even out-and-out rubbish. A significant number of the good and bad plays that people like to go to attract audiences simply by showing life—sometimes quite brilliantly—as it appears to us, as we know it and understand it. The boards are trod by familiar and more or less understandable characters who live through familiar and "natural" situations and destinies. At the same time, everything is skillfully concentrated and enhanced: the char-acters may speak somewhat more wittily, wisely and coherently than people speak in everyday life, but the shift is executed so cleverly and subtly that we are scarcely aware of it. The success of such performances is based on the audience's effortless recognition in it of everything they know well (or at least the part of it that can be expressed), while at the same time, everything is just slightly "better" than they know—which, taken together, is a guarantee of audience identification. Theater of this type faithfully describes life, yet in a certain sense, precisely because of its fidelity, it more or less lies about it: an artful rendition of the surface (not leaving a single crack for mystery to show through) essentially obscures any view beneath it. And even if such performances excite general interest (everyone understands them and they don't offend anyone), in reality they have no telling impact on the life of society: they recapitulate what is generally known, generally accepted and generally acceptable; they do nothing to develop genuine social self-knowledge and self-awareness.

The source of the electrifying atmosphere that attracts me to theater is a success of a kind too, but only of its own kind; i.e., it is quite distinct from the colorful range of what is generally thought of as successful, and in fact it may (only very approximately, of course) be characterized in counterpoint to the type I've just mentioned (which is why I stopped to deal with it). Instead of seeing and immediately recognizing life as they know and understand it and delighting in that, the audience becomes party to an unexpected and surprising "probe" beneath the surface of phenomena which, at the same time as it gives them a new insight into their own situation, does it in a way that is comprehensible, credible and convincing on its own terms. This kind of theater allows us to see beneath the surface of phenomena, to see their inner coherences, the questions they raise, their hidden meaning, how they bear witness, in a "model" way, to man's general situation in the world. This kind of theater neither instructs us, nor attempts to acquaint us with theories or interpretations of the world, but by "probing" beneath the surface, it somehow inspires us to participate in an adventurous journey toward a deeper understanding, or rather to a new and deeper questioning, of ourselves and the world. This can be done in many ways: through a playful yet inexorable extrapolation of the hidden logic of things; by opening up an unusual level of fantasy; by constructing an uncommon way of looking at, describing and reconstructing phenomena; by exploiting particular forms of abbreviation, metaphor, humor, special tonality, special bias and obsession. What takes place onstage is generally unusual, odd, one-sided, astonishing, "open to discussion"; yet it is comprehensible because it has an order of its own and its own orderly way of disturbing that order. We witness something we hadn't realized before but we discover, to our surprise, that this biased and one-sided view, oddly enough, has its own special truth, justification, authenticity. True, we identify with something here too, but it is a "higher" kind of identification. We identify with a certain way of seeing and thinking, with a certain kind of fantasy and humor, with a certain special "order." Or we may not identify with it at all, but simply experience it suddenly, know it and feel it as something possible, as something we can enter into, understand, follow. Our enjoyment comes from a new understanding of ourselves: we consciously experience something that had hitherto existed in us only as a potential; we encounter something which, though new for us, we are able to "go along with" (which is not quite the same as agreeing with it). To a considerable extent, then, we're delighted because we suddenly see more deeply into ourselves, into our inner potential and, through that, into "Being itself." It's as though the theater had carried us with it to a path leading along a dangerous mountain ridge—and to our astonishment, we can walk along it, though we'd never before suspected that such a path existed or that we were capable of negotiating it. The author of the play or the creators of the performance, of course, are no more clever or knowledgeable than anyone else. They are not taking us somewhere they are familiar with and we are not. Everyone goes through the adventure together, and it's equally surprising, tantalizing and disturbing for us all.

I would say that it is precisely this joint participation in an unusual journey, this collective uncertainty about where the journey is leading, this delight in discovering it together and finding the courage and the ability to negotiate and enjoy the new vistas together—it is all this that creates a remarkable and rare sense of community among the participants, this exciting sense of mutual understanding, of a "new brotherhood." A certain one-sidedness in the shared experience (not everyone does, can or wants to share it) suggests that there is more being generated here than mutual understanding of something; frequently as well, there is an understanding directed against something and someone. This necessarily strengthens the new sense of community, and thus when such theater enters into the general awareness of society, it is always somewhat controversial, but that's exactly what makes it genuinely fecundating as well.

In general, it might be said that the source of this sense of community is not a communal identification with the "order of things," but communal participation in the "order of the spirit."

Kisses, Vašek

105

December 5, 1981

Dear Olga,

I live in anticipation of our meeting, which I assume will take place during my half-term hearing; I'm trying to eat less so I'll look nice for you, but it's not working out very well. There is nothing particularly new in my life, except perhaps that I've chalked up one minor success and one minor failure. The success: there was a small display of books for sale here and I ordered (you can pay from your savings!) a couple of good volumes (including Musil), which for a month or two might ease the catastrophic lack of significant reading matter. The failure: I was lulled by the relative tranquillity here (both generally, and within myself) and was not sufficiently on my guard (I should have known better, particularly at this time) and an unintentional lapse on my part turned against me, one result of which is that, except for the news, I won't be able to watch television for two months. Still, there is a positive side to it: occasionally I'll be alone in our little chamber, with peace and quiet for my own things. . . . I'm looking forward to what I hope is my second to last Christmas in prison, or rather to the walnut cake I intend to buy for the occasion. Most of all, however, I'm looking forward to the visit! I thank Ivan for letter 46; I'm waiting impatiently for the other letters he promised. Naturally I'm very interested in the results of his study of logical paradoxes, and I'd also be pleased if he could write me more about those "anticybernetic" theories he once mentioned. So he has quite enough to write me about.

*

Collective perception is, of course, one of the factors on which the ability of theater to create that special sense of community is based, but it is not peculiar to theater (we perceive other genres, like film, collectively as well) and it is certainly not enough in itself. The decisive thing here is something else: in the theater, the work we are watching is not finished, but instead is being born before our eyes, with our help, so that we are both witnesses to its birth and, in a small sense, its co-creators as well. In other words, what we are looking at in theater is not a dead thing created by a living person, but the actual living person, creating the work now, before us and with us. This entices us on that "pathway of adventure" in a quite different and far more compelling way than even the most persuasive "dead" invitation could do. An immediate existential bond is created between the work and we who perceive it; the work can only come into being and take place as a social ("interpersonal") event; seeing it is more than just an act of perception, it is a form of human relationship. It is not only the actors onstage who make this event happen—through their living presence, their actions and their lives—but the people in the audience as well. Film, television and works of visual art, etc. are essentially what they are even without viewers, but theater simply cannot exist without an audience, not just because plays are not usually put on in empty halls, but also because even if they were, it would still not be theater in the deepest sense of the word.

But this does not exhaust the matter: the deepest roots of theater's special ability to create that "festive" sense of community also lie in something else, something I can't properly describe and which grows out of the ancient essence of theater as ritual. It is a kind of immediate and vivid enactment of the very mystery of human existence. The viewer remains himself, a living, thinking, consciously acting person, and yet at the same time, for this precisely limited "festive" time, he steps outside himself and, as part of the agenda (that is, on the basis of a social agreement—or convention), he relinquishes his own identity and assumes that of another (the one being represented). It is this that points toward the real mystery of human existence and human identity, actualizes that mystery, brings it to the foreground of our awareness, opens it anew. The duality of his hour upon the stage amplifies, or rather poses, in a direct, situational way, the question: who is it? In other words: what is man? The distance between the actor and his role, and between us and the action onstage (we know it isn't a "regular" piece of life, but a piece of life that is "deliberately" representing a different piece of life), is precisely what throws us directly into the "heart" of the mystery of our own existence, the mystery of the "order of the spirit." In this sense, the author Ivan mentioned is undoubtedly right to see, in our ability to perform, something that makes us human.

Man is the only animal that reflects upon himself, upon the mystery of his existence and the mystery of his ability to reflect upon himself, and as such he is the only creature capable of "stepping outside himself" in order to point to himself.

The electrifying atmosphere of community I am talking about does not therefore derive solely from the fact that theater is a particular kind of existential event (many things can be that), but an event in which a human existence, existentially, makes present the mystery of itself— and does so not only through the meaning of what it does (that "probe" beneath the surface of phenomena), but also in how it does this—that is, through itself (through presentation and representation). It is only when illuminated and made meaningful from within by this "self-particularizing of existence" that the event of theater becomes most intrinsically itself. It is only to the degree that we ourselves experience this self-particularizing of existence in the theater that we also feel its uniqueness, its specialness and its "celebratory" nature—in other words, qualities that are always inseparable from the kind of theatrical atmosphere I have in mind.

At the same time, an obvious assumption and aspect of this genuine theatrical process of coming to an understanding is, as may be clear from what I've already written, coming to an understanding about the conventions that make all this miraculous "self-particularizing" possible and that mediate it. But I'll come back to that next time—

Kisses, Vašek

106

December 12, 1981

Dear Olga,

My impression is that the main event of last week—my "half-term" hearing—was a success: no untoward occurrence prevented you from coming (the presence of Zdeněk and Nikolaj delighted and moved me—thank them very much!); before the hearing I managed to drink my morning tea, I said what had to be said for the sake of propriety and was able (I think) to maintain the degree of dignity attainable in the given (and rather absurd) situation. The proceedings were formally correct, I was neither humiliated nor ridiculed, I was even mildly tickled by that forgotten form of address—"Mr."—and in the end everything, though in an appropriately simplified form, came to pass just as it should. My final feeling, therefore, was one of harmonious joy, thanks, among other things, to the fact that I had not fully realized, until it was "officially" confirmed, that the greater (and I hope the worse) part of my sentence is now over with. At the moment I'm concentrating entirely on the coming visit and reading Musil in my free time. It's just what I need: it allows me to be in contact, for a while each day, with cultivated language and a clever text. (Besides the Musil, I bought the *History of Architecture in the 20th Century,* a book on the significance of the heavenly bodies in human history, and Chekhov's short stories.)

*

I have always stressed the importance of convention in theater. The point is that theater is already, in essence, a convention in itself. People are agreed that the playhouse is divided (by a curtain) into stage and auditorium; that those who watch the play will sit in the auditorium and those who perform it will do so onstage; that one side will not intervene physically, at least, in the life of the other; that those who perform will not step out of their roles during the performance, and that those who watch understand that what happens on the stage is merely performed and therefore not real life, or more precisely, that it is real life, but representing a different life.

These few elementary conventions give birth to a complex network of other conventions, many of which are more subtle and less obvious, and it is this complex structure of conventions that both establishes and opens up the rich world of their potential disruption, by liberating the enormous potential of emotional, semantic and aesthetic material concealed within that disruption. The more subtle and structured this "order for disrupting order" is, the richer its potential.

As for myself, I am fond of theater that respects some of the basic theatrical conventions, depends on them, uses them in its own way and then—only after having embraced them, as it were—begins gradually and unobtrusively to overturn, travesty and disrupt them. The more rigid and straightforward the original convention, the more suggestive, it seems to me, can the process of its dramatic "violation" ultimately become. Thus the real power of the result is directly proportional to the rigidity of the initial situation and to the dramatic decorum and the layered complexity with which that situation is dealt. I have often realized, and stressed, that where everything is allowed, nothing has the power to surprise. Chaos and caprice are boring; they are "entropic": one quickly wearies of their sameness. Art, like the entire "order of the spirit," is intrinsically antientropic. Its effectiveness is based on penetrating to ever higher levels of articulation. (I am using the words "articulation" or "structuredness," of course, in their most general sense, that is, I am not referring to merely mechanical articulation. Precisely the contrary, in fact: the higher the level of articulation, the less it can be reduced to mechanical models.)

I am not overly fond of the various superficial ways of bringing the audience and the stage closer together, for example, by doing away with the proscenium, positioning the stage in the middle of the auditorium, pestering the audience by having the actors walk among them or even drawing them onto the stage. For the most part I find it embarrassing, sterile and willful. Genuine contact—intellectual, existential contact, that is—is displaced by superficial contact, mere mechanical or physical contact which usually results in a deeper alienation. Actors and audience alike are out of sorts; the agreement between them has been broken, not because the inner logic of the intellectual adventure demanded it, but merely because they lacked the imagination to do anything else. We may observe, in any case, that the less capable theater is of addressing the spirit in a genuinely lively way and drawing one into an "event of the spirit," the more conspicuously it draws attention to itself, whether it be through a variety of special effects, or by having the actors pester the audience. (This "pestering" is almost inevitably unnatural because the actors are suddenly called upon to perform as though they were not performing at all, in other words, the performance contracted for is replaced by ordinary lying.) Do you remember that avant-garde play we once saw together in London? Everything was "unconventional" right from the start: the actors flew over our heads on some kind of trapezes, a donkey wandered about the stage and perhaps through the audience as well, etc.—and it quickly began to bore us, until at last all we could focus on was our fear that someone or something would fall on our heads. At the time, I realized with particular clarity that nothing is quite so mutually exclusive in theater as caprice and surprise.

But to come back to where I began: it seems to me that the convention of "performance"—an outgrowth of theater's ancient roots in ritual—is precisely the "trick" on which that miraculous "enactment" of the mystery of human existence is based: it is only when a person who is physically present "here and now" begins to perform that he takes that fateful step "outside himself" that allows him, "here and now," to demonstrate the mystery of his own humanity, i.e., the mystery of human existence altogether. In other words: it is only by consciously making theatrical convention a part of our enterprise that we can create a springboard for a "flight of the spirit." Without that springboard, every theatrical attempt to "fly" will merely be a sad exercise in self-deception—like the flight of the avant-garde actors in London over our heads.

*

This letter will probably reach you shortly after the visit and just before Christmas. Spend Christmas Day the way you like best; do something nice in my stead and try to fulfill a single wish of mine: that you write something like a "Christmas diary" and send it to me. Wish your mother and all your family a lovely Christmas for me, and to Ivan, Květa, the boys (I know you'll give them something too), to Andulka, all our friends and all people of goodwill that you meet.

Kisses from your "apparent recluse,"

Vašek

107

December 19, 1981

Dear Olga,

Although shortly before the visit I was quite at ease with myself, calm, cheerful, in a conversational mood, no sooner had the visit begun than I once more found myself in that strange state when my mind seems scattered, my throat dries up, I feel cold inside, I stammer and, in short, am not myself. It is probably something like a conditioned nervous reflex and one day I will write more about it (as a general comment on the phenomenon of prison visits). Of course it must be said that this time it was not nearly as strong as last, thanks to which the visit too, was not such a wash-out—on the contrary, I feel very good about it. We said what could be said, and it was even my impression that, more than on other visits, I gained an insight, through various details, into the atmosphere of the life you live and I understood a number of things that haven't been quite clear to me. Moreover the news you brought was all (relatively) good, including one item that particularly pleased me. On the whole, I told you nothing, but in any case, what could I have told you? I've become increasingly aware that some experiences are simply not communicable—and even less so under these circumstances. Both of you looked good; Ivan was even nattier than during recent visits in Heřmanice and you were not only chic, but you were wonderfully got up as well; it helped me to relax, though I didn't let on very much. As always, I was fully satisfied with the parcel; it differs from my directives only in small details. . . .

*

I would say that the social nature of theater has three zones or spheres that grow out of one another:

1. The first consists of the immediate social aspect of each individual performance. It derives from the existential bond that comes into being "here and now," creating that short-term communal feeling in a specific audience and which is essentially a single, unrepeatable phenomenon. All of the other and more profound social aspects of theater must go through this phase: without the individual performances and their audiences, no other lasting impact of theater on society is either possible or thinkable.

2. Just as every individual performance, through its unconditional "here-and-nowness" and through the immediate response that helps to create it, is firmly anchored in its time (it cannot be understood and appreciated later, as a novel or a picture can), so theater itself, in the wider sense of the word—the theater as institution—is anchored in the life of society only through its actual presence. It cannot influence the social climate after the fact, but again, only through the response it evokes at the time, a response which helps to create it both as an institution and a concept. Nevertheless, it is obvious that in this case the social aspect is wider and deeper and more than just a onetime social event. This "second sphere of sociality," deriving directly from the first and related to it, means that the theater as an institution (that is, the kind of theater I believe in, love and have had the good fortune to work in) is never just an institution: it is a focus (or more precisely,

one of the focuses) of social life and social thought, an irreplaceable component of the "spirit of the nation," a small organism, bound by thousands of threads to the great organism of society and playing an irreplaceable and actual social role within it. It has its own audience, which is not just the mechanical sum of its regular and occasional audiences but again, something more: a special kind of community. The theater is frequented and loved above all by a certain kind of people, i.e., people with certain interests, a certain way of thinking, a certain sense of fantasy and humor, people who are open to the theater in question and who identify with it. These people gradually come to understand each other better, and the theater even provides them with a kind of "code" that makes communication among themselves easier.

But in another sense, too, there is usually more involved here than the audience for a particular performance. These people in fact no longer merely go to see this given performance, they go to "their" theater somewhat as they would to their own spiritual home; they go for the vision of the world it provides and for its atmosphere; they go to it as if it were their own club, i.e., in order to be among their own kind. (This is why I consider everything "around" the theater important too: the atmosphere in the performance space and the building, the genius loci, the life in the foyer, the exhibitions, the programs and posters, the comportment of the box-office attendants and the ushers, etc., etc.) The sociality of this second circle, therefore, is something more lasting, more complex and more profound than the atmosphere of a two-hour experience. But here, too, there are limitations: it directly affects only a small portion of society and it is also limited in time. Sooner or later, a theater loses its identity, its atmosphere is gone, the sense of community among its audience dissipates, and that "spiritual home" irretrievably vanishes into the mists of time. The information that remains in the histories of a theater is only a weak and often misleading reflection of its former atmosphere, which can simply never be re-created. (Let us recall, for instance, how "unre-creatable" the Liberated Theatre is. We know everything about it—and at the same time, we know nothing at all.)

3. And yet: nothing that has once happened can be made to "unhappen," either in the metaphysical sense (everything is present in the "memory of Being"), or in the social sense. Each event that has had any impact on the "spirit of society," even in the smallest backwater, has somehow—be it ever so insignificantly—altered that

"spirit" as a whole. Something happened to it that cannot now be made to "unhappen"; it is a tiny component in the large context of thousands of other events, yet it does, after all, influence society a little. Something within society is, and always will be, slightly different than it was before. Obviously then, theater does not transcend itself (its "second sphere of sociability") in time only, but also in space, as it were. Even though in its heyday, its entire audience may have comprised only a tiny percentage of the population, yet indirectly, in some mysterious and complex way, it had an impact on the awareness and the self-esteem of society as a whole—somewhat in the way certain stimulants (like tea, to remain with prison reality), though they only have a direct physiological impact on a tiny part of our organism, make us feel generally different and better after consuming them. This transcendence in space and time that defines theater's "third sphere of sociality" is, of course, deeper and further-reaching in proportion to how deeply and urgently and clearly the theater makes that controversial "probe" beneath the surface of life, or rather to how inventively and daringly it addresses society. In terms of genuine social impact, the daring is far more important than how many people were originally addressed. From a certain point of view, a single performance for a few dozen people can be incomparably more important than a television serial viewed and talked about by the entire country. But more about that next time—

* * *

My wish for you, Ivan, Květa and myself for the New Year is that nothing even remotely like my (needlessly extended) study sojourn will happen to us, and that we will be as cheerful, healthy and hopeful as we have been so far. I also wish a positive mind and perseverance in the faith that things have a meaning to all our friends, of whom I would like to mention today Juliana, whom I think of during the day, Jarmilka, who appears to me in my dreams, and of course Andulka, who appears to me by day and in my dreams—all of which, I should add, takes place in your continuous and especially profound presence (in my mind and in my heart).

I kiss you, Vašek

108

December 26, 1981

Dear Olga,

. . .

Two days before Christmas (I had just had an attack of melancholy but it had nothing to do with Christmas) I wanted to be alone for a while after work, so I went into the little courtyard here. Snow was falling thickly through the murky twilight; I was alone and suddenly it struck me how odd it was that in other circumstances this sad and barren place can make me feel so much joy in being alive. All it takes is sunshine, green grass and flowers—and suddenly one is filled with hope and faith in the meaning of things, including one's own life. How are we to explain this mysterious connection between the immediate atmosphere of a place and the state of the human spirit? How can something as vitally important as the attitude of a person toward his own life be affected by something as incidental as the weather or the season?

When we talk of "the meaning of life," we usually have in mind an existential phenomenon, that is, something that only man, as a "being that questions itself," can seek and aspire to—as a key to his own life. This is how I understood "the meaning of life" in my own reflections on the subject, which of course—regardless of how I came at it—always led to the conclusion that each "existential" meaning ascribed to life essentially means some kind of contact with the mystery of "meaning altogether," i.e., the meaning of Being, in other words, meaning as a metaphysical phenomenon. . . .

I certainly do not think that man has a patent on meaning; I merely think that he alone is capable of putting it to himself as a question. From that point of view, of course, he is exceptional. It really does seem to me true that consciousness, and the "re-creation" of the world through consciousness (the creation of the order of the spirit), is an independent miracle, as it were, in the history of the miracle of Being as a whole. Sooner or later, man had to realize his exceptional nature, so it seems to me more than just a historical error. Obviously, this recognition lies behind the tragic split between European humanity and the biosphere, nature and the universe (the present destruction of the planet, and thus of man himself, are part of its terrifying consequences). But doesn't the most essential cause of this split lie, not in man's having understood his own peculiarity, but his inability to deal with the burden of this understanding? In other words: instead of deepening his humility and wonder before the world that gave birth to his consciousness and, through that consciousness, revealed itself to him anew, this "awareness of the miracle of his own awareness" led him, on the contrary, to an arrogant feeling of superiority over all other forms of Being. And another question: did not man first of all have to separate himself from the world, understand his own uniqueness and the responsibility deriving from that, before—on a higher level this time (as in some Hegelian spiral)—returning to the world and becoming an integral part of it more effectively this time? Is it not possible, therefore, to see the fundamental, dramatic question confronting present-day humanity in this way: what will we accomplish first: this "return to the future" (as opposed to a romantic, illusory return to the past); in other words, will we achieve a new, more profound and more adequate integration of ourselves with the universe? Or will we culminate the tragic work of our own hubris and destroy it all, including ourselves?

To return to the prison courtyard: what is actually happening when it begins to turn green in the spring again in bud and flower and perfume, when things come to life again? What in fact is that change, that its consequences can be so far-reaching? One important thing happens, I think: all at once, what yesterday still seemed no more than an agglomeration of dead, isolated, accidental and purposeless entities now begins to appear as nature—nature, with its own great and mysterious order, its own direction, its countless births and deaths, its own life. We see that something exists that links, with countless hidden but common laws and tendencies, the grass, the flower beds, the trees and everything they represent and remind us of; something that gives them worth, that underlies both the infinite (antientropic) diversity of their existence as discrete entities and the unfailing concord of their natural coexistence; something that breathes into them their beauty and that through them, displays and celebrates itself and inspires celebration. It is a small example, I think, of how Being manifests its own meaning, or rather, how the meaning of Being makes itself knowable through Being. And whom does it "prod," shake up or speak to? To man, as one who, though a part of that Being himself, is at the same time a being who can perceive Being as Being, consciously experience it and generalize about it; who can relate its manifestations to each other, to

Being as a whole and to himself; who can know about those relations; who has the capacity to be amazed and to ponder on all of this, and who can even be aware of his own amazement and wonder at it and think about his thoughts and about how he thinks about them. In other words: man, whose quest is always—whether he admits it or not—an aspiration toward "the absolute meaning of Being," is suddenly confronted with a set of phenomena that reveal themselves as expressions of an integral Being, and with Being that reveals itself to have meaning. And thus, in fact, an encounter takes place: the existential longing for meaning encounters a powerful "metaphysical-physical" signal of meaning and its "obvious" manifestation. And just as a human being who longs for meaning is open to the world, ready to hear its promptings, decode its signals, draw from it its deepest connections and its references to the order of Being—and thus infuse it with meaning—suddenly, the world too is, as it were, ready to infuse that existence with meaning: it intensifies its signals, it behaves in an "obvious" manner. We are then overcome by a feeling of joyous meaningfulness because we suddenly feel that the thing we have been constantly reaching out for is almost physically within our grasp, because it is not just we who are greedily open to it; our counterpart, too, has opened itself to us. It is not just we who long for contact with the meaning of Being, but the meaning of Being itself, if it can be put that way, reaches out to us. I feel like saying that a kind of mystic cooperation occurs: our need to discover our own meaning by touching "absolute meaning" entices this meaning out of what surrounds us, and what surrounds us, on the contrary, entices from the deepest regions of our being our own veiled certitude that meaning exists, which is, the certitude of life itself. Through this cooperation, through this encounter, through this contact, of course, what in fact happens, in an odd, roundabout way, is an encounter between the meaning of Being and Being itself: for Being first had to call itself into question, through man, so that through his search for the "meaning of life," through its own manifestations in the world that surrounds him and ultimately through the encounter of one with the other, Being could return to itself and be fulfilled. But would anything like this peculiar self-fulfillment (a small preview of the vision of the "great" re-union of Being with itself through man as the one who expelled himself from Being so that he could "see" it and then, as "one who can see," returned to it) be possible at all if man, at a certain phase in his development, had not acknowledged his own "uniqueness"—along with all the dangers concealed within this "acknowledgment"?

———

I have survived the prison Christmas, my melancholy is gone and my paunch has grown.

I kiss you,
Vašek

109

January 1, 1982

Dear Olga,

My brief return to the question of "meaning" interrupted my meditation on theater and I'd like to continue the interruption today by bringing up the relationship between identity and responsibility. The atmosphere of the moment (it is New Year's Day) is an invitation to deal with loose ends and moreover, my thoughts on the theater are nearing the point where I'll have to pick up on that theme anyway. In a letter of long ago (unsent, like so many others), I managed to describe the matter with some exactness, and of course I won't be able to repeat the performance (which is why I've put it off for so long). Nevertheless, my sense of order compels me to overcome my distaste for saying something badly that I had once said better.

*

To a certain extent, our actions are always illuminated by responsibility. What this means is that we can always justify them in some way, defend them in advance, stand behind them, own up to them, identify with them, consider them correct or, if not correct, then at least come to terms with that. The essence of this responsibility is a constant tension between our "I," as the subject of our actions, and our experience of something outside ourselves—a "law" or seat of judgment ruling on our behavior, an "investigating eye" that will not be deceived because it sees all and remembers it well, an infinitely wise and just instance of authority that alone can follow and understand the most subtle intricacies of our decisions and the motives behind them, and can pass final judgment on them, an authority whose "stand" (irrevocable) means more to us, for some reason, than anything else in the world. Human responsibility, then, as the word itself suggests, is responsibility to something. But to what? What is this omnipresent, omnipotent and undeceivable instance of authority and where in fact does it reside?

At first it usually seems simply to be our environment—the people, creatures and things around us. Indeed, this higher instance of authority does most frequently seem to be embodied in what surrounds us—and the closer and dearer those things are to us, the more powerfully its presence in them seems to be. On closer examination, however, we soon see that this particular "incarnation" is far from exhausting or explaining the matter; there is always something "more," something "outside," something that transcends it. After all, those around us are ignorant of many of the actions we take with that higher authority in mind, nor will they ever find out; they don't understand much of what we do in that regard and they never will—and yet we do it all the same. Sometimes we simply call this "transcendence" conscience, and in doing so we localize it within ourselves. Some go further and explain this "inner voice" as the joint product of innate emotional dispositions, upbringing, convention, etc. Yes, all of those are certainly ways in which this higher authority approaches us. But reducing it to a mere coagent of those "circumstances" will not get us very far: we always experience responsibility most powerfully when it compels us to act not only against prevailing opinion, but against our own so-called natures as well. And just as a human being—the human "I"—is not (or not only) an accumulation of circumstances, neither is its "partner," the higher authority to which it permanently relates, merely an agglomeration of fragmented accidental qualities. On the contrary, as soon as we begin to communicate with it on even a slightly more serious level, it quickly starts to lose the specific outlines it once had in our everyday dealings with it (e.g., when it was "incarnate" in our notionally fixed principles or in our friends); we seem to leave that world of separate entities, we lose the feeling that we can depend on it—or rather that anything from that world can, in and of itself, provide us with a fully reliable standard— and we suddenly find ourselves relating (subconsciously, perhaps) to something that, though extremely difficult to grasp, is crucial: a totally integral instance of authority that pervades everything we know, yet cannot be reduced to any known thing or person. Individual quanta—be they our own "natural" urges or the watchful eyes of those around us—seem to dissolve in its deeper context, which, in a way, they had only represented. They cease to constitute the highest authority, and that authority, as it were, constitutes them, breathes into them what takes them beyond themselves and makes them what, to us, they really are.

But again: what in fact is this "final instance of authority"? What else but the "absolute horizon of Being," against whose background and out of which anything first becomes itself; the absolute horizon of Being as a "system of coordinates" providing everything that exists with a place, a context, a meaning, a discrete existence, and thus, ultimately, genuine Being. It is, therefore, the "experience of all experiences," the measure of all measures, the order of all orders. Indeed: if I know what I have done and why, and what I do and why, if I can really stand behind this and (in private, perhaps) own up to it, I am thereby constantly relating to something stable, something I "win" from my "unstable" surroundings, and thus I myself ultimately become "relatively stable"—something graspable, something that possesses continuity and integrity. In short, I am "someone", i.e., identical with himself. By standing today behind what I did yesterday, and standing here behind what I did elsewhere, I not only gain my identity, but through it, I find myself in space and time; if, on the contrary, I lose my identity, time and space must necessarily disintegrate around me as well.

In this sense, therefore, responsibility establishes identity; it is only in the responsibility of human existence for what it has been, is and will be that its identity dwells. In other words, if human identity is the irreplaceable locus of the "I" in the context of the "non-I," then human responsibility is what determines that locus: the relationship of the former to the latter.

Patočka said that the thing most peculiar to responsibility is that it is "ours, everywhere." I think this is so because the world is everywhere, "surrounded" or "infused" with its absolute horizon, and that we can never step beyond this horizon, leave it behind us or forget about it, regardless of how hidden it is (and in any case it is always hidden: it is in everything, and nowhere does it exist in and of itself). It may be only our own imaginary construct—but in that case, so is the whole world. Does it matter, though, whether we use the word "Being" or the word "imaginary construct"? In doing so, we cannot escape our responsibility, not even by a fraction of an inch!

*

But we don't even want to, do we?

I kiss you,
Vašek

110

January 9, 1982

Dear Olga,

. . .

Regarding Zdeněk N.'s remarks: I feel there is more than mere intellectual quibbles preventing me from professing faith in a personal God. Behind those "quibbles" lies something deeper: I have not had the mystical experience of a genuine, personal revelation, that supremely important "last drop." No doubt I could simply substitute the word "God" for my "something" or my "absolute horizon" but that would hardly be responsible. I am trying to describe the matter as precisely as I can, as it appears to me and as I feel it; in other words, I don't wish to feign certainty where none exists. I admit to an affinity for Christian sentiment and I'm glad it's recognizable; nevertheless, one must be extremely cautious in such matters and weigh one's words well (as a matter of fact the archbishop of Prague himself once told me this when we were discussing the matter). There are many other aspects to a faith in the Christian God, such as belief in the divinity of Christ, in the Immaculate Conception of the Virgin Mary, etc.—and I take all that too seriously to pass off as belief various more or less figurative acceptances of those things. . . .

It's obvious to me that there is no such thing as "mereness"; things appear to be "mere" when one is alienated from oneself and the context of Being, overpowered by a sense of absurdity and hopelessness, when one loses touch with meaning and surrenders to Nothingness (the prison courtyard in winter). (I can't even be criticized for disdaining the animal sphere of life: after all, I am known—among other things—for my epicureanism and, moreover, I am a dog trainer of many years standing.) The misunderstanding lies in something else: my formulations are taken too seriously, literally, as though they were definitive. For the sake of simplicity, brevity, expressiveness, and also because I can't be precise all the time, I formulate things this way one time and that way another, as it suits me and as the context requires; I don't claim that any of my formulations are definitively valid. My language is somewhat figurative, abbreviated, tentative, the terms are chosen for the occasion and are meant to serve only in particular sentences or to make specific observations. Which compels me to stress again something I've already written several times before: that my meditations are not, nor are they meant to be, a philosophy, much less a philosophical system intended to add to the common property of mankind in that department. They are more the testimony of a man—myself—in a particular situation, of his inner murmurings. They are only (perhaps) an existential document (like poetry), an imprint in progress of the flow of my inner life, nothing more. I can vouch for myself, as a man who is subjected to certain forms of distress, but not for my formulations as such; I am prepared at any time, without torture and in good conscience, to withdraw or alter any of them. I have neither the education nor the experience to be a true philosopher. Nothing I write has been conceptually worked out beforehand—I clarify it in the act of writing. (I am not trying to excuse rash or random formulations, nor am I rejecting the opinions of professionals—on the contrary: they inspire me greatly.)

. . .

On New Year's Day I saw *The Bartered Bride* on television and it was one of the most beautiful experiences I've had in recent times. Tears came to my eyes during almost every aria, and I was extraordinarily touched and moved by it. It's odd how such things affect a person here. There are probably several reasons for it, one of which is no doubt the absolute lack of anything pretty, pure, moving, emotional in the atmosphere in which one has lived so long. Whenever I am feeling emotionally vulnerable I am struck with a great sense of regret. It's interesting, though, that I never feel sorry for myself, as one might expect, but only for the other prisoners and altogether, for the fact that prisons must exist and that they are as they are, and that mankind has not so far invented a better way of coming to terms with certain things.

Kiss Kamila, Zuzana, Anička and Otka for me, and give my greetings to Zdeněk Neubauer and Docent Palouš, who took the trouble to read and comment on my letters. And naturally, to Ivan and his whole family!

I kiss you,
Vašek

111

January 16, 1982

Dear Olga,

When I'm with you, I naturally speak and behave somewhat differently from how I speak and behave when I'm with my case officer; in both cases I am—without necessarily being aware of it—a slightly different person. Of course you too are a different person when speaking to me and speaking to someone else, and all three of us are different when we meet at a visit. That is why each of these encounters has an essentially different atmosphere. Each atmosphere can, in turn, have a thousand variations, depending on our moods, our changing relationships, the events that came before or after, the spatiotemporal circumstances of our encounters, etc. What is important and interesting here is that each atmosphere is a discrete phenomenon which each of us—in his own way—influences but which, as such, transcends our individual wills and perhaps even our collective will. It may be explicable as the active sum of all the influences that make it up, but only to the same degree that human life, for example, is explicable as a complex of biochemical processes. In other words, it can't be fully explained this way, because all the factors, in addition to being cocreators of the atmosphere, are also part of a "higher order," subordinated to its own "game rules" that transcend psychological explanations in the same way that human existence transcends biochemistry. But what is this "higher order"? I think it is nothing more and nothing less than the order of "intersubjective psyche," i.e., what we might call the "collective spirit," something that has its own identity, continuity, integrity and mood. As a matter of fact our language recognizes and frequently employs categories like "mob psychosis," the "mood" or the "will" of a certain community, "the climate of the times," "the behavior of the nation" (or even its character!), "social consciousness," "class consciousness," etc. Obviously, therefore, we cannot do without the primly suppressed assumption that a "collective spirit" exists. Which is in itself, I think, more than telling.

All that, of course, is merely the tip of the iceberg—that is, the territory of "physical collectivity," whose "spirit" can, after all, appear to be woven from the more or less "visible" strands of immediate social interaction. But is the substance of the "collective spirit" limited to trivial matters like the mood in lineups for meat, in a platoon before the attack or in a nation before an uprising? Are there not thousands of infinitely more subtle, complex and important ties—from the biological, the political and social to the purely spiritual—which weave together people of widely different eras, cultures and civilizations? Are we not wedged into complex social, economic and cultural structures that necessarily mediate as well the extensive spiritual integration of modern humanity? Then, too, none of us knows what is lodged in our subconscious, what archetypal experiences we've inherited from thousands of years of human existence, what tortuous byways they follow before finally surfacing in our "existential praxis." Even less do we understand the mysteries of the "psychic field": what if individual existences are really only nodes in a single gigantic intersubjective network?

Yet any "collective spirit" is only the "physical" preamble to the metaphysical fact I once called "the order of the spirit." And that is my main concern here.

For some time, I've had the unshakable feeling that the order of the spirit—like the order of Being—has its own special memory as well. Every intellectual act, once it has taken place, is "recorded" first in the memory of Being, like everything that has happened, and a second time in the memory of the spirit (which of course is also part of the history of Being, so we might say that the intellectual act is recorded twice in the memory of Being as well: once "directly" and once as a part of the history of the spirit. This essential "duality" of everything spiritual, by the way, is very important and I shall come back to it, because, it has a number of specific implications, especially for art). I firmly believe that what I understand by the order of the spirit has its own "spirit" (or is it "metaspirit"?), its "superidentity," its horizon—in short, something that maintains its continuity across epochs, cultures, civilizations and the entire history of humanity (or humanities?), something that is its backbone, its axis, its center of gravity, its direction, its mysterious "mission" within the order of Being. Here and there, the continuity and integrity of the order of the spirit are generally easy to discern; elsewhere they are disputable, even well hidden, and sometimes, try as we might to perceive them, they simply seem nonexistent. I feel that they exist—though I can't say exactly why—quite independently of whether they can be grasped or not. I am simply convinced that every means by which man has tried to give expression to his spirit leaves its imprint on the history of the order of the spirit or in the memory of the spirit, that through all this, the order of the spirit, with antlike diligence, probes and tests the limits, the possibilities and the dimensions of humanity's freedom and responsibility; that everything in it is somehow secretly tallied, stored and evaluated (including the possibility that man abandon it for good, as erroneous). Doesn't the fact that one has managed to create something—though it may seem to have had no other impact—mean something in itself? Does not that alone say something and promise something? Does it not thus expand the range of what can be done, and of how far one may go? Every work of the spirit is a small reenactment of the miracle of Being, a small re-creation of the world—and is not this essential and unique transcendence of its material existence enough to guarantee it a lasting place in the history of the spirit and lasting participation in the "spirit" of the order of the spirit—that special attempt on the part of Being at its own great re-creation?

To sum up: I'm convinced that each spiritual act is an integral part of the order of the spirit, that the order of the spirit is present in each act just as the entire river is present in an eddy, and that every such act irrevocably alters the order of the spirit, just as every eddy, though it may last no more than a minute, has irrevocably changed the river. And none of this is altered by the fact that we will never know what effect it actually had on the river. We only know that it happened, and that therefore it had to happen for some reason and that the river would not be what it is had it not happened. . . .

I kiss you,
Vašek

112

January 23, 1982

Dear Olga,

As you may or may not have noticed, my last letter was a subtle way of preparing to return to my thoughts on theater. I can now summarize and conclude that passage about the social nature of theater with the claim that unlike any other artistic discipline, theater enters the memory of the spirit exclusively through the multiform "collective spirit," or rather, through that part of it that I have called "the tip of the iceberg," the part that grows out of a physical collectivity. Not only is theater already, by its very nature (as one of the arts), an "intersubjective" event, that is, a product of that "higher order" which every collective psychicality is, but also, through the various forms of the physical collectivity and its "collective spirit," it becomes what it is in the wider sense as well—as an institution and a cultural phenomenon. If theater, as I have written, is an existential phenomenon par excellence (it is always bound to the human "here and now"), then it is also an "interexistential" (or, perhaps more precisely, a "superexistential") phenomenon. This is far from being a merely theoretical distinction: it allows us to differentiate between theater and special cases, like certain kinds of body art or the happening, where the art also resides in an existential "here and now"; mainly, however, it points to a very important fact known to every theater person: that theater works intrinsically with a rather different kind of psychic material than anything else which does not emerge from an immediate human community (such as film and television, for example, genres which are otherwise relatively close to theater). Each performance has its own special atmosphere (something like each of your visits here with me), which obeys the special laws of the collective psyche and cannot be reduced to an imaginary sum of those who take part (audiences as a whole behave differently from each individual member in them; and the cast of different productions of the same play—though it may involve some or all of the same actors—always creates a different "collective spirit" onstage). All this, however, becomes far more complex in the second and third spheres of sociality, through which theater must pass before it attains its "definitive" cultural (and therefore spiritual) identity, and so too its definitive locus in the order of the spirit and its memory. (How much easier, in this regard, is it for a poem, say, or a drawing. Theoretically, at least, they can skip all that: although their place in the history of the spirit also consists in the absolute sum of their objectivized cultural impact—in other words, of everything they ever meant to anyone and every response they ever evoked—they do not intrinsically depend on that, because it is not the intrinsic medium of their physical existence and therefore not of their spiritual dimension either.)

I will leave an investigation of the specific consequences and expressions of these peculiarities of theater to experts (by the way, very little has had so much nonsense written about it as the relationship between theater and society); here are only a few general remarks.

The "adventurous path" that theater (or at least the kind of theater I'm concerned with here) invites us to travel down can be as steep, as treacherous and as special as it likes, but it must also be so artfully blazed that it can be found by a "collective spirit" capable of going along it, or rather of opening it up. The point is that if theater wants to be theater at all, it can't very well go beyond the limits of what its contemporaries are capable of experiencing, and what any contemporary "collective spirit" is fitted to experience (this, too, has countless concrete consequences!). In short, the theater can attract, provoke, shock the people of its own time in a variety of ways, it can draw out of them their many hidden proclivities, but it must always do so in a way that still allows that to happen, that leaves something to be attracted and drawn out, so that shock may still be experienced as shock. Whatever it is theater attempts to do with the "collective spirit," it can only accomplish it by connecting with what is already there. (Real theater people, of course, don't usually give these things much thought; they rather feel them at the heart of their talent; it is not a sad and limiting duty, but on the contrary an exciting challenge.)

As an event in the "collective spirit," the theater is naturally bound by a complex "metabolic" system to its own age and society. It is an organ in the large organism of society and its time, necessarily influenced by everything that influences them. It is a confluence of their currents—be they ever so hidden. Like it or not, theater is always more or less connected to everything by which the "collective spirit" lives— to its hidden and open themes, its dilemmas, to the existential questions that manifest themselves to it or as it manifests them, to the sensibility, the emotivity of the age, its moods, its thought and expression, its gestures, its visual sensibilities, its life-style, fashion, etc. etc.

Theater connects up with all of that in one way or another; it reflects and cocreates it, analyzes and alters it, parodies and negates it; all of that is always more present in theater than in anything else.

As a spiritual and social focus of its time, theater is also bound of course to the social structure (and ultimately, to the power structure) of its time. Regardless of how controversial its entry into the "collective spirit" may be, the mere fact that it exists as a social fact and a social institution testifies to the social structure of its time, means something within it, somehow helps to create and determine that structure as a whole. Everyone who has seen and taken part in it (and therefore helped create it) becomes a little different than he was before, so that even whatever he tries to achieve, or not, as an active member of the social structure, how he thinks and what he does, is influenced (no matter how remotely) by this experience. In fact this is true for everyone, whether they see it or not. To have been a contemporary of the Liberated Theatre, the Theatre on the Balustrade, the Činoherní Klub, etc. means—inevitably—to have been a "part" of the same "collective spirit" that made those theaters possible and that was created by them. Again, this cannot be without consequences. (A succinct illustration: the Liberated Theatre could not have existed in this country at the same time as the Terezín Ghetto.)

Sooner or later, the mark left by a theater on the "collective spirit" will vanish: those who remember it will die, their memories will fade, all the documents (including the plays) will perish, and in the "collective spirit" of other times and other cultures nothing will remain, except perhaps for an almost theoretical "glimmer" deep in its unconscious layers. And that, clearly, is the moment when the theater definitively leaves the anteroom of the "collective spirit" and enters the mysterious chambers of the "mere" memory of the spirit.

It is something like Ivan's eddies: theater is an eddy in the river; it is we who make it, of course, but through it we also try the nature of the river; we make it, and then we observe the swirling water, which of course is now irrevocably unlike what it was before we intervened. After Samuel Beckett, we live in a different world than we did before him. The eddy he set in motion will, of course, subside and eventually vanish altogether, or entirely different eddies will disturb the waters. But though to all appearances it may seem that everything is as before and that nothing has actually happened, this is not the case: that eddy will swirl on forever in the memory of the spirit as a tiny part of that great and extravagant activity through which the order of the spirit fulfills its mission in the order of Being. And just as the river is what it is only because that eddy once appeared in it, the order of the spirit struggles through to achieve its own secret superidentity in this work as well.

*

. . . I'd like to tell you about a dream I had recently (twice in a row, in fact, over two nights): I was on what they call temporary parole and went to Hrádeček; there were many strange people there and I was astonished to realize that during my absence everything had been restored to the way it looked fifteen years ago when we bought it (the walls we put up were knocked down, and those knocked down put up again, the original furniture everywhere, along with stuff the Kulháneks had left, etc.). I made a long, eloquent speech to you about how all the alterations we had made over the years were an expression of our common will, our common taste, our common life, that we had invested so much thought, energy and money in it that it was a kind of material imprint, a material confirmation, of our "collective spirit," our two-in-one identity, and that by restoring it, you had in fact betrayed all that. Whereupon you informed me that your closest friend was now Jirka Němec and that the new appearance of Hrádeček was merely an expression of your common will and of his spiritual influence on you. To which I replied that you couldn't take Jirka that seriously, that his penetrating intellect had lost its "credibility" when he "jumped off the train." If he hasn't already left, give him my regards, wish him luck, and I'd prefer you didn't let him read this—or if you do, then with the proviso that I won't be held responsible for my dreams. . . .

I kiss you,
Vašek

113

January 30, 1982

Dear Olga,

Your letter came at the same time as Květa's letter and Ivan's, and my first impressions have become lumped together into a rather depressing entity. None of them—looked at matter-of-factly—provides sufficient cause in itself for depression, nor do they taken as a whole, but there it is: you become unusually thick-skinned here, but I suppose the price you pay is occasionally having something snap inside you (all it takes is a slight nudge, the kind you might not even notice outside) and suddenly, you become as oversensitive as a girl in puberty. Of course depressions in many forms are nothing new with me, it's just that I don't write about them because by nature I'm loath to make my personal feelings public; I tend, rather, to hide behind certain depersonalized (or apparently depersonalized) constructions, either in my plays or now, in these meditations. But if you find a "personal note" lacking in my letters, then here it is: I will deal with this depression, right away, to capture it on the wing.

Your reference to lack of a "personal note," though it was well meant, of course, disturbed me slightly and this influenced my reading of the other letters. My sister-in-law's letter, however sweet and touching, deepened my discomposure when I realized she feels I never remember her (though in fact I send her greetings at least every other letter). This prepared the ground for Ivan's letter, which brought the disaster to a head: Zdeněk N.'s brilliant, profound yet brief remarks on my first letters about the theater made me feel absolutely disgusted with my meditative letters. Suddenly, I saw them as a constant babbling of banalities which—and then only in the best of them—grind and sweat their clumsy way to conclusions that have long been obvious to clever people and expressed a thousand times better in clever books I haven't read. (I felt a little like a hedgehog who has been digging himself a den for months in the darkness and then suddenly, a ray of daylight invades the gloom and he is utterly beside himself. Which, by the way, is nothing out of the ordinary here: I've noticed that many prisoners who've been here longer than me—I mean for years—have something hedgehoglike about them: their lives are a habitual, daily repetition of precise and polished routines; they go about in a kind of mild somnolence, following well-worn ruts, and are extremely irritated, even outraged, by any disturbance. Given that experience, however, it is extremely important when a little normal light is cast into my burrow from time to time—without regard for how I might feel about it: if only to help preserve my nonhedgehoglike essence.) Nor was I particularly pleased to discover that many of Zdeněk's ideas overlap with what I intend to write about in my next few letters; on the contrary, it only made me more depressed, not so much because they will now seem like clumsy repetitions of what he wrote, but because I realized what a pain it is not to be able to express oneself coherently and at a single go, but always to have to break it up into little pieces. Then to top it off, there were all those horrendous reviews of *The Mountain Hotel.* For someone like myself—so full of self-doubt—the only possible response was heartfelt agreement: I was suddenly convinced that all the good reviews were wrong and the bad ones right, since they were merely saying out loud what I have secretly thought all along: that the play is "rubbish."

There—my depression has been poured onto the page and there it shall remain, even though I know it will pass. Does it serve some useful purpose? Perhaps: such states are a part of my identity too, and what kind of "existential testimony" would my letters be if they tried to hide them?

*

Written a day later: I have already observed more than once that my extraordinary willingness to run myself down must be taken with a grain of salt: in a rather odd way, it goes hand in hand with considerable stubbornness and persistence. And so, to yesterday's passage, I must add that I never once doubted that my next letter would again be "meditative" and that at least 12 more meditative letters would follow—for such is my plan, and it's not my habit to back away from my plans so easily. In the final letters—that is if things work out as planned—the themes of all the preceding cycles (identity and Being—myself—the meaning of life—the theater—and ultimately the long neglected theme of myself and my prison sentence) will gradually be interwoven, like a girl's pigtail or a Christmas loaf to conclude the "megacycle" and then I'll give the meditative letters a bit of a rest. The thing is, I find them quite exhausting, and because of them I can't watch television over the weekend, read or just relax (and in the summer, moreover, I'd like to be able to get some sun on my face in the courtyard). Then after the rest—sometime in the fall—I'll start again on something else, perhaps some personal reminiscences, I don't know yet.

. . .

By the way: I manage to write my meditative letters once in rough and once in final form, which of course takes all the time I can give to it; if I'm dissatisfied, either with the rough copy or the final draft, I can only send it off as it is, or skip a week—and for various reasons I don't want to do that. This is the first time I've tried doing it the way I am today—instead of writing it all on Saturday, I've written the rough draft during the week and the final draft on Saturday—and it's simply not working: I have no time left for anything, including the letter, while as a result of my interrupted concentration, I float through prison life like a typical jailbird. . . .

I have only now dared to reread those letters (except for the reviews of *The Mountain Hotel,* just to make sure), when I'm copying this one out. I wasn't depressed at all this time. And the fact that Z.N. carried through what I only suggested and that he expressed (in his own words) much of what I am getting ready to write myself—even that brings me pleasure. I'm learning not to be startled by the daylight. I send a particularly warm cousinly kiss to my sister-in-law—may she no longer think I don't think about her.

I kiss you,
Vašek

P.S. The book Ivan asked about is: R. Droessler (from the German Democratic Republic): *When the Stars Were Still Gods.* The telegram from my sister-in-law did not arrive. What film was it you saw me in, and where?

P.P.S. After copying the letter, the weekend seemed empty somehow, so I roughed out another letter. In other words: a victorious finale to a week in the life of my spirit!

114

February 6, 1982

Dear Olga,

. . . Every existential event has its own particular spiritual aspect or dimension through which it leaves its mark on the memory of spirit, and which is as intrinsically a part of that event as gravitation is of mass or radiation of its source. The degree to which this aspect is clear and significant, however, may vary a lot, and derives from the scope and intention of the given event in somewhat the same way as the power of a gravitational field is an expression of mass, which is understandably different in a neutrino from what it would be in a superheavy cosmic object. Moreover, this spiritual aspect of everything existential may be considered an expression of the capacity of existence—through questioning, reflecting upon itself and transcending all situational horizons—to "repeat the miracle of Being," to "re-create the world." Consequently each work of the spirit is, in this sense, a "re-created world." After all, we speak of the world of Leonardo or Dostoyevsky, of Heidegger, Newton or Einstein, and these are described as new ways of grasping the world or even of representing it, but what I would stress, rather, is that such representations always involve its re-creation wherein the newly created world always bears the imprint of its origins: it has an existential coloring, because it is founded on a specific manner of thinking and a specific quality of imagination and it is built in the spirit of its own autonomous laws. . . .

Drama, too, is this kind of small world in and for itself, with its own laws, its own space, its own time, atmosphere and causality, a world in which everything happens in the spirit of its own logic. Yet there is something special here: compared with the other arts—or at least those that bear comparison with it—the world of plays seems somehow more firmly planned and predetermined, its laws are more immediately obvious, more detailed and more consequential. What in other cases is an outgrowth of mere hints and suggestions rests in drama on a firm order. Yet though drama may at first seem, of all the arts, the most bound to "the order of things," i.e., to the phenomenal aspect of what is around us and what we call the "world" and "life," I personally feel that this is not so: for does not the openly "artificial" order to which the world of plays submits and by which it is created point, on the contrary, to the autonomy of its world?

This peculiar feature of drama has specific causes and consequences. Note that the experience of theater takes place in a space-time continuum; we can't see a play in installments; we can neither jump backward nor forward in it; we can't even stop the action, or move it ahead; it can last neither a month nor two minutes; it usually occupies an evening, during which we are condemned to experience it in one piece. All of this is far more important than most people suppose. It makes special demands not only on the structure of a play, but on all the laws of its world, which within the given plan, must be fleshed out in a way that is consistently comprehensible. It must be constructed in a way that can be tolerated, that is, so people will actually come to see it, so the theater, in other words, can exist at all. A play, quite simply, must stake out that "adventurous trail" and challenge people to go down it, and in the limited time available, the audience must be given an inkling at least of why it should make the effort to show up at the head of the trail (i.e., come to the theater) in the first place. The more tortuous the path, the sooner and the more precisely it must be made obvious which way it is leading. Only where the "coordinates" of the created world are set forth with real precision, clarity and intelligence is it possible for a character in the play to manage, in the space of two hours, to fall credibly in love, marry, divorce, grow wiser, go insane, etc.

At the same time, the artifice of the world of plays is emphasized in a special way, in that this world is not just a lifeless object (a picture, a book) challenging us to enliven it with our imaginations: we are drawn straight into it by living people, who directly represent it to us and who are both in it and not in it. This tension between the actual, existential "here and now" of those who perform (and those who observe them) and the imaginary "here and now" of what is performed (and observed), this existential incarnation of the play's world, is a source of confusion. It is deliberate confusion, that confuses by being deliberate, that perplexes by reckoning on perplexity. At the same time, it is less confusing than anything else; its artifice counts on the fact that at any moment it may cease to seem like artifice, at which point it proves its worth as artifice. It is literally a "living" fiction, it admits to being a fiction, and deals with itself on those terms. (The very word "play" emphasizes the heightened importance of rules; no game can be played without rules.)

There are many consequences of all this, but I will mention only one here: the playwright himself ends up being surprisingly bound by the world he creates. In some ways he is far less free to do whatever he feels like doing than he would be in a poem, a film or a painting; he soon finds himself miraculously caught up in the rules of his world, and ultimately he becomes the first "victim" of his own creation. The sovereign ruler becomes a humble subject, the re-creator a mere hand-maiden of the miracle of re-creation. It would seem that Being, more transparently here than anywhere else, is in command of its own re-creation by the creator. (Isn't this also a characteristic feature of magic?) What the playwright does transcends him in a remarkable way: he is the first to find himself on the path of adventure and he is as curious as anyone else about where it will lead him. Often, he finds that he has demystified something he had no intention of demystifying, something he didn't even know could be demystified. It is as though Being "itself," through his creative act, desired to shatter the world of appearances which, as Zdeněk properly pointed out, is only reinforced by television serials. (You'll no doubt recall times when I wrote things I felt called upon to apologize for, but never to change: I knew I had no right to do so.) But beware: the author of a television serial is no less pulled along by his creation. The difference is just that what pulls him along is the "order of things," the automatic nature of phenomenal events, not true Being. Of course it could happen to anyone: the danger of falling for "pseudoconcreteness" is lurking everywhere. Thus, although Being can, through the power of its "will to manifest itself," appear even where mere appearance was to have been the "pull," it is also true that mere appearance can insinuate itself where Being was to have been the "pull." Therefore we must always be extremely cautious about what in fact is motivating us. In other words: none of us has it easy, and with these words of wisdom I will finish for today.

*

Some information about my private life: one of my front teeth, which I had always trusted and which had always been faithful to me, unexpectedly betrayed me: it began to ache terribly. On Monday I'm going to the dentist to see if it has to come out. In addition, I have a slight cold, a temperature, and I feel sluggish—so I'm being allowed to lie down over the weekend. In the longer term, I'm healthy; my backside, in general, serves me well, and even my elbows are only mildly painful. Still, I don't know why I can't shake the feeling that my organism is only functioning on its word of honor, as it were.

The price increases have hit Mars cigarettes, unfortunately, so now I spend my entire monthly honorarium for exactly 16 packs, which lasts me twenty days. . . .

Today is Sunday, I'm taking pills, drinking tea, lounging on my bed and perspiring a little. I'm content. Greetings to Lada L. Have someone send you *The Wall* by Pink Floyd.

I kiss you,
Vašek

115

February 13, 1982

Dear Olga,

.   .   .

Every play, especially when compared to other literary genres, has a certain heightened "meaningfulness" about it. The event, the story, the situation, the conflict, etc.—in short, what is actually happening in the play—is usually intended, more directly than in other genres, to say, mean, capture or evoke something specific, important, something of general interest and concern to everyone. In drama, that "probe" beneath the surface of life seems more urgent and abrupt, the veil of appearance seems more quickly, deliberately and manifestly rent asunder (drama is a favorite domain of all forms of demystification), the concealed Being of things is revealed far more aggressively. (Again, I would illustrate this by a comparison with television: it's not hard to imagine a television play telling an interesting or moving story simply because it is interesting or moving, or because its sole purpose is to acquaint us with someone's life story or a historical event, or a social or working milieu. In other words, while television can get away with being "informative," even in the best and widest sense of the word, very few people, I suspect, would come to the theater to see a play so conceived, no matter how good it might be. No, our expectations of the theater have a rather different foundation. Of course this works the other way too: a play written for theater seldom works on television the same way it does onstage.) In drama, this heightened "meaningfulness" (it's not only a question of what we see, but far more of why we see it) is coupled with the fact that a play works naturally and intrinsically with abbreviation and compression, with a certain schematism, bias, a tendency to play on one string, and even to employ direct forms of "sign language." Rather than attempting to cover a broad range of themes and issues, it tries to go straight to the essence of things as quickly as possible. And regardless of how ambiguous, blurred, vaguely provocative, incomplete or irreducible to any conceptual model the heart of what it ultimately "says" is, everything that happens on the stage happens in such a way that the "message" (or the challenge or the appeal) can emerge as quickly and obviously as possible. This is naturally related to the heightened importance of "artificiality" in

drama: very few of the everyday events that surround us are in themselves—as they display themselves to us—structured in a way that allows a "message" (i.e., the manifestation of Being) to radiate from
them with any immediacy or clarity. For that to happen, one really
needs either to create a structure "artificially," or to find a bold way of
"amplifying" the occurrence (an extreme example: Beckett's "amplifi-
cation" of an ordinary situation when a woman at the beach buries
herself in the sand in *Happy Days*). This, I would stress, has a general
validity; that is, it is as true for Greek and Roman drama as it is for
Elizabethan tragedy, for Chekhov or Ibsen as it is for Ionesco. But there
are also qualities here that account for the fact that modern drama is
so frequently thesis-ridden, so infected—either deliberately or involuntarily—with didacticism or ideology. Such an approach, it seems to me,
usually throws the baby out with the bathwater: instead of trying to
construct onstage the kind of world that would of itself—through the
power of its own logic—allow Being to display itself rapidly and clearly
(in a way that the playwright, of course, has surmised from the beginning but which dramatically transcends everything in his original surmise), it does precisely the opposite: first it endeavors to re-create
Being completely (by nondramatic means) and then it subordinates the
world of the play to a single purpose: it must reconstruct, with no loose
ends, what had already been created. The actual act of "re-creating the
world" is thus, in fact, taken out of the theater and moved elsewhere—
into the ideologist's study. (As you know, I respect Brecht, but it's a
cool and polite respect; frankly, I only like his non-Brechtian moments,
when the thing, as it were, becomes bigger than he is.) A second pitfall
inherent in drama's "artificiality" (and this happens occasionally in
so-called absurd drama, or at least in its derivative forms) is the use of
allegory and symbol, which can (though they need not) be at odds with
theater's most fundamental and mysterious mission: that is, with the
way the "message" of the play, because it has many levels of meaning,
always transcends the playwright's intentions. (This, in fact, is simply
a different version of the same error a thesis-ridden play commits: it
treats the world of the play not as a world unto itself, with its own life,
manifesting something "itself," but merely as a mechanical copy or
transcription of something that was completely clear already.)

Aristotle wrote that every play must have a beginning, a middle and
an end and that what comes must follow from what went before. As
long as we don't take it too literally, I think he hit, with brilliant simplicity, on another extremely important consequence of the special nature

of the theater: the importance of structure. The space-time continuum that is so unique to the theater makes merciless demands on it that have a distant analogy only in music. Almost every day over many years, I watched performances in the theater (not just of my own plays), and I had occasion to realize again and again how immensely important—and how little appreciated by people with no personal experience of it—the composition of a play is. Even small errors in rhythm, timing or the distribution of motifs can turn a play that was otherwise wonderful into bad theater. I have even observed that small rhythmic differences in different performances of the same production can sometimes lead to success and sometimes to failure; that is, one performance may create (or help to create) that magnificent and unique sense of community in the audience, whereas another may reduce it to a mechanical assembly of apathetic individuals. The composition and development of motifs, the way they are arranged, repeated, reinvoked, combined, interwoven, connected, gradated and brought to a climax, their precise location—all these things—whether they be emphasized or disguised, whether they are more the result of conscious effort or "merely" of a sensitivity to the matter—are what make a play a play.

As you must have noticed, what I say about drama in general reveals—in its angle of vision and emphasis—something quite clearly as well about who is saying it. I don't deny this; on the contrary I would stress the fact that this is my personal view of the subject and that it is quite deliberately leading up to remarks of a confessional nature, that is, about what I, as playwright, am trying to do in drama or what attracts me most to theater.

*

I've been through a hellish week: the combination of an aching tooth and being in prison (one multiplies the impact of the other) belongs to the trials of Job. For the first time since May 1977, when you brought me home from prison, I wept (!) Don't worry, no one saw me. I'm not counting, of course, my response to *Libuše, The Bartered Bride,* etc. It happened at the height of my agony when I was denied permission to lie down after work. (Later I won permission.) I'm sorry, in a way, that there wasn't a hint of altruism in it this time; it came from a chemically pure self-pity. I might be excused by the fact that I wasn't quite myself, and it was, to a considerable extent, a physiological thing. A short time ago, I lanced my gums with a needle, a quart of pus ran out and the pain stopped. I sterilized the needle in a flame and I

am taking penicillin, so I trust I won't get sepsis and die before morning and that I may be around awhile longer to burden the world with
my identity.

I kiss you,
Vašek

P.S. Written Sunday, February 14: I'm not dead yet, just intoxicated
with penicillin and everything.

116

February 20, 1982

Dear Olga,

First of all, the fact that I was born such as I was, then my early
childhood experiences (I once wrote about them) and finally the experience of an undeserved, and therefore—I felt—a necessarily rather
metaphysical exclusion (as a bourgeois child I was, as you know, a
permanent target of class warfare)—all of this has obviously led, somewhere in the deepest level of my relationship to the world, to a powerful
existential uncertainty: a heightened sensation that there is a barrier
between me and those around me, a tendency to suspect others of
plotting against me, combined with a fear that such conspiracies are
justified, in other words, a sensation of generalized guilt. The lack of
self-confidence flowing from that, my exaggerated sense of shame, my
inappropriate awkwardness, my disproportionate respect for the authorities, my heightened sensitivity to all forms of gaucheness and an
amplified fear of my own gaucheness, my nervous fear of unforeseen
situations and doubts about my ability to acquit myself well in them—
all these are the symptoms or consequences of those deep-seated uncertainties. I think they represent a circle of feelings that are rather
transparently connected with the tendency of my writing: I have always
been intensely aware of matters like the alienation of man from the
world, the dehumanization and the incomprehensibility of the "order
of things," the emptiness and unintentional cruelty of social mechanisms and their tendency to become ends in themselves, how things
get out of control, fall apart or, on the contrary, evolve to the point of

absurdity, how human existence tends to get lost in the mechanized contexts of life, how easily absurdity becomes legitimate, the apparent nature of the "real" and the ludicrousness of the "important," etc. This experience of the world (at many points so akin to Kafka's) would obviously show up in my writing no matter what I wrote.

The almost aggressive energy with which I'm constantly trying to capture all this, either in play-writing or other ways—an energy that not only drives me to get involved in things and occasionally to burn my fingers (and I am even willing to go fling myself into prison for my cause), but also makes me appear to many (it is not my place to say whether rightly or wrongly) as a ruthless debunker, a fearless demystifier, if not a radical and a rebel—that energy may seem paradoxical and incomprehensible in someone whose life is dominated by the kind of feelings I outlined above. Actually, however, there isn't much of a contradiction at all; in fact, these things may well belong together. May not the very feeling of being uncertain in the world or of limping lamely after it be the most effective spur to catch up to it and grasp it? After all, the stronger one's sensation of being "outside the world," the more powerful may be his longing to "conquer" it, that is, to demystify it and call it by its proper name. Is this not, in fact, a form of defense through attack? In other words: perhaps the most essential source of energy for my constant attempts at a "proper grasp" of the world is precisely the feeling that it is my destiny to be aliened from it, a secret fear that I can never acquit myself well in it. (By the way, the roots of my controversial stance are not only to be found in the structure of the specific "non-I" into which I was cast by fate, but very probably lie deeper, which is to say in my relationship to "the world altogether": if, for instance, I were a West German, I would probably be trying, at this moment, to stop the construction of a new runway in Frankfurt, collecting signatures for a petition against the installation of Pershings and Cruise missiles, and voting "Green." The long-haired young people who are doing this, and whom I have the opportunity of watching daily on the television news, are essentially my brothers and sisters, which by the way is nothing new for me: when I was in the USA in 1968, I seldom felt better than in the company of rebellious young people.)

My encounter (more or less accidental) with the theater has been exceptionally fortunate, because theater gives me—at least from the perspective I adopted in my recent letters—an opportunity for that "aggressive" grasping of a world that is constantly eluding me—and in three immediate ways:

1. As a social phenomenon par excellence theater enables me to bridge—not superficially but very essentially—the gap separating me from the world of "others"; in this way I become a participant and a cocreator of interexistential Being, i.e., I become part of the community that theater can create. (I have already written that in, and despite, everything I am an extremely sociable person.)

2. The particular aptitude of the theater to rend asunder, quickly and sharply, the "world of appearance" affords me the most direct opportunity to demystify things (to serve "the tendency of Being to manifest itself") and in this way, to bolster my constantly endangered inner stability.

3. As one who always feels a little outside the given order, or on its margins, I have, understandably, a heightened sense of order (wasn't that, too, characteristic of Kafka?). The importance of structure, organization, composition that is proper to theater—I simply mean the importance of its order—cannot fail to attract me. (Who should be more interested in order than one who is constantly disputing it?)

I think that this attempt to "report on myself" is the key to what might be called the poetics of my plays (which is why I'm talking about all this). They have been referred to as examples of "model drama" and they have also been included in the school of "absurd theater." While I have no particular objections to such classifications, it doesn't particularly interest me (where an author belongs is for the critics to decide, not him). I would characterize my poetics simply as an attempt to acknowledge and develop, purposefully and "publicly," those general characteristics of the theater and drama that I've been writing about in preceding letters. My personal ideal as a playwright is to bring that antientropic structuredness "publicly" (not, in other words, by trying to camouflage it—everyone is doing that) to such a state of perfection that it hides itself, as it were, and what it loses in flamboyance is transformed into dramatic tension. This demystification should be so shrewdly handled that almost no one notices how it happened and, at the same time, almost everyone realizes, with astonishment, that it has in fact happened.

*

A concluding remark: naturally I have dramatized this bit of self-analysis somewhat, and thus oversimplified it (I am, after all, a pretty normal person). But perhaps a dramatist may be excused for dramatizing (and anyway, isn't it just a parallel "report" on his methods applied to himself?).

*

Thanks for the brief but sweet letter, and to Ivan for the blessed package of three letters. For the time being, just a telegraphic response: (1) Ivan should write me such letters as often as he pleases. It is never easy to find the time to read and digest them thoroughly, but I am always happy to struggle with the task. (2) I found the remark about the value of a "voice from the burrow" very encouraging; I had thought that at the very most, their "burrowlike" quality could only give my thoughts a curiosity value. . . .

*

Greetings to Andrej, his Andulka and our Andulka too.

I kiss you,
Vašek

117

February 27, 1982

Dear Olga,

I think that the theme of human identity has always been intrinsically related to the phenomenon of theater. There are no doubt many reasons for this, but I'll mention only two:

1. The mysterious ambiguity of human participation in the theater inevitably leads to it. Man in this context is not merely "what he is and, at the same time, what he knows he is," he is also a being that, aware of its own Being, represents or stands in for another being (or power) that knows of its own Being, thus acting as a medium for the manifestation of "Being in general" and retrospectively, therefore, for his own Being as well. Given this primal essence of theater, it follows that a question has always haunted theater, from its early beginnings down to the present, and from the moment a performance begins the last line is spoken, the question of identity: "Who

is it?" At the same time, the question is not present merely in general onotological terms, that is, as a disturbing undertone in the general harmony of a play, nor as a part of the atmosphere. It has a concrete presence as well, in the sense that it is "drama-creating." There are countless illustrations of this—from dramatic "recognition" in the theater of antiquity (Jocasta recognizes that Oedipus is Oedipus, Oedipus recognizes that Jocasta is Jocasta, etc.), through dramatic revelation of "who is who" in Shakespearean tragedy (Lear recognizes the true identity of his daughters, we recognize Lear; *Hamlet* is about who Hamlet is and what he becomes when he recognizes who Gertrude and Claudius are and what they have become, etc.), through all those Elizabethan, Molièrean, Goldonian, Nestroyovian and other comedies that involve disguises, doubles, mistaken identities, nonrecognition, recognition, derecognition (I once tried this myself at the end of *The Garden Party*), up to and including—to choose appropriately disparate examples—*The Bartered Bride* on the one hand (where everything revolves around the concealing and revealing of Jenik's identity) and Pinter's *The Caretaker* on the other (a play about Davies' identity, lost and then sought for in vain), or his *Homecoming* (climaxing in the shocking revelation that the female lead, whose name I've forgotten, is a prostitute). Taken all round, you realize that in one way or another, every play involves the gradual disclosure of someone's true identity and the breaking down of his mystified identity, or, to put it more generally, every play raises, in a complex fashion, the question of identity as the most fundamental question of existence.

2. . . . The world of the theater is occupied by people and, as a world that moves rapidly toward self-revelation, it always revolves logically around the rapid "exposure," the "undressing" or the dramatic verification of human identity or identities—the reason being, of course, that in establishing identity, something more might be revealed, something from the realm of "Being." At the same time, the "pull" to which the playwright, as a medium, is subject can't help but move him in that direction: the very logic of the world of plays, i.e., the logic of situations, relationships, events, interests, pressures, social forces, etc., as they operate in this world, inevitably forces a confrontation between the way people legitimate themselves and the way they really are. The veils of appearance in which they are shrouded and concealed are torn aside and through labors,

trials and everything the play subjects them to, it "makes of them" what they are ultimately given to become or what that "world" must ultimately make of them.

. . .

All of modern art (in the wider, more general sense) and modern drama (in the narrower, more particular sense) addresses the great theme of "the crisis of human identity." Why is this so? Certainly not because playwrights have all agreed or decided to do so, but simply because this theme (others might call it something else) is the central issue now facing the "collective spirit" of humanity. It is the basic task to be performed in the process of "self-referencing," a task that, simply by virtue of its own weight (the power of Being's will to self-revelation), is accomplished through the artists and, as it were, over their heads. Again, it is no accident that this process is most obvious in the theater: as the most "efficient channel" (i.e., a genre well-equipped to rapidly reveal matters of central importance) and as the most social genre (i.e., the one most closely and "metabolically" bound to what the contemporary "collective spirit" is, and even to how it reflects upon itself), it must perform this task. It is, as we say, "stronger than us."

From time to time I read desperate laments in the papers about the dearth in today's drama of "positive heroes," of wholesome, self-assured, integrated, responsible and at the same time (as they say) "full-blooded" and "juicy" (ugh!) dramatic characters who triumph over the evil world (as in the past), and how all attempts at creating such characters turn out pale and lifeless "paper" figurines, and how the theater is swarming with "caricatures," subversives, flakes, petty bourgeoisie, backstabbers, losers and dreamers, etc. Next, I read that playwrights have to "mobilize their reserves" and set things right, and I have to laugh quietly to myself. As if those poor wretches (who often try so hard) could help it! As if it could be any other way! As if the mirror makers were responsible for how we look in the mirror of contemporary drama! The issue, after all, is not whether there are or are not heroes or cowards around us, whether the former or latter predominate and which deserve to be put on the stage, but something entirely different: the structure of present-day humanity, its potentials, the dangers it faces, its perspectives, its principal questions and its true condition. And it is not the playwrights' intentions but only the profundity of the revelations they mediate that determines what comes across as truthful, authentic (and ultimately cathartic) and what, on the contrary, is merely falsehood, appearance, fairy tale and ideological hogwash.

. . .

Shortly after I announced in my last letter that I was well, I was overcome by fevers, headaches, sore throats, coughs, etc.; I staggered about with them for two days in the hope that they would pass; on Wednesday I was admitted to the clinic, where I still am. I was pretty miserable, but it's better now. I'll be fit by the time the visit is due, I hope. . . .

I kiss you,
Vašek

118

March 6, 1982

Dear Olga,

Not long ago, while watching a report on cows on the television news, I realized that the cow is no longer an animal: it is a machine that has an "input" (grain feeds) and an "output" (milk). It has its own production plans and its own operator whose job is the same as the job of the entire economy today: to increase output while decreasing input. The cow serves us quite efficiently, really, but at the cost of no longer being a cow, in the same way that Northern Bohemia is an important source of fuel (that is, if an admixture of brown coal and clay can be called fuel) at the cost of ceasing to be a part of our homeland and becoming something between the surface of the moon and a garbage dump. Such "details," I think, are graphic illustrations of what has happened to this civilization and what will, sooner or later, bring about its demise (if "something" doesn't happen first, something we are all hoping for without really being able to imagine it): man has grasped the world in a way that has caused him, de facto, to lose it; he has subdued it by destroying it, like Ivan's scientist, who kills a creature to keep it from thrashing about under his microscope. The most profound causes of this tragic process are, I think, obvious: it is a crisis in our experience of the absolute horizon. This crisis, which has grown out of the very intellectual and spiritual structure of our civilization and is continually deepened by it, leads to a loss of sensitivity toward the integrity of Being, the mutual coherence between existences, their autonomy; the secret meaningfulness of the phenomena of this world vanishes (they are neither secret, nor meaningful anymore); everything is reduced to "merely what it is." Most important of all, the crisis in our experience of the absolute horizon inevitably leads to a crisis in the intrinsic responsibility that man has to and for the world, which includes responsibility to and for himself. And where this responsibility is lacking—as a meaningful basis for the relationship between man and his surroundings—his identity, the unique position in the world that this relationship gives him, is inevitably lost. Thus, the circle is closed, and can be summed up aphoristically: by robbing the cow of the last remnants of her autonomy as a cow, man has, at the same time, robbed himself of his human identity and thus become like a piece of livestock himself. Indeed, the herdlike nature of the consumer life, perfectly expressed in the modern high-rise housing developments and whose perfect instrument is television, the breakdown of man into individual and anonymous functions (producer, consumer, patient, voter, etc.), his utter loss of power in the face of anonymous social macrostructures, his complex adaptation to the general "moral" norms, which means surrendering his claim to anything that transcends the horizons of the herd life—all of these are ways in which human identity sinks into a deeper and more complete state of crisis.

How does this crisis manifest itself? In thousands of ways: man caught up in the "self-perpetuating" structures of society becomes a molecule with the same properties as those structures; that is, he loses his face, his will, his power of speech and becomes a materialized cliché, as it were. He grows used to being manipulated and ultimately he identifies internally with that manipulation, which means he surrenders himself all over again. Deprived of the horizon of history—to which, as a subject of that history, he might establish some kind of creative relationship—he sinks into "timelessness." Deprived of the "concrete horizon" of home (if, for example, we live on a housing estate, it makes little difference where it is, for high-rise developments are the same the world over), he finds himself in an anonymous "nonspace," since the breakdown of existential space and time and the breakdown of human identity are connected. He blindly identifies with the irrational flow of the "world of appearances" and gives up trying to understand the world and his responsibility for it. This blurs the human "I" and makes it uncertain: the locus of that connection between what was or should be and what is has been shifted once and for all outside itself and outside the sphere of man's proper concerns, which of course destroys any connection between what he is in a given moment and what he is at any other time. Thus in ceasing to vouch for himself and his life, he necessarily loses the self-assurance and dignity of an autonomous personality and becomes a lump of mud, entirely dependent on his affiliation to the mire. (And incidentally, is it not sadly symptomatic that by far the greatest concentration of strong individuals—no matter how wretched the manifestation of that individuality may be—can be found, as I have had occasion again and again to confirm, in prison?)

The world modern man creates is an image of his own condition, and in turn, it deepens that condition. It is a world that, as they say, has got out of hand. It is driven by forces that utterly betray particular horizons and particular responsibilities. At the same time, the stronger these forces are, the stronger their momentum becomes and the harder they are to control and thus, the stronger the magnetic field dragging man deeper and deeper into his own helplessness, alienation, depersonalization and ultimately—something that may represent the bottom itself—into a state of apathetic contentment with his condition.

Of course the discovery that things are so bad is nothing new: there are thousands of books dealing with the problem from various points of view. Modern man is industrious and he knows how to compute, so that he has already tried, many times, to determine where the world he has created is heading, and he has frequently declared his inability to do anything about it.

Is there really nothing to be done?

If I consider the problem as that which the world is turning me into—that is, as a tiny screw in a giant machine, deprived of human identity—then there is really nothing I can do. Obviously I cannot put a stop to the destruction of the globe, the growing stupidity of nations and the production of thousands of new thermonuclear bombs. If, however, I consider it as that which each of us originally is, or rather what each of us—irrespective of the state of the world—has the basic potential to become, which is to say an autonomous human being, capable of acting responsibly to and for the world, then of course there is a great deal I can do.

For example, I can try to behave in a way I think is proper, a way I am deeply convinced everyone should behave—that is, responsibly. To the objection that it makes no sense, my response is quite simple: it does!

*

I've just received your letter (the news of your illness distressed me a great deal) and Ivan's; thank you for both of them. After this letter you will get two more "meditative" letters (I have them all ready—I've cut back my plans somewhat) and then I'm looking forward to being able to (a) merely receive meditative letters and delight in them; (b) write (in a single draft) about chance occurrences, trivialities, a variety of things and at the very most, now and again, to respond in an improvised fashion to the wealth of letters received. I am feeling with increasing intensity the need to take a rest and also the danger of becoming too wrapped up in my thoughts, too dependent on them; I fear they will no longer lend meaning to my life here and begin to cause unbearable complications (prison is an institution set up to allow one an absolute minimum of time to spend on something else). Along with that, I haven't the strength (at least not now) to reconstruct my letter of long ago on a "worldview." Perhaps its basic idea could be summarized like this: Being has many aspects, and it always shows us the one to which we are somehow receptive; any attempt to absolutize one level of how we perceive it, one perspective, one "face," inevitably leads to error. Therefore I am loath to identify with any closed philosophical system; some things speak to me more, some less, and I am capable, quite eclectically, of entertaining different, but parallel, intellectualizations. The need to hide behind a finished and self-enclosed system is felt by those whose identities have been somehow "disturbed"; anyone who is more or less sure of his identity will have no qualms about drawing from the widest variety of barrels, and perhaps even about blatantly changing his mind (at least about some things). The best possible idea, I believe, is one that always leaves room for the possibility that things are, at the same time, utterly different. In that regard I would refer (and I hope I won't vulgarize it again) to Ivan's idea that the act of communication is more important than its "moribund product." My problem, then, is that on the one hand, I am driven (as Z.N. properly pointed out) by what is sometimes an almost painful need for self-manifestation; on the other hand, however, I am terrified (more and more) of all the "moribund products" of this need, because no sooner do I produce them than I feel at once how imprecise they are (even though I don't exactly know why: Ivan's letters usually reveal the reason). It would be wonderful if one could just go on writing constantly, receiving reactions to it and then reacting to them by fine-tuning one's formulations, developing them further, by correcting them (and recanting!). But that is precisely what I can't do here. . . .

*

I kiss you,
Vašek

119

March 13, 1982

Dear Olga,

While it's true that I touched on this subject briefly when I was still in Heřmanice, I feel I should stay with it a little longer. I'm referring to the contradiction that many have seen, or see, between those efforts of mine which they say betray me as an incorrigible "idealist" who is always willing to have another go at smashing down the wall with his head and to believe, naively, that he can change the world and, on the other hand, my writing, which they say betrays me as a pessimist and a skeptic, if not an outright nihilist, incapable of believing that anything can ever turn out for the best.

Well, I'd like to put the matter in perspective.

1. When a person doesn't remain entirely silent, when he says what he thinks out loud now and again and simply behaves as his sense of responsibility dictates, this doesn't mean he is an "idealist" or a "dreamer," that he harbors any illusions or that he sanctimoniously believes he can change the world by behaving in a certain way (on the contrary: such people are more likely to display good-humored self-deprecation than the various "realists," for whom the wry, knowing smile is more typical); it merely means that he is trying to behave "normally," i.e., freely and with dignity, in harmony with himself, and that his fundamental state of mind is faith and his fundamental need in life is for meaning. (The more like folly this seems, the worse it is for the context in which it seems so.)

2. When a review of *The Mountain Hotel* remarked that the play came

out of the very depths of my despair, I had to laugh. Because I write with such difficulty, and because I am so seldom satisfied with my writing, I often write in a state of agitation, depression, unhappiness and despair. When, on the contrary, my work goes well—in happy moments—and proceeds as I had imagined or even better, I rejoice and am as happy as a child. In other words it's obvious that how I feel when I write is related exclusively to how the work is going, and on the whole has nothing to do with what the writing is actually about. It is inconceivable to me that the source of my writing or my desire to write might be despair, and in any case I don't know why I, of all people, should feel hopeless. I simply observe the world around me with absorption and deep interest; I select from it motifs that speak to me personally and which I feel have that special inner charge from which—if properly understood and developed—an important "message" may radiate, perhaps more clearly than from anything else, a message related to what I understand as "central themes." From such motifs, with happy absorption, I ultimately build my plays as tiny artificial constructions. The better my work goes, the more I am drawn along by "self-manifesting Being" and the greater my joy. If people call my plays absurd, depressing, upsetting, shocking, or even—as they say—"dead-end," then this is certainly not because I have surrendered to such moods while writing them, but simply because it seems right, because I was "pulled" that way by the thing itself, because it seemed the most authentic way of touching on the "central themes" and opening them up in a suggestive way, because I suppose that way corresponds to my general experience of the world—quite simply, because I like it that way, it entertains me that way, and I consider it to be "just right." And if I do manage to get something right, I try to forget I wrote it and imagine going to the theater to see it as a member of the audience. My impression then—however absurd, tragic, depressing or cruel it might be—is that despite its upsetting qualities, and indeed through them, it would certainly uplift me cathartically and delight me, perhaps to the point of tears. I would be delighted to hear things being called by their proper names once more, delighted that Being was supremely revealed and therefore that all was not yet lost. Indeed, such an experience can't possibly depress me; on the contrary, it greatly strengthens my conviction that everything makes sense somehow: our life, our toiling and moiling, our godforsaken world; in short, that there is some genuine hope left. What really depresses me on the stage is something completely different: the slimy, insinuating, clever, seductive, devilishly ethical lie.

3. After this clarification, it should be more or less obvious why there is, in fact, no real contradiction between what is (mistakenly) taken for my "naive idealism" and what is (mistakenly) taken for my "pessimism": they are merely two intrinsic and (in my personal feelings) inseparable sides or aspects of the same existential tendency. Only because I believe in the meaning of Being and because I need to touch it continually by trying to make sense of my own existence in the world, I can and must struggle constantly against nonsense and constantly write about it with as much joyful radicalism as I can muster; only by ceaselessly squaring accounts, through my writing and all the rest of it, with nonsense and by ceaselessly holding up the mirror to its constant victories, can I strengthen in myself the experience of meaningfulness and give substance to my faith. And if, at the outset of this "futile" commitment and my writing about "futility," there is faith, a feeling of meaningfulness and joy, then at the end of it the faith is deepened, the meaningfulness strengthened and the joy is supreme: for it is the joy of those who have tasted the "life in truth."

*

Well, our visit is over with! I'm exceptionally pleased with it; of those we've had in Plzeň, it seemed the best. I also have (among other things) the impression that it gave me, more than others, a glimpse of the strange world that lies beyond the walls and which is obviously quite different from the one I once left. You really looked well; I say again to emphasize that I didn't tell you so just to be polite. The parcel was sensational; as far as I can remember, you met absolutely every one of my whimsical demands, at least taking into account both parts of the parcel, i.e., the one I took with me and the one you took away. . . . After the visit I was, as usual, in my peculiar, absently elevated state of mind: it always takes a while to digest and sort out so many bits of information, impressions and experiences. I prefer being alone at such times, and sometimes, if possible, I walk about—and only after a certain interval of inner relaxation am I able to return to my burrow, that is, to return to the routines of my daily life.

. . .

I kiss you,
Vašek

120

March 20, 1982

Dear Olga,

The moment is approaching when I will have served three years, and thus two-thirds, of my sentence, and this is certainly a reason for giving some thought to it.

All things considered, it seems increasingly clear that my prison term is merely a necessary and inevitable phase of my life, and in fact it's a little surprising that it was so long in coming. After all, for eleven years, if not more, I'd been more or less anticipating or assuming it would come. Of course I didn't know when, how long and what the concrete reasons for it would be, but essentially it was clear that it must happen: the "mass" of my spirit and the field of gravity through which I fly are such that my flight couldn't very well have ended anywhere else. In fact looking back, it even seems to me that after those two unsuccessful "runs" at it, I subconsciously did everything I could to ensure that the inevitable would finally happen. So the question is not whether it had to happen, but "merely" how I've come to terms with it and what I've made of it. My grand plans (to study, write, "work on myself," etc. in prison) have proved immensely naive, of course; I had no idea what it would be like here (despite having heard so much about it—but the experience may indeed be impossible to communicate to anyone else). And so of all that only one thing has remained: the chance to prove—to myself, to those around me and to God—that I am not a lightweight as many may have seen me, that I stand behind what I do, that I mean it seriously and that I can take the consequences. . . . In any case, it was a deliberate choice on my part and I can't be accused of making a virtue of necessity after the fact. At the same time, I have no desire to become a professional martyr; my position followed quite naturally and logically from the logic of the situation as it evolved, and from the inner logic of my attitudes and my work, in other words, from my own identity. To put it more simply: I had to act as I did; there was simply no other way. . . .

The fact that I so often return to the themes of identity, responsibility, etc. in my letters is certainly no accident. After all, I can't very well not ask myself why I "have to" act as I know I must and where this imperative comes from. I put these questions to myself not because I have ever doubted my decision, but because it interests me—if I may put it this way—as a "thing in itself." When I consider all this from various angles, I come to three simple realizations:

1. The world seems (among other things) to grow out of an eternal struggle between two fundamental tendencies of Being: its will (entropic) to make things uniform, to dissolve and blend together all its particular expressions and homogenize itself entirely; and its creative or creatorial (antientropic) will to defend, strengthen and cultivate the uniqueness of all its richly varied manifestations and to develop them in the direction of ever higher (more structured) forms. On the human level, the former tendency finds its misshapen extension in what I call "the order of death"; the latter—among other things and in particular—in the irrepressible "will to self," i.e., the will of a person to be what he is or wants to be, to be himself, and in the best way possible to defend and enlarge the self—that is, in his "will to identity." Defending one's identity in the context of the "non-I" (and above all face-to-face with its diabolical aspect, the order of death) is only possible if one has a solid, lasting, life-giving and meaningful relationship with the "non-I." That, of course, means gradually overcoming all relative, apparent, changeable and transitory horizons, and seeking in oneself and one's experience of the world, "the absolute horizon of Being" and relating to it. That is the only key to responsibility. And it is only through a responsibility so discovered that one finds and strengthens one's own uniqueness, one's identity, and fulfills one's longing to be oneself.

2. What does "responsibility" mean in this extreme sense, responsibility not only to the world, but also "for the world," as though I myself were to be judged for how the world turns out? Whence comes this strange and clearly impractical and "unrealistic" essence of the moral law, that which is called "good"? I think the answer is clear: that curious feeling of "responsibility for the world" can probably only be felt by someone who is really (consciously or unconsciously) in touch, within himself, with "the absolute horizon of Being," who communicates or struggles with it in some way, who draws from it meaning, hope and faith, who has genuinely (through inner experience) grasped it. . . . In other words: by perceiving ourselves as part of the river, we accept our responsibility for the river as a whole (which is folly in the eyes of all proprietors of dams and particular horizons).

3. I have often been compelled by the thousands of odd things about the milieu in which I find myself, to think about what human dignity is, where it comes from, and why people cling so firmly to it. Now I think I know: the will to dignity is only another aspect, another dimension, another expression of the "will to self," i.e., the will to uniqueness, to one's own identity. Whereas humiliation—as a typical expression of the "order of death"—attempts to destroy human identity (its highest ideal is to transform existence into inorganic matter and scatter it throughout the universe), defending one's dignity means above all protecting one's identity, one's self, as an irreplaceable human being.

But getting back to myself: I have made no "sacrifice," I'm not playing at something, nor being provocative, nor flirting with fate nor calculating on a particular outcome. I am merely defending my own identity in conditions I did not invent, and doing so in the only way possible, by attempting to be responsible and dignified. Not to do so as a matter of course and in a sporting spirit, as it were, would mean giving up on myself, merging with my surroundings, losing my dignity, ceasing to be. But a word of caution: human dignity is not measured by what liberties the "non-I" takes, but only by what liberties the "I" takes. One can therefore defend one's dignity anywhere, at any time; it is not a onetime decision, but a daily and rather demanding "existential praxis": the danger of becoming a doormat is always there, just as there are always opportunities not to become one. Clearly, then, there is far more to it than my decision, in the name of defending my identity, to spend some time where I am now. It is more important how I spend my time here, whether even here—and precisely here!—I can remain myself, with everything that is part of me. In this regard, the "meaning" that my imprisonment ultimately retains is not as simple as it first seemed. But you certainly know what I mean.

What will be, I don't know. For the time being, I only know that in spite of all the trials, I have not yet—I hope—become a lightweight, that is to say, I have preserved my identity, put its credibility to the test and defended my dignity. What good this will bring the world I don't know. But for me it is good. There is no certainty that I will ever write anything worthwhile again, but I am sure that I would never write anything worthwhile again if I had failed. So the future is open. I am full of hope, doubts, determination, uncertainties, plans, fears. For the time being, I'm sure of only one thing: it will always be a cliff-hanger, not only for me, but with me as well. But you know that, don't you?

I kiss you,
Vašek

121

March 27, 1982

Dear Olga,

. . . Three quotations from an interview with Edward Albee, which I read in a certain popular magazine: "I think about a work for the stage the way one thinks of a string quartet." "The audience generally wants theater to confirm its traditional preferences, to preserve the status quo, to entertain rather than upset. When I consider people's complacency, what upsets me is the thought that theater could actually be an adventure." "This process (thinking over a play before writing it) takes me anywhere from six months to a year and a half." And by the way: today is the International Day of Theater; there was a nice speech about it on television. (You're making a mistake not to watch the television news. I've just learned, for example, how many thousands of liters of gasoline is saved by a team of four horses, and again, what an advantage it is to have a blacksmith in the village.) . . .

This summer, I'm going to stop drinking tea and cut down on my smoking (you can't get tobacco here); I'm quite looking forward to it for—as Heidegger writes—"We do not lose by renunciation, we gain. We gain the inexhaustible strength of simplicity." . . .

Today, for the first time, I sunned my face, using the cream you brought; I felt wonderful in the sun. . . .

I have the feeling—and someone who should know once confirmed that feeling—that my *Beggar's Opera* could do well in New York, of course with a proper translation (the more so considering that less attractive plays of mine did well there). As far as I know, Věra Blackwell has never translated it. Perhaps it could be tried now. As you know, I've long wanted to see the extravagant response to other plays of mine balanced by greater attention to this seldom performed play, about which I have—which is somewhat comical—fewer reservations than any other play. . . .

I've written this letter in about 6 minutes flat and it probably looks like it. But for the time being, I intend to write only letters like this. I'll return to my calligraphic meditations when the sun stops shining.

I kiss you,
Vašek

122

April 3, 1982

Dear Olga,

.　.　.

You recently complained that events have deprived you of your most pleasurable way of filling the time. If you don't want to look after the flat, which I very much regret, I have another task for you till the end of my sentence: to build up a philosophical library so that when I return, I shall learn at last how it all is (you have no idea how hungry I am for such reading matter; I miss it a hundred times more than grilled chicken and wine). Buy everything that comes out; comb the secondhand bookstores; buy, or put on long-term deposit in our place, the libraries of emigrating friends; gather from clever people and according to their advice everything possible, in print, duplicated (including university texts), typewritten, have them sent from abroad, etc. etc. Naturally I'm most interested in modern philosophers (at random: try and get *Introduction to Christianity* by Ratzinger—will they give you *Being and Time?* Mainly in Czech (chances are I'll still understand it best) but particularly important things (unavailable in Czech) can be in English or German.

Many greetings to the returnees; I'm celebrating with them.

And now, something more for Ivan about the cosmological theory I read about in a popular magazine: the entire universe, they say, is something like a jug, but nothing can get out past its throat because of an enormously powerful gravitational field. If we could get out, however, we would see the universe as elementary particles of matter, because size or length are somehow circular values: the largest is equal to the smallest. The Russians came out with that theory; what I like best about it is how remarkably similar it is to the childhood vision we've probably all had early in life—that the whole world is a dewdrop, and in every little dewdrop is the whole world.

If I don't count one punishment for not fulfilling the quotas at Ostrava, all the disciplinary punishments imposed on me (I've had at least ten so far, I think) have had something to do with writing or reading, with letters and books. It seems that this lifelong source of complications for me (and now for us) has always managed, somehow, to evade my anxious efforts—here at least—not to get into trouble pointlessly. No matter—it's simply destiny.

The tooth that was so painful has turned slightly blue and is obviously dead. Perhaps it can be corrected someday; I don't suppose I'll ever be a handsome fellow, but teeth should at least look like teeth.

· · ·

That's all for today; "lights out" is approaching. Perhaps I'll add something tomorrow.

After rereading Ivan's letter: L.'s idea that "someone has to start," that responsibility establishes an asymmetrical ethical situation, and that it cannot be preached, but merely borne, corresponds absolutely to my experience and my opinion. (In other words: I am responsible for the state of the world. After all, that was what we meant five years ago too.) I would even add that imposing suspiciously heavy demands on others is usually an unfailing sign of unwillingness to take them upon oneself. An inseparable aspect of the crisis of identity is a conflict between words and deeds, which is related to the phenomenon of specialization: experts in responsibility need not themselves be responsible, because that is not what they're paid for. In any case, I've often addressed that problem in my plays: you may remember that the most coherent ethical speeches are usually delivered by the weakest characters and the greatest villains.

I wish you (probably belatedly, even though there's a week to go) a Happy Easter!

I kiss you,
Vašek

123

April 10, 1982

Dear Olga,

. . . The mass exodus of our closest friends makes me feel a great sense of loss, perhaps even more than it does you, but I've learned to accept it as a part of my punishment. (Ajda will probably be leaving us soon; she's getting on in years, and I don't expect ever to see her again.) All we need now is for Ivan, Andulka and Zdeněk to leave—and we'd find ourselves in an exile more genuine than all our friends: we'd be exiles in Prague.

On Easter Thursday at 4 p.m. I started a serious fast (I only allowed myself tea), and a short while ago—i.e., on Easter Saturday morning—I ended it. It wasn't very good; you get used to regular meals here and when you can't use the fast for contemplation and meditation, but have to be constantly on the go, in normal prison fashion, you become grumpy, irritable and susceptible to melancholy. And the rotten weather makes it worse (I assume you didn't go to Hrádeček).

. . .

I came across a good book: *Herzog,* by Saul Bellow. I'm about half-way through it and among other things, it's about the crisis of intellectuality in conditions of complete intellectual freedom. The main character—a professional thinker about the world, i.e., a philosopher—has read everything (obviously without having to work hard or run any risks in tracking things down), can say whatever he wants and write about anything at all—without anything ever happening (either in general terms or to him). But his thoughts are constantly in a whirl until at last it drives him batty. (It is more complex and multifaceted than this; I'm just looking at one aspect of it.) A professional with "words" goes mad in a situation where words have no weight. He clearly lacks what we do not, which is to say a situation in which words have so much weight that you must pay quite dearly for them. "Chance" (I put the word in quotation marks for Zdeněk) always seems to bring to hand something that fits precisely into my meditations. In my last letter, I wrote of the conflict between words and deeds. Words that are not backed up by life lose their weight, which means that words can be silenced in two ways: either you ascribe such weight to them that no one dares utter them aloud, or you take away any weight they might have, and they turn into air. The final effect in each case is silence: the silence of the half-mad man who is constantly writing appeals to world authorities while everyone ignores him; and the silence of the Orwellian citizen.

A part of my punishment is watching, daily, the television news. It is very instructive and interesting. By now I know the foibles of all the announcers (Kraus and Čírtek have poor breath control and thus their phrasing of the text is wrong—if Radok could hear them he'd explode; Kotvová, like some of the other female announcers, pronounces her vowels in an open fashion like the girls in Žižkov, which has a particularly comic effect when it occurs in economic jargon and bureaucratese—in phrases like "mobilizing our reserves"—etc. But the main thing, of course, is the deepening day-by-day degeneration of official Czech. Each instance has profound reasons behind it and would be worth a separate analysis, but here are a few random examples: the notion of "few" or "little" is expressed as "not all" or "not every." Instead of "wood," they say "wood material." The familiar hypertrophy of passive, "impersonal" verbal constructions, the most popular of which, "at the present time," is "resulted." Thus instead of "they met," they say, "a meeting resulted"; instead of "he died," "death resulted"; instead of "I forgot," "a lapse of memory resulted," etc. It can be, and is, used in practically every sentence (or: its use can, and does, result). Most interviewees, responding to an announcer's question, start by saying "Well now." In every sentence the verb "to ensure" appears at least twice, and the phrase "a whole series of . . ." at least three times. ("Well now, in our country too, a whole series of problems resulted, but then a whole series of measures were taken to ensure that they wouldn't result again.") Etc. etc. etc. But my interest in the television news doesn't stop at a study of the language; it is instructive in many other ways too.

Written toward evening: the final traces of yesterday's melancholy have vanished—not only because the rain and snow have stopped and the sun is shining again, but also because something bright has happened in my prison life as well. (After every Calvary comes the Resurrection.)

Congratulations to Klaus on his approaching seventieth birthday. I'd like to take the occasion to say several things, but above all this, that I have found him to be a genuine professional who not only understands his business and conducts it well, but does so with love. I don't know if there are many people like him in his field, but I suspect not. Among other things, this means that he does not understand culture as a means of making a profit, but profit as a means of spreading culture. Moreover, it is almost astonishing and perhaps rare to find an author and a publisher who not only have never, in almost twenty years of working together, had any collisions, controversies or problems, as is usually the case, but quite the opposite: their working relationship has only improved and deepened. Furthermore, it's not insignificant that for a long time now that relationship has been complemented by genuine friendship. Steadfastness and fidelity are qualities which I especially value in this schizophrenic world, and I am happy that despite all the external complications, the many ups and downs, interruptions and eccentricities of my career as an author, we have maintained that fidelity in our relationship, or more precisely, he maintained it toward me. And finally, I'd like to recall one fact that is extremely important to me: if it weren't for Klaus and the fact that he once took the rather large risk of backing a new Czech author who was entirely unknown abroad (and moreover whose plays were full of untranslatable linguistic brain twisters), perhaps no one today (apart from a few old-timers at home from those long-ago days when my plays were performed in my own country) would remember me as a playwright. But even if that were not the case, the fact that my plays are speaking to audiences in so many countries is largely due to Klaus and his extensive, persistent and notoriously precise and thorough work. So I thank him for all of this and I hope—no doubt along with many other writers—that he will continue in the same fashion for a long time to come, which means that he will continue to be as I know him: healthy, vigorous and full of energy. . . .

I kiss you,
Vašek

P.S. I've just discovered that all my cigarettes have been stolen: Ah well—

126

May 1, 1982

Dear Olga,

I haven't had any news from you or Ivan for a long time, and you probably haven't from me either: don't expect letter 124, it won't get to you. Although it wasn't very important, I'll try, for the sake of neatness, to recapitulate briefly what was in it (except for the passages that might have caused it not to be sent). I don't know yet whether letter 125 made it (or rather will make it) to you. . . .

I have come to terms, more or less, with the departure of our friends. I was cheered most of all, of course, by the news that I am a doctor. (Am I really a doctor? Or has the degree yet to be conferred? Or are you the doctor, since you accepted it for me?) It's a pity Mother never lived to see it; she always wanted us to be doctors. That it cheers me and makes me want to joke about it is, of course, a consequence of the situation in which I found out about it (my new title contrasts charmingly with my real position here), but it does not mean in the least that I don't feel honored. On the contrary, I appreciate it a great deal and—like other such honors—it helps me to live here; I see it—among other things—as an indication that what I am doing is understood. Would it be appropriate if I were to write a nice note of thanks for the university? (To do so, of course, I would need to know more details— which faculty granted it to me; if there was any concrete mention of what it was given for; who the dean is, etc.)

In that unsent letter I reacted rather belatedly to Ivan's remark that now (when my sentence is half over) time will pass more quickly. Well, exactly the opposite is true! All experienced prisoners say that the closer you are to the end, the more it drags on and the harder it is to bear. When I was in pretrial custody, I felt it was all the same whether I got three, five, seven or ten years, because in every case it is infinity— and infinity, as we know, equals infinity. But I've realized for some time now that it's not the same at all, and it makes a devil of a difference how much you get. Over time, you become internally reconciled somehow with the length of your sentence; your whole nervous system becomes imperceptibly synchronized to it, or is set to go off (like an alarm clock)—so that you end up feeling that if you had to stay a day beyond your sentence, you couldn't stand it, and were they to let you go early, it would completely throw you off. This subconscious distribution of strength also explains why time goes more slowly toward the end: the alarm clock is winding down, on its last legs, and at any time, it could stop completely. I'm not surprised, therefore, at people who success-fully survive a long sentence only to crack up when they get home. For such reasons, getting out of prison can be a dangerous moment in one's life. But my return is still in the unforeseeable future, so there's no need—at least not for me personally—to get too excited about it.

———

A small addendum to the news about the state of my health: (1) the inflammation in my gums has subsided; obviously it wasn't serious; (2) I've had a temperature since yesterday; perhaps it's the flu coming on; (3) I forgot to mention that I have a hernia again (in the same place I once had an operation for it); so far it's not too bad, but at some point an operation will probably be necessary.

*

A couple of details (on a "personal note"): I've finished reading *Herzog* and I'm continuing in Musil. I miss Herzog; he grew on me, but at the same time, I'm reading Musil with renewed gusto; one enjoys him more with each interruption. . . .

Twenty-five years ago in the army, I made a significant discovery: if I smoked a cigarette in front of a mirror, focused entirely on that and observed the smoke, it was very soothing and increased the enjoyment I got from smoking. Here, I do it almost daily (once—after supper and after cleaning my teeth), and on Saturdays and Sundays twice (after lunch and after supper). People around me have gotten used to this peculiar habit of mine, but of course it means I have to see myself up close every day and confront my own unsightly prison aspect (my shaved head looks like a rugby ball; a dirty complexion, bags under my eyes, etc.). I always try to enhance my looks as best I can for visits, but I'm still surprised that you always say how well I look.

My favorite sentence from *Herzog:* "To God he jotted several lines."

I'm glad you have new records; not long ago, I wanted to write you to get hold of *The Wall.*

I've started studying German a little; I only study English from time to time. In my last English session I learned and incorporated into my vocabulary several rather ridiculous constructions and words, literal translations from prison slang.

An interesting thing: the person I still dream about most often is Miloš Forman. Ever since I've been in prison, he's never let me alone. What does that mean? Is it perhaps an incarnation of my ancient dream to become a film director? Or does he—the most successful of my buddies from my youth—wish to remind me constantly of what I have not achieved in life? God knows! On the contrary, I am not at all surprised that in my dreams (and when I am awake too) various girlfriends appear and try, in all sorts of clever ways, to seduce me (a while ago, for instance, it was Běla. Give her my greetings!).

*

Sunday evening: nothing came (your last letter is from April 7); this afternoon I had a mild attack of anxiety which I fended off by reading Musil. I wouldn't mind a couple of months of straight custody or isolation; this sardinelike collective life—with people constantly bumping into each other, and that odd structural change that the human substance undergoes when compressed together for long periods— is beginning to get to me. Greetings to your mother and a kiss for Andulka.

I kiss you,
Your Vašek

127

May 8, 1982

Dear Olga,

. . .

And now to Levinas:

1) First of all, I'm terribly grateful to Ivan for copying that essay for me. His sporting ambition to stir up my thoughts has been truly realized: the essay is magnificent, almost like a revelation, and it is compelling me to rethink many things more carefully. (Which naturally will not be without influence on my thoughts for the cycle of letters I have planned.) I'm not up to a sustained, coherent response yet; I have to experience and digest it properly; nor do I wish to jump ahead of myself pointlessly. For the time being, then, only three telegraphic remarks:

2) My understanding, to this point, of some things—at least in their articulated form—has probably displayed shortcomings similar to those Levinas criticizes in the greatest philosopher of our time: that he viewed existence, human subjectivity and humanity too instrumentally (something like a lighted passageway, containing nothing more than

what passes through it—or rather, like something defined chiefly in terms of what it is not, that is, by its position in the non-I) and that the human subject—as that which should be put back into the "category of reasons" and which is not merely "outside" itself—was perhaps declared as such, but remained unexplained in any greater detail, so that ultimately it must have seemed like an abstraction. I will have to find a better way of formulating the relationship between responsibility and identity. (Responsibility does establish identity, but we are not responsible because of our identity; instead, we have an identity because we are responsible, wherein we find ourselves in a state of responsibility before having decided for it, before we could choose to be responsible at all. Our responsibility, therefore, is not an aboriginal creative act of the "alert" spirit in search of itself and defining itself in the world; this spirit—through life experiences—merely recognizes it in the experience we have of ourselves. In that sense, then, "responsibility discovers itself"; in that sense identity too probably really does have the paradoxical constitution Levinas claims for it: it is founded on the fact that we are not merely ourselves; it constitutes itself as something definite by transcending itself, by grasping or understanding that transcendence.) I am looking forward to the time when (inspired by Levinas) I can examine this more closely than I have so far.

3) Two small concrete remarks: a) I have always felt that the revolt of the young (in its expansive pre-ideological or pre-linguistic phase) was an extraordinarily important phenomenon. (I even saw in it the first signal of an "existential revolution," the return of man to himself.) Not only does Levinas confirm this impression, he explains it as well. b) I also consider as very precise the idea that "people seek themselves in the vulnerability of slaves." Is this not also confirmed by our experience of meaningful community, born out of the alien nature of the non-I, of understanding it (which deepens alienation), accepting it, from this very vulnerability? (I refer you to the final section of "The Power of the Powerless.")

4) In Levinas, I sense a storehouse not only of the spiritual traditions and millennial experiences of the Jewish people, but also the experience of a man who has been in prison. It's there in every line, and perhaps this is another reason why it speaks to me so vividly. . . .

Your Vašek

128

May 15, 1982

Dear Olga,

.   .   .

I had a fruitful week: Levinas's text, which Ivan copied out for me, set my thoughts aspinning, but after about two or three days they gradually began to fall into place until finally a reasonably precise scheme for another cycle of meditative letters came out of it, along with a great eagerness to get started. Many things that had been mixed up in all sorts of ways in my mind, and about which I wrote something different each time, have become fairly clear; gaps in my conclusions and breaks in continuity have disappeared and that moment has arrived when, preoccupied with what one wants to say, one would dearly love to destroy everything one has said so far (which unfortunately is impossible in the given situation). Luckily, ironing sheets is not very intellectually demanding and it allows me to think about my own matters undisturbed while I work (I am slowly learning how to think even without a pencil and paper). My idea is for a shorter cycle of about fifteen letters, but they will be more homogenous and concise—more, in fact, like one continuous meditation in fifteen installments. (I actually have only thirteen letters planned out so far, but I expect I'll occasionally run over.) The theme is in no way original: roughly the same as those of my earlier letters—yet differently (and perhaps somewhat more systematically) conceived and executed. If the earlier letters were a rather clumsy and haphazard survey of the terrain, this series should be—God willing and myself able—a somewhat more supple and better organized report on it. Naturally each can be read independently of the other; but read in sequence, the former should be to the latter as a long list of words is to a short sentence. I don't know yet whether to begin with the next letter, or later, after the visit, perhaps. However it is, I'll almost certainly be incapable (technically) of writing it in one go, in consecutive letters (I'll only write it when external conditions are bearable and my inner mood is appropriate); thus the "meditative" letters will be irregularly interspersed with "ordinary" ones; they shouldn't be hard to tell apart (even when half the letter is one way and the other half another). I had planned to rest for the summer, but as you can see, I haven't held to the plan. Perhaps it's all right, though it will be—as always with me—a great tribulation. I haven't resolved the question of whether or not Ivan should write me long philosophical letters while I am working on the meditations; I want them, look forward to them and need them, but at the same time I know that they will break my thread and thwart my efforts to spin it (i.e., remind me that everything is otherwise anyway). So I'll leave it up to Ivan (some kind of compromise would probably be best). And another thing: not only will much of what I write be clearly influenced by that excerpt from Levinas (occasionally it will be something like a lay commentary on it), but no matter how well it fits together, I doubt that it will be in any way original. As it fell into place in my mind, I was dogged by the feeling I'd read it all somewhere before. This time, however, it doesn't matter at all: I don't aspire to originality, I just want to clarify some things again and better for myself—and if others have done it long before me, so much the better: it will prove that I haven't gone off the track. Nor will it matter if I become bogged down in new errors, schematics and banalities. At least I'll have something to change, correct and improve next time. You can have your eyes opened all your life, which means the same as being out to lunch all your life. If this weren't so, life would no doubt be very boring.

*

I just happened to discover that my being derailed by Ivan's letters has a physiological cause: apparently it's been determined that some positive psychological and emotive impressions and experiences cause the human body to secrete a substance that excites the nervous system and stimulates various biological functions—somewhat as coffee, alcohol, pep pills, drugs, etc. do. Here—except for the occasional cup of tea—one has no stimulants, not to mention any positive psychological and emotive experiences. At the same time, however, one needs them as much as calories and vitamins—and that gives rise to the many psychological and social disorders that are so common in prisons. Yet if you do manage, in spite of it all, to experience something positive (like an opera on television, a meaningful letter from home, and so on), it is clearly such a major event for your stimulus-starved nervous system that you are quite beside yourself (as when a lifelong teetotaler drinks a liter of rum all at once). . . .

I've read an article in *RP* about how the main cause of criminality in this country is that the requisite social homogeneity of the population has not yet been achieved. This unintentionally confirms the main impression I've had from prison, which is that all forms of criminality are related somehow to the antientropic nature of life (Levinas: the boundless proliferation of human acts) and to the intrinsically contra-dictory nature of the human subject, ultimately untransferrable to any-thing "outside" it. In an ideally homogenous society there will be no criminality because there will be no human life. Evil must be dealt with, of course, but getting rid of the weeds by destroying the crop is truly not the best way to go about it. . . .

I kiss you,
Vašek

IV. Letters 129–144

Plzeň-Bory

May–September, 1982

129

May 22, 1982

Dear Olga,

Birth from the maternal womb—as the moment one sets out on one's journey through life—presents a telling image of the initial condition of humanity: a state of separation. Of release. Of breaking away. The human race becomes distinct from the animal kingdom; a living cell comes into being in a dead ocean; a planet that will one day be occupied by man becomes self-sustaining: in these events can be read the history, or the prehistory, of a constant, and constantly recurring, state of separation. The idea that the human spirit and reason are constituted by a severing of something from the hidden spirit and reason of Being is one that is constantly occurring to us in one form or another, and at the very least, it suggests that "separation" is a fundamental experience that man has of himself and his existence in the world. With the advent of humanity, however, something intrinsically new has appeared, something that ultimately is not referrable to anything else, something that is, but is no longer spontaneously in "Being as such"; something that is, but somehow "otherwise," that stands against everything, even against itself. The miracle of the subject is born. The secret of the "I." The awareness of self. The awareness of the world. The mystery of freedom and responsibility. Man as a being that has fallen out of Being and therefore continually reaches toward it, as the only entity by which and to which Being has revealed itself as a question, as a secret and as meaning.

It seems to me that the notion of separation as humanity's starting point helps us establish our bearings when we explore the stage on which human existence is constituted and its drama unfolded.

Separation creates a deeply contradictory situation: man is not what he has set out into, or rather, he is not his experience of what he has set out into. To him, this terrain—the world—is an alien land. Every step of the way, he comes up against his own "otherness" in the world and his otherness vis-à-vis himself. This terrain is essentially unintelligible to man. He feels unsettled and threatened by it. We experience the world as something not our own, something from which meaning must first be wrested and which, on the contrary, is constantly taking meaning away from us. No longer protected and hidden by spontaneous, unseparated participation in Being, we are exposed to what Being, for us, has become by virtue of our separation—the world of existing entities. Exposed and vulnerable to it. On the other hand, we are no longer what we have become separated from, either: we lose the certitude of Being, of our former rootedness in its integrity, totality and universality, of our involvement in its general "identity." In other words, we are no longer identical with Being. We do not experience it simply, from "inside," but only as our own alienation from it. The certitude of our being in Being has irredeemably become a thing of the past, clouds have darkened the sky and we are flung into the uncertainty of the world. A recollection of this past, its birthmark and the ineradicable seal of our origins in it go with us every step we take. But even that, to a considerable extent, is alienated from us (if only because we reflect upon it) and as such, it is in fact a part of what we have been thrown into or what we have fallen into and what drives us—in the alienness of the world—into situations we do not fully understand, which we suffer, but cannot avoid.

This inner echo of a home or a paradise forever lost to us—as a constitutive part of our "I"—defines the extent of what we are destined to lack and what we therefore cannot help but reach toward: for does not the hunger for meaning, for an answer to the question of what—in the process of becoming ourselves—we have become, derive from the recollection of a separated being for its state of primordial being in Being? From the other side, the alien world into which we are thrown beckons to us and tempts us. On the one hand we are constantly exposed to the temptation to stop asking questions and adapt ourselves to the world as it presents itself to us, to sink into it, to forget ourselves in it, to lie our way out of our selves and our "otherness" and thus to simplify our existence-in-the-world. At the same time we are persuaded over and over again that we can only reach toward meaning within the dimensions of this world, as it lies before us, by being open to the opening out of meaning within the world.

Thus is man alienated from Being, but precisely because of this he is seared by longing for its integrity (which he understands as meaningfulness), by a desire to merge with it and thus to transcend himself totally. As such, however, he is also alienated from the world in which he finds himself, a world that captivates and imprisons him. He is an alien in the world because he is still somehow bound up in Being, and he is alienated from Being because he has been thrown into the world. His drama unfolds in the rupture between his orientation "upward" and "backward" and a constant falling "downward" and into "now." He is surrounded by the horizon of the world, from which there is no escape, and at the same time, consumed by a longing to break through this horizon and step beyond it.

The absurdity of being at the intersection of this dual state of "thrownness," or rather this dual expulsion, can understandably give a person a reason (or an excuse) for giving up. He may also, however, accept it as a unique challenge enjoined upon his freedom, a challenge to set out—by virtue of all his thrownnesses—on a multisignificational journey between Being and the world (and thus, at the same time, to establish the outlines of his identity); to undertake it, aware that his goal lies beyond his field of vision, but also that precisely and only that fact can reveal the journey, make it possible and ultimately give it meaning; to fulfill uniquely the enigmatic mission of humanity in the history of Being by submitting to his destiny in an authentic, thoughtful way, a way that is faithful to everything originally good and therefore effective, and to make this entirely lucid acceptance of his entirely obscure task a source of sage delight to him.

. . .

I kiss you,
Vašek

130

May 29, 1982

Dear Olga,

Several days ago, during the weather report (it precedes the news on television each day, so I see it regularly), something went wrong in the studio and the sound cut out, though the picture continued as usual (there was neither the announcement "Do not adjust your sets" nor landscape photographs, as there usually is in such cases). The employee of the Meteorological Institute who was explaining the forecast quickly grasped what had happened, but because she was not a professional announcer, she didn't know what to do. At this point a strange thing happened: the mantle of routine fell away and before us there suddenly stood a confused, unhappy and terribly embarrassed woman: she stopped talking, looked in desperation at us, then somewhere off to the side, but there was no help from that direction. She could scarcely hold back her tears. Exposed to the view of millions, yet desperately alone, thrown into an unfamiliar, unexpected and unresolvable situation, incapable of conveying through mime that she was above it all (by shrugging her shoulders and smiling, for instance), drowning in embarrassment, she stood there in all the primordial nakedness of human helplessness, face-to-face with the big bad world and herself, with the absurdity of her position, and with the desperate question of what to do with herself, how to rescue her dignity, how to acquit herself, how to be. Exaggerated as it may seem, I suddenly saw in that event an image of the primal situation of humanity: a situation of separation, of being cast into an alien world and standing there before the question of self. Moreover, I realized at once that with the woman, I was experiencing—briefly—an almost physical dread; with her, I was overwhelmed by a terrible sense of embarrassment; I blushed and felt her shame; I too felt like crying. Irrespective of my will, I was flooded with an absurdly powerful compassion for this stranger (a surprising thing here, of all places, where in spite of yourself you share the general tendency of the prisoners to see everything related to television as a part of the hostile world that locked them up): I felt miserable because I had no way of helping her, of taking her place, or at least of stroking her hair.

Why did I suddenly—and quite irrationally—feel such an overwhelming sense of responsibility for someone whom I not only did not know, but whose misery was merely transmitted to me via television? Why should I care? Does it even distantly concern me? Am I any more observant or sensitive than others? (Perhaps, but does that explain anything?) And if I am, why was I so affected by this, of all things, when today and every day, I see incomparably worse forms of suffering all around me?

After having read only one short excerpt in Ivan's letter, I don't feel I can judge the breadth and depth of meaning that the idea of responsibility has in Levinas's philosophical work. But if Levinas is claiming that responsibility for others is something primal and vitally important, something we are thrown into and by virtue of which we transcend ourselves from the beginning, and that this sense of responsibility precedes our freedom, our will, our capacity to choose and the aims we set for ourselves, then I share his opinion entirely. In fact I've always felt that, though I didn't put it to myself that way. Yes, a boundless and unmotivated sense of responsibility, that "existence beyond our own existence," is undoubtedly one of the things into which we are primordially thrown and which constitutes us. That responsibility—authentic, not yet filtered through anything else, devoid of all speculation, preceding any conscious "assumption," nontransferable to anything else, inexplicable in psychological terms—exists, as it were, before the "I" itself: first I find myself in it, and only then—having in one way or another either accepted or rejected this thrownness—do I constitute myself as the person I am.

In itself, the incident with the weatherwoman was insignificant, yet it vividly confirmed all of this within my own tiny frame of reference— not only because it happened in the atmosphere evoked by my having read that excerpt from Levinas, but mainly, I think, because it was such an incisive representation of human vulnerability. And if, in that moment, I felt such a powerful sense of responsibility for this particular woman and felt so entirely on her side (though common sense tells me she is doubtless better off than I am and probably never gives me a thought, if she knows about me at all), then this was likely because the more transparently vulnerable and helpless humanity is, the more urgently does its misfortune cry out for compassion. This dramatic exposure of another, void of all obfuscating detail and all "appearances," reveals and presents to man his own primordial and half-forgotten vulnerability, throws him back into it, and abruptly reminds him that he, too, stands alone and isolated, helpless and unprotected, and that it is an image of his own basic situation, that is, a situation we all share, a common isolation, the isolation of humanity thrown into the world, and that this isolation injures us all the same way, regardless of who, concretely, happens to be injured in a given instant.

· · ·

Just as there is no escape from the world we are condemned to live in, so there is no escape from our unfulfilled connection with the universality of Being, from the painful presence of its absence in us, from this constant appeal to transcend ourselves, from the beckoning of our source and our destination. Speculating about where that endless, boundless and unreserved, prerational and prerationalized responsibility for another and for others comes from, I realize that it can only be one of the ways that separated being remembers its ancient being-in-Being, its presubjective state of being bound to everything-that-is, its intrinsic urge to break out of its self-imprisonment, step outside itself and merge once more with the integrity of Being. The vulnerability of another person, therefore, touches us not only because in it we recognize our own vulnerability, but for reasons infinitely more profound: precisely because we perceive it as such, the "voice of Being" reaches us more powerfully from vulnerability than from anything else: its presence in our longing for Being and in our desire to return to it has suddenly, in a sense, encountered itself as revealed in the vulnerability of another. This cry from the depths of another's fate arouses and excites us, mobilizes our longing to transcend our own subjectivity, speaks directly to the latent memory of our "prenatal" state of being-in-Being; it is, so to speak, stronger than everything else ("rational") within us—we suddenly find ourselves compelled to identify with Being, and we fall into our own responsibility. From this point of view, responsibility for others manifests itself as a revitalized or actualized responsibility "for everything," for Being, for the world, for its meaning. It is a revitalized involvement in Being, or rather an identification with what we are not and what does not touch us; it is the manifestation of a primordial experience of the self in Being and Being in us; the expression of a deep-seated intention to cover the world with our own subjectivity. Compassion, love, spontaneous help to our neighbors, everything that goes beyond speculative concern for our own being-in-the-world and what precedes it, these genuine "depths of the heart" can thus be understood as a unique part of what the world of human subjectivity becomes, evolves toward and how it flourishes when it is thrown into its source in the integrity of Being, and of how that subjectivity constantly strives toward and returns to that integrity—while at the same time being astonished by it—just as I was astonished at the sympathy I felt for the meteorologist, caught unaware by the sudden breakdown of television technology.

. . .

I kiss you,
Vašek

131

Dear Olga,

Perhaps it is clear by now that thrownness into the source in Being and thrownness into the world are not two separate, independent conditions, but that each one shapes the other and that in fact they are only two dimensions of the same occurrence or two parallel expressions of the same initial event, that is, the act of "separation." We don't experience thrownness into the source in Being until we have been separated from its integrity and thrust into the alienness of the world, and on the contrary, we experience thrownness into the alienness of the world only through our "otherness," as separated Being. In other words, if we did not originate in Being, we would not know the experience of being thrown into the world, and if we did not exist in the world, we would not know the experience of originating in Being. The disintegration of Being into an "I" that is constituting itself, and a "non-I" (i.e., the world) surrounding it, creates both an experience of the world, its alienness and thrownness into it, and an experience of a sundering from Being and thrownness into a "longing" for it. Only by transcending these experiences can the "I" once more merge—or more precisely: "quasi-merge"—with the world, or rather with Being.

Separation—as a state that lies between Being and the world and forms the "stage" on which the "I" constitutes itself—is a profoundly contradictory state, and this is naturally projected into both interacting "thrownnesses" of the "I" that is constituting itself. These states of thrownness are deeply paradoxical—and in three ways:

1. I have already written that the state of thrownness into responsibility for another exists "before the 'I' itself." That is true of our thrownnesses in general, but oddly enough the opposite is also true: in order for thrownness to be thrownness at all, there must be something to be thrown; in order for any kind of thrownness—as a particular experience—to be an experience at all, there must be something to experience it. Thus thrownness precedes the "I," but the "I" also precedes the thrownness. But that is precisely what is important: after all, it is through thrownness, by it, in it (on its "stage"), that the "I" is constituted—and what else is this process of "constitution" than a coming into being, a defining, a forming, a ripening—in other words, precisely that simultaneity of nonexist-

ence and existence, or rather the emergence of existence from nonexistence? This tension between the unconstituted and the constituted state of the "I," constituting itself on the "stage" of its thrownness, may be considered the first paradox of thrownness.

2. The distinguishing feature of the "I"—in each of its phases (even though to a different extent in each phase)—is consciousness, the consciousness of self and of the world, of reflection and self-reflection, the fact that the "I" is, and at the same time knows that it is, which includes a more or less developed awareness of its own thrownnesses. What is called the "mind" thoroughly permeates our "I" (though with a different intensity in each case), along with everything that happens to it and around it; it is through this dimension that the "I" becomes itself. The mind, as perception, of course, means distance, detachment. The second paradox of thrownness is the tension between its Being and its self-perception, that is, between thrownness as a state the "I" is simply in and cannot *not* be in, and a certain distancing that the mind and its ability to reflect assumes and provides, in other words that which reveals and recognizes thrownness as such.

3. The third paradox of thrownness consists in the contradiction between, on the one hand, what the "I" that constitutes itself through that thrownness is submerged in, what the "I" relates to under its impulse and what it longs absolutely to identify with (i.e., with Being, or the world, as the case may be), and, on the other hand, the inevitable impossibility of that identification, which flows from the very essence of its "separation." To merge entirely with the integrity of Being or, on the contrary, with the world, would mean the total collapse of the "separation" and thus of the "I," as it has constituted itself, and even of the world as it has fallen into place around the "I" while the "I" was constituting itself. (This is why I talked a while ago about "quasi-merging" and a "quasi-unproblematical" existence in the world.) The "I" is also the horizon of the "I"; a boundless, limitless "I" would mean the end of the "I," the world and of course of all thrownnesses.

I think that these three paradoxes—examined on the terrain of our thrownness into our origin in the integrity of Being—point to three expressions of it, which can be differentiated—purely for the requirements of the moment—by placing them in a kind of "historical" order:

1. I wrote about the first one last time: a spontaneous sense of responsibility "for everything," which becomes actual when we take responsibility for another and for others. I would say that this instance of thrownness into our origin in Being is "historically the oldest": here, the emerging subjectivity of the subject aspires toward the whole of Being; the "I of our I," our embryonic "primal-I," the primal core of our "I" or its "genetic code," that "preprimordial" "I" which, as it were, has not yet fully experienced and reflected upon the world, and therefore upon itself in its separateness and its imprisonment within itself; the "I" helplessly and limitlessly showing itself (Levinas: "exposing its vulnerability"), disregarding its borders and horizons, its vulnerability and its own thrownness into the world, longing to be in everything and to stand behind everything, to be inside everything and to be everything regardless of the outcome and the consequences for one's existence in the world, to be in Being in a way that betrays the freshness and the as yet unhardened nature of the memories of the "prenatal" phase of nonseparation. Is this "pre-I" already our "I"? In some way, of course, it is—for what else could experience (albeit with spontaneous impetuosity) this responsibility "for everything"? And yet, in the fullest sense, it is not: it has not yet clearly perceived its limits and its limitations, its separation and its uniqueness, the demarcation line between itself and the "non-I" and therefore the reality of what it is itself. The fullness and boundlessness of the "I-ness" of this "I" is so far only quite weakly illuminated by mind, by self-perception; though it exists, and exists as fully as a separated being can, it is not yet sufficiently aware that it exists, and mainly how it exists; and after all, what makes the "I" in the first place is the full awareness of its own being as a separated being. This "I" is not yet open to its own freedom; it is prior to it, to its choice and self-choice, to its responsibility for itself, to its own identity. It is authentic, but not yet autonomous. I'm even tempted to say that it is unreliable, in a certain sense. The immediate and unproblematic transcendence of this "I," or "pre-I," has not only not yet been identified as transcendent (not knowing its own limits, this "I" is not yet aware of having stepped beyond anything), but it has not yet even been subjected to the test of knowing the radical unattainability of what it strives toward. In other words: I want to be my meteorologist and I don't know that it won't work. There is a strange ambiguity about this state of humanity: on the one hand it stands behind everything that is noble in the world; on the other hand

from it leads a road—as I will try to show later—to the greatest horrors in human history.

. . .

I kiss you,
Vašek

132

June 12, 1982

Dear Olga,

2. If at first, without giving it a thought as it were, I became my meteorologist, then an instant later I saw my identification (or rather quasi-identification), realized what had happened and gave it a name: I discovered that it was "responsibility for another" (or rather compassion, a longing to take the embarrassment "upon myself," a sense of involvement, of common experience, of suffering through the suffering of another). I was surprised by my state and even somewhat ashamed of it (in other words, I was ashamed of my shame—or "co-shame"); I therefore stepped back from it (i.e., from myself, from my "pre-I"), aware of how disproportionate it was, even as I knew it was inevitable; ultimately, I understood it as a brief encounter with the experience of thrownness into a state of responsibility "for everything." This trivial example illustrates that reflection, mind, consciousness—as the second manifestation of the state of thrownness into our source in Being— appears to be a "historically more recent," i.e., a "more advanced," dimension of our "I." (A subject and its dimensions are indivisible, yet some dimensions emerge, develop and begin to function later than others, as it were: it is in this sense that I speak of "historicity" and for those reasons, I put it in quotation marks.)

What in fact are mind, reflection, consciousness? I would say that we can refer to these dimensions of the "I" as a certain "replication" of the Being of separated being. Through separation, Being irrevocably loses its primordial "prespiritual" and "presubjective," spontaneous and unproblematic participation in the integrity of Being. At the same time, however—because it is rooted in Being by virtue of its origins—it carries that loss within it as a part of its own essence: it is thrown into it, i.e., into "homesickness" for the integrity of Being and into a longing to "repossess" Being, to contain it, to capture it. I say the mind is an expression of our thrownness because—as it seems to me—it is essentially nothing other than another aspect of the individual's effort to "repossess" the fullness of Being. Our irrepressible need to go beyond all situational horizons (*RP*'s formulation), to ask questions (we are, after all, "questioning Being"!), to know, to understand, to get to the bottom of things, to open them up, that inescapable need (we have, after all, been thrown into it) which clearly transcends any utilitarianism with regard to our existence in the world and how we "acquit ourselves" in it—what else is it but, again, just one of the forms of that endless striving toward the lost integrity of Being, the "I" 's longing to include Being in itself once more, or merge with it, to bridge the gap of its own separation, to return to Being and—through fully being in Being—to "understand" it fully as well, from the inside? Thus we are both "somewhat" rooted in Being and "somewhat" outside it, and our mind is in fact a kind of bridge that attempts to span that "gap" by substituting, reconstructing, re-creating what we are not, or what we don't have, what is on the far shore of that "gap." So though we are only "half" in Being, yet in a sense we are so doubly, wherein through this second "half-being" we attempt to replace the loss of the first: perceiving, knowing, appearance, understanding, grasping, becoming aware—all of these are degrees or modes of how our "half-Being" strives toward its missing second half, strives to re-create it. The world—as constituted through the constitution of the "I" and as we try to understand it—is in fact (among other things) that which the lost fullness of Being has become for us, that behind which we anticipate it and in which we seek it, through which we try to penetrate to it. The world—as it constitutes itself through us—repeats the miracle of Being, the miracle of creation.

Again, in the essence of the mind there is transcendence, the effort to step beyond all horizons. From this, of course, it also follows that the mind violates its own horizon as well; we reflect on our ability to reflect; we know that we know; we know that we know that we know; we know that we have been separated, we know of our thrownnesses, we know of the unattainability of what we strive toward, and we know that we cannot help but strive toward it; we know what we don't know and what we cannot know—so that the more radically we step beyond our limitations, the better we know them, and the better we know them, the more obviously we step beyond them.

If "responsibility for everything"—as "historically the earliest" or, in a sense, the most profound, expression of our thrownness into the source in Being—patently ignores our limitations, the borders of our subjectivity and our imprisonment within ourselves and the "reality" of our thrownness into the world, then the mind, on the other hand, already knows these borders and can evaluate them. It can perceive our separateness and understand the implications for its existence in the world of everything the "I" does. It begins to experience the mysteries of time, continuity, duration, evolution, cause and effect, accident and necessity, of how it and the "non-I" permeate and limit each other. Thus the mind gradually opens the "I" up to its own freedom; it forms the basis of that freedom, mediates the "I"'s relationship to it, its self-definitions and self-identifications (possible only at some remove); it opens the "I" up to its own thrownness; it is the instrument of its maturation. It first opens up, in the true sense of the word, the space for that mysterious activity that our "I" is. That which is not transferable to anything else, nor completely explicable in terms of anything outside itself—the genuine and most profound mystery of our "I"— can only fulfill, develop and manifest itself in the environment that it creates itself through its consciousness, its mind. The miracle of the "I" takes place every second of every day—on a stage that we can attempt to describe in one way or another (what I am doing here is one such— half-poetic—attempt), but the "I" is not itself the stage, and is therefore not explicable in those terms. By examining this stage, however, our "I"—among other things—constantly constitutes and "makes" itself. . . .

Without my consciousness, through which my "I" rose above itself in order to reveal and understand, in my somewhat ridiculous feeling of responsibility for the meteorologist, my own responsibility for "everything," to project it into space, time and the world and ultimately, to assume for itself "the responsibility for its own responsibility"— without these functions of consciousness, my responsibility would simply not be responsibility. If Levinas is saying that true responsibility precedes language and speech, he is not entirely correct: it precedes them "slightly," in the first rush of its primordial growth; but it is not here really, fully, completely—as something genuinely human—until the mind establishes itself firmly in the "I," by virtue of which the "I" recognizes and names itself, and its responsibility as responsibility, poses it as a question and brings it out of the timelessness and limitlessness of dreaming and longing into the limitations of the space and time of the world and the reality of human tasks. Levinas himself, in fact, provides the best proof of this: for he himself did precisely this when he expressed what he did, and thus, somewhere in Plzeň, stirred up the thoughts of a prisoner who then had to rethink many of the things he'd always thought about, and who thus became—perhaps—slightly better than he was.

. . .

I kiss you,
Vašek

133

June 19, 1982

Dear Olga,

3. Again, I call to mind that distant moment in Heřmanice when on a hot, cloudless summer day, I sat on a pile of rusty iron and gazed into the crown of an enormous tree that stretched, with dignified repose, up and over all the fences, wires, bars and watchtowers that separated me from it. As I watched the imperceptible trembling of its leaves against an endless sky, I was overcome by a sensation that is difficult to describe: all at once, I seemed to rise above all the coordinates of my momentary existence in the world into a kind of state outside time in which all the beautiful things I had ever seen and experienced existed in a total "co-present"; I felt a sense of reconciliation, indeed of an almost gentle consent to the inevitable course of things as revealed to me now, and this combined with a carefree determination to face what had to be faced. A profound amazement at the sovereignty of Being became a dizzying sensation of tumbling endlessly into the abyss of its mystery; an unbounded joy at being alive, at having been given the chance to live through all I have lived through, and at the fact that everything has a deep and obvious meaning—this joy formed a strange alliance in me with a vague horror at the inapprehensibility and unattainability of everything I was so close to in that moment, standing at the very "edge of the finite"; I was flooded with a sense of ultimate happiness and harmony with the world and myself, with that moment, with all the moments I could call up, and with everything invisible that

lies behind it and which has meaning. I would even say that I was somehow "struck by love," though I don't know precisely for whom or what. Once, in one of my letters, I reflected upon this experience; now I think—at least in the perspective of these essays—that I understand it better.

Evidently there exists an experience in which the longing of separated Being for remerging with the integrity of Being is satisfied, as it were, in the most mature and complete manner. That experience is typically and most profoundly human: it is the experience of meaning, and of meaningfulness. The need for meaning and the search for it—regardless of their form, their strength or their depth, or how definite or indefinite they may be, though they be nothing more than a vague sensation of the absence of "something" without which life is worthless—accompany the human "I" from its beginning right through to its end. They are inseparable and its most important dimension (because it embraces all the rest), its maturest and most complete expression, and the instrument of its self-constitution. Perhaps it could be said that the "I" is, in fact, this search for meaning—the meaning of things, events, its own life, itself. Certainly this dimension of its longing for "Being in Being," or rather this aspect of its thrownness into its source in Being, is somehow the "last" to come to light: it is something more than just the spontaneous intention of the "pre-I," in which there are still echoes of the "prenatal" state of nonseparation; it is even something more than the vigorous effort of the mind to grasp Being by perceiving and throwing light on it; these intentions are, of course, present in the "I," but they do not explain it entirely: it transcends them—by virtue, for example, of how it contains them within itself, mutually increases their strength and consummates them: paradoxically, the "I" seeks fullness of participation, but an alert participation, one that already knows of itself; it seeks a totality of merging, but a totality—so to speak—that is fully aware of its own unrealizability.

The experience of meaning is thus, essentially, the maturest or "highest" form of the "I"'s quasi-identification with the integrity of Being. It is the experience of genuine "contact," but contact as something both autonomous and integral—paradoxical as that may be. Perhaps it might be described as the experience of "counterpoint" between the "voice of Being" in the "I" (in its source) and the "voice of Being" in the "non-I" (in the world), wherein the meaning of this counterpoint does not just lie in a harmony that amplifies the original quality, but in the new quality it brings, a quality that knows neither of the two intersecting voices. It is in this counterpoint that it first seems possible (if only for a fleeting moment) to hear a suggestion or an echo of the as yet unfamiliar theme from the symphony of Being. The semipresence of Being in the "I" and its hidden presence in the "non-I" encounter each other here for an instant as "insight," a joyous sensation of participation and the vertigo that comes with it. The reflection of Being in the "I" renders us open to the mystery of Being in the "non-I"; Being concealed in the world, or the Being of the world, opens itself up to us. It is a meeting of two opennesses—but opennesses that are directed exclusively toward each other: it is not just that we seem to be here because of Being, but that Being seems to be here because of us. The greatest attainable closeness, fullness and completeness of Being would therefore seem to call forth the greatest degree of fullness and completeness of the "I."

Perhaps it will now be clear why I link the experience of meaning with what I called the third paradox of our thrownnesses: the nearest we can come to the fullness of Being also gives us the clearest indication of how unattainable it is; the most mature identification is most powerfully revealed as quasi-identification. Joy has an undertone of horror, tranquillity of anxiety, good fortune a touch of the fatally tragic. This experience reveals to us that in complete and unlimited identification, total insight, utter happiness, lies the end of the "I," death. It is by no means accidental that at the very heights of meaningfulness, happiness, joy and love, the specter of death inevitably appears with particular clarity. The experience of meaning also differs from less mature expressions of our longing for Being in that it contains within it—while at the same time, oddly enough, losing nothing of that sense of supreme happiness—the most forceful awareness of futility. But is it not precisely this that brings it closest to the contradictory essence itself of human life and the human mission?

Being spellbound within me and Being spellbound within the world can join hands anytime, anywhere and in any way: when I look into the crown of a tree or into someone's eyes, when I succeed in writing you a good letter, when I am moved by an opera on television, when a passage from Levinas sets my thoughts swirling, when our visits work out, when I understand the meaning of my compassion for the weather-woman, when I help someone or when someone helps me, when something important happens, or when nothing in particular happens at all. But whenever and however it happens, such moments tend to be rare and fleeting. Given the contradictory nature of separated Being, it can't be any other way and it is right that it should be so: after all, the uniqueness and the unpredictability of such moments combine to create their meaning: it is the meaning of "islands of meaning" in the ocean of our struggling, the meaning of lanterns whose light is cast into the darkness of our life's journey, illuminating all the many meanings of its direction.

.   .   .

I kiss you,
Vašek

134

June 26, 1982

Dear Olga,

You may remember how upset I was that earthlings left such a mess on the moon, like a bunch of city people on a Sunday evening littering the banks of a pond with refuse from their sausages and mustard. Everything that was too heavy and no longer necessary the astronauts simply left scattered around the landing module; and in addition there is all manner of scrap metal strewn about on the moon (the now inactive Lunachod, rockets that have made hard or soft landings, etc.). Millions of years after our civilization has ceased to exist and its last traces on earth have turned to dust, the junkyard we have left behind us will remain unchanged on the moon, a sad monument to our advanced civilization. This distresses me not just because I'm essentially a tidy person; the reasons go far deeper: there is in it a rather melancholy symbol. I mention this because my meditations are edging toward—among other things—an analysis of the situation that this symbol illustrates.

But to be systematic: if so far I've been considering the self-constitution of the "I" from the aspect I have called "thrownness into the source in Being" I must now look at this remarkable occurrence from the other side, that is to say, from the point of view of our "thrownness into the world."

1. It seems to me that the natural opposite of the spontaneous, boundless, unseparated "pre-mental" sense of "responsibility for ev-

erything" (I described my sympathy for the weatherwoman as a small instance of this) is the experience of the alienness of the world. The as yet immature "I"—that "pre-I" which (rightly or not) I recognize in Levinas's philosophical category of "youth"—unthinkingly, and with a marvelous radicalism, strives to attain the world, as if this world, this "non-I," were at once fullness itself, the totality of Being, as though the "I" had not been fatefully separated from it and as though it were possible to flow back into it effortlessly and identify with it entirely. Yet this effort, though extremely important in the entire subsequent history of the self-constituting "I" (perhaps the most important effort of all), inevitably and repeatedly comes to grief and ruin because it repeatedly comes up against the inexorable rampart of separation. The "pre-I"—which is as yet incapable of getting enough distance on itself (in other words: as yet inadequately armed with a mind)—can only experience such collisions and failures as abrupt encounters with alienness and as the absurd and incomprehensible disfavor of fate. This "historically oldest" or, in a sense the most submerged state of the "I," then, is inseparable from primordial wonder, misunderstanding, anxiety, a sensation of helplessness and of vulnerability, of being thrown into a hostile environment with no sense of direction—and of course of the growing tendency toward frustration and a spontaneous desire to escape or capitulate. My impression is that something of the "I" 's primal experience can be detected as readily in the child's longing to return to his mother's embrace, to hide from the evil world behind her skirts, or to destroy everything he finds alien and unresolvable, as it can in the fatal and impenetrable omnipotence ascribed by primitive peoples to nature or the deities. Yet in this stratum of our initial experience of the world are to be found the deepest roots of that broad-crowned tree representing all the many and often quite sophisticated ways in which the "mature I" gives up on Being, or turns away from it, betrays its source in Being and denies its intrinsic orientation toward it. This giving up on Being means, of course, nothing more and nothing less than capitulating to the world as it presents itself to us, i.e., chiefly the world of things, surfaces, stereotypes, seeming, of frantic consumption, of selfishness, apathy and questionable practices, the only kind of world—this world—that can be seen through the optics of such resignation.

Obviously, the paradox of the "I" that has not yet fully understood and accepted its own separation, that has not yet, as it were, quite recovered from no longer being an unproblematic participant in Being "from the inside," that is both "somewhat" existent and "somewhat" nonexistent as yet—this paradox is projected into the "I" 's ambiguous and deeply unstable relationship with its own thrownness. In a magnificent and emotional way, it feels that it is "everything" and unreservedly responsible for everything. At the same time, it is continuously shaken and shocked to despair by the incessant and incomprehensible collapse of its dream. To the same degree that it is disposed immediately and completely to accept the task of putting the world "right," or actually to be that "right," it is likewise prone at any time to bow down before the world and become despair personified because it believes that "nothing is possible." Still half in nontime, nonspace and the nonworld, this "pre-I" does not, nor can it yet have, a developed sense of its own continuity, that elementary assumption and parameter of humanity and any kind of human identity (Sartre: "Man is the history of man"). In its unpredictability, this immature "I" is thus truly unreliable, and in a certain sense it can be quite horrifying: one never knows what to expect of it, yet one can hardly hold anything against it. And even though the most intrinsic source of morality, good, humanity and all "later" forms of meaning may be rooted in its intention to transcend itself, yet genetically encoded within this intention are the preconditions for all sorts of evil, even for what may the most dangerous evil of all, the road to which, they say, is paved with good intentions. The point is that this "pre-I"—though its sense of responsibility is limitless—is at the same time, oddly enough, extraordinarily irresponsible. Because it does not understand its own limitations, it cannot as yet be fully responsible for itself (as a separated being). It cannot even be responsible for its own responsibility, i.e., for its continuity and consequences in space and time (what, in fact, is responsibility that does not stand behind its own yesterdays?), for its beginning and its end, for its restrictions and limitations. It cannot ensure that at any time, the limitlessness of its "preprimordial" responsibility will not become boundless despair. Overlooking, or not yet fully experiencing and reflecting upon, its own state of separation and thus upon its own horizons, still submerged in the "prenatal" vagueness of the borders between itself, as a separated being, and the integrity of Being from which it has been separated, it does not experience and probably cannot yet fully experience the most important thing of all: the absolute horizon of its own transcendence, that is, the immeasurable horizon of that Being which is radically outside it and to which it relates through its sense of responsibility. In other words: this "young I" 's responsibility, for all its purity and boundlessness—and in fact, in a certain sense, precisely because of those qualities—is essentially irresponsible, because it is not yet fully and genuinely a responsibility "toward" anything. Only a genuine (conscious, "alert") entry into the world, time and space, and only a perception of one's own responsibility as being for them and in them, can shape responsibility as a relationship and help it to discover that it is responsibility not only for something, but also toward something; that it is not just an outpouring of the "I" into its infinite surroundings, as though there were nothing "outside," but that it is, at the same time, a call "from beyond," demanding that the "I" render an account of itself.

. . .

I kiss you,
Vašek

135

July 3, 1982

Dear Olga,

2. The emerging "I" gains its first experiences when its longing for the lost fullness of Being collides with the barrier of its own state of separation. Through these experiences, both what is experienced (the world and the "I" in it) and that which experiences (the "I" that knows of itself and of the world) are established. The "I" begins to exist as a subject—that is, as the subject of those experiences—and becomes "an existence," i.e., separated being that is aware of itself and its own state of separation. In the beginning, therefore, there is unfreedom, dependency, blind (or rather still blinded) thrownness; the "I" as an object of its own thrownness and as a milieu from which it will arise (i.e., the stage of its own self-constitution). Obviously its initial experiences—in fact its first "existential" experiences—are what first fully transform it into "an existence," primarily by awakening the consciousness, the ability to reflect, mind. This means that the "I"—already aware that it exists—is continually stepping outside itself in order to return to itself once more and, through this "circulation," it inevitably matures—becomes itself. The existential experience—which opens the

spatiotemporal world to the "I"—also opens up the "inner world" as the proper stage for the activity that the "I" represents, and it sets this activity in motion: the "I" begins to understand its own thrownness, and thus it extricates itself from blind dependence on it; it becomes free, begins to "make itself up," to choose, to want, to write its own history and thus to define its own identity.

The intrinsic orientation of the "I" toward Being means, of course, a will to be. As the "I" begins to take stock of its situation and understand its separation, it begins to understand as well that "to be" means "to be in the world," that is, to exist in it. And here we encounter, in a new form, the profoundly paradoxical nature of human existence: the "I" can only approach the kind of Being it longs for (i.e., in the fullness of Being) through its own existence-in-the-world, and the manner of that existence. It can neither skip over that existence, nor get around it, nor avoid it nor ignore it. On the other hand, however, to focus one's attention exclusively on existence-in-the-world as such and thus substitute the means for the end means inevitably to reject the fullness of Being. To succumb entirely to existence-in-the-world means to block entirely any chance of coming in contact with Being; it means a loss of Being, not to be. Existence, therefore, is a kind of permanent balancing act between the unattainability of Being and succumbing to existence-in-the-world. A constant search for what can never completely be found: a way of best achieving all the demands of that existence-in-the-world without, at the same time, ever succumbing to it, of constantly striving toward Being, not to the detriment of one's existence-in-the-world, or by denying it, but through and by it. Exsitence-in-the-world is, after all, a temptation and a seduction: it drags one down into the world of things, surfaces, frantic consumption and self-absorption; it offers, as the most advantageous alternative, a kind of "setting up shop" among the demands of one's "existence-in-the-world"; it offers identification with them, a chance to forget oneself among them—and thus, it constantly distracts the "I" from itself, from its orientation toward Being. It manages, therefore, successfully to conceal precisely the goal to which it is supposed to lead one and, creating the illusion that it is assuring his passage toward Being, it leads him in precisely the opposite direction: toward meaninglessness, nothingness and non-Being. For succumbing to existence-in-the-world is in fact surrendering to the "non-I." In renouncing the transcendental dimensions of his "I," man renounces its paradoxical essences, disrupts that fundamental tension from which its very existence, subjectivity and ultimately its identity all stem, dissolves himself in aims and matters that he himself has defined and created, and finally loses himself in them entirely. He becomes a mechanism, a function, a frantic consumer, a thing, manipulated by his own manipulations. At the same time, the most treacherous and insidious form of this descent into the "non-I" is the one that appears most effective in overcoming the alienation of the world: the one that drives man to take the world—as the milieu of his existence and therefore as the only proper object of his attention—"by storm," as it were, to overpower it and rule it. At the end of this apparent control of the world lies self-enslavement, nothing more: in assuming that he rules the world and has thus liberated himself, man—dominated by his own "dominion"—loses his freedom: he becomes a prisoner of his own "worldly" schemes, dissolves himself in them and ultimately discovers that by apparently eliminating the barriers to his existence-in-the-world, he has merely succeeded in losing himself. The integrity of the free "I," always open to the fullness of Being and—in all the freshness of its "preoriginal" intentions and despite their ultimate futility—constantly striving toward it, has vanished. Continuity and identity have vanished. The subject, its freedom and its will, have been lost and all that remains is an intersection of different aspects of the "non-I": "the subject no longer belongs to the category of reasons," "man is outside" (Levinas), the "I," in a roundabout way, has returned to its initial unfreedom and has become the alienness of the world (few things can make me feel more anxious and alienated than a scientific "explanation" of my "I"—whether as a biological, psychological or political phenomenon).

As man becomes a full existence, he is confronted with the central task of coming to terms with his own thrownnesses—both into an orientation toward Being and into his Being-in-the-world. And each moment, he is confronted with two basic alternatives: he can seek a way of living out his Being-in-the-world in such a way that he might touch Being, not turn away from it, listen, as a matter of course, to "what is unexpressed in the language of the world" and thus accept the world permanently as a partly opened doorway to Being; or he can simply turn away from Being, accept his existence-in-the-world as his ultimate direction and meaning (in reality a pseudomeaning), enter fully into its service and thus give up on the difficult and demanding "voice of Being" in himself and in the world, i.e., to give up on himself as a subject and as "separated Being," to alienate himself from his own most proper, enigmatic essence.

These alternatives, of course, are also the alternatives of human responsibility: either the primordial, "irresponsible" "responsibility for everything" gradually takes on—through its existence-in-the-world, space and time—the dimensions of the responsibility of the "I" for itself and responsibility "toward" (in other words, becomes "the responsibility of man for his own responsibility") and thus leads man to a permanent, and permanently deepening, relation with the integrity of Being—or else man devalues such responsibility, retreats from it, renounces it (with the help of a wide range of self-deceptions) and replaces it with a utilitarianism that is completely tied to the demands of his existence-in-the-world. His morality is then the morality of the "hypothetical imperative" (for instance, he cares for others—including those who have yet to come—only to the extent that is useful and practical within the terms of his own existence-in-the-world), or it is a "reified" morality, that is, a morality whose measure is no longer a fresh, radical ongoing confrontation with his own source in Being and with the experience of contact with its integrity, but one that is measured only by its fidelity to itself as a human creation, which, though it may originally have come out of a genuine transcendence toward Being, has for a long time now only been living the autonomous life of something man accepts as one of the accessories of his existence-in-the-world. As I will try to show, by conserving the now distant intention of the "pre-I," such a morality creates the illusion that the original intention is still alive and, in the process, deludes man so profoundly that it ultimately makes it possible for him to commit any evil whatsoever in the name of good.

. . .

I kiss you,
Vašek

136

July 10, 1982

Dear Olga,

3. Orientation toward Being leads to that central existential quest, the quest for meaning. It is not a quest after the purpose or function

of one particular entity in relation to another particular entity within the framework of a world constituted in any particular way, but a quest that goes beyond the horizon of all entities and beyond the horizon of the world as well. In this matter, man treats both the world and himself as the subject of his quest. He seeks with his entire being, and in that quest, his being is entirely transformed, as the world is entirely transformed in it as well. The object of the quest is Being itself. As an existential experience, this quest cannot be "answered," not in any specific way. The only possible response to it is another experience— the experience of meaningfulness as a joyful encounter with the unity between the voice of Being within us and the voice of Being in the world, an encounter that first gives both these voices a full voice, as it were, and thus opens the Being of the world up to us at the same time as it opens us up to that Being. In other words: the world becomes genuinely meaningful to one who is questing for meaning—and not just as that part of his experience which is still waiting to be assimilated, but also as that very process of assimilation, that is, as a result of the active entry of the "I" into the primordial alienness of the world and an image of its Being in that world.

And indeed: the world of an "I" that is oriented toward Being is different from the world of an "I" that has succumbed to its existence-in-the-world. Nothing in the former world is entirely defined by its function; everything, in a way that is unclear, somehow transcends both its function and itself as well; everything in it seems turned toward Being, its harmony, its infinitude, its totality and its mystery; everything mirrors the openness of the subject that is assimilating itself into this world, mirrors its humble wonder—and terror—at the sovereignty of Being, its longing for Being's touch and its irrepressible hope.

Precisely these hard to grasp but vitally important dimensions are fatally lacking in the world of the "I" that has settled for mere existence-in-the-world: this is a world of functions, purposes and functioning, a world focused on itself, enclosed within itself, barren in its superficial variety, empty in its illusory richness, ignorant, though awash in information, cold, alienated and ultimately absurd. (It is eloquently symbolized by high-rise housing, which guarantees accommodation by denying a real home: without a genius loci to transcend its function as a source of accommodation, it transforms the mystery of the city into something that merely complicates life: there is no adventure in trying to find someone in a high-rise complex, it is merely a tiresome process.) It is a world of exteriority, extension and expansion, a world of taking power, of ruling and conquering: we conquer continents, mineral resources, the air, the energy trapped in matter, outer space. The aim, however, is simple conquest and when it is all over the familiar scenery of the conquered territory emerges: continents are turned upside down, the bowels of the earth plundered, the atmosphere polluted, the energy trapped in matter released in the form of thousands of atomic warheads capable of destroying civilization and the surface of the planet ten times over. And having successfully conquered outer space, we now have a junkyard on the moon, a small prefiguration of what this civilization is preparing to make of the planet on which it arose.

Surrender to existence-in-the-world means the creation of an imbalance in the intrinsic intentions of existence and thus a denial of its dramatically contradictory essence, a contradiction that could be—if acknowledged—the mainspring of a flourishing of existence becomes, when banished beyond its borders, its graveyard. Thus the world constituted by this surrender grows out of a crisis of human integrity, a crisis of the inner world, a crisis of the subject as subject. It is an expression of the crisis of human responsibility, and at the same time it continues to deepen that crisis. Surrendering to existence-in-the-world, therefore, means falling into a vicious circle in which helplessness, seeking compensation in orgies of power, increases by degrees until at last man—like Goethe's sorcerer's apprentice—can merely gape uncomprehendingly at what has come from his high and mighty illusion of understanding.

How can this vicious circle be broken? There would seem to be only one way: a revolutionary turning toward Being. The first condition for such an about-face, of course, is a recognition of the viciousness of this circle. Modern man has already, I think, come to just such a recognition: it is contained in the experience of absurdity.

A flower, a fish, a galaxy, a neutrino, man's nervous system—anything that is not the work of man—can awaken in us feelings of amazement, horror, joy and a whole range of other emotions, but they cannot, in themselves, awaken a sensation of absurdity. That feeling is always evoked by something man does, by human institutions, thoughts, products, relationships, actions, etc. Absurdity is the experience that something that has, should or could have aspired to meaning—that is, something intrinsically human—does not do so at all, or else has lost it. It is, therefore, the experience of losing touch with Being, the experience of a disintegration of the power to confer meaning, the experience of a humanity that has discovered it has defrauded itself, "lost its way"—and which, for that reason, turns back to its proper track: in the awareness of meaning's absence, the longing for meaning announces its presence again. If "meaning" is an entirely human category, then this is doubly true of "nonmeaning": it is a human experience not just because man has it, but also because man only has it when confronted with what he has already done. It is the experience of the "I" oriented toward Being with the "I" that has surrendered to existence-in-the-world; it is the experience of man alone with himself. And even if that experience revives, or is reminiscent of, that primordial experience of the alienness of the world, the experience of absurdity—as a relatively late experience of the "mature I"—is far from being identical with that recollection: for in absurdity, the alienness of the world is not something that needs to be there; it is not something into which we have been "preprimordially" thrown; on the contrary, it is something that does not have be there, and into which, in a sense, we throw ourselves. For isn't this precisely the point where true absurdity begins?

The moon is not absurd. What is absurd is the junkyard man has left on it: it is not the moon, but the junkyard that lacks the slightest transcendence toward Being and its mysterious order, or the slightest reflection of the wonder, the humility and the hope of someone who aspires to Being. There is in it only the desolation of things torn from their context, the arrogance of conquerors who expect that the captives and the vanquished will clean up after them, the despair of those who do not relate to eternity, but only to the present day. The absurd—because in its pride it is ludicrously inappropriate—expansion of mere occupancy, paid for by a loss of the capacity to make oneself at home. Man here enters the universe not as a wise participant in its order but as its arrogant destroyer, carrying into space only unbelonging, disorder and futility. It is the calling card of fallen humanity, which has ejected from the module of its existence in the world—as something too heavy and no longer necessary—the most important thing of all: its meaning—and thus, to its belated astonishment, it has placed that existence-in-the-world face-to-face with the threat of extinction. Thus a turning away from Being in the philosophical sense of the word points ultimately to a non-Being that is terrifyingly nonphilosophical.

. . .

I kiss you,
Vašek

137

July 17, 1982

Dear Olga,

For many years now, whenever I have thought about responsibility or discussed it with someone, a trivial illustration has come to mind: at night, I board the rear car of a tram to go one stop. The car is empty, and since the fare is paid by dropping a crown into a box, not even a conductor is present (this self-service system, as far as I know, is no longer used on Prague streetcars). So I have the option of throwing the fare into the box or not: if I don't, no one will see me, or ever find out; no witnesses will ever be able to testify to my misdemeanor. So I'm faced with a great dilemma, regardless of how much money I happen to have with me: to pay or not to pay? From the point of view of my existence in the world, it clearly makes sense not to pay, since putting a crown in the box amounts to throwing it down the drain. Still, it troubles me; I hesitate, think about it; in fact I might even be said to agonize over it. Why? What, after all, is compelling me to pay? Certainly not fear of the consequences if I don't—for my misdemeanor will never be discovered, nor will I ever be brought to trial. It is not even a desire to demonstrate my sense of civic duty, for there is no one either to condemn me for cheating or commend me for paying. My friends, fellow citizens, the public, society, the transport commission and the state itself are all, at this moment, sound asleep, quite outside my dilemma, and any instrumental regard for their opinion would be obvious nonsense. The conflict is entirely my own, and my concern, or lack of it, for opinion is simply not a factor. But more than that: in this dispute, not even the extent of my concern, or lack of it, for the general good is germane: clearly, my night ride in the streetcar will cost society what it will cost whether I pay or not, and clearly it is of no concern to the transport commission whether my crown shows up in their ledgers or not. Why, then, does something urge me to pay? Or conversely, why does the thought of not paying make me feel guilty?

The problem is deeper than it would seem at first. I know I should behave as everyone should; I know it's right to pay, that one should pay; that is how I was taught, and I accept that; I respect those who so taught me and who so behave. My upbringing, my sense of propriety, my habits, my sense of duty and responsibility to the whole, instilled in me throughout my life—all of these are certainly factors in my dilemma, but merely background factors, as external, essentially, as matters such as the amount of the fare, how much money I have with me, how far I am going, the chances of someone seeing me, etc. etc. The influence of my upbringing or the extent to which I accept the general moral norms explains the nub of my dilemma as little as all the other external factors, which together bear somewhat the same relationship to it as the scenery, the stage and the lights bear to the drama that unfolds with their help.

Let us examine, then, the structure of this drama: I think everyone must realize, from his own experience, that what is going on here is a dialogue. A dialogue between my "I," as the subject of its own freedom (I can pay or not), of its ability to reflect (I give thought to what I should do) and of its choice (I will pay or I won't) and something that is outside this "I," separated from it and not identical with it. This "partner," however, is not standing beside me; I can't see it, nor can I quit its sight: its eyes and its voice follow me everywhere; I can neither escape it nor outwit it: it knows everything. Is it my so-called "inner voice," my "superego," my "conscience"? Certainly, if I hear it calling me to responsibility, I hear this call within me, in my mind and my heart; it is my own experience, profoundly so, though different from the experiences mediated to me by my senses. This, however, does nothing to alter the fact that the voice addresses me and enters into conversation with me, in other words, it comes to my "I"—which I trust is not schizoid—from the outside.

Who, then, is in fact conversing with me? Obviously someone I hold in higher regard than the transport commission, than my best friends (this would come out when the voice would take issue with their opinions), and higher, in some regards, than myself, that is, myself as subject of my existence-in-the-world and the carrier of my "existential" interests (one of which is the rather natural effort to save a crown). Someone who "knows everything" (and is therefore omniscient), is everywhere (and therefore omnipresent) and remembers everything; someone who, though infinitely understanding, is entirely incorruptible; who is, for me, the highest and utterly unequivocal authority in all moral questions and who is thus Law itself; someone eternal, who through himself makes me eternal as well, so that I cannot imagine the arrival of a moment when everything will come to an end, thus terminating my dependence on him as well; someone to whom I relate entirely and for whom, ultimately, I would do everything. At the same time, this "someone" addresses me directly and personally (not merely as an anonymous public passenger, as the transport commission does).

But who is it? God? There are many subtle reasons why I'm reluctant to use that word; one factor here is a certain sense of shame (I don't know exactly for what, why and before whom), but the main thing, I suppose, is a fear that with this all too specific designation (or rather assertion) that "God is," I would be projecting an experience that is entirely personal and vague (never mind how profound and urgent it may be), too single-mindedly "outward," onto that problem-fraught screen called "objective reality," and thus I would go too far beyond it. Whether God exists or not—as Christians understand it—I do not and cannot know; I don't even know if that word is an appropriate label for the call to responsibility I hear. I know only this: that Being (which is, after all, easier to posit than the being of God) in its integrity, fullness and infinity, as the principle, direction and meaning of everything that is, and as the most profound and, at the same time, the broadest "innerness" of everything that exists (I intend to write about this in more detail) takes on, in the sphere of our inner experience that I am writing about here, an expressly personal outline: its voice, as we receive it—because we are "tuned in to its wavelength" (i.e., because of our source in it and our orientation toward it)—seems to emerge from a particularly "unseparated" subjective aspect of Being, with its own infinite memory, an omnipresent mind and an infinitely large heart. In other words: the Being of the universe, at moments when we encounter it on this level, suddenly assumes a personal face and turns this, as it were, toward us. The extent to which it acquires this face from our limited and deeply anthropomorphic imaginations, or, to be more precise, how much of this experience can be attributed to the one who is having it and how much to what causes it, is of course impossible to judge, nor does it make sense to try: to ascertain that would require climbing above the particular experience and all our other experiences too, that is, it would mean abandoning oneself, one's state of separation and one's humanity, to become God. But however it is, one thing seems certain to me: that our "I"—to the extent that it has not been entirely successful in suppressing its orientation toward Being, and becoming completely absorbed in its existence-in-the-world—has a sense of responsibility purely and simply because it relates intrinsically to Being as that in which it feels the only coherence, meaning and the somehow inevitable "clarification" of everything that exists, because it relates and aspires toward Being with all its being, because it hears within and around itself the "voice" in which this Being addresses and calls out to it, because in that voice it recognizes its own origin and its purpose, its true relevance and its true responsibility, and because it takes this voice more seriously than anything else.

. . .

I kiss you,
Vašek

138

July 25, 1982

Dear Olga,

Five years ago something happened to me that in many regards had a key significance in my subsequent life. It began rather inconspicuously: I was in detention for the first time and one evening, after interrogation, I wrote out a request to the Public Prosecutor for my release. Prisoners in detention are always writing such requests, and I too treated it as something routine and unimportant, more in the nature of mental hygiene: I knew, of course, that my eventual release or nonrelease would be decided by factors having nothing to do with whether I wrote the appropriate request or not. Still, the interrogations weren't going anywhere and it seemed proper to use the opportunity and let myself be heard. I wrote my request in a way that at the time seemed extremely tactical and cunning: while saying nothing I did not believe or that wasn't true, I simply "overlooked" the fact that truth lies not only in what is said, but also in who says it, and to whom, why, how and under what circumstances it is expressed. Thanks to this minor "oversight" (more precisely, this minor self-deception) what I said came dangerously close—by chance, as it were—to what the authorities wanted to hear. What was particularly absurd was the fact that my motive—at least my conscious and admitted motive—was not the hope that it would produce results, but merely a kind of professionally intellectualistic and somewhat perverse delight in my own—or so I thought—"honorable cleverness." (I should add, to complete the picture, that when I read it some years later, the honor in that cleverness made my hair stand on end.) I sent the request off the following day and because no one responded to it and my detention was prolonged again, I assumed it had ended up where such requests usually end up, and I more or less forgot about it. And then one day lightning struck: I was given to know that I would probably be released, and that in the process, "political use" would be made of my request. Of course I knew right away what that meant: (1) that with appropriate "recasting," "additions" and widespread publicity, the impression would be created that I had not held out, that I had given in to pressure and backed down from my positions, opinions and all my previous work; in short, that I had betrayed my cause, all for a trivial reason—to get myself out of jail; (2) no denial or correction on my part could alter that impression because I had undeniably written something that "met them halfway" and anything I could add would, quite rightly, seem like an attempt to worm my way out of it; (3) that the approaching catastrophe was unavoidable; (4) that the blot it would leave on me and everything I had taken part in would haunt me for years to come, that it would cause me measureless inner suffering, and that I would probably try to erase it with several years in prison (which in fact happened), but that not even that would rid me entirely of the stigma; (5) that I had no one but myself to blame: I was neither forced to do it, nor offered a bribe; I was not, in fact, in a dilemma and it was only because I'd unforgivably let down my moral guard that I'd given the other side—voluntarily and quite pointlessly—a weapon that amounted to a heaven-sent gift.

This was followed by a brief period of desperate attempts to avoid the unavoidable—and then it happened, and all my worst fears were more than fully realized: I came out of prison discredited, to confront a world that seemed to me one enormous, supremely justified rebuke. No one knows what I went through in that darkest period of my life (you may be the only one who has an inkling): there were weeks, months, years, in fact, of silent desperation, self-castigation, shame, inner humiliation, reproach and uncomprehending questioning. For a while I escaped from a world I felt too embarrassed to face into gloomy isolation, taking masochistic delight in endless orgies of self-blame. And then for a while I fled this inner hell into frantic activity through which I tried to drown out my anguish and at the same time, to "rehabilitate" myself somehow. Naturally, I felt how tense and unnatural my behavior was, but I still couldn't shake that sensation. I felt best of all, relatively speaking, in prison: when I was locked up a second time I caught my breath a little, and the third time—until today—I have finally managed, or so I hope, to overcome it. And in fact it hasn't been until today— more than five years later—that I've been able to rise above the whole affair and assess it more evenly: I've only now begun fully to realize that the experience wasn't just—from my point of view, at least—an incomprehensible lapse that caused me a lot of pointless suffering; it had a deeply positive and purgative significance, for which I ought to thank my fate instead of cursing it. It thrust me into a drastic but, for that very reason, crucial confrontation with myself; it shook, as it were, my entire "I," "shook out of it" a deeper insight into itself, a more serious acceptance and understanding of my situation, of my thrownnesses and my horizons, and led me, ultimately, to a new and more coherent consideration of the problem of human responsibility. That is also why I am coming back to that event now: to examine—from today's point of view—what it showed me, and how. I think that without such a passage, these meditations of mine would be incomplete: why should they try and cover up their most intrinsic existential origin, and on what more appropriate basis should their assertations be founded if not on what, in fact, set them in motion?

1. The central question I came back to again and again was this: how could it have happened? How could I have done something so transparently dubious? Was it a temporary confusion of the senses brought on by the strange atmosphere of my first imprisonment, along with the relatively skillful way I was interrogated, the rather unfortunate strategy I adopted to defend myself (though originally there were rational reasons for it), my entirely false grasp of the situation and my completely wrong assessment of it? Or was it just the rather banal psychosis of a tenderfoot prisoner? Did the position of my lawyer who, I mistakenly believed, was transmitting the perceptions of those close to me play a part in it? Did I not give too free a rein to some qualities in me that were entirely unsuitable to my position and situation—my tendency to trust where inappropriate, my politeness, my silly faith in signs of good intentions on the part of my antagonists, my constant self-doubt, my effort to get along with everyone, my constant need to defend and explain myself, combined with an utter inability to be a burden to those around me? Was it a major error in thinking, an expression of subconscious physiological fear, or was it simply a wrong assessment, the kind anyone could have made (usually without such far-reaching consequences)? In this and other ways, then, I interrogated myself, but regardless of how I responded, I still felt I had left the essence untouched, that I was getting no closer to an explanation and that this way would never bring me even relative peace of mind. I've known for some time now why this was, but only now have I

learned, perhaps, how to articulate it: the mistake lay not in answering the questions wrongly, nor in wrongly assessing the significance of the various factors involved (which in any case modified and combined with each other), but rather in the very way I posed the questions, which originated in an unconscious effort to localize the essential cause of my failure somewhere "outside," beyond the borders of my real "I" (the "I" of my "I"), in "circumstances," "conditions," external factors or influences, into some alienating "psychological process"—that typically modern way of excluding the self from the "category of blame." Yes, my questioning was essentially only a desperate attempt to hide from myself the hard fact that the failure was mine—exclusively, essentially and fully mine—that is, was a failure of precisely that "I of my I" which then professes such astonishment at that failure, which tries to explain it away at all costs, inconspicuously shift its roots to the "non-I," put some distance between itself and the failure and thereby free itself. This dividing of my self—the source of my questioning—which kept getting deeper, this splitting of my "I" into an alien, prior and incomprehensible "I" that failed, and a living, present, genuine "I," genuinely mine, which does not understand and condemns the former "I" (bitter because it must bear the consequences of the former's actions)—all that was simply an unacknowledged attempt to lie my way out of my responsibility for myself and shift it onto someone else, as it were. Today, the hidden motives behind this attempt are clear to me: accepting full responsibility for one's own failure is extraordinarily difficult, from the point of view of the "interests of our existence-in-the-world," and frequently it is virtually unbearable and impossible, and if one wants to live even slightly "normally"—i.e., exist in the world (guided by the so-called instinct for self-preservation)—one is irresistibly driven to ease the situation by dividing the self, turning the matter into an unfortunate "misunderstanding": those entirely warranted reproaches cannot possibly be addressed to me, but to the other, who has been mistakenly identified with me. Obviously if one stuck complacently to this approach, it would lead to the disintegration of one's own identity. For it is only by assuming full responsibility here for one's own elsewhere, only by assuming full responsibility today for one's own yesterday, only by this unqualified assumption of responsibility by the "I" for itself and for everything it ever was and did, does the "I" achieve continuity and thus identity with the self. This is the only possible way it can become something definite, limited and defined, related to its environment in a graspable way, not dissipated in it, not haplessly caught up in its random processes. To relinquish this full responsibility for oneself, to compromise one's integrity and sovereignty, not to widen and strengthen, but on the contrary, to narrow and weaken the control of one's "I" over one's actions (including those ascribed to the "instincts"—another alibi that shifts the blame from the "I" to the "non-I"), ultimately means only one thing: to turn away from Being, to give up on one's own mysterious connection—in one's origins and aims—to its fullness and integrity, to cancel out one's complex way of relating to it—and to disintegrate into fragmentary, isolated, self-enclosed events, interests and aims that lack any transcendence beyond one's "existence-in-the-world," to dissolve in that existence and thus in the "non-I" and so, ultimately, to deprive oneself of genuinely human being, that is, being as the inner coherence, direction, transcendence, meaning and purpose of human existence, anchored in the fullness of Being and oriented toward it. In other words: it means dissolving oneself in the world, in the world of phenomena, particular aims, random occurrences, isolated things, "merenesses" and disjointed worries. It means apparently simplifying one's life—but at the cost of losing oneself, the miracle of one's separated being which, precisely because of its separation, aspires toward the integrity of Being. It means losing the identity that is anchored in Being and reliably related to it, that is, the only thing that holds our "I" together and makes us truly human. To know all this and express it, obviously, is in no way difficult; but it is not easy to experience it existentially, as I learned through hard personal experience. For there is nothing like experiencing failure to give you a more intense understanding of responsibility—that is, if you manage to open yourself to it wholly and without prevarication—as responsibility for one's self.

It is not hard to stand behind one's successes. But to accept responsibility for one's failures, to accept them unreservedly as failures that are truly one's own, that cannot be shifted somewhere else or onto something else, and actively to accept—without regard for any worldly interests, no matter how well disguised, or for well-meant advice—the price that has to be paid for it: that is devilishly hard! But only thence does the road lead—as my experience, I hope, has persuaded me—to a renewal of sovereignty over my own affairs, to a radically new insight into the mysterious gravity of my existence as an uncertain enterprise, and to its transcendental meaning. And only this kind of inner understanding can ultimately lead to what might be called true "peace of mind," to that highest delight, to genuine meaningfulness, to that endless "joy of Being." If one manages to achieve that, then all one's worldly privations cease to be privations, and become what Christians call grace.

. . .

I kiss you,
Vašek

139

July 31, 1982

Dear Olga,

2. Another question arises, however: why did I agonize so long over how it could have happened when there was nothing I could have changed in any case? Why did I torment myself endlessly with the need to find an "explanation" at any cost? And above all: why did no "explanation" satisfy me, nor relieve my despair? After all, those around me—my friends and the public—eventually accepted and came to terms with my failure, understood it somehow, or even forgave it or quickly put it out of their minds. Why could I not—and cannot still—forget it, when no one would think of reproaching me now, assuming anyone were still concerned?

The answer, I think, is obvious: the source of my torment was and is the same as that which tells me I should pay in the night streetcar—not in words, but more urgently: through a kind of complex "pressure" on my heart and soul, a pressure that, oddly enough, is far more intelligible than the most eloquent words. In this case—just as it did in that—it silently and incisively demasks all my halting equivocations. Ultimately—now as then—it does not give me rest until I have paid: then a crown, and now the "bill" for my own failure. It is, again, that to which, through all my relationships, I alone relate and to which, through all my responsibilities, I alone am ultimately responsible: the mysterious "voice of Being" that reaches my "I" "from outside" more clearly (so clearly that it is usually described as coming "from above") than anything else, but which, at the same time—paradoxically—penetrates to a deeper level than anything else, because it comes through the "I" itself: not only because I hear it in myself, but above all because it is the voice of my own being, torn away from the integrity of Being and thus intrinsically bound to it, of my own being considered as my deep-seated dispositions (developed or betrayed in one way or another), of my sense of rootedness and orientation, of my direction, task and meaning, of my true and unique human limitation and fulfillment. There is a slight but emphatic difference in the impact of this cry—or tormentingly reproachful silence—in the case of an unpaid fare on a night streetcar and a personal failure that betrays dozens of brave people who trusted in me and followed me without complaining of the sacrifices entailed. And yet it is still essentially the same voice. If we are immediately thrown into our original "responsibility for everything" because, by virtue of our "pre-I," we still have one foot, as it were, in the original fullness of Being and our mind has not yet emerged with sufficient clarity to make us aware of our state of separation and present to us the necessity of existence-in-the-world and, of course, the temptations locked within it—if, then, we are not yet capable of reflecting the "voice of Being" on that level, then only later—in the forge of living trials and through them, as we mature into ourselves—do we find ourselves in a genuinely "alert" confrontation with that voice, in that never-ending "dialogue" with it at the crossroads where Being and existence-in-the-world part ways, and only then do we have the real freedom to decide, over and over again, what we will pursue and what we will turn away from. In other words: we really only discover and begin to understand, accept and fulfill our genuine responsibility—as responsibility for oneself and responsibility "toward"—through alert "existential praxis," through the trials and tribulations we undergo, and the tasks that arise—and of course through our own failures as well. Only thus is our responsibility made manifest to us—and conversely, it is only in such activity and on its basis that we can betray that responsibility.

But to return to my story: I have my failure to thank for the fact that for the first time in my life I stood—if I may be allowed such a comparison—directly in the study of the Lord God himself: never before had I looked into his face or heard his reproachful voice from such proximity, never had I stood before him in such profound embarrassment, so humiliated and confused, never before had I been so deeply ashamed or felt so powerfully how unseemly anything I could say in my own defense would be. And the most interesting thing about that confrontation, which in an utterly new way revealed my responsibility as responsibility "toward," was this: if my request had ended up in the chief prosecutor's wastebasket and I had come out of prison a hero, I might never have experienced it at all! In other words: it was shame—anticipated at first, and later experienced directly—before those closest to me, my friends, acquaintances, the public—shame, that is, before actual, erring, imperfect people, who essentially knew nothing about the real inner and outer development of my case (regardless of whether they were right or wrong to condemn or defend me), it was shame, in other words, before that "relative," accidental, ephemeral and indeterminate "concrete horizon" of my relating that, to my astonishment, put me in the sharpest confrontation I had ever experienced with the "absolute horizon" of my relating, i.e., with the Being of the world and my own being, with that "personal face" which Being, in moments like this, turns toward me. Thus it is not so at all that there are two separate and remote worlds, the earthly world of erring people who are of small account, and the heavenly world of God, the only one who counts. Quite the contrary: Being is one, it is everywhere and behind everything; it is the Being of everything and the only way to it is the one that leads through this world of mine and through this "I" of mine. The "voice of Being" does not come "from elsewhere" (i.e., from some transcendental heaven), but only and exclusively "from there": it is "the unuttered in the language of the world" that Heidegger writes about in his *Holzwege,* it is only what is in that language and behind it, what gives it significance, coherence, weight, direction, meaning; it is that by which that language most profoundly addresses us and has an impact on us, opens us up to ourselves, to our true being, to our "being in Being."

3. By casting doubt on my sense of responsibility, the shock I experienced, of course, cast doubt on my identity as well. Everything I was, for myself and for others, suddenly found itself open to question. I had to assume that those around me were justified in asking—and I had to ask with them—who I really was. Was I still the same person my entire previous history had defined me as, or was I now someone else, someone who, in extreme circumstances, knuckles under and who is not—as the previous one was—entirely reliable? I don't know how much and how long those around me mistrusted me after that incident (I anxiously avoided inquiring into the matter), but I assumed—with typical extremism—that I had lost everyone's confidence, that no one would ever fully trust me again, that I had been tactfully struck off the list of the "living." Along with my former identity, then, my whole

former sense of rootedness, of position, of what I was to those around me was necessarily shaken (probably more so in my feelings than in fact). But that, too, was immensely useful: it enabled me not only to understand (it's something that everyone knows theoretically) but to experience, in a directly physical way, the fact that one's identity is never in one's possession as something given, completed and unquestionable, as an entity among entities, as something one can husband like anything else, that one can use, depend on, draw on and, every so often, give a new coat of paint. I had to learn the hard way that the opposite is true: one can, at any time—in the space of a few minutes— deny one's entire history and turn it upside down: all it takes is a moment of inattention, of self-indulgent relaxation, of careless trust that one is what one is, and must be so always. I understood that my identity is what I seek, do, choose and define, today and every day; that it is not a path I once chose and now merely proceed along, but one that I must redefine at every step, wherein each misstep or wrong turn, though caused only by neglecting one's bearings in the terrain, remains an irradicable part of it, one that requires vast and complex effort to set right. The maturing of the "I" into itself is not, therefore, merely an accumulation of bits of knowledge and action that cover one's original state of nakedness and vulnerability with layers of clothing and armor, but a constant confrontation with one's own source, with one's own thrownnesses, with one's own orientation, demanding each instant to return in full seriousness to the "core of things," to pose the primordial questions again and again, and from the beginning, constantly, to examine the direction one is going in. And regardless of how honorable a history a human existence has, it can never rest on it as one would on a pillow, but must be ever mindful that nothing it has is pre-paid and that it remains as "naked" and virginal as ever, face-to-face with the same original choice and just as vulnerable to the "voice of Being" and to the temptations of existence-in-the-world. Human identity, simply put, is not a "place of existence" where one sits things out, but a constant encounter with the question of how to be, and how to exist in the world. Who knows whether, in my case, it wasn't some kind of rescue operation mounted by fate: what if that purifying shock—perhaps at the very last minute—plucked me from the inconspicuous pathway leading to the harbor of that reified, alienated, fetishized and ultimately entirely false "morality of merits" that Levinas talks about, that "morality for the press," that especially dangerous— dangerous because especially confusing—way of giving in to existence-

in-the-world as a complacent deal made with one's own institutional-
ized discomfort?

. . .

I kiss you,
Vašek

140

August 7, 1982

Dear Olga,

My family, friends, acquaintances, fellow prisoners, the unknown
weatherwoman, my fellow passengers in the streetcar, the transport
commission, those who go to see my plays, the public, my homeland
and the state power-structure; countless relationships, tensions, loves,
dependencies, confrontations, atmospheres, milieus, experiences, acts,
predilections, aims and things with which I am loosely or closely connected—all of that forms the "concrete horizon" of my relating, because all of it is my world, the world as my home, the world in which
I am rooted in a complex way, to which I ceaselessly relate, against the
background of which I define myself, through which I simply am. It is
the world of my existing, such as it presents and opens itself to me, as
I make myself at home in it, as it constitutes itself for me through my
experiences and as I—in one way or another—make it meaningful.
Thus my "I" creates this world and this world creates my "I." And yet:
my existence in this world and the way I relate to my "concrete horizon" cannot be explained, as it may seem at first, by some one-sided
and unqualified clinging to them as such, by surrendering to their
actually existing, isolated, relative, self-exhausting, phenomenal and
superficial manifestations. It depends, rather, on something else: on
the extent to which I direct my existence-in-the-world toward Being;
not, of course, toward Being as something outside the world and which
can be attained only by "leapfrogging" or ignoring the world, but on
the contrary, toward Being as something that is "in the world" far more
radically than anything the world declares and offers itself to be at first
sight: that is, toward its own Being, i.e., to the very Being of this world.
This can only mean that through my life, through the experiences and

trials I undergo, I gradually penetrate beyond the different horizons of my "concrete horizon," I attempt to widen them, to step past them, to see beyond them, to get to what is on the other side of them—until ultimately I aspire toward a place beyond its ultimate, conceivable limit, the "horizon of all my horizons," to what I call "the absolute horizon" of my relating. And only then—as I gradually come to realize (though failure to do so won't change the essence of things)—does this horizon breathe into my world, my existence in it and the way I relate to my "concrete horizon," its proper substance, coherence, meaning, perspective and direction; it is this which, in the language of the world—as that which is "unexpressed" in it—first addresses me in a way that truly demands commitment, and thus ultimately becomes the only true, firm and final focus of my relating to the world and my existence in it, the only true, firm and final background of my self-constitution and self-definition, the only genuine, and genuinely determining "coordinates" of my true identity. Thus if it seemed at first that my responsibility—as responsibility "toward"—simply meant responsibility toward my immediate surrounding, to my "non-I," to my world and thus to my "particular horizon," then it is obviously not entirely true: I am genuinely, fully and reliably responsible for my immediate surrounding only if that responsibility is permeated by, based on and subordinated to responsibility toward my "absolute horizon." Any form of clinging to that surrounding as such inevitably ends up as "worldly" utilitarianism. To put it another way: if the ticket box in the streetcar and the reproaches of those around me for my failure are only what they first seem—the former something that stands for the anonymous expectations of an institution for which I care as little as it does for me, and the latter the perception of individuals who are as prone to error as I am, who are insufficiently informed of the event and likely to forget it in time, then neither instance will complicate my existence-in-the-world to any extent, neither will transmit the more profound "voice of Being" to me, and this will allow me to swim painlessly through life from one "worldly" event to another, without overtaxing myself with the question of who I really am. But if I am oriented toward Being, both these events are something infinitely more than that: they are manifestations of a single, integral Being, and through its imprecise and ephemeral language—and exclusively in that language—I am addressed by the quite precise and indestructible "voice of Being," which for me is everything: the highest and most unqualified authority, integrating and giving meaning to everything, a light in which I first become a genuine human being, i.e., an existence that is identical with itself.

Briefly put: "the absolute horizon" of my relating is what I call "Being."

But what is it, this rather cryptic "Being"? I've been using the term for too long now not to feel that the time has come to throw a little light on it. I'm not entirely happy doing so: its blurred, "soft" and unclear quality suits me, for it corresponds precisely to the mysterious haziness of what I am indicating by the term; I like the fact that in every context or sentence it has a slightly different semantic coloring, and I know that any attempt to define it will, at the same time, impoverish, flatten and weaken its uncertain semantic radiations. But I wouldn't be quite serious if I tried to avoid such a task altogether.

First of all, then: my only truly certain and indisputable experience is the experience of Being in the simplest sense of the word, that is, the experience that something is. At the very least, there is I, the one having the experience, there is the experience as such, and there is, and must be, intrinsically, something that I experience; and if I alone existed—which seems highly unlikely, though theoretically, of course, not out of the question—and everything else were merely my dream, this would still be true: for even a dream is an experience, an experience of something, and thus it too is a form of Being. If I try, in all honesty, to examine this trivial experience of Being more closely and describe it, if possible, in words, then it seems most appropriate to divide it— and here I am certainly influenced, though in no way bound, by the fragments of modern philosophy chance has cast my way over the years (in any case, that is technically impossible: how can one be bound by something one doesn't properly know?)—essentially into two basic layers. The first layer—apparently more definite, more tangible, but in fact rather problematic because it is relative—includes all my direct experience of the world and myself as they manifest themselves to me on various levels of perception. The second layer—far less direct and vivid, yet incomparably more profound and essential—is the experience of "Being" in the sense that I am using it here. The first of those layers is related, obviously, to my state of separation, my thrownness into the world. The second, on the contrary, grows out of my thrownness into the source in Being, my recollections of it and my longing for it. But what does the second experience—evidently the more primordial and firmer, however deeply concealed it may be and drowned out by the incessant clamor of everyday life—what in fact does it mean or say? Essentially, it is an assumption (or a feeling? a conviction? a certainty? a faith?) that everything I experience on the first level is not, somehow, exhausted by itself, is not "just that" with "nothing more to it," but rather is a situational, partial, superficial assembly (limited by my perspective and locked into it) of fleeting, confusing, isolated—or once again, merely superficially and accidently linked—expressions of something infinitely more consistent, absolute and absolutely self-defining. There is here an undeniable intimation not only that "there is something behind it all," but also that somewhere in the fathomless depths (i.e., fathomless to me) of everything that exists there is something beyond which there are no more "beyonds" and beyond which there is, therefore, nothing to be, because in it is the "last of everything," of every entity. This true being of an entity, internally intimated, contains the entity's complete history, coherence and "logic," the direction and tendency most proper to it, its essence, intention and "mind"; the endless summation of all causes, connections and reflections of which it forms the intersection and through which it is connected to everything else; all the possibilities of its concealment and manifestation; its true position in the context of everything that was, is and will be; its total "explanation" and final "meaning," if these most human categories may be used here. Everything I experience—on the first layer—as something that exists in one way or another is thus given by its being, which, though concealed from my view, nevertheless declares or manifests itself to me through that existence. Through its being, however, everything that exists is firmly anchored in the being of everything else, in other words, in the integrity and fullness of "absolute Being"—not only as the being of everything that exists, but "Being in itself," "Being as such." Being in this sense of the word is not, therefore, simply a kind of nail on which everything hangs, but is itself the absoluteness of all "hanging"; it is the essence of the existence of everything that exists; it is what joins everything that exists together, its order and its memory, its source, its will and its aim, what holds it "together," as it were, and makes it participatory in its unity, its "uniqueness" and its meaningfulness.

Perhaps it is sufficiently clear that the experience of Being, as I mean it here, is not just a philosophical thesis that can be accepted or rejected with no further existential implications. (To understand it thus would ultimately mean transforming Being into no more than a kind of floating entity among entities and thus hopelessly to reify and alienate it from itself.) By this experience I mean something essentially different and more profound: an intrinsic longing to arouse, through the conduct of one's existence in the world, one's own hidden, slumbering, forgotten and betrayed being and through this being—which is anchored in the integrity of "absolute Being" and separated from the "I" that is constituted from it and to which that "I" is intrinsically oriented—to touch once again that fullness and integrity of Being, at a distance, perhaps, but fully aware this time; through that "counterpoint" of one's own being and that of the world, to reach toward the principle unity of Being; to accept this unity and "uniqueness" as a binding system of order and the final vanishing point of all its existence in the world, and to relate to it as the absolute horizon of all one's horizons. In other words: the experience of Being is not merely an idea or an opinion: it is a state of the spirit and of the heart, the key to life and one's orientation in life, to one's way of existence; it is not merely one experience among many: it is the experience of all experiences, their veiled starting point and their veiled end. It is a genuinely human journey, arduous and beautiful for what it entails—all the way from the injunction to pay attention to the incorruptible voice that is everywhere calling us to responsibility (which exists even where we are out of sight of the world of our existence) to that highest delight, as we experience it fully and completely in those fleeting moments when the meaning of Being is brought home to us, when we find ourselves on the very "edge of finitude"—face-to-face with the miracle of the world and the miracle of our own "I."

· · ·

I kiss you,
Vašek

141

August 14, 1982

Dear Olga,

Orientation toward Being as a state of mind can also be understood as faith: a person oriented toward Being intrinsically believes in life, in the world, in morality, in the meaning of things and in himself. His relationship to life is informed by hope, wonder, humility and a spontaneous respect for its mysteries. He does not judge the meaning of his efforts merely by their manifest successes, but first of all by their "worth in themselves" (i.e., their worth against the background of the absolute horizon). In this general sense, however, believers are all those who do not surrender to their existence-in-the-world, regardless of whether or not they acknowledge a God, a religion or an ideology, and even regardless of whether they admit or deny that there is a transcendental dimension to their way of existence-in-the-world. The state of mind that has given in to existence-in-the-world is, on the contrary, a state of total resignation (regardless of how it disguises itself). Somewhere in the depths of his spirit, man feels that nothing matters. He is concerned for nothing but his purely "worldly" interests, which are his sole responsibility, and he behaves morally only insofar as, and only when and where, it is expedient to do so, when his actions are visible, for instance. (He would certainly not pay his fare in the night streetcar were he alone.)

When I wrote that human identity is not a path that is chosen once and for all but rather must be constantly reestablished and that a person is in fact always "naked," I had in mind, among other things, the fact that faith, as a state of mind, cannot be "reified" into something complete, something given for all time and no longer problematic, which then requires only to be served, without constantly having to go back over elementary questions. Such a reification ceases to be faith as an orientation toward Being and becomes a mere clinging, an orientation toward entities, things and objects (however abstract) and thus ultimately only a covert way of surrendering to existence-in-the-world. "Responsibility for everything," that intrinsic intention of the "pre-I" (i.e., the "I" that has not yet managed to "forget" entirely its source in the fullness of Being and its belonging to everything that exists), is precisely the disposition that, primordially, renders one open to the "voice of Being" and permits one "subsequently"—as an "I" that is already maturing into itself—to hear this voice in the first place, to understand, respect and begin to take it into account. For this reason, "responsibility for everything" is not only the starting point for all future ("mature") responsibility, but is also an inseparable and constant aspect or dimension of it in the present. Constantly reflected upon, developed, controlled and projected by the mind into the spatio-temporal reality of human duties, it also constantly controls the outbursts and tricks of the mind and through its authenticity, measures, criticizes and provides direction; and if the mind keeps it on a tight "leash of reality," responsibility also holds the mind on the same leash (because a mind unhitched from its existential context can easily end up in the same timelessness and unreality as a "responsibility for everything" that has not been developed by the mind). The maturing or self-discovery of responsibility is not, therefore, a gradual distancing from its original source rooted in the "prenatal" experience of the integrity of Being, nor an emancipation from it, but on the contrary, an increasingly profound, conscious and thoughtful drawing on that source. And our permanent "nakedness" before fundamental questions (which goes along with being exposed to a parting of the ways, the wonder of our "I" at its own freedom and undoubtedly as well that primordial shame that Levinas talks about) is in fact only an injunction to pay constant attention (or constantly return) to that "premental" source of our self-transcendence. It is only by constantly giving those roots their due, by being mindful of them, faithful to them, prepared to confront them and measure ourselves by them, that we are capable at all of seeking our own absolute horizon, relating to it with the same élan, tirelessness and "youthful" seriousness and listening, with the same enthusiasm, to the "voice of Being." And it is only a constantly open view, unobstructed by our former successes, into the primordial absoluteness of those demands that keeps us from every temptation on the part of worldly interests to drown out that voice, falsify it, replace it with a stage prop or, instead of listening to it, to become its prompters. In general, then: the precondition for genuine responsibility and thus for genuine identity, and the condition of alert choice and self-choice that keeps to the proper path, is something that might be called a constant, deepening turbulence of the mutual illumination, verification and augmentation of everything primordial, everything that has been achieved, everything intended and acted upon, spontaneously felt and worked out by the mind; a kind of unceasing dramatic confrontation between primordial vulnerability and achieved experience, between the primordial limitlessness of self-transcendence and the reflected limitations of separation, between the primordial radicalism of the unbridled intentions of the "pre-I" and the deliberation and stability of their self-aware projections into the world of our earthly "existential praxis."

I speak of this because it might throw some light on the essence of a very dangerous way of—almost inadvertently—tragically ruining everything: fanaticism.

What is fanaticism? I would say it is nothing other than this reified, mystified, fetishized and thus, self-alienated faith (with consequences—at least in terms of the immediate human suffering it causes—essentially worse than all the direct ways of surrendering to existence-in-the-world). At the beginning of fanaticism—as in the case of a genuine orientation toward Being, perhaps even more limitlessly—is a feeling that one is "responsible for everything," and this feeling is all the more boundless, of course, the more one feels threatened by the shock of alienation from the freshly perceived world. The emerging mind reflects on the situation and latches onto this expansive intention of the "pre-I" in an effort to provide quick protection against imminent collapse (the fall into hopelessness), and tries, come what may, to give it a fixed form, for all time, on the projecting screen of the reality of human separation. But precisely at this moment, the "I" commits a fatal error, which is extraordinarily seductive to a lazy mind, a weak character and everyone who, though he may be intrinsically and almost physically averse to turning away from Being, at the same time suffers a fatal lack of the intellectual and moral courage (including the courage to go it alone against everyone and deny oneself the advantages of mob possession of ideas) which, in extreme circumstances, a true orientation toward Being cannot get along without; in other words everyone who cannot resist the attractive force of self-deception, the kind that hides surrender to existence-in-the-world beneath the illusion that it is a particularly radical form of orientation toward Being. The essence of this error is the notion that transferring primordial self-transcendence from the boundlessness of the dream to the reality of human actions is a one-shot affair, that all you have to do is "come up with an idea" and then blindly serve it—that is, create some intellectual project that permanently fixes and fulfills the original intention—to be relieved of the duty and effort of constantly aspiring toward Being: for in its place there is a handy substitute—the relatively undemanding duty of devoted service to a given project. Being is thus, in fact, represented by a maquette of itself: by a thesis; that is, by an entity among entities, a thing among things, which can then be made to serve one as easily and mindlessly as one's car or cottage and which—if it fails or does not work out—can just as easily be traded in for another. (Indeed: the more fanatical a person is, the easier it is for him to transfer his "faith" to another object: Maoism can be exchanged overnight for Jehovahism or vice versa, while the intensity of the dedication remains unaltered.) In this case, surrendering to existence-in-the-world is obviously masked by the illusion that one is serving an intellectualized point of contact with Being. All of this, however, hopelessly disrupts and even stops outright that essential and life-giving turbulence of the "pre-I"'s intentions, which mutually check each other, and the alert reflection on them: both the truths that are "preprimordially" and "prementally" perceived and the truths arrived at by insight and experience. Fanaticism inevitably stunts them and eventually they both die out: the monster of the constructed project—by its very nature—rapidly evicts them both from the soul of the "believer" and ultimately eliminates them in reality as well, and in the end, it can only persecute genuine morality and ban genuine thinking because it feels threatened and condemned by both of them, and with good reason. "Responsibility for everything" and human rationality have snapped the chain that kept them both under control, and thus they lose touch both with reality and with Being—and lumped together in a rational (or "rationally mythological") plan for general salvation, they career through the world, wiping out everything alive and living, true and truthful, lopping off the head and limbs of everything that transcends or eludes the given project, that resists it or that simply can't be explained in terms of it. In the name of universal salvation (no one is asked, of course, if they care to be saved) the doors are ultimately opened—because the means justify the ends and self-control has perished—to all the horrors of bureaucracy, repression, high-handedness, violence, terror and terrorism. (The connection between childish enthusiasm, mindless rationalism and merciless violence is, of course, familiar enough: the dreamer becomes the worst bureaucrat and the bureaucrat the most conscientious organizer of mass extermination, because rigid rationalism is the most accessible substitute for living thought, so difficult of access to the "pre-I"'s one-dimensional thought.)

In other words, a fanatic is someone who, without realizing it, replaces the love of God with the love of his own religion; the love of truth, freedom and justice with the love of an ideology, doctrine or sect that promises to guarantee them once and for all; love of people with love of a project claiming that it—and it alone, of course—can genuinely serve them. To put it in general terms, it replaces a difficult orientation toward Being with a more facile orientation toward the human product, claiming exclusive rights—as a representative of the human "I"—to mediate contact with Being. Thus wrapping its existential nakedness, and its exhausting, lifelong openness to questions, in the flag of its own responses, fanaticism may make life simpler—but at the cost of hopelessly destroying it. Its tragedy lies in the fact that it takes the beautiful and profoundly authentic longing of the human "pre-I" to take the suffering of the world upon itself and transforms it into something that merely multiplies that suffering: an organizer of concentration camps, inquisitions, massacres and executions. By the time one finally realizes what has happened, it is usually too late. The danger that flows from this "tiny flaw" in the mechanism of how the "I" is constituted is as old as human history and is certainly not the main danger in the world today (even though it has something in common with it). Nevertheless, it is especially relevant now: the general turning away from Being so typical of contemporary civilization provides fertile soil indeed for various forms of fanaticism, which are short-circuited responses to that turning away.

. . .

I kiss you,
Vašek

142

August 21, 1982

Dear Olga,

We live in an age in which there is a general turning away from Being: our civilization, founded on a grand upsurge of science and technology, those great intellectual guides on how to conquer the world at the cost of losing touch with Being, transforms man its proud creator into a slave of his consumer needs, breaks him up into isolated functions, dissolves him in his existence-in-the-world and thus deprives him not only of his human integrity and his autonomy but ultimately any influence he may have had over his own "automatic responses." The crisis of today's world, obviously, is a crisis of human responsibility (both responsibility for oneself and responsibility "toward" something else) and thus it is a crisis of human identity as well. But a warning here: all this does not mean in the least that the experience of Being and the orientation toward it have vanished entirely from the structure of contemporary humanity. On the contrary: as that which in humanity is failing and breaking down, and which is constantly betrayed, duped and deluded by humanity, they are both, in fact, latently present in the structure of humanity, be it only in the form of fissures and faults that must be filled at all costs to preserve appearances—both on the surface and "inside." The point is that morality seldom sees itself as purely utilitarian, and even less would it admit publicly to this. It always pretends, or tries to persuade itself, that its roots go deeper, even in matters less extreme than fanaticism. Would anyone, for example, dare to deny that he had a conscience? There are no two ways about it: the "voice of Being" has not fallen silent—we know it summons us, and as human beings, we cannot pretend not to know what it is calling us to. It is just that these days, it is easier to cheat, silence or lie to that voice (think of the many ways science gives us to do this!). The source of this latent regard for Being, therefore, is not merely convention (that is, a reified morality of traditions which, from the point of view of our existence-in-the-world, it would be a pointless faux pas to ignore publicly) but rather it lies deeper: in our thrownness into our source in Being from which—so long as we remain people and do not become mere robots—we cannot extricate ourselves and which—though it might exist merely as "memories of memories," "homesickness for homesickness" or "longing for longing"—exposes us to that voice. And regardless of how selfishly we act, of how indifferent we remain to everything that does not bring us immediate benefit (the kind that is fully rooted in the world of phenomena), regardless of how exclusively we relate to our utilitarian "here" and "now," we always feel, in some corner of our spirit at least, that we should not act that way and that therefore we must find a way to defend and justify our actions, and by some "mental trick," gloss over its disaccord with something we are simply no longer capable of striving toward. It makes no difference whether, to that end, we invoke the somewhat mystical claim that "all is lost anyway" or on the contrary, the illusion that our bad behavior serves a good cause.

All of this—the turning away from Being, the crisis of the absolute horizon, of genuine responsibility and thus of genuine identity as well, along with heightened efforts to "satisfy" the betrayed "voice of being" by mystification—is transferred or projected, understandably, into the behavior of various "interexistential" formations as well: society, nations, classes, social strata, political movements and systems, social power groups, forces and organisms and ultimately even states and governments themselves. For not only do all these formations shape and direct contemporary humanity, humanity shapes and directs them as well, since they are ultimately the product and image of humanity.

And just as man turns away from Being, so entire large social organisms turn away from it—if I may put it that way—having surrendered to the same steadily increasing temptation of existence-in-the-world, of entities, aims and "realities" (whose attractions are merely strengthened by surrendering to them). And just as man conceals his turning away from the world and himself by pretending that it is not a turning away at all, so these social organisms hide their turning away from the world and themselves in an analogical fashion. For this reason, we may observe how social, political and state systems, and whole societies, are inevitably becoming alienated from themselves. The difficult and complex task of serving primary moral ideals is reduced to the less demanding task of serving projects intended to fulfill those ideals in a concrete way; and, when such projects have won the day, there is a further reduction to the even more comfortable task of serving systems allegedly designed to carry these projects out; and finally, it degenerates into a situation, common enough now, in which the power that directs these systems (or more precisely "possesses" them) simply looks out for its own interests, or else the systems, in a purely utilitarian fashion, adapt themselves to the demands of that power. By now, the behavior of social power, of various establishments and finally of whole societies (which either identify with the given power, or adapt to it, or simply surrender to it) has become utterly self-serving, alienated many times over from the original ideals and has degenerated into the "realities of existence-in-the-world," and at the same time, of course, it still persists in operating in the name of the morality of the original—and long since betrayed—ideals. One consequence of this alienating process is the enormous conflict between words and deeds so prevalent today: everyone talks about freedom, democracy, humanity, justice, human rights, universal equality and happiness, about peace and saving the world from nuclear apocalypse, and protecting the environment and life in general—and at the same time, everyone—more or less, consciously or unconsciously, in one way or another—serves those values and ideals only to the extent necessary to serve himself, i.e., his "worldly" interests—personal interests, group interests, power interests, property interests, state or great-power interests. Thus the world becomes a chessboard for this cynical and utterly self-serving "interplay of interests," and ultimately there are no practices, whether economic, political, diplomatic, military or espionage, which, as means sanctified by an allegedly universal human end, are not permissible if they serve the particular interests of the group that carries them out. Under the guise of the intellectually respectable notion of "responsibility for everything" (i.e., for the "welfare of mankind")—that is, pretending to relate to the absolute horizon—huge and uncontrollable forces and powers are in fact responsible only to the particular horizon from which they derive their power (e.g., to the establishment that put them in power). Pretending to serve the "general well-being of mankind," they serve only their own pragmatic interests, and they are oriented exclusively toward "doing well in the world" and expanding and proliferating further—wherein that very expansion and proliferation which flows directly from the expansive essence of focusing on existence-in-the-world is interpreted as service to "higher things"—to universal freedom, justice and well-being. This entire mendacious "world of appearances," of grandiose words and phraseological rituals is, again, merely the tax that one who has surrendered to existence-in-the-world pays—on the social level this time—to his "recollection of conscience," i.e., to his duty to respond, in this formal and ritualistic fashion, at least, to the languishing "voice of Being" in his indolent heart.

The tension between the world of words and the real practices of those in power is not just directly experienced by millions of ordinary, powerless people, nor thought about only by intellectuals, whose voices those in power either ignore (in some places) or pay "too much" attention to (in others), nor is it pointed out only by minorities in revolt. The power in society can actually see it better than anyone else, but only in others, never in itself. In such circumstances, however, it is not surprising that no one believes anyone and that everyone uses the contradiction between someone else's words and deeds to justify a deepening of the same contradictions in himself. It may even appear that those with fewer inhibitions in this regard will ultimately triumph and crush the others. So the power structures apparently have no other choice than to sink deeper and deeper into this vicious maelstrom, and contemporary people—if they take any interest at all in such "great matters"—apparently have no other choice than to wait around until the final inhibition drops away.

Naturally I am not underestimating the importance of international talks on arms limitation. I'm afraid, however, that we will never attain a peace that will permanently eliminate the threat of a nuclear catastrophe as long as mutual trust among people, nations and states is not revitalized to a degree far greater than has been the case at any time in the past. And that, of course, won't happen until the terrifying abyss between words and deeds is closed. And that, in turn, won't happen until something radical—I would even say revolutionary—changes in the very structure and "soul" of humanity today. In other words, until man—standing on the brink of the abyss—recovers from the massive betrayal he commits every day against his own nature, and goes back to where he has always stood in the good moments of his history: to that which provides the foundations for that dramatic essence of his humanity (as "separated being"), that is, to Being as the firm vanishing point of his striving, to that absolute horizon of his relating.

But who should begin? Who should break this vicious circle? I agree with Levinas when he says that responsibility cannot be preached, but only borne, and that the only possible place to begin is with oneself. It may sound strange, but it is true: it is I who must begin. One thing about it, however, is interesting: once I begin—that is, once I try—here and now, right where I am, not excusing myself by saying that things would be easier elsewhere, without grand speeches and ostentatious gestures, but all the more persistently—to live in harmony with the "voice of Being," as I understand it within myself—as soon as I begin that, I suddenly discover, to my surprise, that I am neither the only one, nor the first, nor the most important one to have set out upon that road. For the hope opened up in my heart by this turning toward Being has opened my eyes as well to all the hopeful things my vision, blinded by the brilliance of "worldly" temptations, could not or did not wish to see, because it would have undermined the traditional argument of all those who have given up already: that all is lost anyway. Whether all is really lost or not depends entirely on whether or not I am lost.

. . .

I kiss you,
Vašek

143

August 28, 1982

Dear Olga,

If, through the armor-plate of indifference to the problems of others—which you must wear in prison to keep you from falling apart—there suddenly penetrates something as absolutely unlikely as the predicament of an unknown meteorologist on the television screen, it is not to be taken lightly: it tells us something about the mysterious essence of the human "I." And indeed: man is the only creature capable—almost "absurdly"—of taking upon or "relating to" himself something that does not, in any determinable way, affect his immediate existence in the world (or at least not in a way commensurate with how he relates to it). This reaching beyond all horizons of determinable utility derives—it would seem—directly from one's "otherness" as "separated Being," that is, from one's capacity to experience Being not only as the existence of something (useful or threatening in one way or another) but also as something that establishes, links and unites the existence of everything that exists, and through which one is in fact ultimately touched by all that exists. (Which doesn't mean that one really "relates" to everything at all times and to the same degree. How much a particular expression of Being that visibly reaches beyond the structure of his "worldly" interests genuinely affects a person existentially depends on the receptivity of his unique "I," and the extent to which Being manifests and opens itself to that particular "I" at that moment.) At the same time, the focus or matrix, as it were, of this human self-transcendence is, and always has been, the existence of others—experienced either directly or indirectly, in a variety of ways. And regardless of how much the "I" ultimately transcends this matrix (and a person could conceivably become more absorbed by the neutrino than by the fate of his own wife), the "I" cannot be constituted without it: it is only through a "you" (the first "you," naturally, is the mother), only through a "we," that the "I" can genuinely become itself. This is the territory on which it has its first experiences. In the nearness and love of another it comes to know its home; in its alienness and unworthiness it knows the alienness of the world; in the mystery of the "I," it first encounters the mystery of self. In short, in the experience of the other it experiences everything that it means to be human: the world, Being, its own separateness, its thrownness, its horizons. On this territory, the first questions arise, a person's responsibility matures and his identity forms. It is here that he begins to grasp his subjectivity, its vastness and its limits. In the eyes of others, he sees his first view "from the outside" and first reads the "voice of Being." Face-to-face with the existence of his neighbor, he first experiences that primordial "responsibility for everything" and thus becomes a special creature capable of fellow feeling with a complete stranger, of loving even that which he does not erotically desire or on whom he is not dependent for his existence-in-the-world (such as the "love" of a dog for its master) or of feeling ashamed of statements made by someone with whom he has no more in common than the fact that they are both people. Ultimately, therefore, even the very absolute horizon of our relating is not something abstract that floats high above the heads of our neighbors, but something we approach through the medium of their disturbing existence—just as in the unhappy eyes of my meteorologist, the very secret of "Being itself" called out to me and irresistibly pulled me into a repeated participation in its fullness and totality. . . . Another person, in short, is the only entity capable of opening the human heart, in the sense that we have understood that notion over the centuries.

If the orientation of man toward Being grows out of this matrix, the only way it can be effectively carried over into "the reality of human tasks" (and thus broaden the hopes for humanity today) is through a radical return of the "I" to that life-giving matrix: any genuine renewal of its orientation toward Being means primarily a radical and profound renewal of all forms of "interexistentiality," that is, a radical and profound change in the relationship of the "I" to the "you" and thus, a newly meaningful substance to human communality. A better outlook for human communality—and thus for the world—does not, therefore, lie in new ideas, projects, programs and organizations as such, but only in a renaissance of elementary human relationships, which new projects can at the very most only mediate. Love, charity, sympathy, tolerance, understanding, self-control, solidarity, friendship, feelings of belonging, the acceptance of concrete responsibility for those close to one—these are, I think, expressions of that new (or more precisely: continually renewed and betrayed by all of human history) "interexistentiality" that alone can breathe new meaning into the social formations and collectivities that, together, shape the fate of the world. An integral part of any communality thus renewed, of course, is the "turbulence" I described in the authentically responsible "I"; only a constant mutual illumination and mutual "checking" of elementary moral intentions against actual "social practices" can guarantee that any new communality will not succumb to the same self-reification, self-fetishization and self-alienation (resulting in the same dull discipline of sects, proliferating bureaucracies of party and government administrations, the corruption of establishments and the despair of the powerless masses) that we know so well in the traditional structures of contemporary society. Every meaningful communality must constantly confront its actions with its intended aims, reassess itself to make certain it is not terrorizing or fanaticizing itself and the world with its reified "truth." It must constantly—here, now, at once and everywhere—withstand the temptation to be utilitarian and weigh what is true against what is a lie, what is genuine against what is false, what is moral against what is immoral, what is life-giving against what is deadening. It must never forget that the first little lie told in the interests of truth, the first little injustice committed in the name of justice, the first tiny immorality defended by the morality of "things," the first careless lapse in this constant vigilance, means the certain beginning of the end.

Are there any visible signs that such an "existential revolution" is happening in the world today? I can't help feeling that if you are open to hope, you can find timid signals in many things: in movements of youth in revolt such as have broken out periodically since the 1950s, in genuine peace movements, in varied activities in defense of human rights, in liberation movements (as long as they don't degenerate into mere attempts to replace one kind of terror with another), in various efforts at religious and ecumenical revival, in ecological initiatives, in short, in all the constantly recurring attempts to create authentic and meaningful communities that rebel against a world in crisis, not merely to escape from it, but to devote their full efforts—with the clear-sighted deliberation and humility that always goes with genuine faith—to assume responsibility for the state of the world.

. . .

I kiss you,
Vašek

144

September 4, 1982

Dear Olga,

Among the thousands of remarkable events that create the miracle of Being and its history, the event which I have called here the constitution or the genesis of the human "I" has an entirely revolutionary significance. Unlike all other events, this one touches, in a special way, the very essence of Being, the very "Being of Being." Man is not merely an entity among other entities, that is, something merely different from all the others, but an entity which, in a direct way, "is otherwise." He is not merely distinguished from other entities by what he is (by the fact that he is essentially more structured, for example), but chiefly by how he is, the fact that his very being is essentially different from the being of anything else outside him. I have tried to describe this deeply ontological "otherness" (experimentally, more in a literary fashion and purely for the needs of the time when my letters are read) as "a state of separation": on the one hand, we "know ourselves" and "know the world," and on the other hand, we in fact know nothing about ourselves or the world, and knowing this of ourselves—and that we alone know this—we necessarily experience ourselves as something that has somehow "fallen" out of or been "separated" from the order of the universe and the general manner of Being. With anything else it seems the other way around: a particular entity "knows" neither itself nor the world; as an unproblematic (i.e., unseparated by its "self-knowledge") expression of the totality of integral Being, however, it also "knows everything," or rather it "possesses" itself completely "from within." These two dimensions of all existing entities (i.e., lack of "self-knowledge" and complete "self-possession" "from inside") are, at the same time, embodied as it were in the two fundamental levels of our experience of Being: the dimension of "not knowing" is the basis of what we experience as the world of entities, phenomena, things, that is, of everything I have called "the world"; and the dimension of hidden and total "self-knowledge of the universe" is the object of our inner experience, which I have called simply the experience of "Being." That double layer of our ontological experience is essentially the experience of our double thrownness: our thrownness into the alienness of the world, which brings home or manifests to us our "separateness," our vulnerability and our lostness, and our thrownness into the original integrity of Being and into our "longing" for it. (By the way, it would seem that, logically, the world and the entities that make it up must have come first, and that only subsequently could man have been thrown into it. In fact, however, that is not so: man and the world come into being at the same time, as two "dimensions" of a single act of separation, because the world, i.e., the world of entities, is nothing other than Being, or rather the Being of the "non-I," as it manifests itself to and through the constituting "I." Thus the world is Being made external, made manifest to us, "made existent" by our otherness; it is a declaration or an expression of Being that is structured and defined by the kind of existential, mental and sensory openness and limitations we possess.

That is why I wrote—and I can't remember if I made it clear enough—that when the "I" is constituted, the world is constituted along with it. In any case, thrownness into the source in Being is a similar matter: it is separation from the integrity of Being that first establishes that source as a genuine source, i.e., as a more or less conscious experience of the secret bond between the "I" and the universe—or more precisely, between me and what is "beyond me," as it were, and beyond each of my "exteriorities.") Our thrownness into the world, then, makes present to us our separation; our thrownness into the source in Being, on the contrary, awakens in us that intrinsically human self-transcendence: the longing to step beyond all our concrete horizons and thus to touch again the lost fullness of Being, somehow to "possess" it again (and thus to overcome our state of separation), issuing in the experience of "quasi-identification" as an alert contact—that is, fully aware of itself—with "absolute Being," that mysterious principle and essence of everything that is. An important and special circumstance, one that throws light on many other things, is that both these experiences of ours are far from being merely noetic instruments; they have profound existential and moral substance and implications: while "Being"—as the absolute horizon of our relating—is for us—as a "voice" and a "cry"—identical with a moral order (as though Being were not only the "reasoning mind" of everything that exists, but its "heart" as well), the world, or rather existence in it, is a temptation for us to cling in a more complacent fashion (because of indifference to the difficult "voice of Being") to superficialities, immediate aims, details, to adapt ourselves to the flow of phenomena while giving up on their meaning (leading inevitably to the weakening of one's own Being). Behind this notion is a sensation of the ambiguity, the instability, the contradictory and paradoxical nature of the human position. Our ontological "otherness" in fact chiefly expresses this: only man, for instance, can pose the question of meaning, yet he can never come up with an exhaustive answer to it (since it would mean not being what he is—"separated from Being"); he alone experiences, or rather through his experience constitutes, the world as that into which he has been thrown and in which he is condemned to exist, yet at the same time, he alone knows that by succumbing to that existence-in-the-world, he will irrevocably lose himself; he alone is capable of alertly experiencing Being as the true background of everything that exists, but at the same time he alone is fated to be outside that Being and condemned never to be fully inside it. Yet the paradox of this paradoxical nature of human being is that in it resides—at the same time—the source of all its beauty and misery, its tragedy and its greatness, its dramatic florescence and its continual failures.

I think that religious archetypes accurately mirror the dimensions of this ambiguous essence of humanity—from the idea of paradise, that "recollection" of a lost participation in the integrity of Being, the idea of a fall into the world as an act of "separation" (is not the apple of knowledge in fact the "knowledge of the self" that separates us?), the idea of the last judgment as our confrontation with the absolute horizon of our relating, right down to the idea of salvation as supreme transcendence, that "quasi-identification" with the fullness of Being, to which humanity is constantly aspiring. And the fact that all the short-circuited attempts of fanaticism to organize a "heaven on earth" inevitably lead to an earthly hell is more than clearly expressed in the reminder that the kingdom of God is not "of this earth." Indeed: a relatively bearable life on this earth can only be secured by a humanity whose orientation is "beyond" this world, a humanity that—in each of its "heres" and each of its "nows"—relates to infinity, to the absolute and to eternity. An unqualified orientation to the "here" and "now," however bearable that may be, hopelessly transforms that "here" and "now" into desolation and waste and ultimately colors it with blood.

Yes: man is in fact nailed down—like Christ on the cross—to a grid of paradoxes: stretched between the horizontal of the world and the vertical of Being; dragged down by the hopelessness of existing-in-the-world on the one hand, and the unattainability of the absolute on the other, he balances between the torment of not knowing his mission and the joy of carrying it out, between nothingness and meaningfulness. And like Christ, he is in fact victorious, but by virtue of his defeats: through perceiving absurdity, he once again finds meaning; through personal failure, he once more discovers responsibility; through the defeat of several prison sentences, he gains a victory—at the very least—over himself (as an object of worldly temptations); and through death—his last and greatest defeat—he finally triumphs over his fragmentation; by completing, for all time, his outline in the "memory of Being," he returns at last—having rejected nothing of his "otherness"—to the womb of integral Being.

The same thing in fact applies—this must be added for the sake of completeness—to these meditations of mine: they are a defeat because in them I have neither discovered nor expressed anything that hasn't already been discovered long before and expressed a hundred times better—and yet they are, at the same time, a victory: if nothing else, I have at least managed, through them (overcoming more banally exterior and profoundly interior obstacles than I would ever wish upon anyone who writes anything), to pull myself together to the point where I now feel better than when I began them. It's strange, but I may well be happier now than at any time in recent years.

In short, I feel fine and I love you—

Vašek

Notes

page 28: "Has Mejla been there with Klíma?" Possibly a reference to a cycle of songs written by the Plastic People of the Universe based on the writings of the Czech philosopher Ladislav Klíma. See Glossary of Names.

page 30: "it would be good if ——— came." The name was blacked out by the prison authorities.

page 33: "that trip to the USA." In August, the authorities offered to release Havel if he would accept an invitation to go to the USA on a "study trip." He refused because he believed the authorities would not allow him back into Czechoslovakia.

page 35: "the premiere in Vienna." Probably Havel's one-act play *Protest,* which premiered on November 17, 1979.

page 36: "Ahoj." An informal Czech greeting and farewell. Pronounced "ahoy."

page 37: "with photos of the funeral." Havel was let out for two hours to attend his father's funeral. He attended it under escort, and was accompanied by the prosecutors.

page 38: "those complications in 1977." When Havel was released from prison in May 1977, a routine letter he had written asking to be let go was deliberately misquoted in the media to make it appear that he had promised to be less active in Charter 77. See Letter 138 for more details.

page 41: "fet." Czech prison slang for a drug "fix."

page 42: "some inappropriate speculations." See Letter 138 for a fuller explanation.

page 43: "*Tvář.*" A critical journal in the 1960s. See the Introduction for details of Havel's part in the *Tvář* affair.

page 52: "*Audience.*" A one-act play by Havel written in 1975. It premiered in Vienna's Burgtheater on October 7, 1976. Havel and the actor Pavel Landovský subsequently taped a performance of the play.

page 60:   "those for whom freedom was a fresh joy at Christmas." On December 22, 1979, four of the original ten arrested were released from detention. They were Jiří Němec, Jarmila Bělíková, Václav Malý and Ladislav Lis.

page 63:   "the Canadian edition of my plays." Sixty-Eight Publishers in Toronto brought out a collection, in Czech, of Havel's full-length plays from the 1970s, called *Václav Havel: Hry 1970–1976 (Václav Havel: Plays 1970–1976)*. *The Conspirators* was one of them.

page 64:   "green is the color of hope." Havel signed this letter with a green felt-tipped pen.

page 67:   "able to reflect upon the change with others." Václav Benda and Jiří Dienstbier, two of Havel's codefendants, were sent to the same prison as Havel.

page 68:   "to make me choose it." Havel is referring here to exile.

page 71:   "my former lawyer's legal dispute." Havel's former lawyer was Dr. Josef Danisz, who had been charged with "slandering a public official" after a too energetic defense of Jaroslav Šabata against charges of attacking a police officer. In January 1980, Dr. Danisz was sentenced to ten months in prison and disbarred for two years.

page 78:   "top nutritional category." Prisoners were punished for not fulfilling the quotas, among other things, by being given less food.

page 82:   "my tattooed friends." Havel means his fellow prisoners, who often tattoo themselves in prison.

page 82:   "We are fortunate." Havel means himself, Benda and Dienstbier.

page 82:   "a visit from Prague." Havel, Benda and Dienstbier were visited by police officials, possibly their interrogators.

page 91:   "Libuše's final vision." In Smetana's strongly patriotic nineteenth century opera, Libuše, the heroine who is gifted with prophecy, has a vision of Prague as a city whose glory shall touch the heavens.

page 99:   "Jirka and Dana." Jiří Němec and Dana Němcová, two members of the Committee to Defend the Unjustly Prosecuted (VONS) who were arrested along with Havel. Ječná is the name of the street in Prague where they lived.

page 104:   "love letter." In an interview with Karel Hvížďala in 1985, Havel said, "Kamila Bendová once wrote Vašek Benda that, unlike his letters, mine did not contain a single affectionate word. Vašek showed this to me, and I tried to write Olga a love letter. The result was a queer specimen in which, as Vašek said, the only genuine emotion was anger at Kamila for putting me up to it." Havel left this letter out of the collection.

page 114: "that 'last supper' at the Fregata restaurant." On the night before his arrest, Havel and other members of VONS met at a favorite restaurant called Fregata.

page 115: "máčo." Czech prison slang meaning "crazy." Pronounced "macho."

page 185: "my new situation." Dienstbier and Benda were transferred from Heřmanice prison under escort; Havel had no idea where they had been transferred.

page 209: "the sounds of my mother tongue." Havel means the sounds of Czech spoken with a Prague accent, as opposed to the strong Ostrava dialect.

page 214: "local micropark." A small prison exercise yard.

page 238: "BUY HOFMANNSTHAL!" A translation into Czech of the Austrian poet and playwright Hugo von Hofmannsthal (1874–1929) had just appeared.

page 277: "jumped off the train." Emigrated.

page 289: "model drama." A technical term used in Czech drama criticism to describe plays that present typical human situations schematically, almost metaphorically, in ways that are not intended to be "realistic."

page 296: "my letter of long ago on a 'worldview.' " A reference to letter 78, which Havel erroneously believed had not been allowed through.

page 300: "those two unsuccessful 'runs' at it." Havel is referring to two periods when he was held in custody, the first in 1977, when he was arrested in connection with Charter 77, and the second in January 1978, in connection with a police provocation at a railway workers' ball (he was released and the charges dropped on March 13, 1978).

page 305: "what we meant five years ago too." A reference to the appearance of Charter 77.

page 309: "the news that I am a doctor." Havel was awarded an honorary doctorate by York University in Toronto, Canada, in the spring of 1982.

page 312: "Levinas." Havel's brother Ivan sent him a translation of a text by the French philosopher Emmanuel Levinas. The text referred to is "Sans identité," from the book *Humanisme de l'autre homme* by Emmanuel Levinas (Montpellier, 1972).

page 312:   "The Power of the Powerless." This essay, in which Havel discusses the problem of dissent in modern totalitarian states, was written in 1978 and was published in English in 1985 as the title essay in an anthology of essays on dissent by Czech authors.

Glossary of Names

ANDREJ: Usually, but not in every case, refers to Andrej Staňkovič, a Czech poet.

BONDY: Egon Bondy, the pen name of a Czech poet, novelist, philosopher.

ČERNÝ: Jiří Černý, a Czech popular music critic.

CHARLIE: Karel Soukup, Czech singer and songwriter. Now living in France.

ČINOHERNÍ KLUB: Literally the Play Club, a small actor-oriented theater in Prague; with the Theatre on the Balustrade, it enjoyed a great vogue in the 1960s.

DANISZ: Dr. Josef Danisz, who was Havel's defense counsel at the time of Havel's arrest. See note for page 71.

DEJVICE: A residential quarter of Prague where Havel and Olga were living at the time of his arrest.

DIETL: Jaroslav Dietl, the author of many serials and sitcoms for Czechoslovak television. Died in 1986.

FANTÔMAS: Popular villain in French fiction; bald-headed à la Kojak. Fantômas enjoyed a vogue among European intellectuals in the 1930s.

FIALKA: Ladislav Fialka, a mime and director of pantomime at the Theatre on the Balustrade.

FORMAN: Miloš Forman, Czech film director now living in the United States.

GOTT: Karel Gott, Czech pop singer.

GROSSMAN: Jan Grossman, literary critic and theater director; worked at the Theatre on the Balustrade and directed Havel's plays.

GLOSSARY OF NAMES

GRUŠA: Jiří (Jirka) Gruša, a Czech poet and novelist now living in West Germany.

HEJDÁNEK: Ladislav Hejdánek, Czech philosopher.

HOLAN: Vladimír Holan (1905–1980). A Czech poet.

HORNÍČEK: Miroslav Horníček, a comic actor and monologist.

HRADČANY: The Prague castle, its precincts and environs; seat of the President of the Republic.

HRADEC KRÁLOVÉ: A large town and administrative center in northeast Bohemia, the region where Havel's cottage is located.

IVAN: Havel's brother Ivan.

JARDA: See KOŘÁN.

JARMILA: Jarmila (or Jarmilka) Bělíková, a VONS activist. See note for page 60.

JIRKA G.: See GRUŠA.

JIRKA N.: See NĚMEC.

JIRKA P.: See PALLAS.

JIROUS: Ivan Jirous, also known as Magor; Czech art historian and artistic manager of the Plastic People of the Universe.

JULIANA: Juliana Stritzková-Jirousová, a Czech painter married to Ivan Jirous.

JURÁČEK: Pavel Juráček, screenwriter and director who helped create the "New Wave" of Czech cinema in the 1960s.

KAČER: Jan (Honza) Kačer, an actor and director in the Činoherní Klub in Prague.

KACHYŇA: Karel Kachyňa, a Czech film director.

KAFKA: Vladimír Kafka, a liberal book editor in the 1960s; died shortly after the Soviet invasion in 1968.

KAMILA: Kamila Bendová, Václav Benda's wife.

KLAUS: Klaus Junkers, Havel's literary agent and publisher, head of Rowohlt Verlag in Hamburg, West Germany.

KLÍMA: Ladislav Klíma (1878–1928). Czech philosopher and novelist.

KOBLASA: Jiří Koblasa, Czech artist now living in West Germany.

KOHOUTOVÁ: Terezka Kohoutová, daughter of Czech writer and playwright Pavel Kohout.

KOŘÁN: Jaroslav Kořán, a Czech translator.

KRKONOŠE: The Krkonoše Mountains lie in the border region between Northeast Bohemia and Poland.

KUSÍN: Vladimír Kusín, a translator.

KVĚTA: Havel's sister-in-law, Ivan's wife.

LÁĎA L.: Probably Ladislav Lis, a member of the Central Committee under Dubček, now a member of VONS; arrested with Havel et al. but later released. See note for page 60.

LANĎÁK: Pavel Landovský, a friend of Havel's, an actor and playwright now living in Vienna.

LIBERATED THEATRE: See WERICH.

LIBÍČEK: Jan Libíček, an actor connected with the Theatre on the Balustrade.

LINHARTOVÁ: Věra Linhartová, a Czech writer now living in Paris.

LOPATKA: Jan (Honza) Lopatka, Czech literary critic and editor. Lopatka edited the Czech edition of *Letters to Olga*.

MAGOR: See JIROUS.

MALÁ STRANA: A historical quarter of Prague on the left bank of the Vltava river.

MEJLA: Milan Hlavsa, bass player and composer for the underground rock group the Plastic People of the Universe.

MELODIE: Czech pop-music monthly.

MLADÝ SVĚT: A weekly tabloid published in Prague and aimed at young people.

MUCHA: Alfons Mucha, Czech painter (1860–1939).

NĚMEC: Jan (Honza) Němec, Czech film director now living in the United States.

NĚMEC: Jiří (Jirka) Němec, Czech psychologist and philosopher; member of VONS arrested along with Havel and released in December 1979. Now living in Vienna.

NEUBAUER: Zdeněk Neubauer, a Czech philosopher.

NVU: Napravně vychovný ústav: Correctional Institute.

OTKA: Otta Bednářová, former journalist and member of VONS sentenced with Havel.

PALLAS: Jiří (Jirka) Pallas: Czech record producer living in Sweden; brought out a gramophone version of Havel and Landovský performing Havel's one-act play, *Audience.* See letter 14, page 52.

PALOUŠ: Radim Palouš, Czech philosopher.

PANKRÁC: Pankrác prison, in Prague, which has hospital facilities. Prisoners in serious condition are sent there for medical examination and treatment.

PAPP: Joseph Papp, artistic director of the Public Theater in New York. Papp had sent Havel a letter of invitation to the United States; Havel refused to go. See note for page 33.

PATOČKA: Jan Patočka (1907–1977), Czech philosopher; with Havel, one of the three founding spokesmen of Charter 77.

PRÁŠIL: Baron Prášil, a mythological hero of European folklore who performed fabulous feats of strength and daring.

PUZUK: A childhood nickname for Havel's brother, Ivan.

RADOK: Alfred Radok, Czech theater director; died 1976 in exile.

RP: Rudé právo, the official Czech-language Communist party daily newspaper, published in Prague.

ŠAFAŘÍK: Josef Šafařík, born 1907; philosopher and essayist. His writings had a great influence on Havel in his formative years.

SCHNEIDER: Jan (Honza) Schneider, drummer for the Plastic People of the Universe.

SHKLOVSKÝ: Russian formalist critic.

SLAVÍK: Otakar Slavík, a Czech painter now living in Vienna.

SMOLJAK and SVĚRÁK: Ladislav Smoljak and Zdeněk Svěrák, an acting and play-writing team.

T.G.M.: Tomáš Garrigue Masaryk (1850–1937), Czechoslovakia's first president, from 1918 to 1935.

TOPOL: Josef (Pepík) Topol, Czech poet, playwright, essayist and translator.

TRINKY: Karel Trinkiewicz, a Czech painter now living in West Germany.

TŘÍSKA: Jan Tříska, Czech actor now living in the United States.

TVÁŘ: An independent journal of literature and criticism begun in the 1960s. See the Introduction for details of Havel's part in the Tvář affair.

VĚRA: Věra Jirousová, a Czech poet; former wife of Ivan Jirous.

VODIČKA: Vladimír Vodička, director of the Theatre on the Balustrade.

VYSKOČIL: Ivan Vyskočil, Czech playwright and actor.

WERICH: Jan Werich (1905–1980), a writer and actor who, together with Jiří (George) Voskovec (1905–1981) established the Liberated Theatre (Osvobozené divadlo) in Prague in 1927. During the Nazi occupation, Voskovec and Werich emigrated to the United States. After the war they returned to Czechoslovakia. Werich remained to run the Theatre ABC in Prague, where Havel worked as a stagehand in the 1950s. Voskovec went back to the United States, where he made a career as an actor.

ZDENĚK: Usually Zdeněk Urbánek, a Czech writer and translator of Shakespeare, among others. A longtime personal friend of Havel's.

ZDENĚK N.: Zdeněk Neubauer, Czech philosopher.

ŽIŽKOV: A working-class quarter of Prague.

ZLÍN: Now Gottwaldov, a manufacturing city in Moravia.

ZUZANA: Zuzana Dienstbierová, Dienstbier's wife.

Index

A Note About the Author and Translator

Václav Havel was born in Czechoslovakia in 1936. Among his plays, those best known in the West are <u>The Garden Party, The Increased Difficulty of Concentration, The Memorandum, Largo Desolato</u> and three one-act plays: <u>Audience, Private View,</u> and <u>Protest.</u> He is a founding spokesman of Charter 77 and the author of many influential essays on the nature of totalitarianism and dissent, including "An Open Letter to Dr. Husák" and "The Power of the Powerless." In January 1983, for reasons of health, he was released from prison before his sentence was completed. In 1986 he was awarded the Erasmus Prize, the highest cultural award in the Netherlands.

Paul Wilson (translator) lived in Czechoslovakia for ten years, working as a translator and English teacher and playing with an underground rock band, The Plastic People of the Universe. He was expelled in 1977. He has translated the work of several Czech writers, including Josef Škvorecký and Bohumil Hrabal. He now lives in Toronto.

A Note on the Type

*This book was set in a digitized version of a type face
called Baskerville. The face itself is a facsimile reproduction
of types cast from molds made for John Baskerville (1706–1775)
from his designs. Baskerville's original face was one of the
forerunners of the type style known to printers as "modern face"
—a "modern" of the period A.D. 1800.*

DESIGNED BY CLAIRE M. NAYLON